D0850014

CAMBRIDGE CLASSICAL TEXTS AND COMMENTARIES

26

CALLIMACHUS: THE FIFTH HYMN

CALLIMACHUS

THE FIFTH HYMN

EDITED WITH INTRODUCTION AND COMMENTARY

BY

A. W. BULLOCH

University of California, Berkeley

CAMBRIDGE UNIVERSITY PRESS

CAMBRIDGE

LONDON NEW YORK NEW ROCHELLE

MELBOURNE SYDNEY

Published by the Press Syndicate of the University of Cambridge
The Pitt Building, Trumpington Street, Cambridge CB2 1RP
32 East 57th Street, New York, NY 10022, USA
296 Beaconsfield Parade, Middle Park, Melbourne 3206, Australia

First published 1985

Printed in Great Britain at
the University Press, Cambridge

Library of Congress catalogue card number: 84-5015

British Library Cataloguing in Publication Data
Callimachus
[Hymni]. Callimachus: the fifth hymn—
(Cambridge classical texts and commentaries; 26)
I. Title II. Bulloch, A.W.
III. Callimachus: the fifth hymn
881'.01 PA3945.A2

ISBN 0 521 26495 2

AP

FOR
PATRICK

CONTENTS

PREFACE

In preparing this edition I have been fortunate enough to enjoy the help and encouragement of many friends and colleagues. Giuseppe Giangrande first interested me in the Hellenistic period and demonstrated what a rich and fascinating area it is for research; from him I learnt much about the tools and techniques of scholarship. I owe much to Michael Silk who gave freely of his time and ideas when I was writing the first draft of the commentary; an early draft benefited greatly from the learning of D.W.Lucas, the late Sir Denys Page, and Hugh Lloyd-Jones, and the final draft was improved by the careful and generous scrutiny of the Editors of Cambridge Classical Texts and Commentaries, Professor Brink, Dr Diggle and Professor Sandbach. Discussions with Charles Murgia helped me improve greatly the section on the transmission of the text. Through every stage of the writing of the commentary I enjoyed the constant support and stimulus of Penelope Bulloch, and this work would be far inferior to what it is had it not been for her extraordinary learning and generosity. The late Hermann Gundert of the University of Freiburg im Breisgau was incomparably generous with his hospitality and scholarship when this work was at a crucial stage. Thomas Gelzer has been a continual source of learning and encouragement. The whole work has been subjected to the rigorous scrutiny and learning of my Research Assistant Victoria Stafford who saved me from many mistakes and blunders. The Cambridge University Press exercised great patience and care. Finally Patrick Wilkinson has seen this work at every stage of its development, read and re-read it and made many improvements; he has throughout been guide, teacher and dear wise friend, and to him I dedicate the book with profound thanks and affection. The failings of this edition are entirely my own responsibility; they would have been many more without the help of so many fine scholars and friends.

Berkeley 1983 A.W.B.

PREVIOUS EDITIONS AND COMMENTARIES

First edition of the Fifth Hymn:

Angelo Poliziano, *Miscellaneorum Centuriae Primae ad Laurentium Medicem*, Florence 1489 Chapter 80 (see Section VII pp. 58f).

First complete edition of the Hymns:

Ianus Lascaris, *Callimachi Cyrenaei Hymni*, no date or place of publication; ?1494–6 (see Section VII p. 59)

Aldine edition: Venice 1513 (containing Pindar, Callimachus, Dionysius Periegetes, Lycophron)

After these early editions the most important are:[1]

J.G.Graevius	Utrecht 1697 (containing Bentley's collection of fragments and the notes of Robortelli, Stephanus, Frischlin, Bonaventura Vulcanius, Anna Dacier, Ezechiel Spanheim)
J.A.Ernesti	Leiden 1761 (a re-edition of Graevius with the addition of Ernesti's own notes and important work on the MSS)
C.J.Blomfield	London 1815
A.Meineke	Berlin 1861
O.Schneider	Leipzig 1870–3
U. von Wilamowitz-Moellendorff	Berlin 1882[1], 1896[2], 1907[3], 1925[4]
A.W.Mair	London/Cambridge, Mass. 1921 (Loeb Classical Library, with Aratus and Lycophron)
R.Pfeiffer	Oxford 1949, 1953

There have been few commentaries on the Hymns. That of Spanheim (most conveniently available in Volume II of Ernesti's edition) has not yet been superseded and Schneider's (Volume I) contains much useful material; the commentary of E.Cahen, *Les Hymnes de Callimaque* (Paris 1930: Bibliothèque des Écoles Françaises d'Athènes et de Rome 134.2) is very slight and disappointingly derivative from Spanheim but is 'non plane inutilis' (Pfeiffer).

Cahen's compendious *Callimaque et son oeuvre poétique* (Paris 1929: Bibliothèque des Écoles Françaises d'Athènes et de Rome 134.1) also has

[1] For a survey of the printed editions down to the late nineteenth century see C.Nigra, *Riv. di Filologia* 20 (1892) 414–33.

some useful material. The chapter by Wilamowitz in *Hellenistische Dichtung in der Zeit des Kallimachos* (Berlin 1924) II 14–24 and the extensive essay by H.Kleinknecht, 'ΛΟΥΤΡΑ ΤΗϹ ΠΑΛΛΑΔΟϹ', *Hermes* 74 (1939) 301–50 are the most important modern studies on the Fifth Hymn. The lively monograph by K.J.McKay, *The Poet at Play* (Leiden 1962: *Mnemosyne* Supplement 6) is unreliable (I have discussed McKay's interpretation at the appropriate points in the Commentary).

Abbreviations. I have referred to the above works in the following way:

Previous editions by the name of the editor
Cahen's *commentary* simply as 'Cahen'
Cahen, *C* = *Callimaque et son oeuvre poétique*
Kleinknecht, *LP* = 'ΛΟΥΤΡΑ ΤΗϹ ΠΑΛΛΑΔΟϹ'
McKay, *PP* = *The Poet at Play*
Wilamowitz, *HD* = *Hellenistische Dichtung*

Some useful commentaries on other Callimachean hymns have recently appeared:

G.R.McLennan, *Callimachus: Hymn to Zeus* (Rome 1977: Testi e Commenti/Texts and Commentaries 2: Istituto di Filologia Classica Urbino/Birkbeck College, London)
F.Williams, *Callimachus: Hymn to Apollo* (Oxford 1978)
F.Bornmann, *Callimachi Hymnus in Dianam* (Florence 1968: Biblioteca di Studi Superiori 55)
N.Hopkinson, *Callimachus: Hymn to Demeter* (Cambridge 1984)

ABBREVIATIONS AND REFERENCES

Abbreviations of Greek and Roman authors and their works, modern journals, and the main lexica and encyclopedias (LSJ, *RE* etc.) are those in standard use. I have occasionally expanded an abbreviation for the sake of clarity (e.g. 'Aristoph.' and 'Aristot.' in place of the usual 'Ar.' and 'Arist.'); but I have generally adopted the abbreviations used in Liddell and Scott's *Greek–English Lexicon* and *L'Année Philologique*.

The following is a selection of the editions used for the more fragmentary authors before the Hellenistic period:

Hesiod fragments	R.Merkelbach and M.L.West, *Fragmenta Hesiodea* (Oxford 1967)
Sappho and Alcaeus	E.Lobel and D.L.Page, *Poetarum Lesbiorum Fragmenta* (Oxford 1955)
Other melic poets	D.L.Page, *Poetae Melici Graeci* (Oxford 1962) (references given according to the continuous numeration preceded by *PMG*)
	D.L.Page, *Supplementum Lyricis Graecis* (Oxford 1974) (references given according to the continuous numeration preceded by S, prefaced by *SLG*)
Archilochus	M.L.West, *Iambi et Elegi Graeci* I (Oxford 1971)
Hipponax	O.Masson, *Les Fragments du poète Hipponax* (Paris 1962)
Pindar fragments	B.Snell and H.Maehler, *Pindarus* II (Leipzig 1975^4)
Bacchylides	B.Snell and H.Maehler, *Bacchylides* (Leipzig 1970^{10})
Antimachus	B.Wyss, *Antimachi Colophonii Reliquiae* (Berlin 1936)
Menander	plays: F.H. Sandbach, *Menandri Reliquiae Selectae* (Oxford 1972) fragments: A.Körte and A. Thierfelder, *Menander* II (reliquiae apud veteres scriptores servatae) (Leipzig 1952^2)
Comic fragments	T.Kock *Comicorum Atticorum Fragmenta* (Leipzig 1880–8), 3 vols. (reference to fragment number followed by volume and page)

The following are some of the more important editions of Hellenistic authors referred to:

ABBREVIATIONS AND REFERENCES

Apollonius Rhodius	H.Fränkel, *Apollonii Rhodii Argonautica* (Oxford 1961)
	G.W.Mooney, *The Argonautica of A.R.* (London 1912)
	F.Vian, *Apollonios de Rhodes* (Paris) I 1974, II 1980, III 1981
Bucolici	A.S.F.Gow, *Bucolici Graeci* (Oxford 1952)
Euphorion	As in J.U.Powell, *Collectanea Alexandrina* (Oxford 1925)
	F. Scheidweiler, *Euphorionis Fragmenta* (Diss. Bonn 1908)
Greek Anthology	A.S.F.Gow and D.L.Page, *Hellenistic Epigrams* (Cambridge 1965), 2 vols. (referred to by *HE* and line number(s) according to the continuous numeration)
	A.S.F.Gow and D.L.Page, *The Garland of Philip* (Cambridge 1968) 2 vols. (referred to by *GP* and line number(s) according to the continuous numeration)
Herodas	I.C.Cunningham, *Herodas: Mimiambi* (Oxford 1971)
	W.Headlam and A.D.Knox, *Herodas* (Cambridge 1922)
Moschus	W.Bühler, *Die Europa des Moschos* (Wiesbaden 1960: Hermes Einzelschrift 13)
Nicander	A.S.F.Gow and A.F.Scholfield, *Nicander* (Cambridge 1953)
	O.Schneider, *Nicandrea* (Leipzig, 1856)
Philetas	G.Kuchenmüller, *Philetae Coi Reliquiae* (Diss. Berlin 1928)
	A.Nowacki, *Philitae Coi Fragmenta Poetica* (Diss. Westphalia 1927)
Simias	H.Fränkel, *De Simia Rhodio* (Diss. Göttingen 1915)
Theocritus	K.J.Dover, *Theocritus* (London 1971)
	A.S.F.Gow, *Theocritus* (Cambridge 1952^2) 2 vols.

Callimachus. The works of Callimachus I have referred to as follows: Hymns by simple Roman numerals I–VI, epigrams by the abbreviation *E.* with numeration as in Pfeiffer, and fragments by simple Arabic numerals punctuated with a stop before any line numeration (e.g. '198, 260.21' = 'Callimachus fr. 198 and fr. 260 v. 21'); but I have preceded fragment numbers by 'fr.' or 'Call. fr.' at any point (e.g. in lists of references) where clarity required.

SELECT BIBLIOGRAPHY AND ABBREVIATIONS

(See also p. xii above.)

Ahrens, *DD* — H.L.Ahrens, *De Graecae Linguae Dialectis: II de Dialecto Dorica* (Göttingen 1843)

Arndt–Gingrich, *GNT* — W.F.Arndt and F.W.Gingrich, *A Greek–English Lexicon of the New Testament* (translation and adaptation of W.Bauer's *Wörterbuch*) (Cambridge 1957)

Bechtel, *GD* — F.Bechtel, *Die griechischen Dialekte* (Berlin) vol. I 1921, vol. II 1923, vol. III 1924

Björck, *AI* — G.Björck, *Das Alpha Impurum und die tragische Kunstsprache* (Uppsala 1950)

Blass–Debrunner–Rehkopf, *GNG* — F.Blass and A.Debrunner, *Grammatik des neutestamentlichen Griechisch* 14th ed. rev. by F.Rehkopf (Göttingen 1976)

Boisacq, *DD* — E.Boisacq, *Les Dialectes doriens* (Paris 1891)

Buck, *GD* — C.D.Buck, *The Greek Dialects* (Chicago 1955)

Chantraine, *DE* — P.Chantraine, *Dictionnaire étymologique de la langue grecque* (Paris 1968–80)

Chantraine, *FN* — P.Chantraine, *La Formation des noms en grec ancien* (Paris 1933)

Chantraine, *GH* — P.Chantraine, *Grammaire homérique* 2 vols. (Paris 1958³)

Collitz, *GDI* — H.Collitz (ed.), *Sammlung der griechischen Dialekt-Inschriften* 4 vols. (Göttingen 1884–1915), vols. III and IV² with F.Bechtel, vol. IV³ with O.Hoffmann

Crönert, *MGH* — W.Crönert, *Memoria Graeca Herculanensis* (Leipzig 1903)

Daremberg–Saglio, *DA*	C.Daremberg and E.Saglio, *Dictionnaire des antiquités grecques et romaines* (Paris 1873–1919)
Debrunner, *GW*	A.Debrunner, *Griechische Wortbildungslehre* (Heidelberg 1917)
Degner, *DUC*	R.Degner, *De Dorismi Usu Callimacheo* (Diss. Breslau 1877)
Denniston, *GP*	J.D.Denniston, *The Greek Particles* (Oxford 1954^{2})
Ebeling, *LH*	H.Ebeling, *Lexicon Homericum* 2 vols. (Leipzig 1880–5)
Farnell, *CGS*	L.R.Farnell, *The Cults of the Greek States* 5 vols. (Oxford 1896–1909)
Frisk, *EW*	H.Frisk, *Griechisches etymologisches Wörterbuch* 2 vols. (Heidelberg 1954–1970)
Gautier, *LX*	Léopold Gautier, *La Langue de Xénophon* (Diss. Geneva 1911)
Gildersleeve, *SCG*	B.L.Gildersleeve, *Syntax of Classical Greek from Homer to Demosthenes* (New York) vol. I 1900, vol. II 1911
K–B, *GG*	R.Kühner rev. F.Blass, *Ausführliche Grammatik der griech. Sprache: I Elementar- und Formenlehre* 2 vols. (Hannover 1890–2^{3})
K–G, *GG*	R.Kühner rev. B.Gerth, *Grammatik . . . II Satzlehre* 2 vols. (Hannover 1898–1904^{3})
Lampe, *PGL*	G.W.H.Lampe, *A Patristic Greek Lexicon* (Oxford 1961–8)
Lapp, *TF*	F.Lapp, *De Callimachi Cyrenaei Tropis et Figuris* (Diss. Bonn 1965)
Leumann, *HW*	M.Leumann, *Homerische Wörter* (Basel 1950)
LfgrE	B.Snell and H.Erbse (edd.), *Lexikon des frühgriechischen Epos* (Göttingen 1955–)
Maas, *GM*	P.Maas, *Greek Metre* trans. by H.Lloyd-Jones (Oxford 1962)
Maas, *SJ*	P.Maas, *Sokrates: Jahresberichte des philologischen Vereins zu Berlin* 47 (1921) 136

Mayser, *GGP* — E.Mayser, *Grammatik der griech. Papyri aus der Ptolemäerzeit* 7 vols. (Berlin and Leipzig 1906–34); vol. 1^1 rev. H.Schmoll (Berlin 1970), vols. 1^2, 1^3 rev. Mayser (1938 and 1936)

Meineke, *AA* — A.Meineke, *Analecta Alexandrina* (Berlin 1843)

Meisterhans, *GAI* — K.Meisterhans, *Grammatik der attischen Inschriften* (Berlin 1900^3)

Monteil, *PR* — P.Monteil, *La Phrase relative en grec ancien* (Paris 1963)

Monteil, *T* — P.Monteil, *Théocrite: Idylles (2, 5, 7, 11, 15)* (Paris 1968)

Moulton, *GNT* — J.H.Moulton, *A Grammar of New Testament Greek* 3 vols. (vol. III by N.Turner) (Edinburgh 1908^3–63)

Nauck, *TGF* — A.Nauck, *Tragicorum Graecorum Fragmenta* (Leipzig 1889^2)

Nilsson, *GGR* — M.P.Nilsson, *Geschichte der griech. Religion* (Munich) vol. I 1967^3, vol. II 1961^2

Page, *GLP* — D.L.Page, *Greek Literary Papyri* (Loeb, rev. 1942)

Peek, *GVI* — W.Peek, *Griechische Versinschriften I Grab-Epigramme* (Berlin 1955)

Pfister, *RGR* — F.Pfister, *Die Religion der Griechen und Römer* (Leipzig 1930) (Bursian's *Jahresbericht Supplementband* Band 229)

Powell, *CA* — J.U.Powell, *Collectanea Alexandrina* (Oxford 1925)

Preller–Robert, *GM* — L.Preller rev. C.Robert, *Griechische Mythologie* (Berlin): I *Theogonie und Götter* 1894^4, II *Die griechische Heldensage* i 1920^4, ii 1921^4, iii.1 1921^4, iii.2.1 1923^4, iii.2.2 1926^4

RAC — *Reallexikon für Antike und Christentum* (Stuttgart 1950–)

Risch, *WHS* — E.Risch, *Wortbildung der homerischen Sprache* (Berlin and Leipzig 1974^2)

Roscher, *LM* — W.H.Roscher (ed.), *Ausführliches Lexikon der griech. und römischen Mythologie*

6 vols. (Leipzig and Berlin 1884–1937)

Schmidt, *PH* — C.E.Schmidt, *Parallel-Homer* (Göttingen 1885)

Schmidt, *SGS* — J.H.H.Schmidt, *Synonymik der griech. Sprache* 4 vols. (Leipzig 1876–86)

Schmitt, *NDK* — Rüdiger Schmitt, *Die Nominalbildung in den Dichtungen des Kallimachos von Kyrene* (Wiesbaden 1970)

Schwyzer, *DGEE* — E.Schwyzer, *Dialectorum Graecarum Exempla Epigraphica Potiora* (Leipzig 1923)

Schwyzer, *GG* — E.Schwyzer, *Griechische Grammatik* 3 vols. (Munich 1950–9^3) vol. II rev. A.Debrunner

SH — Hugh Lloyd-Jones and Peter Parsons, *Supplementum Hellenisticum* (*Texte und Kommentare* II: Berlin 1983)

Snell, *TGF* — B.Snell, *Tragicorum Graecorum Fragmenta* (Göttingen) vol. I 1971, vol. II 1981, vol. IV (Sophocles, ed. S.Radt) 1977

Stengel, *GKA* — P.Stengel, *Die griech. Kultus-Altertümer* (Munich 1920^3)

Svensson, *GBA* — A.Svensson, *Der Gebrauch des bestimmten Artikels in der nachklassischen griech. Epik* (Lund 1937)

Thumb, *GD* — A.Thumb, *Handbuch der griech. Dialekte* (Heidelberg) vol. I rev. E.Kieckers 1932, vol. II rev. A.Scherer 1959

Veitch, *GV* — W.Veitch, *Greek Verbs Irregular and Defective* (Oxford 1887)

Wackernagel, *SUH* — J.Wackernagel, *Sprachliche Untersuchungen zu Homer* (Göttingen 1916)

Wackernagel, *VUS* — J.Wackernagel, *Vorlesungen über Syntax* (Basel) vol. I 1920, vol. II 1924

Wifstrand, *KN* — A.Wifstrand, *Von Kallimachos zu Nonnos* (Lund 1933)

Wilamowitz, *GH* — U. von Wilamowitz-Moellendorff, *Der Glaube der Hellenen* 2 vols. (Berlin 1931)

INTRODUCTION

I OCCASION AND COMPOSITION OF THE POEM

The very first line of Callimachus' fifth 'hymn' establishes the theme and tone of the poem:

ὅσσαι λωτροχόοι τᾶς Παλλάδος ἔξιτε πᾶσαι . . .

'You women who are bath-pourers of Pallas, all of you come out . . .'

The occasion is the celebration of Athena, which will involve a ritual bath, and the ceremony, the preserve of women, is about to begin; the voice which addresses the celebrants is never identified, but the speaker, the same throughout the poem, is presumably an official or priestess. More details soon emerge: the setting is Argos in the Peloponnese and Athena's statue is to be taken down in procession to the river Inachus, bathed and returned to the city. Only women may attend the ritual bath, and for them emergence of the cult-statue, presumably from its temple, is a divine epiphany (see on vv. 1 τᾶς Παλλάδος, 3 καὶ ἁ θεὸς . . ., 35 φέρεται, 137 ἀτρεκές, ἀλλὰ δέχεσθε, 139 ὀλολυγαῖς); for the celebration the Palladion *is* Athena and is so addressed (see on vv. 35–56), the horses and waggon which convey the statue are identified with Athena's actual horses and chariot (see on vv. 5–12), and the cult equipment is such as Athena actually uses (cf. on vv. 13–17, 29–32). We are witnesses, or participants, at the scene of the festival, and the poem recreates the religious enthusiasm of the occasion: vv. 1–32 summon the celebrants, giving instructions what equipment to bring, and insisting with mounting agitation on the imminence of Athena's arrival (2–3 the waggon-horses are neighing in anticipation, 14 the waggon's axle is creaking); 33–56 invoke Athena directly, assuring her that the ceremony will be properly conducted now that the celebrants are assembled, and addressing her with increasing agitation (33, 43 ἔξιθ' Ἀθαναία, 55 πότνι' Ἀθαναία, τὺ μὲν ἔξιθι) and appropriate epicletic epithets (43);

57–136 tell a cautionary tale, the blinding of Tiresias who offended the goddess, both as a warning to the profane and, by implication, as encouragement to the pious and initiated; in 137–42 the emergence of Athena is briefly announced at last, the celebrants receive final instructions and the goddess a formal hymnal greeting.

Excitement and religious fervour dominate the mood of the poem, and Callimachus has been so successful in recreating the tension of the ceremony that some commentators have taken the *Bath of Pallas* as an actual cult hymn. Anna Fabri suggested that Callimachus was in fact under commission from Argos and that the Doric element in the language of the Hymn derives from practical circumstance (*hoc poematium Dorice scriptum est, quia tunc Argis erat Callimachus: ideoque cuncta illi gratificari volens eius dialecto utitur: neque enim perpetuo Aegyptum aut Cyrenen incoluit; nam et in Sicilia vixit.* Conveniently cited in Ernesti); more recently H.Staehelin argued that, while the poem was not an actual cult hymn, the tone of intense enthusiasm is too convincing not to have been the product of serious religious involvement (*Die Religion des Kallimachos* (Diss. Basel 1934) esp. 34–7, 54, 58ff.). The practical and methodological objections to this approach do not need to be detailed here;[1] Wilamowitz, *HD* I 182 can hardly be contested when he says: 'jeder Unbefangene muss sehen, dass solche Gedichte in keiner Weise für den Kultus bestimmt sind und auch keine alten Kultlieder widerspiegeln'.[2] Ph.-E.

[1] Since the publication of *P. Oxy.* 1362 fr. 1 (= Call. fr. 178) it has been almost impossible to maintain that Callimachus ever left the continent of Africa (cf. Pfeiffer, *Callimachus* II xxxix). I have considered some of the methodological issues involved in the question of 'religious seriousness' in a study of the Sixth Hymn in *AJP* 98 (1977) 97–123.

[2] Similarly Herter, *RE* Suppl. V 433–4 'Die sechs Hymnen . . . sind rein literarische Erzeugnisse: sie sind nicht für den wirklichen Kultus bestimmt, sondern für die Rezitation im Kreise gelehrter Kunstverständiger, vor allem am Hof, und für die Lektüre; darüber kann heute kein Zweifel mehr herrschen', and *RE* Suppl. XIII 230 'Die Hymnen sind vielmehr, einer wie der andere, rein literarisch wie schon einige vor Kallimachos und nach seiner Auffassung wohl bereits die homerischen

Legrand demonstrated long ago (*REA* 3 (1901) 281–312) that the Fifth Hymn in particular would present insurmountable difficulties of timing and co-ordination if it was written for performance at the Argive festival itself; references to neighing horses (v. 2) and creaking axles (v. 14) are too hazardous for the poem to have been written in advance for a real ceremony, and in any case a liturgical text whose recitation comprehended the entire ceremony, from congregation of the celebrants to epiphany of the divinity, would be unique in practical ritual. The compass of the Fifth Hymn and the careful insertion of references to ceremonial particulars have to do not with realism, but verisimilitude. Indeed the very presence of such details betrays precisely the literary nature of our text. The point has been well made by Paul Friedländer in 'Vorklassisch und Nachklassisch' in *Das Problem des Klassischen und die Antike* (ed. W.Jaeger, Leipzig and Berlin 1931) 35f.: "Von den Bedingungen – kultlichen, staatlichen, gesellschaftlichen –, in denen archaische und klassische Dichtung erwuchs, ist die hellenistische frei. Sie muss erst Gemeinschaft um sich zu gründen versuchen, und muss den Lebenszusammenhang, der nicht mehr gegeben ist, mit Kunst hervorbringen. . . . Kallimachos stellt nicht in einen gegebenen Raum seine Dichtung, sondern er muss mit der Dichtung zugleich den Raum für sie schaffen . . . Dieses Hervorbringen des Nicht-Vorhandenen fordert starke Mittel. Pathetische Wortwiederholungen: . . . ἔξιτε ἔξιτε, σοῦσθε σοῦσθε, Aufruf, Aufforderung, Frage. Die Wahrnehmung wird betont, gerade weil sie (grob gesagt) nicht da ist.' The *Bath of Pallas* is not a hymn written for a ritual but a literary poem skilfully designed to create the illusion of a ceremony actually being performed.

Muster selber'. The attempt by Cahen, *C* 281 to argue for a more restricted 'epideictic' function for II, IV, V and VI 'en rapport direct avec la fête religieuse, en dehors pourtant de son programme cérémonial', seems to me likely only for the Hymn to Apollo (see also H.Herter, *Gnomon* 12 (1936) 454–9).

The mimetic hymn, purporting to be what is actually said by an organiser of a celebration, belongs to a distinct class of Alexandrian experimental poetry, literary drama. Two of Callimachus' contemporaries, Theocritus and Herodas, particularly concentrated on this form, and although the origins of Hellenistic mime are not at all clear (though presumably the tradition of theatrical mime was an important antecedent),[1] we may certainly classify the *Bath of Pallas* with Theocritus' dramatic idylls, both pastoral and non-pastoral, and with Herodas' lively sketches of lower-class life. Both these authors show an interest in religious matters, Herodas in *Mime* 4 where two women make an offering at a temple of Asclepius, and Theocritus in *Id.* 15 where Gorgo and Praxinoa visit Ptolemy's palace and listen to a performance of the 'Adonis' at the Adonis festival. There are important differences between the Fifth Hymn and these poems since the latter are both dialogues and are more concerned with ecphrasis of the palace and temple decorations than with ceremonial itself; but interest in the psychology of religious feeling, even if at different levels, motivates each author, and in Callimachus the long narrative of Tiresias plays a similar part to the descriptions of statues and paintings in Herodas 4. In the Theocritean corpus *Id.* 18 the *Epithalamion for Helen* is closer in style and level to the *Bath of Pallas* as 'situation' poetry, though the idyll is only partially mimetic since it has a narrative introduction; closest in tone and style is *Id.* 2, the *Pharmaceutria*, also a dramatic monologue, and although a personal prayer as against the cult prayer of the Fifth Hymn the idyll nonetheless skilfully recreates a fervid emotional atmosphere and is similarly structured with a central narrative section.[2]

---

[1] Cf. I.C.Cunningham, *Herodas: Mimiambi* (Oxford 1971) 3–17, K.J.Dover, *Theocritus* (London 1971) liv–lxv.

[2] The two poems have some points of detail in common: the use of refrain, address to a second party other than the divinity, reference to circumstantial items of ceremonial equipment, and the use of atmospheric realism

We should also not forget that the hymn form had long been used as a vehicle for a literary fictional occasion. The circumstances of composition and performance of the Homeric Hymns are unknown, but as Allen–Sikes–Halliday, *The Homeric Hymns* (Oxford 1936) lxxxvi point out, our critical evidence indicates that they are 'more literary and less devotional' than other early hymns of which we know. Sappho uses the hymn form in poems composed not for formal ritual occasions but for literary prayer (frr. 1, 2: cf. Denys Page, *Sappho and Alcaeus* (Oxford 1955) 16f., 40ff.), and the 'hymns' which appear in the Theognis corpus (e.g. the introductory hymnal prayers to Apollo in 1–10, to Artemis in 11–14 and the Muses in 15–18, and the address to Apollo in 773–82) mark the complete separation of hymn from cult (cf. Wünsch in *RE* IX 158). In choral lyric (a genre to which Callimachus' three mimetic hymns are closely related) Pindar used the encomion form for poems which were almost certainly not performed as part of a religious celebration (e.g. *P.* 3, *I.* 2), and in tone and mode of writing he is often the precursor of Hellenistic hymnal style.[1]

Thus although Callimachus is the first to write hymns in the mimetic style specifically as illusory enactments or recreations of the festivals of Apollo (Hymn II), Athena, and Demeter (Hymn VI), these poems do not mark a radical break

(with *Id.* 2.35 cf. V 2f., 29ff. and 137ff.). L.Deubner, 'Ein Stilprinzip hellenistischer Dichtkunst', *Neue Jahrbücher für das klassische Altertum* 47 (1921) 376–8 attempted to argue that *Id.* 2 was actually the forerunner and inspiration of II, V and VI: his arguments are unconvincing since they rest on unprovable assumptions about the dating of *Id.* 2 and of V and VI (see below Section V p. 39).

[1] Aptly expressed by F.Dornseiff, *Pindars Stil* (Berlin 1921) 85 'Hier ist nämlich ganz deutlich die Vorstufe einer Haupteigentümlichkeit des hellenistischen, profan-künstlerischen Hymnos . . . Sie sind halb mimisch-chorisch, halb episch-rezitativisch, sie spielen leicht romantisch mit der Fiktion, Begleitgedicht zu einer heiligen Handlung zu sein, und schildern sie doch zugleich, eine höchst kunstvolle Stilmanier, kraft deren es in der Schwebe bleibt, ob der Dichter oder der Festordner eines Chores spricht, ob das δρώμενον Wirklichkeit oder Annahme ist.'

with tradition, for all that they are some of the most masterly examples of a mode in which several Alexandrians were experimenting. Later Bion was to follow with his *Adonis*, a ritual lament, and one of his pupils with the *Bion* (Pseudo-Moschus 3).

Callimachus' mimetic hymns were clearly written for recitation before an educated audience associated with the royal court at Alexandria, but this does not mean that they should be regarded as fictitious in every respect. In presenting a work such as the Fifth Hymn Callimachus will have presupposed that his listeners were well acquainted with festivals of this kind and perhaps even knew something of the Argive ceremony.[1] What we know of bathing ceremonies shows that the details mentioned by Callimachus were thoroughly characteristic of actual ritual. The *Bath of Pallas* (our sole source for the Argive ceremony) describes a ritual in which the statue was taken from its temple to the river, bathed and anointed by women attendants and returned to the city, and the underlying practice, κόϲμηϲιϲ ἀγαλμάτων, is one with which we are familiar from many parts of the Greek world (though our evidence is often fragmentary and late). Formal cleansing (γάνωϲιϲ) of statue and sanctuary was generally an annual matter involving washing down with water, sponging, oiling (χρίϲιϲ) and anointing with perfume (μύρον); a procession of the statue carried around on a waggon and accompanied by χοροί seems often to have followed.[2] Amongst many inscriptions from Delos one, *IG* XI^{2}

[1] Cf. U. von Wilamowitz-Moellendorff, *Bion von Smyrna: Adonis* (Berlin 1900) 10–12 (= *Reden und Vorträge* I (1925^{4}) 298ff.) who rightly emphasises that Bion's poem was written as a recital text for dramatic presentation before a knowledgeable audience.

[2] On the whole process of γάνωϲιϲ see H. Blümner, *Technologie und Terminologie der Gewerbe und Künste bei Griechen und Römern* (Leipzig 1884) III 200ff. In Rome such cleansing of the temple of Capitoline Jupiter was the first duty of the censors on taking office: Plut. *Mor.* 287B διὰ τί οἱ τιμηταὶ τὴν ἀρχὴν παραλαβόντεϲ οὐδὲν ἄλλο πράττουϲι πρότερον ἢ τὴν τροφὴν ἀπομιϲθοῦϲι τῶν ἱερῶν χηνῶν καὶ τὴν γάνωϲιν τοῦ ἀγάλματοϲ;

161A (279 B.C.), a temple account, refers in a short space to: 90f. εἰς κόσμησιν τοῦ ἀγάλματος . . . , τὴν ἅμαξαν ἧι ἄγεται τὸ ἄγαλμα τοῦ Διονύσου Θεοφάντωι ἐπισκευάσαντι . . . , 92f. ἔλαιον . . . μύρον ῥόδινον . . . , 93f. εἰς τοὺς χοροὺς τοὺς γενομένους τοῖς Λητωΐοις καὶ τοῖς Ἀρτεμισίοις καὶ τὸν τῆι ὀγδόηι δᾶιδες . . .[1] The κόσμησις of female divinities often took the form of a cult ritual which involved washing the statue in the sea or a river. Few of these ceremonies are attested for us in any detail, but the one about which we have the most evidence, the Athenian Plynteria, seems to have been very similar to the Argive festival of the Fifth Hymn: the wooden statue of Athena Polias was stripped of its dress and jewellery, taken in procession with a guard of ephebes out of the city to Phaleron, bathed in the sea under the direction of two girls called πλυντρίδες or λουτρίδες, re-dressed and ornamented and returned to the temple.[2] Most of the other bathing ceremonies of which we know involved Hera and seem to have been connected with purification, or restoration of virginity, after her Sacred Marriage with Zeus;[3] however, at Ancyra Athena appears again, this time accompanied by Artemis, in a double bathing ceremony which involved carriage in a waggon down to a lake.[4] Surprisingly we have little explicit testimony that Aphrodite was the object of bath

[1] See T.Homolle, 'Comptes et inventaires des temples déliens en l'année 279', *BCH* 14 (1890) esp. 496–511 and the full citations and discussion in P.Bruneau, *Recherches sur les cultes de Délos à l'époque hellénistique et à l'époque impériale* (Paris 1970) 198ff. on Artemis and 249ff. on Hera.

[2] For detailed description and citation of sources see L.Deubner, *Attische Feste* (Berlin 1932) 17–22, H.W.Parke, *Festivals of the Athenians* (London 1977) 152–5.

[3] Thus in Nauplia, Samos, Plataea: see M.P.Nilsson, *Griechische Feste* (Leipzig 1906) 44–56. Also in Mesopotamia (Aelian, *NA* 12.30).

[4] Nilsson, *Griechische Feste* 255f. Our source is a fifth-century Christian one and tempting parallels with the Argive ceremony (Athena, Artemis ~ Athena, Chariclo) cannot be pressed even though the ritual itself was doubtless an old one; commentators have noted that the ceremony was orgiastic and may have derived from the Phrygian cult of the Magna Mater.

ritual, even at Paphos, though in myth and the visual arts she is frequently associated with the sea.[1]

Thus even though we know nothing about the Argive festival,[2] and indeed know little about the cult of Athena at Argos at all (see Section II below pp. 14–17), our evidence of similar ceremonies elsewhere permits us to reconstruct the ritual in outline from the Fifth Hymn itself.[3] On the day of the festival the women of Argos assembled ready for procession (vv. 1–4 etc.); there is no strong reason to think that the ceremony, or any part of it, was restricted to women of particular class or age (as was the Demeter festival of the Sixth Hymn, vv. 128–33), unless the first line ὅϲϲαι λωτροχόοι . . . πᾶϲαι is taken as being implicitly exclusive (i.e. referring to all who qualified as initiates rather than to the bath officials specifically). The question whether the festival was restricted to women of unmarried status has to remain open; only v. 34 παρθενικαί offers any textual support for this, but the word occurs in a phrase which is a standard periphrasis for 'daughter' (see Commentary ad loc.), and although ritual celebration of virgin goddesses was often

---

[1] In Sicyon the temple of Aphrodite was barred to all except the two servants of the god, one of whom was titled λουτροφόροϲ. We know that in the early third century B.C., at least, the temple of Aphrodite Pandemos at Athens was cleansed annually, but the cult image seems to have been washed in position: *IG* II² 659.24 καὶ περιαλεῖψαι τοὺϲ βωμοὺϲ καὶ πιττῶϲαι τὰϲ [ὀροφὰϲ] καὶ λοῦϲαι τὰ ἕδη· παραϲκευάϲαι δὲ καὶ πορφύραν ὁλκήν . . . (cf. Deubner, *Attische Feste* 215f.). For a useful survey of the evidence for all divinities see R.Ginouvès, *Balaneutikè* (Paris 1962) 283–98 'Bains de statues et de divinités', and cf. also E.Fehrle, *Die kultische Keuschheit im Altertum* (Giessen 1910) 170–6.

[2] The introductory note in the ancient scholia is of no demonstrable value since it contains nothing which could not be derived from the text of the Hymn.

[3] It should be emphasised here that Cahen's extraordinary conclusion (*Hymnes de Callimaque* (Paris 1930) 218–20) that the Fifth Hymn deals with Athena's arrival in Argos by chariot from Olympia is completely erroneous and is based on misinterpretation of ἔξιτε in vv. 1–2 and failure to realise that the waggon (v. 14) was a standard vehicle in ceremonies of this kind.

restricted to virgins, the presence in the accompanying myth of Tiresias' mother Chariclo suggests that virginity was not required for Argive Athena's bath attendants.[1] When the women were assembled (33–4) the statue, the Palladion, was placed on the waggon (14) and drawn by horses (mares, naturally) down to the river Inachus. The Palladion was accompanied by an important relic, the shield of Diomedes (35), doubtless as a symbol of protection while the city's talisman was away from the temple (see Commentary on 35–42). In the Athenian Plynteria ephebes went with the procession to Phaleron; there is no explicit mention in the Hymn of similar military accompaniment for the Palladion, but the aetiological myth of Eumedes (36–42) might be taken as implying an escort, and the use of warrior epithets in the address to Athena which closes the myth (43–4) might imply an armed procession which included cavalry (44 ἵππων) and ritual banging of shields (44 cακέων . . . πατάγωι).[2] Men were excluded from the ritual bath even if not from the procession (51–4, 57–136), and the river was reserved exclusively for the ceremony (44–51). Before the statue was bathed the horses, and possibly the waggon, were washed in the river (5–12 the first attribute of Athena (see Commentary), mention of which is logical only if it arises from part of the actual ritual: see Commentary ad loc.). The Palladion was stripped of its costume, whether before it left the temple as in the Athenian Plynteria or at the river as the Tiresias narrative suggests (70–2), bathed, and then given formal κόcμηcιc with plain oil and a ritual comb (18–32 the second attribute of Athena, explicitly designed to reinforce instructions given to the celebrants in 13–17). As at Athens the statue will then have been reclothed and driven back to the city; mention of the battle against the Giants in 7f. may be due to

[1] See also Commentary on 45 ὑδροφόροι, 47 αἱ δῶλαι.

[2] In Sparta Athena Χαλκίοικοc was celebrated by a procession of armed young men: Polyb. 4.35. Cf. Wilamowitz, *HD* II 18.

the fact that in Argos as at the Athenian Panathenaea the war was depicted on the peplos.[1]

No more than this can be inferred from the text of the Hymn,[2] but we may take it as established that although the Fifth Hymn was not designed for performance at the actual Argive ceremony it was none the less full of realistic detail. Callimachus' audience will certainly have recognised that the ceremony in which the poet was inviting them to participate imaginatively was typical of such bath rituals; what will probably have been new and entertaining to them is the particular Argive festival and the myth associated with it, for knowledge of which Callimachus drew on his antiquarian researches in the Alexandrian Library.

Finally, we should not rule out the possibility that the setting of the Hymn in Argos had some connection with the Ptolemaic royal family's interest in tracing their descent back to the best Macedonian ancestry. From the time of Ptolemy I propaganda that the Ptolemaic line was very closely connected to that of Alexander the Great and the Macedonian royal family was widely disseminated, the key ancestor for the Ptolemaic and Macedonian lines being Argaeus.[3] Although

---

[1] See Commentary on vv. 7f., 70 πέπλων. As Wilamowitz, *HD* II 14 pointed out, if the Argive ceremony, like the Athenian, involved clothing the statue in a new peplos the 'Ενδυμάτια referred to by [Plut.] *de mus.* 1134C may have been part of this ritual.

[2] We may wonder whether a beauty contest preceded the festival; this would give an added dimension to the second mythological exemplum in vv. 18–28, the Judgement of Paris. Theophrastus fr. 111 Wimmer (= Athen. 609F) records that at Elis the festival of Athena was preceded by an ἀγὼν κάλλους the winner of which led the procession to her temple. Competitions were an important feature in the Athenian Panathenaea, including one for εὐανδρία in which physical appearance was important: see A.Brelich, *Paides e Parthenoi* (Rome 1969) 338ff. and cf. Deubner, *Attische Feste* 34.

[3] For the concern over the ancestry of Ptolemy I and the important link to the main Macedonian line through his mother Arsinoe or, according to clever rumour, even through Ptolemy being the bastard son of Philip II, see K.J.Beloch, *Griechische Geschichte* IV 2 (Berlin 1927[2]) 176–7, W.W.Tarn, 'Two notes on Ptolemaic history', *JHS* 53 (1933) 57–68. The

the town of Argos with which the Argeads were connected was actually situated in northern Macedonia, it was the practice even in the fifth century to give them a more romantic and flattering origin by making Peloponnesian Argos their homeland and thus giving them an ancient and impeccable Dorian descent, through Temenus, from Heracles and Dionysus. This ancestry, based on an early member of the family fleeing from Argos to Macedonia, is recorded as early as Herodotus 8.137, Thucydides 2.99.3, and, in a variant form, Euripides, *Archelaus* (frr. 228–64 Nauck); Isocrates, *Philip* 32 could even say to Philip Ἄργος μὲν γάρ ἐστί σοι πατρὶς ἧς δίκαιον τοσαύτην σε ποιεῖσθαι πρόνοιαν ὅσην περ τῶν γονέων τῶν σαυτοῦ. Contemporaries of Callimachus emphasised this Doric, Argive connection: Theocritus 17.16–27 stressed the descent of Ptolemy I and Alexander the Great jointly from Heracles; at Theocritus 15.96ff. the Adonis-song for the festival at the Ptolemaic royal palace is sung by the daughter of an Argive (v. 97); and in Theocritus 24 (which is given no specific setting) it is Argos that is most prominent as the place where Alcmene and Heracles are renowned (cf. vv. 78, 104ff.).[1] Callimachus' Fifth Hymn contains no overt political references, but Argos was a place of unusual significance for his Ptolemaic patrons, and their interest in Heracles as an ancestor may be behind the, to us puzzling, reference to Eumedes at vv. 35–42 (see Commentary).

---

importance of this ancestry was such that Satyrus, in his work on the demes of Alexandria, traced the full genealogy from the Ptolemies back through Heracles to Dionysus: see the summary quoted in Theophilus (*FGrHist* 3C 631 F 1) now supplemented by *P. Oxy.* 2465 fr. 1. Many of the demes of Alexandria were given names from the generations of this Macedonian royal genealogy: see P.M.Fraser, *Ptolemaic Alexandria* (Oxford 1972) I 44–5 and notes.

[1] For the possible Ptolemaic setting of Theocritus' *Heracliscus* (*Id.* 24), and its connection with Ptolemaic ancestry, see Ludwig Koenen, *Eine agonistische Inschrift aus Ägypten und frühptolemäische Königsfeste* (Beiträge zur klassischen Philologie 56: Meisenheim 1977) 79–86.

II ATHENA, TIRESIAS AND ARGOS

The first line of the Fifth Hymn identifies the Argive cult-statue as the famous Palladion from Troy (see Commentary on v. 1 τᾶς Παλλάδος). Early tradition, from the *Little Iliad* on, had it that after the Greeks besieging Troy learned of the protection afforded by the Palladion, Diomedes and Odysseus succeeded in stealing the talisman and making the city vulnerable to attack;[1] after the sack the departing Greeks took the statue with them, and various states in historical times claimed to possess the authentic image, amongst others Argos, Sparta, Athens and Rome (see Nilsson, *GGR* I 435f.). The Argive claim to own the Trojan Palladion was based, naturally, on the part played in the theft by the city's own hero Diomedes (Paus. 2.23.5, Plut. *Mor.* 302D), who on his return after the Trojan war also dedicated the temple of Athena Oxyderkes at Argos in thanks for her lifting the darkness from his eyes in an incident at Troy (*Il.* 5.127; Paus. 2.24.2).[2] Diomedes was intimately associated with both Athena and Argos (Preller–Robert, *GM* II 302–6, Roscher, *LM* I 1023–7), but the ancient sources have no more to tell us about the Argive Palladion and the temple in which it was housed; about the relic of Diomedes' shield we have no information beyond the bare mention in our Hymn (see Commentary on vv. 35–42). Modern archaeological investigations have added little to our knowledge. In 1956 W. Vollgraff published the full results of his 1902–6 excavations and

---

[1] For a convenient summary of the most important material see Frazer on Ovid, *Fasti* 6.421; also Jebb–Pearson on Sophocles, *Lacaenae* (*The Fragments of Sophocles* II 34–6). For a full survey see Roscher, *LM* III 1301–33.

[2] At Sparta the temple of Athena Ophthalmitis was said to have been founded by Lycurgus because the Lacedaemonians saved him from losing his one remaining eye (Paus. 3.18.2). Preller–Robert, *GM* II 303 suggest that Pausanias' explanation of Argive Athena's Oxyderkes title was his own notion, and that the name in fact derived from the belief that the real Palladion could roll its eyes (Virg. *Aen.* 2.172f. and Servius on *Aen.* 2.166).

the sanctuary of Athena Oxyderkes seems to have been identified on the slopes of the Aspis hill (which adjoins the higher main citadel, the Larisa) next to the temple of Apollo Pythaeeus; amongst several other temples to Athena mentioned by Pausanias the one on the Larisa, close to the temple of Larisaean Zeus (Paus. 2.24.3), has been identified by an inscription as being that of Athena Polias.[1] Scholars have debated which of these two sanctuaries is likely to have housed the Palladion, and Wilamowitz (*HD* II 14), Kleinknecht (*LP* 311f.) and Cahen all accept the Oxyderkes temple.[2] However there are strong grounds for thinking that the Palladion stood in the main Larisa temple of Athena Polias: it is in this sanctuary that excavation revealed a terracotta representation of an armed Athena, Argive coins depict a Palladion placed on a hill which resembles the Larisa citadel, and Paus. 2.25.10 reported that in the temple of Athena at Lessa, between Argos and Epidaurus, was a wooden image *exactly like the one on Argive Larisa* (ξόανον οὐδέν τι διάφορον ἢ τὸ ἐν ἀκροπόλει τῆι Λαρίϲηι).[3] This evidence, slight though it is, seems difficult to resist, and we should probably allow that Diomedes' shield was brought separately from its temple, that of Athena Oxyderkes, to that of Athena Polias whence the Palladion would move in procession to the

[1] W.Vollgraff, *Le Sanctuaire d'Apollon Pythéen à Argos* (Paris 1956) 51–76 'Le temple d'Athéna Oxyderkes'. For Athena Polias see W.Vollgraff, *Mnemosyne* 57 (1929) 208, 217, and for a more recent editing of the inscription see *SEG* 11 (1954) 314.

[2] Wilamowitz assumes, reasonably, that Diomedes' shield was likely to have been housed in the temple which he founded and inferred the location of the Palladion from its association here with the shield; Kleinknecht erroneously argued that Palladion and shield were the same object (see Commentary on vv. 35–42). Cahen gives no reason for his identification.

[3] For the terracotta see W.Vollgraff, *Le Sanctuaire d'Apollon Pythéen à Argos* 53f.; for the coins see F.Imhoof-Blumer and P.Gardner, *A Numismatic Commentary on Pausanias* (1885–7) 39f. Vollgraff had originally argued for the Palladion in the Oxyderkes temple (see *Mnem.* 57 (1929) 218f.), but later changed his mind (*Bull. de l'Acad. Roy. de Belgique* Cl. des Lettres (1938) 39 n. 4).

Inachus.[1] Location of the Palladion in the Polias temple is not without importance for interpretation of the Fifth Hymn: we should beware of assuming that Athena Oxyderkes had anything to do with the Argive Palladion cult or has any bearing on our text.[2]

Although it is unfortunate how little we know about the practical circumstances of the Argive cult of Athena and the background to the *Bath of Pallas* there is, or should be, a salutary side-effect: we should be the more aware that at various points in the poem we probably lack certain crucial items of information which Callimachus could take for granted in his contemporary audience. Furthermore, although Callimachus himself had probably never visited the Argolid and experienced at first hand the cult of which he writes, he did have available major sources of information about Argos and its religious practices which are lost to us. One work in particular seems to have been used by Callimachus: the Ἀργολικά of Agias and Dercylus is known to have been his source in the *Aetia* in the episodes dealing with the Graces (frr. 3–7), Linus and Coroebus (frr. 26–31), and the Fountains of Argos (frr. 65–6),[3] and it is a reasonable assumption that Callimachus may have used the same source for the *Bath of Pallas*.[4] The *Argolica* was a prose work in at least three books, written in mild Doric dialect and dealing with matters of myth (for example Heracles, the Trojan war) and

---

[1] The placing and wording of v. 35 φέρεται δὲ καὶ ἁ Διομήδεος ἀσπίς are not inappropriate for this interpretation: the shield is already present with the celebrants *before* the Palladion emerges from its temple and 'is being carried'.

[2] McKay's interpretation, for example, suffers throughout from an over-enthusiastic preoccupation with eyes.

[3] See respectively the Florentine Scholium 35–6 (Pfeiffer, *Callimachus* I 13), the Diegesis in *P. Oxy.* 2263 fr. 1 col. II 6–8 (Pfeiffer, *Callimachus* II 108), the commentary to Antimachus fr. 179, in *Papiri della R. Università di Milano* vol. primo, ed. A. Vogliano (Milan 1937) no. 17 col. II 14–16 (Pfeiffer on fr. 65).

[4] The suggestion was first noted by B.Wyss, *Antimachi Colophonii Reliquiae* (Berlin 1936) 88 n. 15.

cult; almost nothing is known about the authors, but Dercylus is generally assumed to be the reviser or supplementer of the earlier work of Agias, and the new edition of Agias' work may have appeared only recently and become the standard work on Argos when Callimachus wrote.[1] In the *Aetia* frr. 65–6 Callimachus drew on Agias and Dercylus for information about cult practices connected with the main water-sources of Argos, from one of which, the *Argolica* tells us, women called Ἡρεσίδες carried water back to Hera (cf. Hesych. s.v. Ἡρεσίδες· κόραι αἱ λουτρὰ κομίζουσαι τῆι Ἥραι); the similarity of subject-matter makes it very probable that Callimachus used the *Argolica* also for information about the Argive bath festival of the Palladion, though we have no explicit evidence for this.

Callimachus may well have derived more from Agias and Dercylus than just the cult. When the festival organiser has finished summoning the Argive celebrants and invoking Athena she turns to the cautionary tale with the words μῦθος δ' οὐκ ἐμός, ἀλλ' ἑτέρων (v. 56). The disclaimer is standard, as also is the general phraseology which leaves any actual source unidentified (see Commentary on vv. 55f.), but the plural ἑτέρων is notable. This plural could be generalising, but metrically ἑτέρου would have been equally possible (and more likely if his source had been Pherecydes as many commentators have assumed: see below) and we should consider the possibility that the Tiresias myth was in fact the cult myth associated with the actual Argive festival and that Agias and Dercylus reported this in their *Argolica*.

The version of the blinding of Tiresias narrated in the Fifth Hymn is particularly unusual.[2] The account more frequently

---

[1] For surviving fragments of the *Argolica* see Jacoby, *FGrHist* 3B 305 (pp. 7–10 and 757), and for background and discussion *FGrHist* 3b (Kommentar) pp. 17–24 and 3b (Noten) pp. 10–13. Callimachus' pupil Istros also wrote an *Argolica* (*FGrHist* 3B 334 F 39), and this may possibly reflect a particular interest in Argos on Callimachus' part.

[2] L.Brisson, *Le Mythe de Terésias* (Leiden 1976) is disappointing on the

given is that first found in Hesiod, *Melampodia* fr. 275, according to which Zeus and Hera, quarrelling about whether the man or the woman derived more pleasure from sexual intercourse, turned for arbitration to Tiresias (who had been both man and woman); when Tiresias adjudged that the woman receives nine times as much pleasure as the man, Hera blinded him but Zeus gave him the gifts of prophecy and long life. This was the version to be found subsequently in Dicaearchus (fr. 37 Wehrli), Clearchus (ap. Phlegon, *Mir.* 4 in Jacoby, *FGrHist* 2B 257 F 36), Ovid, *Met.* 3.316ff., [Apollod.] 3.6.7, Hygin. *fab.* 75 etc.[1] Only one author before Callimachus is known to have given the account involving Athena, the fifth-century Athenian mythographer Pherecydes, who is reported in two sources (=Jacoby, *FGrHist* I 3 F 92):

ἦν δὲ παρὰ Θηβαίοιϲ μάντιϲ Τειρεϲίαϲ Εὐήρουϲ καὶ Χαρικλοῦϲ νύμφηϲ, ἀπὸ γένουϲ Οὐδαίου τοῦ Ϲπαρτοῦ, γενόμενοϲ τυφλὸϲ τὰϲ ὁράϲειϲ. οὗ περὶ τῆϲ πηρώϲεωϲ καὶ τῆϲ μαντικῆϲ λέγονται λόγοι διάφοροι. ἄλλοι μὲν γὰρ αὐτὸν ὑπὸ θεῶν φαϲὶ τυφλωθῆναι, ὅτι τοῖϲ ἀνθρώποιϲ ἃ κρύπτειν ἤθελον ἐμήνυε. Φερεκύδηϲ δὲ ὑπὸ Ἀθηνᾶϲ αὐτὸν τυφλωθῆναι. οὖϲαν γὰρ τὴν Χαρικλὼ προϲφιλῆ τῆι Ἀθηνᾶι ⟨ ⟩ γυμνὴν ἐπὶ πάντα ἰδεῖν· τὴν δὲ ταῖϲ χερϲὶ τοὺϲ ὀφθαλμοὺϲ αὐτοῦ καταλαβομένην πηρὸν ποιῆϲαι· Χαρικλοῦϲ δὲ δεομένηϲ ἀποκαταϲτῆϲαι πάλιν τὰϲ ὁράϲειϲ μὴ δυναμένην τοῦτο ποιῆϲαι τὰϲ ἀκοὰϲ διακαθάραϲαν πᾶϲαν ὀρνίθων φωνὴν ποιῆϲαι ϲυνεῖναι, καὶ ϲκῆπτρον αὐτῶι δωρήϲαϲθαι κράνειον, ὃ φέρων ὁμοίωϲ τοῖϲ βλέπουϲιν ἐβάδιζεν.

[Apollod.] 3.6.7

πηρωθῆναι δ' αὐτόν ⟨φηϲι⟩ Φερεκύδηϲ ἰδόντα τὴν Ἀθηνᾶν λουομένην ἐν τῶι ⟨ ⟩ παρθένον ὑπάρχουϲαν καὶ κορευθεῖϲαν ὑπ' Ἀπόλλωνοϲ εἰϲ τὸ ⟨ ⟩ καίεϲθαι μέλλειν ὑπὸ Εὐήρου τοῦ πατρὸϲ ⟨ ⟩ εἰϲ ἄνδρα μεταβαλέϲθαι γνώμηι τοῦ θεοῦ καὶ μίαν τὴν ⟨ ⟩ γενέϲθαι . . .

Schol. T *Od.* 10.493

Both texts are lacunose but complete enough to show that in

Athena–Tiresias version and fails to consider any comparative material. Cf. below.

[1] Phlegon, *Mir.* 4 also lists Callimachus among those who told this version; Pfeiffer itemises this as fr. 576 but we may wonder whether Phlegon was not confused. For a full list of sources see Roscher, *LM* v 182ff.

outline Pherecydes' account was very similar to that of Callimachus, and modern scholars have assumed that Callimachus was consciously drawing on the mythographer for an unusual version of a standard story.[1] Further support for this has been found in the fact that Callimachus seems to characterise Athena with features more appropriate to Artemis than to the unfeminine warrior-goddess: Wilamowitz, *HD* II 23 'Passt es sich für Athena im Walde zu spazieren und in einer Quelle zu baden oder für die Jägerin Artemis? Hat Athena wie jene einen Chor von Gespielen um sich? Und ist der Abklatsch nicht deutlich, wenn Teiresias auf die Jagd gehen muss?' And with that flourish Wilamowitz concludes that Pherecydes made up his story from that of Artemis and Actaeon, an incident which Callimachus himself mentions in the course of the narrative (vv. 107–18); he was tentatively followed by Cahen (p. 232) and by L.Radermacher, *Mythos und Sage bei den Griechen* (1938) 51f. However Wilamowitz' argument that the Tiresias–Athena encounter is based on the Actaeon–Artemis story is weak, since the bath of Artemis is not mentioned before the Fifth Hymn itself, and some scholars have argued that it is the Artemis story which Callimachus has remodelled on the basis of the Athena myth.[2] In any case the assumption that feminine attributes and associations are unsuitable for Athena needs examining more closely.

Modern accounts of Athena and the cults associated with

---

[1] Thus, for example, Wilamowitz, *HD* 24 'Wenn er eine Fabel des Pherekydes hervorzieht, so tut er dasselbe wie mit der arkadischen Zeusgeburt im ersten Hymnus . . . er überrascht also auch hier seine Hörer: den Fund des Gelehrten nutzt der Dichter aus'. Cahen p. 232 'le récit de Phérécyde avait quelque chose d'une histoire rare et curieuse, et se recommandait par là au poète érudit.' McKay, *PP* 26–54 has even made this supposed waywardness of Callimachus the basis for his strange interpretation of the Hymn, even though it involves assuming without evidence that pseudo-Apollodorus misreports Pherecydes, and misreading a crucial word in Callimachus (see Commentary on v. 87 ἀφείλεο).

[2] See Commentary on vv. 107–18. Wilamowitz again asserted, without warrant, the early authority of the bath of Artemis in *GH* I 400f.

her often stress her role as a sexually neutral, even masculine, divinity concerned with military protection and maintenance of civic values;[1] consequently the importance of Athena as a feminine deity tends to be underestimated.[2] Yet even in Athens, whose growth in political influence and nationalistic pride promoted increasing emphasis on Athena's aspects as a civic patron, her fundamental association with fertility and sexuality is evident. Some festivals were concerned primarily with growth and increase: the Procharisteria was a spring ceremony connected with fertility,[3] the Oschophoria was a harvest festival involving transvestite celebrants in a procession from the sanctuary of Dionysus to that of Athena Sciras in Phaleron,[4] the Scirophoria (or Scira) involved Athena with Demeter and ritual ploughing which clearly concerned fertility of the crops.[5] Athena's priestess at Athens played a part in the consecration of marriages with the aegis, just as in Trozen brides dedicated their girdle to Athena Apatouria and in Elis Athena was called 'Mother' for having assisted in conception of children.[6] But one of the most illuminating customs is that of the Athenian Arrephoria, at which two

[1] So, for example, Wilamowitz, *GH* II 160–6 who simply omits the non-civic aspects, or Nilsson, *GGR* I 433–44 who dilutes them to a rather puzzling appendage.

[2] Some of the feminine aspects of Athena were treated in detail by E.Fehrle, *Die kultische Keuschheit im Altertum* (Giessen 1910) 169–201, who however is sometimes rather extreme in his interpretations.

[3] *Suda* s.v. Προχαριστήρια· ἡμέρα ἐν ἧι οἱ ἐν τῆι ἀρχῆι πάντες ἀρχομένων καρπῶν φύεσθαι λήγοντος ἤδη τοῦ χειμῶνος ἔθυον τῆι Ἀθηνᾶι . . . ὀνομασθεῖσαν δὲ Προχαριστήρια διὰ τὴν βλάστησιν τῶν καρπῶν τῶν φυομένων. Cf. Deubner, *Attische Feste* 17, Nilsson, *GGR* I 440f.

[4] Deubner, *Attische Feste* 142–7, but in particular see H.W.Parke, *Festivals of the Athenians* (London 1977) 77–81 who rightly stresses the importance of Athena in this festival. Nilsson effectively ignores the ceremony.

[5] Deubner, *Attische Feste* 46–50, Parke, *Festivals* 156–62. The mid-summer Panathenaea also made much use of vegetation, including myrtle the symbol of fertility: Deubner, *Attische Feste* 28f., Fehrle, *Kultische Keuschheit* 181f.

[6] Deubner, *Attische Feste* 15f.; Nilsson, *GGR* I 443f., embarrassed by the association of Athena and sexuality, attempts to dismiss the significance of the Elis story.

young girls carried cult-objects shaped like snakes and phalli between the shrines of Athena Polias and Aphrodite in the Gardens; Walter Burkert has demonstrated (*Hermes* 94(1966) 1–25) that this was a puberty initiation rite and that its counterpart in myth is the story of Athena, Erichthonius, and Cecrops' daughters Aglaurus and Herse. After Hephaestus' unsuccessful attempt to rape Athena the goddess took over the child produced when Hephaestus' semen fell on Earth, and put him in a casket which she entrusted to the daughters of Cecrops with instructions that they should not look inside; when Athena left, Aglaurus and Herse disobeyed, and on seeing τὰ μὴ θεμιτά, Erichthonius and a snake (or snakes), went mad and threw themselves over a cliff.[1] Myth and ritual together here demonstrate very effectively that Athena could be closely associated with matters of sexuality,[2] but there is an additional, if more speculative, point of importance for the Fifth Hymn. The structure of the Erichthonius and Tiresias myths is very similar, and this similarity suggests that the story of the blinding of Chariclo's son is not out of place associated with an Athena cult. In both myths the offence is perception of sexual secrets, against Athena or her representative (Erichthonius was the medium through whom some important aspects of culture were transmitted to Athens,[3] Athena's counterpart who was the strange offspring, like her, of a single parent), by the child or children of a parent who enjoyed the goddess' close patronage; Aglaurus and Herse were killed while Tiresias was only blinded, but the difference is superficial since the crucial significance is that the offender(s) changed state on encountering the divine and experiencing revelation, and for this

[1] Cf. the myth of Eurypylus, who opened a chest which he received after the fall of Troy and on seeing the image of Dionysus which it contained went mad (Paus. 7.19.6–10).

[2] For full discussion and references see the detailed treatment of W. Burkert. Cf. also Deubner, *Attische Feste* 9–17; Parke, *Festivals* 142f. is mystified by the Arrephoria and seems not to know Burkert's article.

[3] For references see Burkert, *Hermes* 94 (1966) 23.

purpose madness and blindness are interchangeable (see below p. 23).[1]

The structure of the Erichthonius–Aglaurus myth, then, suggests that the story of Tiresias' offence against Athena is not inherently implausible and could have been linked to an actual bath ceremony. In other ways too an association between Athena and Tiresias is not inappropriate: both figures are of ambivalent sexual status, Tiresias because of his changes of sex, Athena as a feminine deity with many male characteristics,[2] and Athena is the only divinity who could substitute for Zeus and Hera in a transformation of the more common version of Tiresias' blinding. Here too is the explanation for Athena's gifts of compensation to Tiresias; it is not that she is linked intrinsically with insight and clairvoyance (see Commentary on vv. 107–18), but that these supernatural powers are another form of the madness following encounter with the divine that marks a fundamental change of state. The essential feature after encounter with the divine is metamorphosis: Aglaurus and Herse went mad, Tiresias became clairvoyant, Actaeon changed into a stag, Siproites, who when hunting saw Artemis at her bath, was changed into a woman (Anton. Lib. *Met.* 17.5). Furthermore there is a close link in Greek mythopoeic thought between sexual and extra-perceptive potency or impotency: for example Melampus owed his gift of understanding animal-language to snakes which he once rescued from a burning

---

[1] It is also worth noting that Aglaurus was associated with Athena's bath festival. Aetiological myth connected her with the origins and purposes of both Callynteria and Plynteria: see Burkert, *Hermes* 94 (1966) 12–13, Deubner, *Attische Feste* 21, and in particular Hesych. s.v. Πλυντήρια and Photius, *Lex.* s.v. Καλλυντήρια.

[2] Similarly Aglaurus, as priestess a human counterpart to Athena, was connected with militaristic matters through her lover Ares in myth and in cult as the figure by whom Athenian ephebes swore their oath (in her sanctuary on the rocks where she and Herse threw themselves down from the Acropolis); for references see Burkert, *Hermes* 94 (1966) 12 and cf. P.Vidal-Naquet, 'The Black Hunter and the Origin of the Athenian Ephebeia', *Proc. Cam. Phil. Soc.* 14 (1968) 49–64.

tree, and one of his most notable achievements as a seer was the cure of Iphiclus' impotence;[1] Cassandra's rejection of Apollo's sexuality was punished with clairvoyance which was in turn disregarded. Plut. *Arat.* 32 demonstrates the connection well: according to the Pellenians when their statue of Artemis is moved from its temple it not only causes everybody to divert his gaze but also makes trees past which it is carried become barren and drop their fruit.[2]

Perception and sexuality are both ultra-sensitive in experience of the divine (often interdependently so), and sacred madness, as after encounter with the divine, may cause radical changes in either or both. Tiresias is a pivotal figure in whom this principle is particularly well illustrated (we should not forget that the other major Tiresias myth involves his change of sex after violating two snakes while they coupled), and Athena is not inappropriate as the critical divine catalyst. She is associated with blindness and sterility again in two parallel stories: [Plut.] *Parall. Min.* 17A (= *Mor.* 309E) reports from Dercyllus (= Jacoby, *FGrHist* 3A 288 F3) that Ilus once snatched the Palladion from Athena's burning temple and was blinded (οὐ γὰρ ἐξὸν ὑπ' ἀνδρὸς βλέπεσθαι),[3] and Paus. 9.34.2 tells how the priestess Iodama saw Itonian Athena in the sanctuary one night and was turned to stone.[4]

---

[1] See Roscher, *LM* II 2567–73.

[2] Some scholars emend Artemis to Athena (see *RE* II 1977) on the basis of Paus. 7.27.2–3 and Polyaenus 8.59, but the latter is almost certainly muddled; see W.H.Porter on Plut. *Arat.* 32. Blindness and impotence are also sometimes interchangeable: Amyntor punished his son Phoenix for seducing his mistress with the curse of childlessness according to some versions (*Il.* 9.453–7), with blindness according to others (Eur. fr. 816N, cf. Frazer on [Apollod.] 3.13.8). Betrayal of sexual trust could also be punished with blindness: Daphnis' infidelity caused him to be blinded (Roscher, *LM* I 956–7), and Anchises' revelation of his affair with Aphrodite resulted in blindness according to one version (Servius on *Aen.* 1.617, 2.35, 687).

[3] The blindness was not permanent: as Tiresias received compensatory gifts so Ilus regained his sight after atonement.

[4] Another account from Dercyllus given by [Plut.] *de fluv.* 22.4f. (= Jacoby, *FGrHist* 3A 288 F1) demonstrates how closely blinding and petrifaction

The myth of Tiresias and Athena, therefore, may be an unusual version, but both the structure of the story and its components stand up to analysis: there are no secure grounds for suspicion and, given the present state of our evidence, we should assume that association of the Argive ritual and the Tiresias myth was no invention of Callimachus, but that most probably they were linked in Argive history or local legend itself. This assumption leaves one question unanswered: why should an Argive ritual be accompanied by a myth set in Thebes? To this there is no single satisfactory answer; we can only point to the pertinent close association in myth between Argos and Thebes, through Adrastus who led the first disastrous attack on Thebes for his guest Polynices and through the Epigoni. Tiresias died on the occasion of the second expedition, in which Diomedes took part ([Apollod.] 3.7.3, Diod. Sic. 4.67.1, Strabo 9.2.36), and the Argive capture of the city may have resulted in appropriation of some Theban religious items; the famous seer will have been an obvious focus for any such claims. According to Paus. 9.33.1 Tiresias was actually taken prisoner by the Argives but died on the way to Delphi (where his daughter Manto was dedicated to Apollo),[1] but an important link, perhaps through a relic, may still have been made between him and

are linked. When Calydon inadvertently saw Artemis bathing he was changed into a rock: on the rock grows a plant which, if put into washing water for the face, causes blindness (once again sight can be restored by appeasing Artemis). Mutation into something inorganic is another form of the impotence or sterility associated with divine blindness: cf. the effect of Pellenian Artemis mentioned above p. 23. Other divinities too punish with blindness: Aepytus was blinded when he offended against the sanctuary of Poseidon at Mantinea (Paus. 8.10.3), Erymanthus when he saw Aphrodite bathing (Ptolemy Chennus in Photius, *Bibl.* 146f. Bekker), Lycoergus when he expelled the maenad nurses of Dionysus (*Il.* 6.139). Cf. also Hdt. 6.117, Philostr. *Her.* 132.7ff.

[1] The report in Proclus' summary of the cyclic epic Νόστοι that Tiresias died in Colophon must be a mistake of an ancient epitomiser: see U. von Wilamowitz-Moellendorff, *Homerische Untersuchungen* (Berlin 1884) 178f. However, one tradition reported that Tiresias' daughter Manto emigrated to Colophon (Paus. 9.33.2).

Argos.[1] It would be no surprise to find Tiresias among the many items of myth (of which the most prominent example is Heracles) and early history which connect Thebes and Boeotia with Argos.[2]

III LANGUAGE AND STYLE

The high tone and style which are patent right from the opening words of the *Bath of Pallas* and maintained throughout the Hymn are achieved essentially by a combination of diction which has deep roots in the traditional Homeric/poetic language and a skilfully developed period structure. In vv. 1–56 language and tempo carefully reflect the increasing tension of a religious festival (see Commentary *passim* but particularly on vv. 1–4, 5–12, 13–17, 33–56); in vv. 57–136 vocabulary and phraseology become more heightened and, along with the rhythm, even more pronouncedly epic, reinforced by metre and narrative construction (see Commentary *passim*, but particularly on vv. 57–69, 70–84, 85–95, 107–18, 119–36). That the Fifth Hymn is extremely poetic in language and style may seem to be fairly evident, but it is worth emphasising just how far removed the text was from everyday language of third-century Alexandria. Words and forms which are specifically Homeric are relatively easy to identify, but there are many other items which, although they look ordinary enough, will also have stood out to the contemporary audience as poeticisms or archaisms: many words had changed form in the *koine*, such as v. 5 Ἀθαναία (Ἀθηνᾶ), 16 χρίματα (χρίσματα), 27 ἔρευθος (ἐρύθημα), 30 Ἡρακλέης (-ῆς), 32 σμασαμένα (σμηξαμένη), some words had changed substantially such as 6 ἱππειᾶν (ἱππικῶν), 23

[1] All sources agree that Tiresias' grave was situated by the spring Tilphousa near Haliartos where he died.

[2] For details of the associations between the two areas and the possible historical basis of the interconnections see A.Schachter, 'The Theban Wars', *Phoenix* 21 (1967) 1–10.

διαθρέξαϲα (διαδραμοῦϲα), while other items are simply obsolete, such as 61 iterative optative with historic tense main verb, 64 local ἐπί with dative, 75 ἅμα of accompaniment, 77 qualitative adverbial τι, 96 ἔλεξεν (for details in each case see Commentary).

One of the distinctive features of the Hymn is the dialect coloration; the Fifth and Sixth Hymns have, in addition to their strong poetic language, pronounced Doricisms throughout. Editors have not discussed this aspect of the *Bath of Pallas* very satisfactorily. Some, including Wilamowitz, have even considered that Callimachus may have been writing in his own native Cyrenaean dialect (as if Hymns v and vi had any more connection with Callimachus' family origins than any of the non-Doric poems),[1] while Cahen, after a rambling discussion, was reduced to the romantic vagueness of 'un essai de composition épico-lyrique dans la tonalité dorienne' (*C* 443) and 'une κοινή poétique éolo-dorienne' (*C* 447). The Fifth Hymn uses Doric as part of its 'mimetic' apparatus, to recreate as convincingly as possible (within the poetic framework) the occasion of the festival at Doric Argos. Careful analysis of the language of the Hymn shows that the dialect is for the most part a generic Doric and not specific to any one region, but a few of its features might be characteristic of the Argolid (see on v. 1 λωτροχόοι, 3 ἁ θεόϲ and ἕρπεν, 27 κῶραι, 51 τὸ λοετρόν, 69 ἔϲϲαν). Callimachus' Doric hymns should be seen in their general Alexandrian context: in the same period Theocritus was experimenting with mimetic poems which had 'realistic' use of Doric in presenting the conversations of Sicilian or South Italian countrymen or even Syracusan immigrants in Alexandria, and Herodas wrote mimes in a carefully revived Ionic genre dialect. Callimachus used Doric again in fr. 228, the Ectheosis of Arsinoe,

[1] Wilamowitz, in his third edition of the Hymns (1907), remarks on p. 16 'constat nunc Callimachum in hymnis V et VI patrio sermone usum esse' (cf. *Die Textgeschichte der griechischen Bukoliker* (Berlin 1906) 26); he was followed by W. Vollgraff in *Mnemosyne* 47 (1919) 337–9.

presumably as part of that poem's lyric form, and the fact that v and vi, had they actually been written for performance at the real ceremonies (as were Pindaric choral lyrics), might have been composed in lyric form, may have had some influence on the use of dialect.[1] In itself the mixture of Doric and epic dactylic verse is not unusual; epic forms naturally occur in native Doric epigrams (see Thumb, *GD* i 221f.), and Doric coloration is to be found as early as the hexameter processional ode written by Eumelus of Corinth for the Messenian delegation at Delos (*PMG* 696). Nearer the time of Callimachus Isyllus of Epidaurus combined the two in an inconsistent mixture of epic and Doric forms, and as Wilamowitz stressed (*Isyllos von Epidauros* (1886) 25–8) he was not only a precursor to Theocritus but also part of the more general phenomenon of the Doricising and modernising of the epic tradition.

In the *Bath of Pallas* the Doric element is moderately pronounced, being more severely dialectal than in the lyrics of Attic tragedy, but less extreme than in some of the native Doric lyricists, and slightly less severe than in Theocritus; it strikes a good literary balance. In general the Doric element seems to be internally self-consistent, and is evident even in some very small details: see, for example, on 42 αἷϲ, 106 τέλθοϲ, and perhaps 115 τουτάκι. Even when the immediate context is very strongly Homeric, pronounced Doric elements feature: see on 79 προϲέφαϲεν, 94 ἀηδονίδων. However, as elsewhere in Doric writing within the broader poetic tradition (e.g. Pindar, Isyllus), non-Doric elements stand easily alongside their true Doric forms (e.g. 108, 129 μόνοϲ and 29, 132 μῶνοϲ, εο and ευ [see on 97 βαλεῦ]), and in complete contrast to the detail with which the Doric element features

[1] This point, which has to do with form, should not be confused with Cahen's grandiloquent but vague (and thoroughly unconvincing) attempt to argue that Callimachus represents 'la rentrée du "lyrisme", au sens moderne du mot, dans la poésie' (*C* 295; the theory is asserted at length, entangled by its own inherent contradictions, in 295ff., with a dismissal of the *Bath of Pallas* on 317).

elsewhere, trivial Homeric forms completely oust their Doric counterparts (e.g. 59 Τειρεσίαο, 60 Θεσπιέων, 73 ἔσαν, 89 ὄψεαι, 91 ἐπράξαο, 111 ἔσσεται); even blatantly unnatural hybrids are entirely acceptable (e.g. 89 ἀέλιος, 113 ὁππόκα, 116 λεξεῖται). A number of forms are helpfully Homeric and Doric simultaneously: e.g. 1 ὅσσαι, 9 πράτιστον, 24 τοί, 37 τεΐν, 39 τεόν, 51 τὸ λοετρόν, 67 τελέθεσκον, 77 ποτί, 120 ἐμέθεν.

Homeric diction, however, overshadows any other single linguistic aspect in the poem. The poetic tone is that of the Homeric/poetic language, which is apparent in small details of form and phraseology which have no more exact significance except that they are 'Homeric': see, e.g., on 7 λύθρωι πεπαλαγμένα, 9 ἀλλὰ πολὺ πράτιστον, 9–10 ὑφ' ἅρματος αὐχένας ἵππων | λυσαμένα, 11 ἱδρῶ, 21 χαλκὸν ἑλοῖσα, 29 τῶι καὶ νῦν, 42 οὔνομα, 49 χρυσῶι τε καὶ ἄνθεσιν, 60 εὖτ', 62 ἔργα διερχομένα, 63 ἵνα οἱ τεθυωμένον ἄλσος, 65 ἑῶ ἐπεβάσατο δίφρω, 68 ἀλλ' ἔτι, 71 καλὰ ῥεοίσαι, 73 ἔσαν, 75 Τειρεσίας δ' ἔτι μῶνος, 77 ποτὶ ῥόον ἤλυθε κράνας, 78 σχέτλιος· οὐκ ἐθέλων, 79, 82 ὄμματα νὺξ ἔλαβεν, 89 ἀλλ' οὐκ ἀέλιον πάλιν ὄψεαι, 91 ἦ μεγάλ', 96, 97 δῖα γύναι, 101 ὅκα μὴ θεὸς αὐτὸς ἕληται, 104–5, 105 τὸ πρᾶτον, 111 αἵ τ' ἐν ὄρεσσι, 113 λοετρά, 114 ἄνακτα, 119 ὦ ἑτάρα, τῶι μή τι, 121 ἀοίδιμον ἐσσομένοισιν, 123 οἵ τε πέτονται, 131 ὣς φαμένα, 141 πάλιν αὖτις, 142 σάω.

Rare words, usages, constructions etc. are picked out as special Homeric idiosyncrasies: see, e.g., on 11 ῥαθάμιγγας, 58 φίλατο, 58 ἑταρᾶν, 66 ὄαροι, 76 ἀνεστρέφετο, 92 πρόκας, 92 φάεα, 102 ἀθρήσηι, 103 παλινάγρετον, 103 γένοιτο, 116 λεξεῖται; and existing Homericisms are extended, or new ones created according to Homeric practice: see, e.g., on 54 πανυστάτιον, 72 μεσαμβρινά, 91 δόρκας, 117 ὀλβίσταν, 124 ἄλιθα, 125 θεοπρόπα. Occasionally an unusual feature is illuminated by what we know of the editorial work which Hellenistic writers did on Homer (see on 60 Θεσπιέων, 83 ἑστάκη, 98 εἶπας, 131 κατένευσε), though discrepancies with Aristarchus' later work are noticeable (see on 7 πεπαλαγμένα, 65 ἐπεβάσατο). In general the narrative section concerning the blinding of Tiresias seems to be more pronouncedly Homeric than 1–56 the 'Argive section' (for a confirmatory detail see on 2f. τᾶν ἵππων . . . τᾶν ἱερᾶν).

Occasionally use of Homer goes beyond stylistic atmosphere and select items of vocabulary. There are points in the Fifth Hymn where the reader must know his Homer well enough to be able to recognise that Callimachus is echoing a particular scene or passage from the *Iliad* or *Odyssey*: e.g. at 31f. the ironical vaunting of Athena over Aphrodite will be missed unless *Il.* 14.175ff. is remembered (typically, the main point of contact between the two passages, the 'clue', is a lexical one, πέξηται, as well as the particular memorableness of the Homeric scene); similarly 83f. gain heightened dramatic effect by reminiscence of *Od.* 4.703ff., 93–5 obtain a formal dignity from *Od.* 17.38ff. (again the preliminary link is lexical, v. 92 φάεα), 111–14 are made more menacing and authoritative by recalling *Il.* 5.51ff., and 129 is the more convincing because of its quotation of *Od.* 10.493ff.

But in spite of the wealth of Homeric material on which the Hymn draws throughout, Callimachus is not writing to imitate or reproduce Homer, and it is not possible to construct a line-by-line concordance listing the Homeric source for each word and phrase as can be done to a considerable extent with Apollonius Rhodius (for books I and II of the *Argonautica* see H.Kasseger, *Das homerische Formengut bei A.R.* (Diss. Wien 1967)). Even in passages which are extensively Homeric a non-Homeric element or a variation is often firmly introduced: see, for example, on 65 ἐπεβάσατο, 79 προσέφασεν, 82 ἁ μὲν ἔφα, 94 ἀηδονίδων, 96 ἔλεξεν, 133 πατρώϊα. Callimachus looks to Homer because the *Iliad* and *Odyssey* were *the* great poetic monuments, and a 'given' of Greek culture; but although they were inevitably central for any Hellenistic poet they were not for Callimachus the prime source of creative energy. Callimachus' own critical statements (as in fr. 1) make this perfectly clear as also does his practice, and many modern editors and critics of Callimachus have concentrated too much on the purely Homeric element in the background to his writing.

At the technical level alone much that is poetic or especially literary is not Homeric at all. Examples of poeticisms which are non- (or even anti-) Homeric are: 3 εὔτυκος, 33 καταθύμιος, 43 περσέπτολι, 77 ἄφατον, 102 μισθῶ, 115 τουτάκι, 117 εὐαίωνα, 127 βάκτρον, 142 κλᾶρον. A number of abnormal forms, terms or usages can be described as 'literary': see on 23 διαθρέξασα, 27 ἔρευθος, 32 σμασαμένα, 45 βάπτετε, 47 κάλπιδας, 61 ἐλαύνοι, 62 ἔργα(?), 96 ἔλεξεν. Often a poetic or heightened effect is obtained by the way in which normal words are arranged or formed: see, e.g., on 10 ἔκλυσεν, 16 χρίματα, 18 τὰν Ἴδαι, 31 παγχρύσεον, 37 ἱρεύς, 64 ἐπί, 93 περί . . . λαβοῖσα, 97 μετά . . . βαλεῦ, 105f., 141 ἐξελάοισα. Some of the poetic vocabulary and usage results from Hellenistic innovation: in addition to the 'Homeric' extensions listed above see 21 διαυγέα, 14 ὑπαξόνιον, 25 ἐμπεράμως, 66 χοροστασίαι, 90 παριτέ (?), 103 αὖθι, 126 ὕστερα.

The contrast between Callimachus and Apollonius Rhodius is manifest at the level of small detail (vocabulary, usage, forms etc.) as well as in the broader stylistic features, and the following points should be noted from this Hymn:

4 Πελασγιάδες of Peloponnesian Argos: so often elsewhere, but A.R. follows Homer in calling only Thessalian Argos 'Pelasgian'.

10 ἔκλυσεν: as in normal usage, but in A.R. and Aratus archaically as in Homer.

14 φθόγγον: the form of normal usage, but A.R. has only poetic φθογγή.

20 ἔβλεψεν: a verb of normal usage frequent in C., Theocr., Herodas, *AP*; not Homeric and thus avoided by A.R., Aratus and Nicander.

22 μετέθηκε: normal usage and avoided by C.'s contemporaries.

25 λιτά: an adjective of normal usage frequent in C. and *AP* (once also in Aratus), but avoided by A.R. and bucolics.

26 τᾶς ἰδίας: normal usage, avoided by all except C. and [Theocr.].

41 ἀπορρώγεσσιν: as in normal usage, but as a Homeric archaism in A.R. and Aratus.

62 ἔργα: Homeric but also apparently in literary *koine*; used by C., Theocr., and Aratus, but avoided by A.R.

75 ἁμᾶι: ἅμα as in *koine* in C., bucolics, and 'didactics', but in A.R. with Homeric sense.

82 ἁ μὲν ἔφα: Homeric in tone but not with exact phraseology; A.R. has only the precisely Homeric ὣϲ ἄρ' ἔφη.

95 ἐλέηϲεν: normal usage, but A.R. has only the epic form ἐλεαίρειν.

96 ἔλεξεν: a 'literary' form (not poetic) used by C. and Theocr. but avoided by A.R., Aratus and Nicander.

105 τὸ πρᾶτον: only here and in the strongly Homeric III 23, 113, but often in A.R.

113 λοετρά: A.R. uses only this Homeric plural, but elsewhere C. also uses the singular.

133 πατρώϊα πάντα: an adaptation of Homeric usage, whereas Theocritus has the traditional sense.

It will be noted that Theocritus stands between Callimachus and Apollonius Rhodius, and Aratus more often lines up with Apollonius than Callimachus (see Commentary for more specific details).

IV THE METRE

Alone of Callimachus' six hymns the *Bath of Pallas* is in elegiacs and not hexameters, and in the whole ancient anthology of hymns as part of which the Callimachean collection was transmitted no other abandons the heroic metre.

The various explanations which modern editors have suggested for the metre subscribe broadly to one (or both) of two theories, each of them, it should be said at the outset, very tenuous and insecurely based. First, in 1905 Crusius, following a suggestion of Bergk,[1] argued (*RE* V 2270–1) that the Fifth Hymn was consciously written in the tradition of early Peloponnesian religious elegy. Of this supposed Peloponnesian tradition not a single elegiac verse has survived,[2] and the only testimony to its existence is the dubious pseudo-Plutarch, *de musica* 3, 5, 8 and 9. A careful examination of this

[1] *Philolog. Thesen* II 31 = *Kleine Schriften* II 742.

[2] Editors have long given up trying to convert the 'epigram' of Echembrotus reported by Paus. 10.7.5f. into elegiacs.

rather muddled source reveals that its author(s) had essentially the following information to offer: (1) poetry accompanied by the flute (including elegy) was begun by Clonas, who came from Tegea or Thebes, and was continued by Polymnestus of Colophon, Mimnermus of Colophon and Sacadas of Argos; (2) the latter *may* have been followed by other writers (9 οἱ δὲ περὶ Cακάδαν ἐλεγείων [ποιηταί]) though in Greek of this period οἱ περί . . . is often no more than a periphrasis for the single person mentioned; (3) music festivals were founded first in Sparta thanks to Terpander (a citharode), then in a 'second period' in Lacedaemon, Arcadia and Argos by Thales of Gortyn, Xenodamus of Cythera and Xenocritus of Locri (all writers of paeans), Polymnestus of Colophon (writing orthians) and Sacadas of Argos writing elegy. Little of consequence can be inferred from this scant information, but the early elegists clearly came from all over the Greek world and were not narrowly Dorian, and the festivals of which the elegists and others were regarded as the 'founders' were obviously widely spread geographically.[1] If 'religious elegy' existed as an identifiable genre in the Peloponnese this is not the evidence for it, and Crusius'

[1] A misunderstanding of [Plut.] *de mus.* 9 has led some scholars to imagine that Sparta was the centre of musical activity at this period (most recently D.L.Page in 'The Elegiacs in Euripides' *Andromache*', *Greek Poetry and Life* (Oxford 1936) 216 and A.E.Harvey, *CQ* 5 (1955) 170 n. 4): ἡ μὲν οὖν πρώτη κατάcταcιc τῶν περὶ τὴν μουcικὴν ἐν τῆι Cπάρτηι Τερπάνδρου καταcτήcαντοc γεγένηται. τῆc δὲ δευτέραc Θαλήταc τε ὁ Γορτύνιοc καὶ Ξενόδαμοc . . . μάλιcτα αἰτίαν ἔχουcιν ἡγεμόνεc γενέcθαι· τούτων γὰρ εἰcηγηcαμένων τὰ περὶ τὰc Γυμνοπαιδίαc ἐν Λακεδαίμονι λέγεται καταcταθῆναι, τὰ περὶ τὰc Ἀποδείξειc τὰc ἐν Ἀρκαδίαι, τῶν τε ἐν Ἄργει τὰ Ἐνδυμάτια καλούμενα. This means not 'the first period in Sparta was founded by Terpander, the second by Thaletas etc. . . .', but (note the placing of ἐν τῆι Cπάρτηι prominently before the genitive absolute Τερπάνδρου καταcτήcαντοc) 'the first establishment of musical festivals happened (γεγένηται) in Sparta at the instigation of Terpander, and thereafter Thaletas etc. were primarily the pioneers, because they are said to have introduced the establishment of the Gymnopaedia in Lacedaemon, the Apodeixis in Arcadia, and of the Argive festivals the so-called Endymatia'.

further attempt to analyse the Fifth Hymn as a Terpandrian nomos, an archaising poem looking back to a collection of early Spartan poetry, adds only confusion.[1]

The other theory, which has attracted several modern critics, is Heinze's, that the metre helps to convey the predominant mood of the Tiresias narrative, τὸ ἐλεεινόν (*Ovids elegische Erzählung* 95.1, Herter *RE* Suppl. v 435, Suppl. xiii 240). The presumption here is that at an early stage elegy was, as its name suggests, the metre of threnody and lamentation, furthermore in Doric. The case for this elegiac threnody has been argued most extensively by D.L.Page (*Greek Poetry and Life* (Oxford 1936) 206–30) in an attempt to explain the Doric elegiacs spoken by Andromache in Eur. *Andr.* 103–16; K.J.McKay (*PP* 79–81, 106–14, 122–4) enthusiastically took up the theory to explain the metre and mood of the Fifth Hymn. However two fundamental points need to be made: first, if there was such a thing as threnodic elegy, Eur. *Andr.* 103–16 is the sole obvious example of the supposed genre, and moreover we have no firm documentary evidence for the genre, only the passages of pseudo-Plutarch cited above for Doric religious elegy and Paus. 10.7.4 (who records that at the early Pythian games gloomy elegy accompanied by the flute was performed). Some early elegy *may* indeed have been threnodic (the name clearly suggests some connection between elegy and lament: see the very full evidence cited by Page pp. 206–10), but to assert that all certainly was so, and then to interpret the Fifth Hymn as the single major

[1] Crusius maintained the theory of Terpandrian nomos and suggested the existence of a Spartan Liederbuch on which Callimachus drew, in a supplementary note to 'Dithyrambos' in *RE* v 1225–8; in his article 'Elegie' in *RE* v 2270 Crusius then proposed a Terpandrian analysis for v: 1–12 ἀρχά, 13–32 μεταρχά, 33–42 κατατροπά, 43–56 μετακατατροπά, 57–130 ὀμφαλός, 131–6 cφραγίc, 137–42 ἐπίλογοc. This theoretical schema does little for Callimachus' text (cf. my analysis below on p. 109 and Commentary on 33–56, 57–136). Ph.-E.Legrand, *REA* 3 (1901) 302–5 develops the Terpandrian analysis in more detail; much special pleading is needed to force v into this alien structure. For a full exposé of the inadequacies of the nomos theory see Cahen, *C* 589–600.

instance is rash in the extreme.[1] Secondly, the Tiresias narrative is quite simply *not* concerned with lamentation as such, and is not especially ἐλεεινόν in mood: the whole incident of the encounter between Tiresias and Athena in fact moves to, in Greek terms, a positive solution with the goddess' gifts of compensation. At one level the narrative ends harmoniously with the grimness of the punishment counterbalanced (for a fuller discussion, with qualification, see Section VI below), and if the metre of the poem did not need some explanation the description 'threnodic' would not seem appropriate for the Fifth Hymn.

There is no single, neat reason for the elegiac metre of v. The elegiac couplet was an exceptionally versatile form, and was early referred to as ἔπη (Solon fr. 1 αὐτὸς κῆρυξ ἦλθον ἀφ' ἱμερτῆς Σαλαμῖνος, | κόσμον ἐπέων . . . θέμενος, Theogn. 20, 22, Hdt. 5.113),[2] just as later theoreticians could speak of Mimnermus and Sacadas as writers of ἐλεγεῖα μεμελοποιημένα ([Plut.] *de mus.* 8). In particular elegy was the vehicle of *adhortatio* and public address, and in this respect was an entirely suitable form for one to exhort her co-celebrants on the virtues of Athena; in Sparta Tyrtaeus and in Ephesus

---

[1] Many scholars have expressed scepticism about the existence of Doric threnodic elegy, notably P.Friedländer and H.B.Hoffleit in *Epigrammata* (Berkeley and Los Angeles 1948) 66; recently Bruno Gentili in 'Epigramma ed elegia' in *L'Épigramme Grecque*, Fondation Hardt Entretiens XIV (Geneva 1967) 39–81 (especially 52–64) has re-examined the evidence for a connection between elegy and threnody and offered some strong fundamental objections (cf. also the Entretiens discussion on pp. 83–5). A.E.Harvey in his important article 'The Classification of Greek Lyric Poetry', *CQ* 5 (1955) 157–75 tries to accept the theory of a common origin for elegy and threnody, but, discomforted by the fact that none of the surviving elegies are dirges, he is reduced to arguing that the lamentation took the form of *contemplation*, and that the mood of advice and exhortation which characterises extant (Ionic) elegy developed from there.

[2] Cf. the protest by Wilamowitz, *Sappho und Simonides* (Berlin 1913) 290f. against attributing a specific style to elegy as against epos. In MS S (see p. 57) Lascaris wrote alongside the title of the Fifth Hymn ἡρωελεγεῖοι (Smiley, *CQ* 14 (1920) 66).

Callinus provide particularly explicit examples of directly exhortatory poetry. Nor is the elegiac foreign to hymn poetry: short hymnal addresses and invocations were early to be found, for example in Theognis 1ff., 757ff., 773ff., Solon fr. 13 (parodied by Crates fr. 1); and Strabo 14.1.4 reports that Callinus called on Zeus to pity the Ephesians ἐν τῶι πρὸς τὸν Δία λόγωι.[1] Amongst Callimachus' near-contemporaries Posidippus wrote a similar twenty-five-line hymnal address probably as a preface to an edition of his poems (*SH* 705: full commentary with discussion by Hugh Lloyd-Jones, *JHS* 83 (1963) 75–99). Narrative too was in place in elegy in a mood of reflection or with the tone of address: Mimnermus' *Nanno* seems to have consisted at least in part in continuous narrative, and in the fourth century Antimachus' *Lyde* was certainly narrative in style, and his contemporary 'Pigres' could even translate the *Iliad* into elegiac couplets.[2]

Fragmentary though our knowledge is of pre-Hellenistic elegy, we know enough to see that an elegiac exhortatory 'hymn' to Athena was far from contra-conventional; and two other factors are also relevant to an Alexandrian elegy. First, 'die Kreuzung der Gattungen' had already begun in the fourth century, and shortly before or just contemporarily with Callimachus Hermesianax in his *Leontion* (Powell, *CA* 96–106) and Phanocles in his Ἔρωτες ἢ Καλοί (Powell, *CA* 106–9) had written elegiac poems studiedly in the manner of Hesiod (Herm. fr. 7.1 οἵην μὲν φίλος υἱὸς ἀνήγαγεν Οἰάγροιο . . . , Phanocles fr. 1.1 ἢ ὡς Οἰάγροιο πάις Θρηΐκιος Ὀρφεύς . . .); the hexameter is self-consciously converted into the elegiac distich. Callimachus himself wrote epinicia in elegiacs (frr. 383, 384)[3] and possibly even an epithalamion

[1] Cf. Wünsch in *RE* IX 157f., 167. From the first century B.C. the Fayum has produced two elegiac hymns to Isis by one Isidorus which were inscribed on a wall: *SEG* 8 (1937) 549, 551.

[2] On the origins and range of elegy see also M.L.West, *Studies in Greek Elegy and Iambus* (Berlin 1974) 2–21.

[3] Fr. 383 *The Nemean Victory*, which we now know to have opened Book III of

(fr. 392); similarly a near-contemporary of Callimachus, possibly Posidippus, wrote what was almost certainly an epithalamion to Arsinoe in elegiac distichs (*SH* 961); the papyrus is fragmentary, but the poem seems, like the Fifth Hymn, to have contained an invocation and to have addressed the celebrants.[1] Secondly, other poets were in any case writing hymns in new metres: Castorion of Soli wrote a hymn to Pan in iambic trimeters (Athen. 10.454F, = *SH* 310), and Hephaestion particularly selects for comment hymns and addresses written by Simias in new metres, in cretics to Doris (fr. 13 Powell), in resolved cretics to Dionysus (fr. 15), in anapaestic trimeters to Hestia (fr. 9). A third-century B.C. papyrus offers a hymn to Demeter in couplets of hexameter and tetrameter (Page, *GLP* 91 = *SH* 990).

Thus there is no reason to think that the metre of the Fifth Hymn requires particularly special explanation; certainly Callimachus may have been motivated by a desire to write something slightly unusual and by the challenge of trying to 'bring off' a new type of hymn- and narrative-form (the more so, perhaps, if the Doric Sixth Hymn had already been written: see Section v below), but in the light of what the elegiac tradition already consisted in, and of what Callimachus' own contemporaries were doing, even the description 'experimental' might be rather exaggerated. Appeals to the highly speculative genres of religious or threnodic elegy are unnecessary, and one's suspicions that had we more elegy extant the metre of the Fifth Hymn might appear less unusual

---

the *Aetia*, may possibly have appeared first as an independent poem: see the new Lille papyri, first published in *Cahiers de Recherches de l'Institut de Papyrologie et d'Egyptologie de Lille* 4 (1977) 261–86, in P.J.Parsons, *ZPE* 25 (1977) 1–50 and in *SH* 254–69.

[1] Philetas too may have extended the elegiac as a verse form. His *Demeter* (Powell, *CA* 90f., Kuchenmüller frr. 5–8) was an elegiac poem and seems to have been at least partially narrative. In spite of much modern speculation we know virtually nothing about this work; however, here as often this shadowy figure may have been an important influence on contemporary trends.

are increased by a poem referred to by Aelian – the text has been ignored by most modern anthologists and editors of Callimachus and is worth quoting in full. Aelian, *NA* 11.4 (= *SH* 206) reports a text from, or for, the Argolid town of Hermione:

Δάματερ πολύκαρπε, cὺ κὴν Cικελοῖcιν ἐναργής
καὶ παρ' Ἐρεχθείδαιc. ἓν δέ τι ⟨τοῦτο⟩ μέγα
κρίνετ' ἐν Ἑρμιονεῦcι· τὸν ἐξ ἀγέληc γὰρ ἀφειδῆ
ταῦρον, ὃν οὐχ αἱροῦc' ἀνέρεc οὐδὲ δέκα,
τοῦτον γραῦc cτείχουcα μόνα μόνον οὔατοc ἕλκει
τόνδ' ἐπὶ βωμόν, ὁ δ' ὡc ματέρι παῖc ἕπεται.
cὸν τόδε, Δάματερ, cὸν τὸ cθένοc· ἵλαοc εἴηc,
καὶ πάντων θάλλοι κλᾶροc ἐν Ἑρμιόναι.

Like Callimachus' poem this is an elegiac hymn in mild Doric dialect. Authorship, date and provenance are uncertain,[1] but language and dialect suggest that it is not later than the third century and possibly earlier. The implications for Callimachus are not uninteresting: at the least this rather ordinary text confirms that Callimachus' Doric elegiacs were not so exceptional as vehicle for a hymn, and it also raises the possibility that in the Argolid at any rate elegiacs may even have been a *normal* popular form. We have currently no other evidence with which to test this hypothesis, but we should keep in mind two corollaries: Sacadas the early elegist from Argos *may* have had a local following ([Plut.] *de mus.* 9), and in any case his apparent involvement in the foundation of the Argive festival Ἐνδυμάτια ([Plut.] *de mus.* 9) may have resulted in the type of poetry in which he specialised becoming incorporated in the traditional religious institutions of the area. Perhaps the verse form of the Fifth Hymn,

[1] Aelian is indeterminate when he says καὶ οἷc λέγω μάρτυc Ἀριcτοκλῆc, ὅc πού φηcι: this could imply that Aristocles himself was the author, but since the scholiast to Theocr. 15.64 reports that Aristocles wrote a περὶ τῶν Ἑρμιόνηc ἱερῶν this may have been a prose work which cited an older (?traditional?) hymn. On this Aristocles see *RE* II 936. For introduction and notes to Aristocles' poem see D.L.Page, *Further Greek Epigrams* (Cambridge 1981) 30f.

like the dialect, is local colouring and another aspect of Callimachean realism.

V DATE OF COMPOSITION

We possess no external evidence by which to date the Fifth Hymn. None the less many scholars have attempted an absolute or relative dating for this poem as for the other hymns, even though no theory has yet found more than passing acceptance. For Franz Susemihl (*Geschichte der griechischen Literatur in der Alexandrinerzeit* (Leipzig 1891) I 361) the very fact that the Fifth and Sixth Hymns contained no allusions to court or political circumstances demonstrated that they were composed before Callimachus was fully established in Alexandria and were thus the earliest as well as the best hymns.[1] A.Rostagni (*Poeti Alessandrini* (Turin 1916) 254–6) saw the hymns as a unified collection in which the parody by Asclepiades or Posidippus of v 2 (see Commentary and pp. 40f. below) allowed the Fifth and Sixth Hymns to be allocated to the period 280–275.[2] W.Vollgraff (*Bulletin de l'Acad. Royale de Belgique* Cl. des Lettres 24 (1938) 34ff.) also argued for an early dating for the Fifth Hymn, 278–272, on the tenuous grounds of the political relationship between Argos and Alexandria at that time, and P.M.Fraser (*Ptolemaic Alexandria* (Oxford 1972) I 656) claims that the Hymn 'is to be dated fairly early in the career of the poet' since 'a line of it was filched by his elder contemporary Posidippus', though he adds 'it would be quite wrong to regard it as immature'.

[1] Susemihl found additional support for his early dating in Bergk's proposition that the Fifth Hymn, like the Sixth, was composed as a seven-part Nomos (see Section IV above).

[2] Rostagni's view of the hymns as a collection was based on little more than general assertion, as p. 254: 'E sembreranno allora gl' *Inni* sorgere da un solo periodo storico: serie unica, e compatta, di carmi che, non senza un certo disegno architettonico, trovandosi corrispondere a certe tendenze di forma appositamente esplicate, rappresenti in momento determinato nell' attività del poeta.'

Finally it is worth mentioning three arguments based on stylistic considerations. G.Kaibel ('Observationes Criticae in Anthol. Graec.', *Comm. Philol. in hon. Th. Mommsen* (Berlin and Leipzig 1877) 326ff.) examined the incidence of penthemimeral caesura and bucolic diaeresis and concluded that VI and III were the earliest of the hymns, followed by V, I, II, IV.[1] L.Deubner ('Ein Stilprinzip hellenistischer Dichtkunst' *Neue Jahrbücher* 47 (1921) 376–8) suggested that the innovator of the 'mimetic' poem was Theocritus and that among the Idylls 2 is to be placed close to 15 on account of its religious theme and use of Sophron, i.e. in the 270s; of Callimachus' mimetic hymns II should be dated to the 250s or 240s, while V and VI should be placed close to II ('wegen der gleichen Technik') but earlier because of their use of Doric, VI being the earliest since it follows the model of Theocritus 2 most closely, whereas V, though maintaining the dialect, varies the metrical form. McKay (*PP* 106–24) suggested that VI has to be read in the light of V, which therefore antedates it.

Several of the above theories have useful observations to make on the possible circumstances of composition of the Fifth Hymn, but it is surprising how many scholars, at all periods, have been prepared to make extravagantly confident and precise assertions from the most meagre of data. We have to recognise at the outset of any discussion about dating for this Hymn that at present our evidence allows only inference and speculation and that any conclusions are necessarily very insecure. Thus Kaibel's metrical analysis has a certain appeal, being based on unemotional quantitative data and a simple methodology which presupposes only that as Callimachus advanced as a writer he was more inclined to observe the bucolic diaeresis; however, in the Heracles and Molorcus story of *Aetia* III new papyri have demonstrated that the episode was at least compiled, and possibly composed, very

[1] Kaibel's figures are that in VI, of 139 verses 12 have no bucolic diaeresis; in III, 21 of 268; in V, 4 of 71; in I, 3 of 96; in II, 3 of 113; in IV, 3 of 326; all of the epigrams always observe bucolic diaeresis.

late in Callimachus' career, and of the nineteen hexameter lines now intact in the third and fourth feet no less than *eight* fail to observe the bucolic diaeresis.[1] Now speculation about the political circumstances of a very literary hymn is unlikely to be productive, and if we make assumptions, on general 'interprétative' grounds, about the relationship of the Fifth Hymn and other supposedly similar texts, we are also making covert assumptions about the question of relative date; thus we are left only with specific references between the Hymn and other authors from which to reconstruct a chronology. There are three such instances of cross-references to and from the Hymn (to date editors have discussed only one of these), and they are worth considering separately.

(1) v 2 ~ Asclepiades/Posidippus *HE* 977. We have no date for the epigram; we can attempt only a *terminus ante quem* based on the latest date at which we know the epigrammatists to have been alive. For Asclepiades (along with Posidippus) an honorific inscription from Delphi (*Fouilles de Delphes* III 3 no. 192, not mentioned by Gow–Page) gives us 276/5 or 273/2;[2] for Posidippus we have record of an honour at Thermon (*IG* IX i^2 17.24), once thought to date from *c.* 280, but now datable to 263/2.[3] The implications of this latter date need to be stressed: Posidippus was still alive less than twenty years before Callimachus was writing his latest surviving works (frr. 54–9 + 383 (= *SH* 254–69), 110) and complaining

---

[1] For an up-to-date text of the Heracles–Molorcus episode, including the *P. Lille* fragments, and discussion see P.J.Parsons, *ZPE* 25 (1977) 1–50 and *SH* 254–69.

[2] Wilamowitz, *HD* I 147 n. 5 (followed by Fraser, *Ptolemaic Alexandria* II 813) asserted that the epigram must have been written by Posidippus since chronology made borrowing by Asclepiades from Callimachus unlikely; this is not acceptable since Callimachus was probably already active as a writer in the 280s. However if the arguments given below for dating v after the *Argonautica* (and therefore after at least *Aetia* I and II) are accepted the Hymn may well have been written after we can expect Asclepiades (probably a contemporary of Philetas) to have died.

[3] See Klaffenbach ad loc. Cf. also Fraser, *Ptolemaic Alexandria* II 796, Gow–Page, *HE* II 481f.

of the weight of old age (fr. 1). In 263/2 Callimachus may have been any age between, say, 40 or 60 years old; in other words there is no justification whatever for using the parody by Asclepiades/Posidippus to place the Fifth Hymn early, or even 'fairly early' in Callimachus' career.

(2) v 23–8 ~ Theocritus 18.22–32. The arguments for seeing a reminiscence by Callimachus of Theocritus 18 are given in the Commentary (see in particular on vv. 18–28, 23–8, 23f., 27 ἀνέδραμε, 27–8). That there is a connection between the two poems, and that it is Callimachus who picks up Theocritus, not vice versa, seems clear, but since we have no date for *Id.* 18 and no other apparent links between that poem and other texts, no wider inferences about relative chronology are possible.

(3) v 103 ~ A.R. 2.444f. The connection between these two passages has long been recognised,[1] though the wider affinity between the two contexts has gone unobserved (see Commentary). Spanheim and Schneider assumed that Apollonius was the imitator, but the metrical irregularity of placing proclitic οὐ before the main caesura makes the reverse more likely. Placing of a proclitic before the caesura has no parallel in Callimachus, whereas in Apollonius three other instances occur; furthermore reminiscence of Apollonius adds various dimensions to Callimachus' text, whereas the Phineus episode gains nothing from echoing the Fifth Hymn. If the *Bath of Pallas* is to be dated after at least Book 2 of the *Argonautica* there are additional implications to be considered. First, that Apollonius echoes at least Book I of the *Aetia* is now almost undeniable,[2] and the many verbal contacts between other Books of the *Aetia* and the *Argonautica* (see Pfeiffer, *Callimachus* II Index Rerum Notabilium s.v. Apollonius Rhodius) are probably to be interpreted in the same way; in other words, if the priority of *Argonautica* 2 over the Fifth

---

[1] First by Spanheim; Cahen makes no mention of it in his commentary.

[2] See Pfeiffer, *Callimachus* II xli–xlii, E.Eichgrün, *Kallimachos und Apollonios Rhodios* (Diss. Berlin 1961) 119–39.

Hymn is accepted, we can additionally date the Hymn later than *Aetia* I and II, and also probably than *Aetia* III and IV.[1] Secondly there are reasonable grounds for thinking that *Argonautica* 2 and probably 4 were written *after* Callimachus' Sixth Hymn (the evidence is intricate and I have discussed it at length in *AJP* 98 (1977) 116–21); this means that the Fifth Hymn too was written later than the Sixth.

We have no grounds at present, then, for assigning the Fifth Hymn to a specific period of its author's life, but we can probably place it after a number of other works, some of them of major importance: Callimachus' own Sixth Hymn, *Aetia* I and II (and probably III and IV), *Argonautica* 1 (presumably) and 2[2] and probably 3 and 4, and Theocritus 18. After the Hymn was written either Asclepiades or Posidippus penned *AP* 5.202 (*HE* 974–9).

I append, as a very tentative footnote to the above discussion, two considerations which *might* suggest that the Fifth Hymn was written before the Third Hymn, and, perhaps, the *Hecale*. The arguments are necessarily very tenuous since they concern matters of vocabulary.

(1) At vv. 91f. Callimachus uses the words δόρκας . . . πρόκας. The form δόρξ probably does not appear before Callimachus (again at III 97 and fr. 676.1 which may come from the *Hecale*) and appears to have been formed by him, as

[1] The matter is complicated by our uncertainty about the time and manner of publication of the *Aetia*. There are good grounds for assuming Books I and II to have been published together, and Books III and IV to have been published separately from the first two and at least compiled into their final form very late in Callimachus' career after 246–5; the crucial questions to which we lack the answers are (a) had Books III and IV been published earlier in a different form but still as *Aetia* III and IV? (b) had individual episodes circulated earlier as separate poems, before they were finally compiled into *Aetia* III and IV? For a summary of the main evidence see Fraser, *Ptolemaic Alexandria* II 1006, and for the additional implications of the Lille papyri see P.J.Parsons, *ZPE* 25 (1977) 1–50. Our ignorance about the alleged two editions of Apollonius' *Argonautica* is a further hindrance to clarity in these issues.

[2] In coming after *Argonautica* 1 and 2 the Hymn would be in the company of Theocr. 13 and 22 (which surely postdate Apollonius).

a variation on δορκάς, δορκάδος, by analogy with the Homeric πρόξ which is doublet to προκάς. Since formation of the word is modelled on another Homeric pair of words it seems reasonable to take v 91–2 as its first occurrence, since in that passage the Homeric model, πρόξ, is explicitly given to explain, or key in, the new formation, whereas in III 97 and fr. 676.1 the word is used (in the spelling ʒ-: see Commentary) without supporting Homeric reference.

(2) At v. 92 Callimachus uses the very rare Homeric metonymy φάεα 'eyes' (see Commentary), and its use has the consequence of recalling specifically *Od.* 17.38ff., with considerable effect for the Hymn. φάεα occurs again at III 53, 71, 211 and possibly in *P. Oxy.* 2529 Front 4 (*SH* 282) which comes from the *Hecale* (Back 4–5 = fr. 248). None of the instances in the Third Hymn invoke the Homeric context as does v 92 and it is tempting to argue that this suggests the Fifth Hymn to have been the first instance of the Homeric metonymy and that once so established it was later used without supporting reference to its Homeric origins (the allusion to the Homeric context will also have been more easily established if φάεα had not already been used without such reminiscence in III).[1]

These two points of contact between the two hymns are too slight to bear much weight of argument, but it is worth noting that a dating of the Third Hymn after the Fifth is not incompatible with other evidence: the date of III is far from secure (see F.Bornmann, *Callimachi Hymnus in Dianam* (Florence 1968) vii–xi, who also suggests that a late date, after 246, may be suitable), and if the Third Hymn was written, like the Fifth, *after* Apollonius' *Argonautica* the points of verbal contact between III and Apollonius Rhodius will be reminiscences by Callimachus.[2]

---

[1] There seems to be another connection between the two hymns at v 102 and III 263 (see Commentary).

[2] E.Eichgrün, *Kallimachos und Apollonios Rhodios* (Diss. Berlin 1961) 111ff. argues vigorously for the priority of Apollonius but the evidence is too

VI SOME FORMAL ASPECTS OF THE POEM

The most immediately notable feature of the Fifth Hymn is its success as a mimetic poem, as a re-creation of the tense, excited atmosphere at a festival where the celebrants apprehensively await the epiphany of their goddess. The outward structure of the poem, much more pronounced and carefully calibrated than that of the Sixth Hymn or the Second Hymn, takes the reader as a participant through the stages of mounting excitement from the moment when the celebrants are summoned from their houses to the formal invocation of Athena and her final appearance as she emerges from the sanctuary. The way in which the progression of the festival and the religious enthusiasm are conveyed has already been described (Section I above) and is analysed in detail in the Commentary; what is important to appreciate also is the extraordinary success of the poem as a skilful illusion. First, the Hymn closes right at the moment of Athena's imminent appearance, in other words *before* the ceremony proper, the procession to the river and the ritual bath, has actually begun. Vv. 137f. ἔρχετ' Ἀθαναία νῦν ἀτρεκές· ἀλλὰ δέχεσθε | τὰν θεόν, ὦ κῶραι . . . read like a triumphant conclusion, as if the purpose of the poem has been achieved once Athena emerges, and what would be somewhat incongruous at an actual festival is possible because for his readers Callimachus has already presented the epiphany of the goddess and her ritual bath within the framework of the narrative; the readers of the poem have already experienced vicariously through the Tiresias story what the supposed celebrants are going to experience after the Hymn is over. In

---

slight to warrant his conclusions. The most important points of contact are given by Bornmann, *Hymnus in Dianam* x–xi. The most substantial connection concerns A.R. 3.876–83 and III 15, 110–12, 162; given the absence of any other criteria (Bornmann's concern about the name Amnisus is unnecessary) it seems a priori more likely that the text in which the verbal links are scattered across several passages was written second.

literary terms the occasion is complete, and it is one of Callimachus' considerable achievements that the close does not destroy the poem's verisimilitude, even though this is the most fully 'realistic' of the three mimetic hymns. Secondly, despite the mimetic force of the poem, as a dramatic first-person monologue, the text has all the ingredients of a hymn in the fashion of the Homeric narrative hymns; vv. 1–56 illustrate important ἀρεταί of the divinity by recounting famous incidents in which she participated and excelled (cf. Commentary on vv. 1–32), as well as containing a directly epicletic section (vv. 33–56). By covertly appealing to the familiar formal characteristics of the prayer-hymn Callimachus lends the tone of the *Bath of Pallas* greater religious authenticity; the Sixth Hymn is less sophisticated and less experimental in this respect since there the opening address to the celebrants (vv. 1–9) quickly converts into a standard direct appeal to the divinity herself (vv. 10–23) and the poem approximates more directly to a prayer-hymn.

The poetic complexity of the Fifth Hymn is best evidenced in its use of allusion. Like all Hellenistic dactylic poetry the Hymn establishes itself as high poetry by employing the mode of traditional epic, the *Iliad* and *Odyssey*, in morphology, grammar, syntax, vocabulary, phraseology and rhythm. This is a matter of linguistic texture and diction, not imitation, for even when Callimachus alludes to a whole Homeric turn of phrase (e.g. v. 63 ἵνα οἱ τεθυωμένον ἄλcoc, see Commentary) the purpose is to create a resonance and establish a general narrative tone, never simply to reproduce from a fixed model (cf. Section III above). But Callimachus' readers have to be alert to more than just characteristic features of the traditional poetic language, for where Callimachus does repeat exactly a Homeric phrase or rare word there is usually a specific reference to the scene or context. The most important examples in the Fifth Hymn have been listed above in Section III p. 29. What is significant about these instances for appreciation of Callimachean poetic technique is that often not only does the allusion contribute depth to the Hymn but information essential to understanding the poem is lost if the allusion should go undetected. In vv. 93–5 the description of Chariclo grieving is impressive even if the reminiscence of *Od.* 17.38ff. is not recognised, and Athena's ominous remarks about Actaeon in vv. 111–14 do not depend on identification of the echo of *Il.* 5.51ff. (though in both cases the fact that Callimachus found it helpful and legitimate to underwrite the emotive effect by appealing to Homeric prototypes reveals the profoundly literary nature of this supposedly religious poem). On the other hand at vv. 31–2 ὡς ἀπὸ χαίταν | πέξηται reads strangely until the allusion to *Il.* 14.175ff. has been noticed (see Commentary), and the witty comparison of Athena to Hera beautifying herself before the seduction of Zeus gives bite to the final instruction to the celebrants, after the rather convoluted denigration of Aphrodite and comparison of Athena to Helen in the preceding lines; without the Homeric reference the whole conclusion to the section on the Judgement of Paris is rather flat. Similarly the reference to Theocritus 18 in the preceding lines (see Commentary on vv. 23–8) is extensive and very important to the poem; mention of the Judgement of Paris as one of the typical occasions when Athena excelled is not very convincing in itself, since Aphrodite was the winner on that occasion, and identification of the allusion to Theocritus which compares Athena to the masculine but glorious Helen is essential if Athena is to be established as a real feminine beauty. The setting of a puzzle (why mention the Judgement?) was itself probably part of Callimachus' motivation here, and doubtless also Theocritus' poem had only recently been published and was current in Alexandria; none the less the risk was considerable that the allusion might not be picked up, and that the whole section on Athena's supposed beauty would remain obscure and unsatisfactory. Callimachus' readiness here to rely on allusion to establish his point reveals an inherent weakness in his mode of writing; it is a weakness shared to some degree by almost all the Hellenistic poets, but one to which Callimachus was particularly prone precisely because of his extraordinary intellect and appreciation of intricacies. No other Hellenistic writer was more alert to nuance and levels of meaning or more aware of the subtleties which could be conveyed by literary allusion.

However, for all that the *Bath of Pallas* is a subtle poem which requires fairly close appreciation of its 'place' in the tradition and its relationship to contemporary works, it is in no sense an obscure work. The excitement of the Argive ceremony which frames the poem is convincingly conveyed, directly and forcefully, reaching a climax in the eager invocation of Athena in vv. 33–56; the narrative of the blinding of Tiresias, which starts by contrast on a very calm note, is written in a heightened, more 'epic' style than the first part of the poem, and proceeds in very straightforward linear fashion. In particular the description of Athena and her companion at the spring and the uncanny noonday quiet which sets the atmosphere for Tiresias' intrusion (vv. 70–8) is as direct and powerful as anything which Callimachus wrote; extended descriptive passages (particularly passages of atmospheric description) are rare in Callimachus, whose narrative is generally indirect and rather febrile, and even the story of Erysichthon in the not dissimilar Sixth Hymn has nothing like this passage with its combination of setting and preparatory emotional atmosphere. The punishment of Tiresias is openly dramatic and terrifying; in the two figures of the transfixed boy and the shrieking mother we see the two polar reactions to dreadful godhead, and Athena's calm, measured reply, with its promise of gifts of compensation, provides a clear, and necessary, antithesis to the intensity of what precedes (how adequate Athena's response is in other terms we shall consider shortly).

The structure of the narrative too is simple and throws into prominence the main issues of the encounter between Athena and Tiresias. The arrangement is chiastic:

A[1]	57–69	the friendship
B[1]	70–84	Tiresias' intrusion and punishment
C[1]	85–95	Chariclo's grief
C[2]	96–106	Athena's response to Chariclo's grief
B[2]	107–118	Actaeon's intrusion and punishment
A[2]	119–136	gifts of friendship

The narrative begins with the friendship and concludes with Athena's attempt to mitigate the effects of Tiresias' punishment because of the friendship (v. 120 τεῦ χάριν ἐξ ἐμέθεν πολλὰ μενεῦντι γέρα); the friendship is the central issue and the key question that which Chariclo enunciates immediately on the blinding of her son, v. 86 τοιαῦται, δαίμονες, ἐςτὲ φίλαι; To be sure Athena remains the most important figure throughout the narrative. Even the opening description of her friendship with Chariclo is presented in the form of a list of cult centres (see Commentary on 57–69), and the whole of the second half of the narrative consists in the speech of Athena; in a hymn to Athena the divinity is naturally the focus, or at least the essential factor. None the less both the formal narrative structure and the emotional pace converge to make the awful punishment, along with the questions of loyalty and responsibility, the most prominent issues in the Tiresias story, and structure and pace are explicitly reinforced by the language of the narrative which describes Tiresias' blinding in the vocabulary of high tragedy (see Commentary on vv. 82 ὄμματα νὺξ ἔλαβεν, 93–5, 94–5).

In considering how Callimachus presents Athena and her behaviour towards Chariclo we have to keep two important points in perspective. First, the fact that Tiresias' intrusion on Athena's bath (and that of his mother) was unwitting is not in itself of much significance. At v. 52 the speaker of the ceremony warns the men of Argos to beware that they do not catch sight of Athena οὐκ ἐθέλων, and this phrase is repeated of Tiresias at the climax in v. 78 οὐκ ἐθέλων δ' εἶδε τὰ μὴ θεμιτά, and again of Actaeon at v. 113. The repetition certainly marks an interest by Callimachus in this aspect of the encounter, but it should not be taken as insistence or as emphasis on a central issue; in Greek belief, as in that of many other cultures, when a mortal encounters a god the question of the mortal's intention or responsibility is of little or no account in determining the outcome. An electric shock is effected merely by contact, whether intentional or accidental. Secondly, Athena's protestation of her own relative innocence and her inability to reverse the blindness, along with the offers of gifts of compensation to mitigate the punishment, may seem to a modern reader to betray disengagement and an inappropriate concern with practicalities. However in Greek religion no god was autonomous and no god could alter the larger order of things (of this the most celebrated example is the inability of Zeus to obstruct the death of his own son Sarpedon in *Il.* 16.431–61); furthermore compensation was a very proper concern since an encounter of this kind with a god necessarily resulted in a change of state (cf. Section II p. 22 above), and a fundamental feature of Greek mental categories was balance and counterbalance. The closing scenes of Euripides' *Hippolytus* illustrate both these points well; there are a number of notable similarities of wording with the fifth Hymn.

Theseus has unwittingly invoked a fatal curse on his son, thanks to the contrivance of Aphrodite. When Artemis reveals this to him she has also to explain her own non-interference:

θεοῖcι δ' ὧδ' ἔχει νόμοc· (~ V 100)
οὐδεὶc ἀπαντᾶν βούλεται προθυμίαι
τῆι τοῦ θέλοντοc, ἀλλ' ἀφιcτάμεcθ' ἀεί.
ἐπεί, cάφ' ἴcθι, Ζῆνα μὴ φοβουμένη
οὐκ ἄν ποτ' ἦλθον ἐc τόδ' αἰcχύνηc ἐγώ (~ V 98–100)
ὥcτ' ἄνδρα πάντων φίλτατον βροτῶν ἐμοί
θανεῖν ἐᾶcαι. (1328–34)

When the broken Hippolytus comes on stage he can protest his own innocence:

ὅδ' ὁ σεμνὸς ἐγὼ καὶ θεοσέπτωρ,
ὅδ' ὁ σωφροσύνηι πάντας ὑπερσχὼν (1364–5)

ἔμολέ τ' ἐπ' ἐμὲ τί ποτε τὸν οὐ- (~ v 78, 85)
δὲν ὄντ' ἐπαίτιον κακῶν; (1382–3)

Hippolytus, of course, is not as innocent of all responsibility as Tiresias, but between them he and Theseus have as much reason for dismay as do Chariclo and Tiresias. When Hippolytus and Artemis converse directly, Artemis, like Athena, expresses a certain detachment:

Hipp. ὁρᾶις με, δέσποιν', ὡς ἔχω, τὸν ἄθλιον;
Art. ὁρῶ· κατ' ὄσσων δ' οὐ θέμις βαλεῖν δάκρυ.
Hipp. οὐκ ἔστι σοι κυναγὸς οὐδ' ὑπηρέτης, (~ v 110–12)
Art. οὐ δῆτ'· ἀτάρ μοι προσφιλής γ' ἀπόλλυσαι.
Hipp. οὐδ' ἱππονώμας οὐδ' ἀγαλμάτων φύλαξ.
Art. Κύπρις γὰρ ἡ πανοῦργος ὧδ' ἐμήσατο. (1395–1400)

But she is able to promise that despite her powerlessness to interfere with Hippolytus' fate she will give compensation (a cult in Trozen) as a mark of her affection:

σοὶ δ', ὦ ταλαίπωρ', ἀντὶ τῶνδε τῶν κακῶν (~ v 119ff.)
τιμὰς μεγίστας ἐν πόλει Τροζηνίαι
δώσω· κόραι γὰρ ἄζυγες γάμων πάρος . . . (~ v 127, 128) (1423–5)

Before leaving Artemis herself stresses the unwitting nature of what Theseus has done:

ἄκων γὰρ ὤλεσάς νιν (1433)

The *Hippolytus* helps us to identify the true issues in the Fifth Hymn. Athena's gifts are a necessary counterbalance to the punishment and are appropriately placed at the end of the story; her inability to alter what has happened should not surprise us, and her disclaimer at vv. 98–100 can be accepted. However, the question which Callimachus puts in sharp focus and which is given no easy answer is that of the cost to the friendship with Chariclo. Tiresias offends, receives punishment and compensation, and can have no further complaint by Greek standards; but although he is the ostensible subject of this cautionary tale, he is a κωφὸν πρόcωπον, whose very silence highlights the main emotional crisis in which he plays only an observer's part. It is the friendship, and the concomitant expectations of loyalty, and the grief of a mother whose son's blinding is almost as terrible as his death, which Callimachus has placed at the centre of this poem, and it is the tension between the traditional epic-narrative presentation of conventional religion and the insistent problem of Chariclo's grief which makes the *Bath of Pallas* such a fascinating work.

This tension is not to be explained away as a compositional weakness or imaginative failure on the part of Callimachus; the structure and language of the narrative focus so deliberately and clearly on the unresolved issues that the latter have to be taken as integral to the poem as a whole. In the *Bath of Pallas* Callimachus goes beyond traditional myth and religion and explores another, more intrinsically secular area: What must it have felt like to be *Chariclo*, as a mother? This interest in the psychology of the individual, even within the framework of conventional religion, is characteristic of many Hellenistic writers of this time, in particular Apollonius Rhodius and Theocritus among Callimachus' contemporaries, but it was Callimachus who especially developed what might be called a new realism in his poetry in the spirit of contemporary Hellenistic rationalism. We can see the same direction being taken in the Sixth Hymn, which first presents the crime and punishment of Erysichthon in traditional form, and then explores what might have been the consequences at the very mundane human level.[1] The Sixth Hymn treats the Erysichthon story with black humour, and may seem almost frivolous on a superficial reading. Similarly the Fifth Hymn raises the question of Chariclo's feelings only to offer no satisfactory resolution: Athena's long reply to Chariclo's

[1] I have discussed the Sixth Hymn at greater length in *AJP* 98 (1977) 97–123.

outburst may be appropriate in terms of religious order, but it does not meet the powerful emotional basis of her friend's grief, and the narrator's concluding remark at v. 134 μάτηρ δ' οὔτις ἔτικτε θεάν seems only to underscore with terrible irony the fact that Athena is simply unable to meet Chariclo on her own terms.[1] This is the bleak climax of the Hymn, the outcome of Chariclo's passionate confrontation with her divine friend, and the absence of any tidy solution is not in itself a failing. In Euripides' *Hippolytus* the innocent Theseus is not permitted the luxury of a moral justification for the loss of his wife and son; for him as for Chariclo there is only the bleakness of knowing that catastrophes owe no-one an explanation. So too in the Fifth Hymn Callimachus has identified some of the terrifying implications of the ultimately unequal relationship between a mortal and Athena, and it is sufficient that the disturbing reality of such a liaison be merely exposed.[2]

This 'realism' should not be taken to signify that the Fifth Hymn is a mere literary exercise. Athena is still a divinity to be reckoned with, just as Artemis and Aphrodite in the *Hippolytus* lose no claim on man's attention by their treatment of Theseus. However the focus on Chariclo does mark a shift of emphasis away from pure celebration of the divine

---

[1] H.Staehelin, *Die Religion des Kallimachos* (Diss. Basel 1934) 48f. suggested that Athena does in fact help Chariclo to adjust to the punishment of her son, almost by therapeutic means; this interpretation is too coloured by post-pagan ideas of suffering and redemption.

[2] If Callimachus is to be criticised it is not for the incompleteness of the poem but for the form of the work: as a drama the *Hippolytus* can set Theseus in a tragic mode, whereas the *Bath of Pallas* by virtue of its nature as a hymn inevitably has more restricted dimensions, and for all Chariclo's grief (and Callimachus' narrative power) she comes across as a figure of anguish but not tragedy. It is rather ironical that a fundamental criticism of a work by Callimachus should have to be that its scale is too small, but the impact of what is a profoundly serious poem is reduced in the Fifth Hymn by the form being too limited for the subject-matter and denying any possibility of true universality. By contrast the facetious tone of the Sixth Hymn makes that poem, though less serious, formally more congruent.

(something which the Hymn to Apollo is closer to being) to the more secular concerns of human isolation. In this respect the Fifth Hymn is thoroughly Hellenistic and thoroughly Callimachean: the framework is derived from classical Greek religion, but what gives the poem its energy is fascination with re-creating the human act of celebration, and reflection on the effects of seemingly arbitrary divine 'law' on a loyal mother. There is certainly no basis here for venturing to determine what Callimachus did 'believe' about Athena or any other cult matter, but the orientation of his Hymn is that of the rationalism of third-century Alexandria. Callimachus is not making any aggressive declaration about man as the centre of all things, but the *Bath of Pallas* is a poem about man and his feelings, written for appreciation by an audience with a very strong sense of their own detachment and their own independent intellectual powers as sophisticated readers.

VII THE MANUSCRIPT TRADITION AND THE TEXT

Any reader of Callimachus' Hymns who opens the editions of Schneider (1870) and Pfeiffer (1953) and who compares the text and apparatus criticus of each editor can only be struck by the dramatic advance in our knowledge of the textual tradition achieved by modern research.[1] The economy and clarity which characterises the modern edition is owed to the diligence and insight of several scholars, among them Wilamowitz, of whose editions the first of 1882 was a major advance in properly establishing the MSS tradition and archetype, and the second of 1897 was a radical reassessment incorporating a fresh collation of several of the MSS. But the

[1] In I 9–37, for example (the first complete double page in Schneider), Pfeiffer's text is different in eight places from that of Schneider, and whereas the latter's apparatus criticus is 8 inches long, Pfeiffer's covers a mere 1 inch for the same lines.

two scholars who have contributed more than any other are M.T.Smiley and Rudolph Pfeiffer.

Smiley's was the most detailed study to date: for the first time he undertook a systematically comprehensive collation of almost all the important extant MSS and the *editiones principes*, and presented his results, together with analysis and stemmata, in a sequence of very important articles – *CQ* 14 (1920) 1–15, 57–77, 105–22, 15 (1921) 57–74, 113–25. Pfeiffer's edition of the Hymns was made rather as a supplement to the first volume of fragments, and Pfeiffer makes few claims for his own work, but he is far too modest; Pfeiffer carefully recollated most of the MSS,[1] and his introduction to the Hymns (*Callimachus* II 'Prolegomena' li–xci) is a comprehensive reassessment of the evidence, with a clear and concise outline of the crucial readings for the MSS classification, as well as much that is new on the provenance of the MSS and the copyists responsible for them.

Smiley's work is still fundamental for any editor of the text of Callimachus' Hymns, and his articles contain a great deal that is of considerable interest and is not to be found in Pfeiffer; equally Pfeiffer, in addition to offering a masterly summary of the essential evidence, added much material of his own. There is no need for further extensive collation of the MSS, but some reassessment of part of the transmission, family α, and revision of the stemma codicum, is necessary in view of the recent redating of MS At (see below p. 60); and this seemed an appropriate point at which to give also a brief synoptic survey of the MSS and their history, supplementing and correcting both Smiley and Pfeiffer. In what follows I have described briefly each of the MSS, taking care to give where possible for the main witnesses any information likely to be relevant to reconstruction of their background and

[1] Using Smiley's photographs for most of them; for Λ and G, which Smiley had not seen, he secured specimen photographs, and from S.G.Kapsomenos he obtained a new collation of the Athos MS At, of which very few readings were available to Smiley (*CQ* 14 (1920) 3, 15 (1921) 61).

place in the overall transmission (contents, authorship, ownership etc.), often more fully than in Pfeiffer. I have repeated almost none of the data on which construction of the stemma is based, with the slight exception of family α, since the evidence is well presented in Pfeiffer and does not need to be repeated. My discussion of the archetype Ψ has, as with my descriptions of the extant MSS, a slightly different emphasis from that of Pfeiffer, and attempts a fuller presentation of the evidence for what kind of a manuscript Ψ was physically and for its background. Within the general framework I have tried particularly to indicate the relevance of the evidence for the Fifth Hymn.

Smiley and Pfeiffer provide sufficient data for an editor to establish an independent text, and after careful analysis of their work, and a little very cautious supplementation from Schneider, I have established a new text and drawn up my own apparatus criticus. A list of the places where my text differs from that of Pfeiffer is given on p. 90. I have not recollated any of the MSS, but I have re-examined the two first printed editions of Politian and Lascaris, and this is reflected in my apparatus criticus. Pfeiffer's apparatus criticus has turned out to need correcting and supplementing in a number of places, and where I differ from him I do so quite consciously (see, for example, vv. 5, 16, 18, 25, 38, 49, 78, 87, 93, 130).

The manuscripts

References to the second volume of Pfeiffer's *Callimachus* are cited by Pfeiffer's name alone followed by Roman or Arabic page references. Contents of MSS are listed only briefly, minor omissions and supplements being noted only for the Callimachean portions.

For the main line of transmission of the text 8 MSS are prime witnesses.

F: Milan, Ambrosianus 120 (B 98 sup.), early fifteenth century.

Contents: Apollonius Rhodius, *Argonautica*, *Batrachomyomachia*; [Hdt.] *Vita Homeri*; Maxim. Tyr. diss. 34 Dbn., Orphic *Argonautica* and *Lithica*; *Homeric Hymns* 3–33 and epigram εἰς ξένους; Callimachus I–VI with marginal and interlinear scholia; anon. epigr. (= Pf. test. 23) 1–4.

The Homeric and Callimachean hymns are probably in the hand of George Chrysococces, written at Constantinople between 1420 and 1428.

[Pfeiffer lvi–lvii]

E: Paris, Bibl. Nat. gr. 2763, fifteenth century.

Contents: Orphic *Argonautica* and *Hymns*; Proclus, *Hymns* I–V; Callimachus I–IV, VI, V with marginal and interlinear scholia; *Homeric Hymns* 3–33 and epigram εἰς ξένους; Moschus, ἔρως δραπέτης; Musaeus, *Hero and Leander*; Hesiod, *Op.* and *Scutum*; *AP* 16.92; Hesiod, *Theog.*; Theocritus.

The Callimachus section was not written by the hand which copied Proclus. Between Callimachus VI and V appears a scholium on Lycophron, *Alex.* 35, again similarly placed after VI in e (see below). Smiley suggested that an ancestor of E and e began Lycophron's *Alexandra* immediately after VI and that a scholium therefrom spilled back onto the last page of Callimachus' *Hymns*.

[Pfeiffer lxiii–lxiv]

e: Milan, Ambrosianus 734 (S 31 sup.), fifteenth century.

Contents: Orphic *Hymns*; Proclus, *Hymns*; *Homeric Hymns* 3–33; Moschus, ἔρως δραπέτης; Musaeus, *Hero and Leander*; Callimachus I–VI with marginal and interlinear scholia; Pindar, *Epinicia*.

On the first page is the inscription '*liber iste est mei Marci Antonii de Passeris Ianuensis* [in the margin '*Patavini*'] *et amicorum*', and then below '*I. V. Pinelli*' (1535–1601); Pinelli also owned MS q (see below). Pfeiffer points out that the Callimachean part of e is in the same hand as cod. Laur. 60.14, whose copyist seems to have been roughly contemporary with Politian. After VI is the same scholium on Lycophron *Alex.* 35 which appears in the same place in E (see above).

[Pfeiffer lxiv]

Π: Paris, Bibl. Nat. gr. suppl. 1095, late fifteenth century.

Contents: *Vita Homeri*; [Plut.] *de Hom.*; Homer, *Iliad* with scholia; *Homeric Hymns* 3–33 and epigram εἰς ξένους; anon. epigr. (= Pf. test. 23);

Callimachus I–VI (omitting III 66–145) with marginal and interlinear scholia; Orphic *Hymns*; Proclus, *Hymns*; *Batrachomyomachia*.

Notes at the beginning and end of the volume indicate that the MS once belonged to the Abbey of St Peter at Perugia. The omission of III 66–145 is due to a lost page. In V each distich begins with a large initial letter projecting into the margin. Wilamowitz (ed. 3, p. 11) remarked of the copyist '*Graecum non fuisse* Τροεζῆνος *ostendit, quod in scholio IV 41 semel ei excidit*', and other slips suggest this too.

[Pfeiffer lxv–lxvi]

S: Madrid, Bibl. Nac. gr. 4562 (=N 24), dated 1464.

Contents: Musaeus, *Vita*; *AP* 7.666 (Antipater Thess. on Hero and Leander); *Hero and Leander*; Marcus Musurus on Musaeus; epigrams and Constantine Lascaris etc. on Orpheus; Orphic *Argonautica*, *Hymns*; Proclus, *Hymns*; *Homeric Hymns* 3–33; Callimachus I–VI; summary of *Suda* on C.; *AP* 7.41f. (both on C.); 20 epigrams of C. and more than 470 other epigrams.

After VI is the inscription κτῆμα κωνσταντίνου λασκάρεωσ ἐν μεδιολάνωι ὑπ' αὐτοῦ ἐκγραφέν· ,ᾱῡξ̄δ (i.e. 1464). A number of suprascript changes, marginal additions, and supplements of lacunae were later made by Lascaris himself apparently from the first edition of Politian (S^2).

[Pfeiffer lxviii]

Q: Modena, Estensis 164 (=αW5.16, previously III E 11), late fifteenth century.

Contents: Orphic *Hymns*; Proclus, *Hymns*; Callimachus I–VI with marginal and interlinear scholia; *Homeric Hymns* 3–33 and epigr. εἰς ξένους; miscellaneous notes, glosses etc.

After the *Homeric Hymns* is the subscription γεώργιος ὁ οὐάλλα πλακεντίνος ἔγραψε; all the writing is in the same hand. Q is probably to be dated before 8 May 1492 since Pico della Mirandola then asked Valla to lend him a text of Callimachus' *Hymns* (such a manuscript does not appear in the list of books which Janus Lascaris saw in Valla's collection in Venice in 1490–1). Valla himself later made suprascript corrections, marginal and interlinear notes, and supplements to lacunae (Q^2).

[Pfeiffer lxviii–lxix]

A: Vatican, gr. 1691, fifteenth century.

Contents: Apollonius Rhodius, *Argonautica*; Orphic *Argonautica* and *Hymns*; Proclus, *Hymns*; Callimachus I–VI with marginal and interlinear notes on I 1–44 only.

A, like C, once belonged to Cardinal Bessarion († 1472).
[Pfeiffer lxx]

C: Venice, Marcianus 480, fifteenth century.

Contents: Oppian, *Hal.* and *Cyn.*; Theocritus; Dionys. Perieg.; Nicander, *Ther.* and *Alex.*; Aglaias etc.; Aratus, *Phaen.*; Hesiod, *Scut.*, *Op.* and *Theog.*; Apollonius Rhodius, *Argonautica*; Orphic *Argonautica* and *Hymns*; Proclus, *Hymns*; Callimachus I–VI.

The Callimachean portion of C was written by George of Crete (who also copied MSS B and K – see below). The MS belonged, like A, to Cardinal Bessarion, who gave it to the basilica of St Mark in Venice in 1468.
[Pfeiffer lxx–lxxi]

In addition to the above MSS another, D, from which the Callimachean portion is now missing, was also an important primary witness; however, both first printed editions used D and are thus particularly important.

[D]: Florence, Laurentianus 32.45, fifteenth century.

Contents: Apollonius Rhodius, *Argonautica*; Orphic *Argonautica* and *Hymns*; Proclus, *Hymns*; *Homeric Hymns* 3–7.33.

D finishes abruptly, and it may be to this MS that an entry in the index of the Medici library made in 1495 refers: '*Orphei Argonauta* [*sic*] *et hymni Homeri et Calimachi* [*sic*] *in greco, in membranis*'. Schneider suggested that Lascaris may have torn out the last portion (after 1495) when preparing his first edition.
[Pfeiffer lxvi]

Politian: *Angeli Politiani Miscellaneorum Centuriae Primae ad Laurentium Medicem*, Florence, Antonio Miscomini 13 October 1489, Chapter 80 'Fabula ignotior de Tiresia et Pallade: qua sensus aperitur Propertianus' containing the Greek text and a translation in Latin elegiac couplets. This chapter was reprinted in a composite volume which also contained works by Filippo Beroaldo, Domizio Calderini and Giambattista Pio in Brescia 1496, and again in the Aldine edition of Politian's collected works, Venice 1498.

In this chapter Politian achieves a very beautiful simple typographical style by omitting breathings, accents, apostrophes and interrogation marks, and placing iota subscript in adscript position; he also prints many enclitics and other words (conjunctions, negatives, prepositions etc.) for the most part continuously with what precedes or follows. By a slip vv. 61f. were omitted from the Greek text (although translated in the Latin) in the Florence and Brescia editions – see Commentary on v. 61.

[Pfeiffer lxvii]

Lascaris: *Callimachi Cyrenaei Hymni*; no date, place of publication or printer's name.

Contents: Callimachus I–VI; a Greek poem εἰς Καλλίμαχον with the subscription Λασκάρεως; scholia.

The hymns are printed in Roman capitals, with breathings and accents and with iota subscript placed adscript but half-size; the scholia are in lower case. Each hexameter line of V is marked by a larger capital. The type is the same as that used for a number of other editions by Janus Lascaris printed by Lorenzo di Alopa at Florence, and these, together with the author's poem εἰς Καλλίμαχον, suggest Lascaris as editor, between 1494 and 1496.[1] Pfeiffer rightly stresses the importance of Lascaris' *Journal*, which indicates that in 1491–2 during his travels in the east Lascaris found, or even bought, on Athos in the Lavra a manuscript containing 'Καλλιμάχου ὕμνοι, Βαβρίου μῦθοι etc.': this manuscript is otherwise unknown.

[Pfeiffer lxvi–lxvii, lxxvii]

---

[1] Smiley's suggestion that two editions were published, one by Lascaris without scholia, and one later by Alopa alone with scholia, was correctly rejected by Pfeiffer (lxxvii n.1): the 19 known copies of Lascaris' edition seem all to be the result of one printing, and the absence of scholia in 5 copies must be due to some mechanical omission.

In addition to the above a number of copies of other extant MSS belong to the medieval tradition.

At: Athos, Vatopedi 671 (previously 587), fifteenth century.

Contents: Sophocles' life, *Aj.*, *El.*, *OT*, argument of *El.*; Euripides, *Hec.*, *Or.*, *Phoen.*; *Homeric Hymns* 3–33 and epigram εἰς ξένους; [Hdt.] *Vita Homeri*; Callimachus I–VI with scholia; anon. epigr. (= Pfeiffer test. 23) 1–4.

Pfeiffer followed the general inclination of earlier editors (though subsequently expressing reservations in vol. II Addenda p. 124) to date At to the fourteenth century, thus making it the earliest extant MS of the Hymns and a parallel relative of F. Other evidence was difficult to reconcile with this, however, since all the errors of F, even of the most trivial kind, are repeated in At, and At has additional errors of its own (Pfeiffer lx and 124f.); on their readings one would assume that At is descended from F. N.G.Wilson, *Revue d'Histoire des Textes* 4 (1974) 139–42 has now demonstrated that T.W.Allen's earlier insistence on a later date for At was correct (*JHS* 15 (1895) 149f. and Allen–Sikes–Halliday *The Homeric Hymns* (Oxford 1936²) xxxvi–xxxvii), since the scribe of At was Girard of Old Patras who was active *c.* 1420–43.

[Pfeiffer lvii and 124–5]

G: Vienna, Imperial Library gr. 318, late fifteenth century.

Contents: letters of Phalaris, Mithridates, Alciphron; Pindar, *O.* and *P.*; Musaeus, *Hero and Leander*; Callimachus I–VI.

An entry in the MS records that it was bought at Venice for the Library in 1672 for sixteen florins.

[Pfeiffer lix]

H: Leiden, Vossianus 59, fifteenth (or early sixteenth) century.

Contents: Orphic *Argonautica* and *Hymns*; [Pyth.] *carmina aurea*; Callimachus I–VI; various epigrams; scholia to *Iliad* 2; Musaeus, *Hero and Leander*; Hesiod, *Scut.*; Phocylides; Aratus, *Phaen.*; Nicander, *Ther.* and *Alex.*; Phanocles.

[Pfeiffer lix]

Λ: Florence, Laurentianus suppl. 440, late fifteenth century.

Contents: Callimachus I–VI.

Written by George Moschus, the copyist of I (below). The

first letter of each distich of the Fifth Hymn is in red (minuscule).

[Pfeiffer lviii–lix]

I: Vatican, gr. 1379, late fifteenth century.

Contents (five distinct MSS bound together): (1) some Theocritus, Moschus, Bion etc.; (2) Babrius, *tetrastich.* etc.; (3) Callimachus I–VI; anon. epigr. (= Pf. test. 23); (4) κανονίςματα etc.; (5) Plutarch, some *Lives*.

The Callimachus is prefaced with the inscription '-χ- *hymnos aiunt edidisse tantum modo Callimachum perdifficiles atque elegantiarum plenos. Moschus*', and has at the end the subscription '*Corcyrae conscripsit manu Georgius Moschus Callimachi hymnos hosce anno Domini 1496 iii cal. Maias*', the subscription being in the hand of Pietro Candido. Moschus made a few interlinear and marginal corrections himself, but a later hand (so Pfeiffer against Smiley) made a large number of alterations and additions. George Moschus also copied MS Λ (see above).

[Pfeiffer lvii–lviii]

Anon. Bern.: A few readings from another MS, unidentified and no longer, apparently, extant, are preserved in the margin of a Bern library copy of Vascosan's Paris edition of 1549; the anonymous annotator, datable before 1585 when the book was bought by the library, also recorded some readings, prefaced by ἴcωc and presumably conjectures of his own, which help the text of the Fifth Hymn at 36 and 46. See R.Reitzenstein, *Hermes* 26 (1891) 308ff.

[Pfeiffer lxiii]

q: Ambrosianus 11 (A 63 sup.), dated 1509.

Contents: Orphic *Argonautica* and *Hymns*; Proclus, *Hymns*; Callimachus I–VI with marginal and interlinear scholia.

A subscription on the last page records + $\overline{\alpha\varphi\theta}$ (1509) ὀκτωβρίω $\overline{\kappa\beta}$. ἐν οἰκία κυροῦ μανουὴλ τοῦ πουλλομάτου ... κἀγὼ μιχαὴλcουλιάρδοc ... ἔγραψα. Suliardo (from Nauplia) copied q from Valla's Q in Italy; Nigra, *Riv. Fil.* 20 (1892) 204 remarks that q has all the faults characteristic of

Suliardo's workshop. The MS at one time belonged, like MS e, to I.V.Pinelli.

[Pfeiffer lxix]

B: Vatican, gr. 36, fifteenth century.

Contents: Apollonius Rhodius, *Argonautica,* with scholia; Orphic *Argonautica* and *Hymns*; Proclus, *Hymns*; Callimachus I–VI.

In the same hand as C and K (see above on C); for the most part B is a copy of C.

[Pfeiffer lxx–ii]

K: Vatican, Urbinas gr. 145, fifteenth century.

Contents: Orphic *Argonautica*; Callimachus I–VI; Nicander, *Ther.*

The writing is in two hands, the more elegant and accurate which copied the Callimachus and Nicander being that of George of Crete who also wrote MSS B and C (see above). K was copied from A.

[Pfeiffer lxxi–lxxii]

In addition to these 18 MSS and two printed editions five others should be mentioned (see Commentary on v. 136; cf. Pfeiffer lxxii–lxxvi '*Codices recentissimi e libris impressis descripti et codices nunc deperditi*'):

L: Leiden XXXIII Ru. 7, sixteenth century. 'ex editione iam interpolata (Venet. 1555 etc.) aut ex editione priore cuius margini loci interpolati adpicti erant' (Pfeiffer). This MS appears not to have been collated since Ruhnken.

M: Paris, Bibl. Nat. gr. suppl. 456, sixteenth or seventeenth century. 'ex editione Frobeniana, ut videtur, at lacunis . . . aliunde expletis' (Pfeiffer).

N: an unidentified MS used by F.Robortellus in 1543 in which 'integra habentur' (Rob.) IV 177ff., 200ff., V 136.

O: an unidentified MS used by H.Stephanus in his *Corpus Poetarum Graecorum* of 1566 where 'eidem loci modo allati et VI 23 expleti sunt' (Pfeiffer).

T: Turin, Biblioteca Nazionale B.v.26 (previously CCLXI. B.VI.21), sixteenth century. 'ex editione "interpolata" descriptus, cum notis marginalibus eadem manu additis quae textum scripsit' (Pfeiffer). Destroyed by fire in 1904.

Five other extant MSS seem only to be copies of printed editions: d, Ot, P, Str, cod. Bonon. See Pfeiffer lxxii–iii. Br is a copy of I (Pfeiffer lviii).

R, the Madrid codex gr. 122, was no longer to be found in the Biblioteca Nacionale when Smiley made his collations, and in September 1974 the Director of the Escorial Library, Gregorio de Andres, confirmed to me that the MS is not in the Library.[1] (Cf. Pfeiffer lxxiv.)

The stemma codicum

The impressive work of M.T.Smiley (*CQ* 1920, 1921) demonstrated conclusively that the extant MSS of Callimachus' Hymns belong essentially to a closed tradition, being derived from a number of hyparchetypes which were copied from a single common ancestor (Ψ). Pfeiffer's own supplementary collations confirmed Smiley's results.[2] Smiley's

[1] Dr Andres suggests that R may have been removed from Spain in the nineteenth century. It is worth noting that R, a fine illuminated codex of the fifteenth or sixteenth century containing Callimachus' *Hymns* with scholia, had never been collated. J.Iriarte, *Regiae Bibliothecae Matritensis Codices Graeci MSS* (Madrid 1769) 499f. describes the MS and notes the first words of each hymn and the first and last words of accompanying scholia, together with lacunae; Schneider merely repeated the little that is in Iriarte. Smiley dismissed R as manifestly derived from the *editio princeps* (*CQ* 14 (1920) 5), and the presence of Lascaris' poem placed, as in the *ed. pr.*, between text and scholia, as well as curtailment of the scholia to v at v. 124, certainly suggest an affinity; however, R did diverge in supplementing v 136 (apparently), and vi 14[a], 23 more than Lascaris, and in omitting iv 179 and the beginning of 199. We cannot be confident, therefore, that R had nothing to contribute to establishing the text, especially in view of the copyist's claim to 'fine emendation' in his subscription: καὶ ταῦτα μὲν τοῦ καλλιμάχου διορθώϲει ξιομένηι Ἐγὼ ποντικὸϲ ὁ οὐϊρούνιοϲ [died 1520] ἔγραψα πρὸϲ τὸν γεώργιον τὸν ἀνϲελμὸν μεγαλοπρεπῆ καὶ ϲοφώτατον ἐν τῆι χρυϲοπόλει μναρὸν φιλίαϲ καὶ τοῦ ξενοδοχείου.

[2] Smiley himself made one subsequent modification: he had originally argued that Q was a copy of S (*CQ* 14 (1920) 62–72), but changed his

articles contain a very detailed exposition of the evidence for the interrelationship of the MSS, and Pfeiffer's Prolegomena give an excellent summary and supplementation; there is no need to repeat the evidence here, with the exception of sub-group α. At the time of Pfeiffer's edition six MSS, At, F, G,H,I,Λ, all of the same family, seemed to be derived from a common hyparchetype in the following manner:

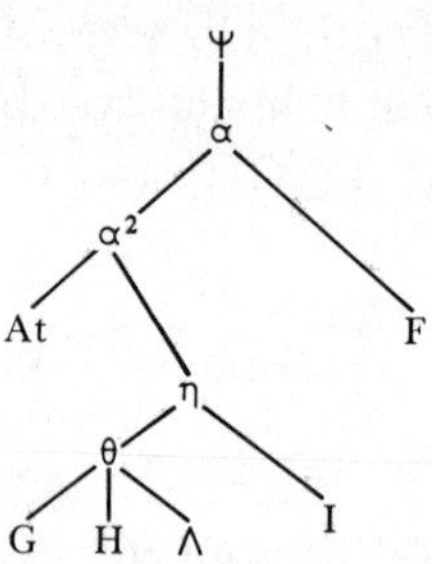

This genealogy was only partly satisfactory since At showed every sign of being a copy of F, reproducing each single one of the latter's errors, while exhibiting errors of its own not to be found in F (Pfeiffer lx). However, on palaeographical grounds such a relationship seemed impossible: F can be dated to 1420–8, while the general inclination of editors had been to place At in the late fourteenth century (though the MS had hardly been examined at all by a properly qualified palaeographer). N.G.Wilson's demonstration in 1974 that At is also to be placed in the fifteenth century removed the only obstacle for regarding At as a copy of F (*Revue d'Histoire des Textes* 4 (1974) 139–42, see above p. 60), and as a corollary to this the relationship of η (G,H,Λ,I) to F needs re-examining. The close affinity of At and η (at least in Hymns III–VI)[1] is

mind when reviewing Breuning's treatment of the Homeric Hymns (*CR* 44 (1930) 148). See also Pfeiffer lxix.

[1] The shared errors of At and η all occur in the last three hymns, but this is probably due to coincidence. The majority of notable errors in most of the MSS and hyparchetypes tend to be bunched in III–VI, which probably reflects developing loss of scribal attention in the course of copying out a difficult set of texts.

evidenced by a number of corruptions which they have in common, of which the most striking is the omission of IV 142f. (see the list in Pfeiffer lxi). Pfeiffer had already remarked that At and η should be treated as gemelli, and the evidence on which this conclusion was based is not affected by the new dating for At. We can now regard η also as a descendant from F and for clarity's sake should redesignate the common parent of At and η; I suggest the symbol μ:

Errors shared by At and η but not found in F are those of the intermediary μ. Errors which are common to At and F but not found in η (listed in Pfeiffer lx) we may regard as having been transmitted in μ but corrected by η; that η was a reasonably capable critic is demonstrated by the corrections noted by Pfeiffer lxi[1] (most are corrections required by metre, and the errors idiosyncratic to At and F also mostly involve metrical infelicities: we obtain the consistent impression of η as a competent metrician rather than a general textual critic).

Thus the number of prime witnesses to the text of Ψ has been reduced to ten for the Fifth Hymn, nine for the others (including the first editions). At and η may be omitted from our apparatus criticus except where they carry the correct reading by emendation. Since F is now the sole transmitter of what Pfeiffer designated as the α sub-group we have to allow

[1] These are IV 126 ὑπάτου η: ὑπάτοιο Ψ, which Pfeiffer notes in his discussion of At and η, and the list of corrections found in η and La. To these ten add III 57 τρινακρίη *P. Ant.* 20, E marg., η: τρινακίη Ψ, 125 λοιμὸς E[c] η: λιμὸς Ψ. At III 55 η corrected to ἄκμαζε, which is metrical but incorrect.

the possibility that F was copied direct from Ψ; however, since F was copied in Constantinople at a time around which, or shortly after which, hyparchetype ʒ was copied from the archetype in Italy (see below p. 71), it is still a reasonable assumption that an intermediary came between Ψ and F and we should continue to posit a hyparchetype α. The stemma codicum can now be drawn as follows:

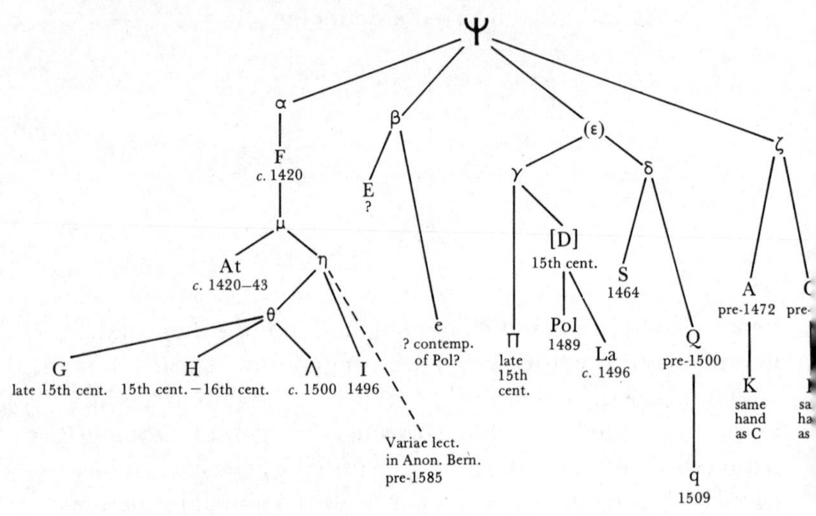

Contamination

The stemma codicum expresses the essential pattern of interrelationships of the extant MSS, but it is worth noting that within this clear-cut framework there is evidence of substantial 'contamination' (cf. Pfeiffer lxxx–lxxxii).

Family γ. In a number of lacunose passages γ offered a more complete text than its gemellus δ (or hyparchetypes β or ʒ); thus at v 128, for example, γ preserved the whole verse, and at v 136 θυγάτηρ. Smiley (followed rather reluctantly by Pfeiffer) suggested that γ had drawn on a MS from family α, but there are some difficulties in this. If γ had an α MS from which to take θυγάτηρ at v 136 we may be surprised that ψεύδεα was overlooked at the beginning of the same line, and equally puzzled that only a few lines further on in the text γ did not turn to the same MS for supplements at VI 13, 15, 18, 22 and 86.[1]

Pfeiffer lxi lists nine passages in which the edition of Lascaris prints emendations found otherwise only in η from family α. Lascaris might have made the corrections independently, and it is certainly relevant that if he was able to consult an α MS he did not use it to supplement the lacunae in his own main exemplar.

Family δ. Pfeiffer lxxviii itemises the scholia found only in Q and e or E, and these together with some shared readings and mistakes suggest some sort of contact between Q and the β family. Smiley, *CQ* 14 (1920) 69f. discussed a number of coincidences between Q^2 and β (including V 27 κόραιϲ EQ^2) and suggested that Valla drew on 'some manuscript, not extant, akin to E and e'. Quandt also concluded that in the Orphic Hymns contamination is evident between Q and β (Prolegomena xxiiff.).

Family ʒ. Smiley, *CQ* 15 (1921) 124 notes a small number of coincidences between Π and ʒ. At the beginning of the lacunose VI 23 ʒ alone recorded the single letter π (thence Q^2); normally the scribe of ʒ simply omitted what he found difficult to read (in V see 17, 107, 108 and cf. the list of passages in Pfeiffer lxxxi).

These instances of contamination are such as to remind us that the extant MSS, and what we can reconstruct from them about the hyparchetypes, do not convey the whole story of the transmission of the text from the archetype. Other external evidence reinforces this conclusion. On 13 June 1428 Francisco Philelpho wrote from Bologna to Ambrose Traversari

[1] At VI 23 γ alone has ἰδέϲθαι at the end of the line where our other MSS have nothing. This is the only place at which γ would be the sole transmitter of the text where Ψ was lacunose, and Smiley ingeniously suggested (*CQ* 15 (1921) 121f.) that γ was copying from a MS with 29 lines to each page and a hole at VI 23 which showed ἰδέϲθαι through from V 109.

about MSS in his possession brought from the East, including one containing 'Orphei Argonautica et hymni, Callimachus';[1] this description (Orpheus and Callimachus but no Homer) would fit only members of the ʒ family in our tradition, but since ʒ was almost certainly copied in Italy itself (see below p. 71) we have to assume that Philelpho's MS is now lost.[2] Again in 1491–2 Janus Lascaris recorded in 'indice codicum repertorum et emptorum' 'Athos, Lavra... Καλλιμάχου ὕμνοι, Βαβρίου μῦθοι etc.' (K.K.Müller, *Zentralblatt für Bibliothekswesen* I (1884) 399); this MS, whether bought or only seen by Lascaris in the course of his travels, is otherwise unknown to us.[3]

Ψ

That each of the sub-groups of our MSS derives from a common ancestor is plainly demonstrated by the many corruptions which they all share (see the attributions to Ψ in my apparatus criticus passim), and in particular by the lacunae to be found in every MS at IV 177ª–8 and 200f.: these two lacunae patently derive from mechanical damage in a single earlier MS. Furthermore there are a number of communally 'sensitive' points in our MSS in III–VI where almost every MS is corrupt or lacunose to a varying degree, clearly owing to the progressive deterioration in the legibility of the archetype from which the hyparchetypes were copied.

---

[1] *Ambrosii Traversarii... aliorumque ad ipsum et ad alios... Latinae epistolae* ed. P.Canneti and L.Mehus (Florence 1759) column 1010, letter no. 875 in the continuous series (= Book 24 letter 32). (No year is given in the date at the end, but the letters on either side of it are from 1428 and Canneti clearly intended it to be placed in that year.) Cf. A.Calderini, *SIFC* 20 (1913) 217 n. 2, 280f.

[2] The MS could have been an intermediary between Ψ and ʒ. Pfeiffer lxxxii rightly dismissed earlier suggestions by Hollander and Maas that Philelpho's MS was our F.

[3] Later, after 1496, Lascaris recorded that he possessed at least two MSS of Callimachus: K.K.Müller, op. cit. 410. See Pfeiffer lxvii.

Thus for example at v 78 probably α was able to read the whole of θεμιτά; β all but the last letter, θεμιτ; ε all but the last two letters, θεμι;[1] ʒ nothing at all; in v this same deterioration in Ψ underlies corruptions and lacunae also at 107f., 128, 131, 136.[2] These 18–20 sensitive points enable the hyparchetypes to be put with some confidence in the chronological order α, β, ε, ʒ.[3]

That Ψ deteriorated in this way was unfortunate, but the nature of the damage does give us valuable evidence with which to construct a fairly detailed identikit description of the archetype. In most cases the damage in Ψ was such as to affect both sides of the page on which it occurred, and the resultant corruptions and lacunae in our MSS regularly group in pairs, with 30 lines separating each of the two passages. The disposition of the last 11 pages in Ψ can therefore be reconstructed, and for v pagination was as follows:

Page	Lines	Damage
v recto	IV 316–26 Title[4] V 1–18	?17?
v verso	V 19–48	?47?
IV recto	49–78	78 } bottom outside corner
IV verso	79–108	107f. } bottom outside corner
III recto	109–38	128, 131, 136
III verso	139–42 Title VI 1–25	VI 15, 18, 23

[1] So γ, falsely supplemented: δ as usual omitted completely part-words which appeared to give no sense.

[2] Also perhaps 17, and conceivably 47.

[3] See P.Maas, *Byzantinisch-Neugriechische Jahrbücher* 5 (1926–7) 206, and the detailed citation of evidence in Pfeiffer lxxix–lxxxi. G.Quandt, *Orphei Hymni* (Berlin 1941) xxix comes to the same conclusion for the Orphic contents of these same MSS. Cf. also M.T.Smiley, *CQ* 15 (1921) 114.

[4] The titles seem to have occupied the space of only one line; H.Hollander,

That Ψ had only 30 lines to each side of its Callimachean section leads to a further inference about its format. From the contents of the extant descendants of Ψ it is clear that the archetype contained the hymns of Homer and 'Orpheus', as well as those of Proclus, and the Orphic *Argonautica*. H.Hollander demonstrated that the part of Ψ which contained the Homeric Hymns had 36 or 37 lines to each side of the page,[1] and G.Quandt that for the Orphic hymns there were 35 lines to each side.[2] The reduced number of lines for Callimachus is to be explained by the presence of the scholia written in with the text, almost certainly interlinear rather than marginal;[3] the scribe who wrote the text spaced out his lines so that the scholia could be added in. The script of Ψ was minuscule: hyparchetype α, for example, misread ἄημα for ἄκμα at III 55, and καύριος for κύνθιος at IV 10.

Furthermore Ψ itself made mistakes which derive from misreading of minuscule script: in V cf. 34 ἀκεστοριδᾶν for ἀρεστ., 83 ἑστάθη for ἑστάκη (and see Pfeiffer lxxxiv). Ψ's own source was therefore a minuscule MS. Moreover Martin Sicherl demonstrated in *Hermes* 88 (1960) 121–3 that for the Homeric Hymns Ψ was preceded by at least *two* MSS in minuscule script; whether or not the same applies to the Callimachean part of Ψ depends on the date of the original hymn collection which Ψ represents,[4] but the possibility should be borne in mind.

Progr. Osnabrück (1886) 9f. established the same for Ψ in the Homeric Hymn to Hermes.

[1] *Progr. Osnabrück* (1886), 8ff.; cf. Wilamowitz, *DLZ* (1886) 991.

[2] *Orphei Hymni* (Berlin 1941) xxixff.

[3] P.Maas, *Byz.-Neugr. Jahrb.* 5 (1926–7) 210 suggested a mixture of shorter interlinear and longer marginal scholia, but Pfeiffer lxxxv pointed out that the scholia are lacunose precisely where the main body of the text had been damaged in Ψ (namely on p. III verso at VI 6, 7–9, 15), and not apparently elsewhere as would have been expected in the upper and lower margins.

[4] Currently we are able to date the forming of the collection only to within a very broad period, the sixth to thirteenth centuries: see below pp. 80, 82.

Ψ was already damaged when hyparchetype α copied his text, and should thus presumably be dated a good deal before our earliest MS (F c. 1420); but the rapidity with which Ψ deteriorated between the copying of α and ʒ suggests that it was written on paper and therefore dates from after the second half of the eleventh century. The physical condition of the MS cannot have been helped by its apparent transference from Greece to Italy, presumably in the fourteenth or early fifteenth century: the provenance of F shows that hyparchetype α was written in Greece, but the last of the hyparchetypes to be copied, ʒ, which drew its text of Apollonius from a Palatine codex, seems to have been written in Italy.[1] Of the intermediate history of Ψ, between Greece (probably Constantinople), in the thirteenth or fourteenth century, and Italy, in most probably the early fifteenth century, we know nothing.

But Ψ was not the only component in the transmission to have suffered damage. At IV 177[b] Ψ had only 9 initial letters followed by a lacuna, and at 200 only a gap. Smiley (*CQ* 15 (1921) 16) had already suggested that these lacunae indicated damage to a page of an ancestor earlier than Ψ which had 23 lines to each side,[2] but the publication in 1948 of *P. Oxy.* 2225 revealed that the damage was much more widespread. The papyrus contains an additional line (now annotated as 177[a]) between 176 and 177, and offers a text superior to that of Ψ at several points between at least 177[a]–188 and 200–12. Clearly the minuscule manuscript from which Ψ copied its text (or, less plausibly, an earlier

[1] In spite of attempts by earlier scholars (for which see H.Herter, Bursian's *Jahresbericht* 255 (1937) 194), the occasion when Ψ was taken to Italy cannot be identified. Giovanni Aurispa in a letter to Ambrosio Traversari dated 27 August 1424 details some of the 238 MSS which he brought back with him to Venice: *Argonautica Orphei et eiusdem auctoris tria alia opuscula et hymnos. Callimachum, quam plurimas Pindari odas. laudes deorum Homeri, non parvum opus.* (R. Sabbadini, *Giov. Aurispa, Carteggio* (Rome 1931) 11). Several MSS would be candidates here: Ψ, β, γ or δ. Cf. Pfeiffer lxxxi–ii.

[2] Cf. P.Maas, *Byz.-Neugr. Jahrb.* 5 (1926–7) 211.

ancestor) had *24* lines to each page-side. At least one page, containing 177ᵃ–199 on the recto side and 200–23 on the verso side, was badly damaged in at least its upper portion covering the first 13 lines of each side – indeed so badly at the top of the recto side that all traces of 177ᵃ had disappeared completely, as had the last half of 178, while on the verso Ψ could detect only the traces of an illegible verse at 200 and only parts of the last half of 201. The outside edge of this page was so damaged that the ends of lines 179, 181, 188, 192 were misread on the recto by Ψ, and on the verso correspondingly the beginnings of 212 and probably 216 (as well as the end of 205) were difficult to read. The copyist of Ψ 'interpreted' his exemplar as best he could, but thereby introduced readings which we can now identify as false.[1]

The damage in Ψ's exemplar may conceivably have been restricted to the one page, but we have no right to assume this, and in fact other evidence points to the pessimistic conclusion that Ψ was an unreliable witness in the transmission, whether through corrupt and damaged predecessors or through its own scribe's attempts to interpret his original. The predominant scholarly assessment earlier this century was very favourable to Ψ; Wilamowitz in 1925 professed himself more and more inclined to follow the archetype (preface p. 8), and Herter in 1931 (*RE* Suppl. v 443.57ff.) declared that Ψ was a thoroughly good representative of the text of the editor Salustius,[2] with the exception only of mechanical error. Since then, however, the main papyri which have been published have undermined our editorial confidence. Pfeiffer pointed out in 1951 that although the papyri show many errors, both orthographical and more serious, they more often conserve the truth where Ψ is false than they have corruption where Ψ

[1] 202 τλῆμον' for δαίμον' could have arisen from damage not in Ψ's exemplar but in an earlier majuscule text; however 188 φαίνω for Φοίβου is clearly a minuscule error.

[2] For Salustius see below p. 78.

is true (liii–liv, cf. lxxxv–vi),[1] and this assessment is corroborated by the indirect tradition too, which is often better than the text of Ψ (Pfeiffer liv). We should remember that the papyrus evidence is no longer scant; more finds will be welcome, but Callimachus was a widely read author and we now have papyrus texts from every century between the first century B.C. and the sixth to seventh century A.D.[2] Throughout this period texts of the Hymns seem generally to have been superior to Ψ, and we can no longer hold the latter in the high regard which was possible fifty years ago.

The absence of the Fifth Hymn from any of the papyri discovered so far is disappointing (especially from the extensive *P. Oxy.* 2258, which has fragments of all the other hymns) but is clearly due only to chance (see below pp. 79f.), and the lesson learnt from the papyri for the other hymns should be applied equally to the *Bath of Pallas*. To a suspicious editor Ψ's text of the Fifth Hymn could be worrying in a number of places; thus damage to another page of Ψ's exemplar may have caused deep-seated corruptions in 17 (fin.) and 41 (init.) which are again 24 lines apart. 17 ὄμμα τὸ τήναc has been questioned, and the repetition at 41 Κρεῖον, although explicable, may have arisen from illegibility of the sort which at IV 179 prompted καρπόν for καπνόν, leading Ψ

[1] The only papyrus text which is inferior to Ψ in a major way is the second-century A.D. *P. Oxy.* 2226 which in Hymn VI lacks 118–37. The omission is at first sight alarming, but the resultant text is neat enough to be the result not of corruption but of an author's alternative version. The section omitted forms a complete unit in itself, a closing ceremonial address to the celebrants: furthermore the papyrus had at least one *additional* line after 138, and possibly more, so that this version closed, apparently, with a more substantial address to the divinity – appropriately enough after the prayer at 116–17.

[2] It is worth emphasising that our latest papyri date from the fifth to seventh centuries A.D., only *c.* 600 years before Ψ. Although the papyri from this late period have a number of trivial errors not found in Ψ, they are superior to our archetype on quite a few substantial points: for *P. Bodl.* (*Ms. Gr. Class.* f. 109) see IV 66, for *P. Oxy.* 2258A see II 2, 7, 8, 35, 36, VI 128, 132.

to import the name from the preceding line. Elsewhere in v Ψ was certainly seriously corrupt at 18, 36, 83, 93, 136.

Ψ and Doric

Although the dialect tone of the language of the Fifth Hymn is relatively mild (see above pp. 26f.), no scholar will be surprised to discover that the dialect features were particularly subject to corruption in the course of 1,500 years of transmission, and in this respect Ψ was a poor witness to what Callimachus wrote. Quite simply, the archetype text was an inconsistent muddle: much had been 'normalised' into non-Doric Greek, but a dialect form which was corrected away at one point was often let stand a few lines further on (e.g. 38 ποτε, but 57 ποκ', 7 φέρουcα but 21 ἑλοῖcα). This process was clearly the result of ignorance and idle chance: scribes misunderstood or 'corrected' individual items, but no-one attempted a systematic rewriting.

This very inconsistency of Ψ is invaluable: editors generally assume, surely correctly, that Callimachus, who was brought up in the Doric-speaking Cyrene, is most unlikely to have used randomly inconsistent forms of the same word or inflexion within one text, and they have standardised Ψ's non-Doric to the Doric elements. This is particularly simple since mild Doric consists largely in basic inflexional transformations (-αν for Attic -ων, ᾱ for original η, -ω for -ου, etc.) and a few standard stem changes (νιν for μιν, etc.). Furthermore 'organic' consistency helps where a form occurs only once in the poem: thus, for example, an author who employs participles in -οιcα and contract futures is extremely *likely* to have used the Doric infinitive ἕρπεν in v. 3 (see Commentary), and 132 μῶνοc similarly suggests correcting to cῶcθε in v. 4 and βωλευτόν in v. 38. Papyri of other similar texts are also generally helpful, both in illustrating the process of corruption at an earlier stage in its development, and in indicating which occasional items may have been completely 'normalised': thus *P. Oxy.* 2226 shows that at VI 92 and 111 Ψ's μέcφα is a correction of Doric μέcτα, and this form should therefore probably be restored at V 55.[1]

Most of the instances of corruption of the Doric forms in the Fifth Hymn are easily identified: because the dialect is relatively mild the consequent damage to the text has been mostly superficial. The following list itemises every point where a dialect form seems to have been offered in corrupt form by Ψ: all corruptions and their correction are discussed individually at the appropriate points in the commentary. The only example of 'reverse' dialect corruption, a hyper-Dorism having been falsely intruded, seems to be 109 where it is difficult to accept that Callimachus himself wrote ἁβατάν.

2 φρυαccομενῶν for -ᾶν, preserving -αν at 2 τᾶν, 3 ἱερᾶν, 6 ἱππειᾶν
3 ἕρπει for ἕρπεν
4 coῦcθε for cῶcθε
5 οὔποτ' for οὔποκ', preserving 57 ποκα, 59 οὔποκα
'Αθηναία for 'Αθαναία, preserving 'Αθαν- at 33, 43, 55 etc.; 'Αθην- again at 16
7 φέρουcα for φέροιcα, preserving -οιcα at 21, 25, but corrupting to -ουcα again at 93 and 25 (some MSS)
8 γηγενέων for γαγενέων
21 ἥρη (Homeric/Ionic) for Ἥρα
27 κόραι for κῶραι
οἷον for οἵαν
28 cίβδηc for cίβδαc
χροιήν (epic/Ionic) for χροϊάν
29 μοῦνον for μῶνον, preserving μῶνοc at 132
36 'Αργείων . . . παλαιότερον for 'Αργείωc . . . παλαιοτέρωc; -ωc corrupted again at 62, 142

---

[1] Another Doric form which *P. Oxy.* 2226 restores to VI is 97 Ποτειδάωνα (Ποc. Ψ). A good impression of the way in which copyists steadily correct away dialect features may be obtained by comparing the Antinoopolis Papyrus (*c.* 500 A.D.) with the MSS in Theocr. 2 and 15. For some examples of the help which papyri can give to restoration of Doric in Theocritus see K.Latte, 'Zur Textkritik Theokrits', *Nachr. v. d. Akad. d. Wiss. in Göttingen* Phil.-Hist. Kl. (1949) 225–32. As a general rule, papyri have demonstrated that the hesitancy of early editors to restore Doric forms consistently in Callimachus and Theocritus was misplaced.

38 ποτε for ποκα (see above on 5)
βουλευτόν for βωλ- (cf. 27 κόραι for κῶραι)
46 τῶν ποταμῶν for τῶ ποταμῶ; Doric singular corrected also at 87, 128, 140
55 μέσφα for μέστα
58 ἑταιρᾶν for ἑταρᾶν
60 ἀρχαίων for ἀρχαιᾶν: see on 2 φρυασσομενᾶν
62 ἵππους for ἵππως; -ως preserved at 5, 13, 15 etc., but corrupted again at 142
65 μιν for νιν; corrupted again at 96, but preserved at 105, 121
67 ὅθ', ὅτ' for ὅκ', preserved at 7, 18
70 ποτε for ποκα, preserving ποκα at 57, 59
83 ἑστάθη for ἑστάκη
84 γώνατα: a possible hyper-Dorism
ἀμηχ- for ἀμαχ-
85 ἐβόησε for ἐβόασε, but original Doric ᾱ preserved in contract verbs at 11, 65, 83, 130
87 τοῦ for τῶ: similar corruption at 46 of τῶ to τῶν
93 λαβοῦσα for λαβοῖσα: see on 7 φέρουσα
96 μιν for νιν: see on 65
99 παίδων for παιδῶν
100 ἁρπάζειν for ἁρπάζεν
105 ἡνίκα for ἁνίκα
κομίζου for κομίζευ, preserving ευ often elsewhere (see on 97 βαλεῦ)
109 ἀβατάν for ἠβατάν
123 ὄρνιθας for ὄρνιχας
124 ἤλιθα for ἄλιθα
128 βιότου for βιότω; masc. sing. gen. similarly corrupted at 140, but preserved at 10, 65, 102
140 Ἰναχίου for Ἰναχίω; see on 128 βιότου

The early history of the text

Although modern scholarship has as yet provided no secure chronology for the composition of the Hymns, no-one has successfully maintained that all six were written at the same time or at only brief intervals from one another;[1] the

[1] Only Theocritus, of the Hellenistic poets, is credited with a curiously compressed active period as a writer. Discussions of T. are generally based on the implicit assumption that 275–270 was the probable date of

collection of the six hymns together was, in other words, the result of a conscious editorial decision. We have no direct evidence that this first editor was Callimachus himself, but probability favours the assumption. Callimachus certainly re-edited the *Aetia* in his old age, and his edition seems to have contained the *Iambi* placed immediately after the long elegiac poem[1] – this could also have been the occasion for editing the Hymns, whether separately or as part of a Collected Works; secondly *P. Oxy.* 2226 contained a version of the Sixth Hymn different from that offered by our MSS – it is possible that there were two author's versions (see above p. 73 n.1), and the occasion for substantial revision of the Hymns might have been, as with *SH* 254–69 (Heracles and Molorcus) and fr. 110 *Coma Berenices*, the compiling of an authoritative edition; finally, the fact that no variation in the order of the Hymns in ancient or medieval MSS has yet come to light indicates that an authoritative edition appeared very early in the transmission of the text.[2]

The history of the text after this early edition lies in almost complete darkness, in which the only aids are presumption and speculation. That the Hymns were indeed much attended to and edited is clear from their frequent citation in reference works and in the editions of other authors (see the running testimonia to Pfeiffer's text), as well as from the medieval scholia and the generally fuller papyrus scholia to

most of his compositions: editorial neatness often supposes that the apparent uniformity of his poetry was due to the briefness of the period in which T. composed. For a recent discussion of the chronology of Callimachus' Hymns and references to other literature see Fraser, *Ptolemaic Alexandria* II 915–17.

[1] R.Pfeiffer, *Hermes* 63 (1928) 339ff. (=*Ausgewählte Schriften* 130ff.), *Callimachus* II xxxvi–vii, I 125.

[2] The earliest papyrus whose ordering of the Hymns is clear is *P. Med.* 18 (second century A.D.), but if the first authoritative edition had appeared long after Callimachus' death we might expect some variation of order between *P. Med.* 18, *P. Oxy.* 2258A, *P. Ant.* 20 and Ψ (cf. the papyri and MSS of Theocritus). The placing of V after VI in MS E was merely the result of a mechanical error (see above p. 56).

Hymns II, III and VI. But curiously we know with certainty the name of not one ancient editor. Theon, the Augustan grammarian, son of Artemidorus, edited the *Aetia* and possibly the *Hecale* (see Pfeiffer xxvii);[1] a scholar who edited several of Callimachus' poems is an obvious candidate for the Hymns too, the more so since Theon edited all Callimachus' major contemporaries. Again, it is difficult to imagine the indefatigable Didymus ignoring the Hymns, and the latter are much cited in the scholia to Pindar and Aristophanes, on both of whom Didymus did substantial work.

For the mysterious and undated Salustius as a possible editor we have marginally more indication (though nothing that qualifies strictly as evidence). *Et. Gen.* s.v. ἀσκάντης mentions Salustius on the *Hecale* (fr. 240), and various citations of that poem in the ancient lexica were probably drawn from Salustius' edition;[2] the same Salustius is cited by Stephanus of Byzantium s.v. Ἄζιλις (πόλις Λιβύης, οἱ δὲ περὶ Σαλούστιον οὐ πόλιν, ἀλλὰ τόπον φασὶ καὶ ποταμὸν εἶναι) in an entry which fits well with Callimachus II 89 Ἄζιλιν. Salustius also edited Sophocles, and the frequent citation of the Hymns in the ancient scholia to Sophocles is doubtless due to an editor of the tragedian who had also worked closely on Callimachus (though a scholar such as Didymus could equally well have been responsible for these).[3] An unknown author wrote summaries of Callimachus' collected poems, including from the Hymns at least I and II, which were reproduced in the papyrus of the early second century A.D. from Tebtunis, *P. Med.* 18, and anonymous scholia are extant in papyri from the first century A.D. (*P. Cair.* inv. 47993[b] to

[1] Fr. 383.4, which was known to Theon, is now known to have come from the *Aetia* (*SH* 254).

[2] See R.Reitzenstein, *Ind. lect. Rostock.* (1890–1) 13ff., Pfeiffer I 228.

[3] On Salustius see Wilamowitz, *Einleitung in die griech. Tragödie* (1895) 198–200, E.Diehl, *Hypomnema* (Riga 1937) 386f., 388f., 398–406, 410, 445f., Pfeiffer xxviii–ix (Gerth, *RE* IA 2.1960 is unsatisfactory). For other editors of C. (Epaphroditus, Archibius, Astyages) see Pfeiffer xxviii.

III), as well as the fourth century (*P. Amh.* 20 to III), the fourth to fifth centuries (*P. Ant.* 20 to II and III), and the sixth to seventh centuries (*P. Oxy.* 2258A to II, III and VI).[1]

Callimachus was much read throughout the Hellenistic and Roman periods, and every century from the first B.C. to the sixth and seventh A.D. is represented by a surviving papyrus text of the Hymns.[2] None of the papyri so far discovered has given evidence of the Fifth Hymn and this is disappointing, especially in the case of the extensive *P. Oxy.* 2258 from which parts of all the other hymns have appeared. At first sight the absence of the only elegiac hymn may seem far from accidental, especially as the *Bath of Pallas* was cited by the ancient grammarians less than the other hymns (including VI positioned last in the collection: compare the testimonia cited by Pfeiffer to each hymn). However there are no other indications that V was ignored in antiquity, or less easily available. In the first century B.C. the poem was clearly known to Propertius: Prop. 2.18.9–10 looks to V 5–6 (see Commentary), and 4.9.53–8 recalls both the whole Tiresias narrative and especially V 101f. Tibullus II 1 is a mock festival poem which closely matches the structure of Callimachus' hymn and echoes its wording at several specific points (see *Proc. Cam. Phil. Soc.* 19 (1973) 81f.). On *Georg.* 4.425ff. L.P.Wilkinson has suggested that Virgil's dramatic technique was learnt from Callimachus V 70ff. (*The Georgics of Virgil* (Cambridge 1969) 218f.). Ovid too almost certainly knew and drew on V. In *Met.* 3.138–252 the account of the destruction of Actaeon is generally very similar to the Tiresias story, and in particular 173–8, describing Actaeon's entry into the bath scene, are verbally very close to V 73–8;

[1] Unfortunately the various papyri overlap too little to determine to what extent the ancient scholia derived from a uniform standard commentary. The Ψ scholia have much in common with the papyrus scholia, but both are sufficiently idiosyncratic to suggest that there was no single ancient commentary for the Hymns and that these poems were regularly re-edited. Cf. also Pfeiffer lxxviii.

[2] For a list see Pfeiffer li–iii, to which add *P. Ant.* 179.

C.Floratos has plausibly suggested that *Fast.* 4.133–62 looks to v, and the opening, 133–40, is particularly close to v 1–32 in tone and articulation.[1] Heliodorus *Aeth.* 4.19.3 may have been written with Callimachus v 78 in mind (see Commentary). Finally, more than four hundred years later the epic writer Nonnus adapts and echoes phrases and lines from the *Bath of Pallas* at numerous points in his *Dionysiaca* (see Commentary on 9–12, 21, 22, 114, 115f., 117). Texts of the hymn were clearly available to each of these authors, and the absence of the hymn from papyri published to date has to be ascribed to a chance of history. We should remember that our papyri are not necessarily a completely representative selection; thus of the *Iambi* VIII–XI have still to appear in papyrus texts apart from the *Diegeseis* summaries.

From the late fourth century A.D. the Hymns seem to have come to occupy a more prominent place in editions of Callimachus. In the few extensive papyrus editions of which fragments survive, the 'epic' poems, *Hecale* and Hymns, were placed after the *Aetia* and *Iambi*, until *P. Oxy.* 1011, of the late fourth century, in which the lost opening pages doubtless began the collection with the Hymns and *Hecale* (order unknown: see Pfeiffer xxii–iii). The Suda records that in *c.* 500 A.D. one Marianus wrote a long iambic paraphrase of the works of Callimachus, apparently in the order *Hecale*, Hymns, *Aetia*, Epigrams (Testim. 24 in Pfeiffer), and similarly the Byzantine (sixth to twelfth century) iambic List of Contents recorded in Ψ once headed a collection ordered Hymns, *Hecale*, *Aetia*, minor poems (Testim. 23 in Pfeiffer).[2] We

---

[1] *Athena* 60 (1956) 128ff. Other possible allusions to v have been suggested: *Fast.* 2.583f. may look to 55f. (cf. F.Bömer's commentary ad loc.: the two lines have a similar shape and function in the narrative as Callimachus' couplet), and E.J.Bernbeck, *Beobachtungen zur Darstellungsart in Ovids Metamorphosen* (Munich 1967) 90 compares the parenthesis at *Met.* 3.336ff. with v 97–106.

[2] *P. Oxy.* 2258, from the sixth or seventh century, also placed the Hymns before *Hecale* (see Lobel, *Ox. Pap.* XX 69), and although the order of the

cannot judge whether the re-ordering of the Callimachus edition was due to an increase in the popularity of the more immediately intelligible (and, to a Christian readership, perhaps more attractive) Hymns over the other, more obscure, works of Callimachus in the late fourth century, or whether it reflects the dominating influence of a recent standard edition (perhaps that of Salustius, if we accept Wilamowitz' speculative dating[1]).

The *Hecale* and *Aetia* may have survived at least until the twelfth century, for the Metropolitan of Athens Michael Acominatus, a pupil of Eustathius, refers to both poems (Testim. 35 and 36 in Pfeiffer, Pfeiffer on fr. 23.3 and in Addenda I on fr. 1.1 and 7.30, and Michael Acominatus ed. Lambros II 345. 10–11 ~ fr. 260.1 as newly edited by Lloyd-Jones and Rea, *HSCP* 72 (1968) 125–45 (*SH* 288)) just as Arethas had done earlier (Pfeiffer xxxii),[2] but the text(s) from which Michael had come to know these poems was doubtless destroyed in 1204 when the Fourth Crusade wantonly plundered Constantinople, and if he did possess an actual copy of his own it was certainly lost when his library was

---

rest of the MS is unknown, that suggests that here again the 'epic' poems preceded the *Aetia* etc. The iambic Contents can be dated only within broad limits since we have only analogy to guide us; Paul Maas, *Byz.-Neugr. Jahrb.* 5 (1926–7) 210 n. 1 remarks that the versification technique would fit well in the circle of Marianus in the sixth century, and in *Byz. Zeitschr.* 17 (1908) 402 (on an iambic paraphrase of the Labours of Heracles) Maas notes that such relative correctness of versification is characteristic of the classic Byzantine periods – i.e. any time down to the seventh century, but thereafter only of the tenth or eleventh centuries. Pfeiffer lv refers to the iambic summary poems collected by Cougny in vol. III of his *Anthologia Palatina* pp. 327–9 which Pfeiffer considers to be post-tenth-century (cf. especially 231).

[1] *Einleitung in die griech. Tragödie* (1895) 198–200. On Salustius see above p. 78.

[2] There is clear evidence that Arethas had read the Hymns (see Pfeiffer's testimonia to I 8, IV 36, VI 3), but none that Michael had done so. If Michael's teacher Eustathius had read them (see testimonia to IV 160, VI 1) he had done so only very cursorily: his reference to the Fifth Hymn replaces Athena with Artemis (1665.45).

scattered on the capture of Athens by Boniface.[1] The survival of the Hymns is owed to the anonymous excerptor who decided to assemble in one collection ancient hymns by a variety of authors: 'Orpheus', Proclus, 'Homer' and Callimachus, together with the Orphic *Argonautica*. For the Callimachean hymns this collector drew on an edition containing Hymns, *Hecale*, *Aetia* and other poems, as is shown by the prefatory iambic poem which he copied out with the Hymns (Testimonia 23 in Pfeiffer), but of his date very little can be inferred. The prefatory poem can be ascribed to only a very broad period (see above p. 80 n. 2), and a similar interest in compiling collections of poems is characteristic of several Byzantine scholars of very different dates.[2] Ψ may have been

---

[1] Michael Acominatus from Chonae was outstanding in his generation for his education and reading; both in Athens and in Constantinople he had painstakingly collected a personal library, but when Boniface finally captured Athens in 1204 Michael fled, ultimately to Ceos, and his books were left to the plundering Christians. See S.P.Lambros, *Athenaion* 6 (1878) 354ff., and on Athens at the time of Michael, K.M.Sutton, 'Athens in the later twelfth century', *Speculum* 19 (1944) 179–207.

The question whether Michael possessed, or had access to, a text of Callimachus is intricate and will need much more detailed research on Michael and his period to be resolved. A major ground for scepticism is that Michael never mentions a Callimachus MS (which, as he would be aware, would be a great rarity) and never ascribes his quotations to a source (contrast his treatment of Nicander and Pindar). The *Aetia* citations might have come from secondary lexicographical sources, and the *Hecale* might have been known in the form of a Byzantine digest which preserved some of the Callimachean vocabulary. For these and other reasons the Byzantinist Margaret Howatson has expressed her scepticism to me that Michael had ever read a proper text of C., though she considers it possible that the *Hecale* may have survived, taken out of its Callimachean corpus, in some literary context of 'wise women'.

[2] The tenth-century Emperor Constantine VII Porphyrogenitus enthusiastically promoted the compilation of anthologies from ancient writers, and it is tempting to date the collection of hymns to that period, contemporary with, for example, Constantine Cephalas' *Palatine Anthology* of epigrams and the lexicon *Suda*; however 350 years later Maximus Planudes was an energetic excerptor from classical authors (see Wendel, *RE* xx 2230–41). P.Maas, *Byz.-Neugr. Jahrb.* 5 (1926–7) 210f. suggested that the hymn collection was compiled at the time of Planudes (when the collection of epic writers in Laurentianus 32.16 was copied); Pfeiffer

copied by, or for, the original compiler himself, but the MS may equally well have been a chance representative of an earlier tradition.

VIII NATURE AND PURPOSE OF THE COMMENTARY

Callimachus has attracted the attention of some of the best classical scholars in the last three hundred years, and each generation has seen a distinguished contribution to the study of the leading Alexandrian poet as well as of his contemporaries. But despite recent work by scholars of the calibre of Wilamowitz or Pfeiffer and commentaries by Spanheim, Ernesti, Schneider and Cahen, to name only the most prominent, much of the fundamental work on the Hellenistic poets remains to be done. This is partly because large quantities of new material have come to light during the last eighty years, primarily through papyri, which continue to provide us with new texts, and partly because the main stream of scholarship, regarding the Hellenistic age as inferior to the Classical period, has not subjected its writers to the same systematic analysis as the 'best authors'; lexica offer Hellenistic material only sporadically and rather randomly (LSJ is notoriously capricious and cursory here), and there is simply not the same accumulated body of material in grammars, commentaries and other technical works to illustrate and explain the details of grammar, syntax, usage, diction and style such as one can usually rely on when dealing with a text from an earlier period.

This Commentary is therefore concerned with groundwork. I have tried to provide the detailed information

lxxxiv points out that we have no evidence of the survival as late as Planudes of the collected works of Callimachus from which the Hymns were copied. P. Chantraine, *Rev. de Phil.* 28 (1954) 283 notes that the collection is unlikely to have been made *between* the sixth and ninth centuries, when the classical poets were completely neglected.

needed, whether on language and diction, 'Realien', or other matters, for an informed and sensitive reading of the poem; in addition to dealing with 'problems' and obvious matters of central interest, I have tried to reconstruct, inevitably through analytical means, what the ancient reader will have taken for granted as part of his cultural or intellectual background when approaching the text of the Fifth Hymn. I have tried never to lose sight of the fact that the ultimate aim of the commentator is to enable the user to *read* the text and to place it in its full literary context, but in a field where so little of the primary data has been systematically collected and scrutinised the only fruitful course was to present at each point the full evidence on which each conclusion is based; I have referred to other secondary works where possible, for the sake of brevity, but where the collected material is not easily available in a standard reference work I have uncompromisingly given full direct citation. A commentary of this kind has to work in part by the process of accumulation; often the individual features noted will seem trivial in themselves, but cumulatively I hope that they will provide a firm perspective for the whole poem.

In the interests of clear presentation the Commentary divides the poem into sections (e.g. 1–32) and, where appropriate, sub-sections (e.g. 1–4). Each section or sub-section is preceded by remarks of a general nature applicable to the whole of what follows and attempting to pick out the major features and points of issue; the detailed comments which then follow concerning individual words and phrases assume a reading of the remarks made at the beginning of the (sub)-section.

One of the main concerns of the Commentary is, inevitably, reconstruction of the language in which the poem was written; for a sensitive and informed reading of a Hellenistic poem above all it is crucially important that detailed points, sometimes of grammar and syntax, often of usage and diction, be well noted by the reader. I have commented on the language, wherever particular features seemed significant, at various levels.

(1) *Grammar and syntax*. In such an elaborately constructed poetic diction as most of the Hellenistic poets use, even the smallest detail of form or inflection can be an important indicator of tone, and I have tried to point out the standard (often Homeric) features of Hellenistic diction as well as the significant exceptional characteristics. An important feature of the whole poem is, of course, the dialect element within and alongside the traditional features of standard poetic diction. Often the dialect forms are of consequence not just for typographical accuracy of the text, but for the tone of the poem as a whole, and I have analysed the grammar and syntax of the Doric element with as full documentation as possible.

(2) *Vocabulary and usage*. This is one of the most important constituents of diction and often one of the least well studied. A large part of this commentary's energy is concentrated on reconstructing at each significant point the status and tone of individual words and phrases. The reader of any text, but particularly of a Hellenistic poem, must have available to him as far as possible the full linguistic and semantic significance of any word or phrase in its context, and must have some idea whether it is 'prose or poetry', 'normal usage or heightened usage', 'a standard poeticism or an archaism' etc. I have therefore tried to give wherever necessary a full documentation and analysis relevant to reconstructing the semantic context. The method of analysis is inevitably different from that employed by the standard lexica and works of reference. These classify vocabulary mostly according to variety of 'meaning' in a rather abstract formalistic way, with little regard for historical development and organic context; my own analysis is rather in terms of the *distribution* and *frequency* of instances. For the most part this semantic approach is self-explanatory; the key factors are the types of authors and contexts in which a word (and its cognates) is distributed,

and, within the constraints of its distribution, the apparent rarity or normality of its occurrence. The most essential prerequisite of this mode of analysis is that the evidence surveyed should be as *complete* as possible: one will draw different conclusions, e.g., about a word which occurs only once each in Sophocles, Euripides, and Menander, and one which, in addition to this distribution and frequency, occurs twice each in Theophrastus and Hippocrates. I have therefore tried to base the analysis of every word discussed in this way on a complete survey of all author indices, and where I give a list of instances without the qualifications 'e.g.' or 'etc.' it should be assumed that I have been unable to find any other instances from the historical period in question. As a result of surveying even apparently obvious usages in this way I have not infrequently come to conclusions very different from those of the standard lexica and reference works; many apparent poèticisms have turned out to be normal usage and many apparent instances of normal usage to be heightened or poetic usages, especially in relation to the *koine*. I have attempted to use as frequently as possible authors such as Aristotle, Theophrastus, Hippocrates, Polybius, Josephus, the Septuagint and New Testament and occasionally Philo, Plutarch etc. as sources from which to ascertain what was normal usage in the *koine*. I need hardly add that such an approach seemed particularly necessary with an author such as Callimachus whose attitude to the mainstream of poetic writing and received critical opinion was so complex and yet whose own diction has been as yet rather inadequately analysed.[1]

(3) *Style*. I have tried wherever possible to draw together the material on points of grammar, syntax, vocabulary and usage and indicate what I believe to be their cumulative effect. Additionally, matters of phraseology and modes of

[1] For a full discussion of the theoretical and practical issues involved in establishing normal and poetic usage see M.S.Silk, *Interaction in Poetic Imagery* (Cambridge 1974) 34–56 and Appendix III (211–23).

expression are commented on, with a view both to setting the poem in its overall literary context (especially in relation to Homer), and to pointing up what appear to be typical elements of Callimachean or Hellenistic style.

In so far as space permitted I have adopted the practice of quotation rather than mere reference for any passage whose appreciation seemed particularly important to the understanding of the Hymn, and where a usage needed elucidating through citation of a parallel I have tried to pick an example which had more than the single shared point in common with the Callimachean Hymn, and have looked for a parallel with similar phraseology or a similar theme.

The translation has no literary pretensions; it is intended as a working version to convey, even if rather baldly, some of the more important qualities of style, diction, tone and manner of the original (though I have found it impossible to reproduce the 'texture' of traditional Homeric/poetic Greek). I hope also that the translation may help to convey more directly some of the points made by the laborious means of scholarship in the Commentary. I have used verse couplets (hexameter alternating with pentameter) because, even though it has no poetic quality, a verse translation can at least suggest some of the effects of rhythm and articulation of the original which would be lost completely in a prose version.

TEXT AND TRANSLATION

DIVERGENT READINGS

My text is the same as that of Pfeiffer except at the following places (my reasons for adopting different readings are explained in the Commentary):

	A.W.B.	*Pfeiffer*
3	ἐϲάκουϲα· καί . . .	ἐϲάκουϲα, καί . . .
4	ϲῶϲθε . . . ϲῶϲθε . . .	ϲοῦϲθε . . . ϲοῦϲθε . . .
25	ἐνετρίψατο	ἐτρίψατο
	λαβοῖϲα	βαλοῖϲα
55	μέϲτα	μέϲφα
58	περί	πέρι
60	ἀρχαιᾶν	ἀρχαίων
75	ἁμᾶι	ἁμᾶ
99	παιδῶν	παίδων
100	ἁρπάζεν	ἁρπάζειν
109	ἡβατάν	ἁβατάν
113	ὁππόκα κ᾽ οὐκ	ὁππόταν οὐκ
124	ἄλιθα	ἤλιθα
136	ἁ θυγάτηρ	αι θυγάτηρ

SIGLORUM CONSPECTUS

At Athous Vatopedi 671
  At^2 = manus recentior in At
C Ven. Marc. 480
E Par. Gr. 2763
e Ambros. 734
F Ambros. 120
Π Par. Gr. suppl. 1095
Q Mut.-Est. 164
S Matr. Gr. 4562
  S^{pc} = S post correctionem
  (Q^2, S^2 vide p. 57)
anon. Bern. variae lectiones codicis alicuius in marg. editionis Vascosanianae nunc in bibl. Bernensi asservatae
La Ianus Lascaris, ed. pr.
Pol Angelus Politianus, hymni quinti ed. pr.

β hyparchetypus, = Ee
γ apographon hyparchetypi ε, = Π Pol La
δ apographon hyparchetypi ε = SQ
ʒ hyparchetypus, = AC
η apographon ex F deductum, = GHΛI (vide pp. 64f.)
Ψ archetypus

ΕΙϹ ΛΟΥΤΡΑ ΤΗϹ ΠΑΛΛΑΔΟϹ

Ὅϲϲαι λωτροχόοι τᾶϲ Παλλάδοϲ ἔξιτε πᾶϲαι,
ἔξιτε· τᾶν ἵππων ἄρτι φρυαϲϲομενᾶν
τᾶν ἱερᾶν ἐϲάκουϲα· καὶ ἁ θεὸϲ εὔτυκοϲ ἕρπεν·
ϲῶϲθέ νυν, ὦ ξανθαὶ ϲῶϲθε Πελαϲγιάδεϲ.
οὔποκ' Ἀθαναία μεγάλωϲ ἀπενίψατο πάχειϲ,
πρὶν κόνιν ἱππειᾶν ἐξελάϲαι λαγόνων·
οὐδ' ὅκα δὴ λύθρωι πεπαλαγμένα πάντα φέροιϲα
τεύχεα τῶν ἀδίκων ἦνθ' ἀπὸ γαγενέων,
ἀλλὰ πολὺ πράτιϲτον ὑφ' ἅρματοϲ αὐχέναϲ ἵππων
λυϲαμένα παγαῖϲ ἔκλυϲεν Ὠκεανῶ
ἱδρῶ καὶ ῥαθάμιγγαϲ, ἐφοίβαϲεν δὲ παγέντα
πάντα χαλινοφάγων ἀφρὸν ἀπὸ ϲτομάτων.
ὦ ἴτ' Ἀχαιιάδεϲ, καὶ μὴ μύρα μηδ' ἀλαβάϲτρωϲ
(ϲυρίγγων ἀίω φθόγγον ὑπαξόνιον),
μὴ μύρα λωτροχόοι τᾶι Παλλάδι μηδ' ἀλαβάϲτρωϲ
(οὐ γὰρ Ἀθαναία χρίματα μεικτὰ φιλεῖ)
οἴϲετε μηδὲ κάτοπτρον· ἀεὶ καλὸν ὄμμα τὸ τήναϲ.
οὐδ' ὅκα τὰν Ἴδαι Φρὺξ ἐδίκαζεν ἔριν,
οὔτ' ἐϲ ὀρείχαλκον μεγάλα θεὸϲ οὔτε Σιμοῦντοϲ
ἔβλεψεν δίναν ἐϲ διαφαινομέναν·
οὐδ' Ἥρα· Κύπριϲ δὲ διαυγέα χαλκὸν ἑλοῖϲα
πολλάκι τὰν αὐτὰν δὶϲ μετέθηκε κόμαν.
ἁ δὲ δὶϲ ἑξήκοντα διαθρέξαϲα διαύλωϲ,
οἷα παρ' Εὐρώται τοὶ Λακεδαιμόνιοι

---

2 φρυαϲϲομενᾶν Meineke: -μέναν Ψ (-μένων F) 3 εὔτυκοϲ E marg., εγȝ: εὔτυκτοϲ FEδ ἕρπεν Schneider: ἕρπει Ψ 4 ϲῶϲθε . . . ϲῶϲθε scripsi: ϲοῦϲθε . . . ϲοῦϲθε Ψ 5 οὔποκ' Pol: οὔποτ' Ψ Ἀθαναία ηPolLa: Ἀθηναία Ψ 7 φέροιϲα La: φέρουϲα Ψ 8 γαγενέων Meineke: γηγ- Ψ 14 ὑπαξόνιον Ee$^{\gamma\rho}$SQΠ$^{\gamma\rho}$Pol: ὑπαξονίων FeΠ(-ίω)La, ss. Q,ȝ 16 Ἀθαναία v. supra ad v. 5 μεικτὰ Wilamowitz: μικτὰ Ψ 17 ὄμμα τὸ τήναϲ om. ȝ, ἔνδυμα δ (ὄμμα S marg., ὤμμα ss. Q) 18 Ἴδαι Stanley et Bentley: ἴδαν Ψ 19 οὔτ' . . . οὔτε Meineke: οὐδ' . . . οὐδὲ Ψ Σιμοῦντοϲ Ψ: fortasse Σιμῶντοϲ 20 ἔβλεψεν EPolLa: ἔβλεψαν Ψ 21 Ἥρα Ernesti: ἥρη Ψ 24 παρ' EPolLa: περ Ψ

ON THE BATH OF PALLAS

You bathpourers of Pallas, come out everyone,
  come out. The mares just now began to neigh,
I heard the sacred mares; the goddess too is ready to come.
  Hasten, fair women of Argos, hasten now.
Never did Athena wash clean her mighty arms
  before banishing the dust from her horses' flanks,
not even when she brought her armour all spattered with gore
  coming from the lawless earthborn ones;
but far the first the horses' necks from under the harness
  she set free, and doused in Ocean's streams
their sweat and grime away, and cleansed all the congealed
  foam from their mouths that champed the bit.
Oh come, women of Achaea, and neither perfumes nor jars
  (I hear the axles creaking on the naves)
neither perfumes for Pallas, bathpourers, nor jars
  (oils with scent are not what Athena likes)
are you to bring, nor a mirror – *her* aspect is always fair.
  Even on Ida when a Phrygian judged the contest
the mighty goddess looked neither into oreichalc
  nor in the transparent eddy of the Simoeis;
nor did Hera, but Cypris took the translucent bronze
  and frequently twice rearranged the same lock of hair.
Athena ran twice sixty double course lengths,
  like the Lacedaemonians by the Eurotas,

ἀϲτέρεϲ, ἐμπεράμωϲ ἐνετρίψατο λιτὰ λαβοῖϲα
χρίματα, τᾶϲ ἰδίαϲ ἔκγονα φυταλιᾶϲ,
ὦ κῶραι, τὸ δ' ἔρευθοϲ ἀνέδραμε, πρώϊον οἵαν
ἢ ῥόδον ἢ ϲίβδαϲ κόκκοϲ ἔχει χροϊάν.
τῶι καὶ νῦν ἄρϲεν τι κομίϲϲατε μῶνον ἔλαιον,
ὧι Κάϲτωρ, ὧι καὶ χρίεται Ἡρακλέηϲ·
οἴϲετε καὶ κτένα οἱ παγχρύϲεον, ὡϲ ἀπὸ χαίταν
πέξηται, λιπαρὸν ϲμαϲαμένα πλόκαμον.

ἔξιθ', Ἀθαναία· πάρα τοι καταθύμιοϲ ἴλα,
παρθενικαὶ μεγάλων παῖδεϲ Ἀρεϲτοριδᾶν·
ὡθάνα, φέρεται δὲ καὶ ἁ Διομήδεοϲ ἀϲπίϲ,
ὡϲ ἔθοϲ Ἀργείωϲ τοῦτο παλαιοτέρωϲ
Εὐμήδηϲ ἐδίδαξε, τεῒν κεχαριϲμένοϲ ἱρεύϲ·
ὅϲ ποκα βωλευτὸν γνοὺϲ ἐπί οἱ θάνατον
δᾶμον ἑτοιμάζοντα φυγᾶι τεὸν ἱρὸν ἄγαλμα
ὤιχετ' ἔχων, Κρεῖον δ' εἰϲ ὄροϲ ὠικίϲατο,
Κρεῖον ὄροϲ· ϲὲ δέ, δαῖμον, ἀπορρώγεϲϲιν ἔθηκεν
ἐν πέτραιϲ, αἷϲ νῦν οὔνομα Παλλατίδεϲ.
ἔξιθ', Ἀθαναία περϲέπτολι, χρυϲεοπήληξ,
ἵππων καὶ ϲακέων ἁδομένα πατάγωι.
ϲάμερον, ὑδροφόροι, μὴ βάπτετε – ϲάμερον, Ἄργοϲ,
πίνετ' ἀπὸ κρανᾶν μηδ' ἀπὸ τῶ ποταμῶ·
ϲάμερον αἱ δῶλαι τὰϲ κάλπιδαϲ ἢ 'ϲ Φυϲάδειαν

---

25 ἐνετρίψατο Meineke: ἐτρίψατο Ψ   λαβοῖϲα ΠPolS^{pc}: λαβῶϲα η, λαβοῦϲα ȝ, βαλοῖϲα FβΠ^{γρ}Laδ   27 κῶραι H.Stephanus: κόραι Ψ, κοῦραι La   οἵαν H.Stephanus: οἷον Ψ, οἵην La   28 ϲίβδαϲ Ernesti: ϲίβδηϲ Ψ   χροϊάν H.Stephanus: χροΐην Ψ   29 τι Bergk: τε Ψ   κομίϲϲατε Ψ: κομίξατε Schneider dubitanter   μῶνον Ernesti: μοῦνον Ψ   34 Ἀρεϲτοριδᾶν Valckenaer: ἀκεϲτοριδᾶν Ψ   36 Ἀργείωϲ anon. Bern., anon. in marg. Aldinae ap. Ernesti: ἀργείων Ψ   παλαιοτέρωϲ anon. Bern.: -ον Ψ   lacunam post v. 36 indicavit Wilamowitz (lectione codicum recepta)   38 ποκα Meineke: ποτε Ψ   βωλευτὸν Degner: βουλευτὸν Ψ   46 τῶ ποταμῶ anon. Bern.: τῶν ποταμῶν Ψ   47 αἱ δῶλαι om. δ (suppl. Q^{2}), ὦ δῶλαι PolS^{2}

the famous stars, and with skill she took and rubbed in
plain oil, the product of her own growing.
Girls, the fresh flush sprang up, with what, early in the year,
the rose, or the pomegranate seed, has for a bloom.
So now too bring something manly, just olive oil,
the anointing oil of Castor, of Heracles;
bring her also a comb all of gold, that she may untangle
her hair, after cleansing her shining locks.

Come out, Athena; here is a company to satisfy you,
daughters of the mighty Arestorids.
Also being carried, Athena, is Diomedes' shield,
this practice that the older Argives
learnt from Eumedes, your own favoured priest;
who once perceived that a death-plot against himself
was being prepared by the people, and fled with your sacred image
away, and settled on the Creian mount,
the Creian mount, where he put you, goddess, upon the sheer
rocks which are now called Pallatids.
Come out, Athena sacker of cities, golden-helmed,
who delight in the crash of horses and of shields.
Today, water-carriers, do not draw – today, Argos,
drink from the fountains, not from the river;
today you slaves should take your pitchers to Physadeia

ἢ ἐς Ἀμυμώναν οἴcετε τὰν Δαναῶ.
καὶ γὰρ δὴ χρυcῶι τε καὶ ἄνθεcιν ὕδατα μείξας
ἡξεῖ φορβαίων Ἴναχος ἐξ ὀρέων
τἀθάναι τὸ λοετρὸν ἄγων καλόν. ἀλλά, Πελαcγέ,
φράζεο μὴ οὐκ ἐθέλων τὰν βαcίλειαν ἴδηις.
ὅς κεν ἴδηι γυμνὰν τὰν Παλλάδα τὰν πολιοῦχον,
τὦργος ἐcοψεῖται τοῦτο πανυcτάτιον.
πότνι' Ἀθαναία, cὺ μὲν ἔξιθι· μέcτα δ' ἐγώ τι
ταῖcδ' ἐρέω· μῦθος δ' οὐκ ἐμός, ἀλλ' ἑτέρων.

παῖδες, Ἀθαναία νύμφαν μίαν ἔν ποκα Θήβαις
πουλύ τι καὶ περὶ δὴ φίλατο τᾶν ἑταρᾶν,
ματέρα Τειρεcίαο, καὶ οὔποκα χωρὶc ἔγεντο·
ἀλλὰ καὶ ἀρχαιᾶν εὖτ' ἐπὶ Θεcπιέων
– ⏖ – ⏖ – ⏑ ἢ εἰc Ἁλίαρτον ἐλαύνοι
ἵππωc, Βοιωτῶν ἔργα διερχομένα,
ἢ 'πὶ Κορωνείας, ἵνα οἱ τεθυωμένον ἄλcοc
καὶ βωμοὶ ποταμῶι κεῖντ' ἐπὶ Κουραλίωι,
πολλάκιc ἁ δαίμων νιν ἑῶ ἐπεβάcατο δίφρω,
οὐδ' ὄαροι νυμφᾶν οὐδὲ χοροcταcίαι
ἁδεῖαι τελέθεcκον, ὅκ' οὐχ ἁγεῖτο Χαρικλώ·
ἀλλ' ἔτι καὶ τήναν δάκρυα πόλλ' ἔμενε,
καίπερ Ἀθαναίαι καταθύμιον ἔccαν ἑταίραν.
δή ποκα γὰρ πέπλων λυcαμένα περόναc
ἵππω ἐπὶ κράναι Ἑλικωνίδι καλὰ ῥεοίcαι
λῶντο· μεcαμβρινὰ δ' εἶχ' ὄροc ἁcυχία.
ἀμφότεραι λώοντο, μεcαμβριναὶ δ' ἔcαν ὧραι,
πολλὰ δ' ἁcυχία τῆνο κατεῖχεν ὄροc.

48 ἐc om. δ (suppl. S^2Q^2) Ἀμυμώναν Meineke: ἀμυμώνην Ψ 49 ὕδατα At^2PolLa: ὕδατι Ψ μείξαc Wilamowitz: μίξαc Ψ 52 μὴ οὐκ E: μ' οὐκ Ψ 53 πολιοῦχον Ψ: fortasse πολιᾶχον Meineke 55 cὺ Ψ: τὺ Meineke μέcτα prop. Pfeiffer: μέcφα Ψ 58 ἑταρᾶν eΠPolȝ: ἑταιρᾶν FE, ἑτερᾶν Laδ 60 ἀρχαιᾶν Meineke: ἀρχαίων Ψ 61–2 om. ȝ spatio duorum vv. post 63 relicto 61 lacunam indicavit Wilamowitz: ἢ 'πὶ Κορωνείαc Ψ (=63 init.) 62 ἵππωc Ernesti: ἵππουc Ψ 64 Κουραλίωι Ψ: Κωραλίωι Schneider 65 νιν Meineke: μιν Ψ 67 ὅκ' Wilamowitz: ὅθ' Ψ, ὅτ' βC 70 ποκα Meineke: ποτε Ψ λυcαμένα F: λυccαμένα Ψ

or else to Amymone the Danaid.
Yes for in fact mingling its waters with gold and flowers
Inachus will come from the nourishing mountains
bringing Athena her bath beautiful. Pelasgian men,
beware lest unwitting you see the queen.
Whoever should see Pallas, the city's guardian, naked
shall look on this city of Argos the very last time.
Lady Athena, you come out, and meanwhile I shall speak
to these women; the tale is others', not mine.

Girls, Athena once loved one nymph in Thebes
out of her companions quite exceedingly well,
the mother of Tiresias; never were they apart.
For even when to Thespiae of old
. . . . or to Haliartus she drove
her horses, passing through the Boeotian fields,
or toward Coroneia, where her bescented grove
and altars lay by the river Couralius,
often the goddess set her upon her chariot,
nor did the nymphs' dalliances or dance
joyously take place but with leader Chariclo;
yet even for her still many tears remained
although she was a companion after Athena's own heart.
Once on a time they undid the pins from their robes
by the fair-flowing fountain of the horse on Helicon
and were bathing; midday quiet took the hill.
Both of them were bathing, and the hour was midday,
and deep was the quiet that held that hill.

Τειρεςίας δ' ἔτι μῶνος ἁμᾶι κυςὶν ἄρτι γένεια
 περκάζων ἱερὸν χῶρον ἀνεςτρέφετο·
διψάςας δ' ἄφατόν τι ποτὶ ῥόον ἤλυθε κράνας,
 ςχέτλιος· οὐκ ἐθέλων δ' εἶδε τὰ μὴ θεμιτά.
τὸν δὲ χολωςαμένα περ ὅμως προςέφαςεν Ἀθάνα·
 'τίς ςε, τὸν ὀφθαλμὼς οὐκέτ' ἀποιςόμενον,
ὦ Εὐηρείδα, χαλεπὰν ὁδὸν ἄγαγε δαίμων;'
 ἁ μὲν ἔφα, παιδὸς δ' ὄμματα νὺξ ἔλαβεν.
ἑςτάκη δ' ἄφθογγος, ἐκόλλαςαν γὰρ ἀνῖαι
 γώνατα καὶ φωνὰν ἔςχεν ἀμαχανία.
ἁ νύμφα δ' ἐβόαςε· 'τί μοι τὸν κῶρον ἔρεξας
 πότνια; τοιαῦται, δαίμονες, ἐςτὲ φίλαι;
ὄμματά μοι τῶ παιδὸς ἀφείλεο. τέκνον ἄλαςτε,
 εἶδες Ἀθαναίας ςτήθεα καὶ λαγόνας,
ἀλλ' οὐκ ἀέλιον πάλιν ὄψεαι. ὢ ἐμὲ δειλάν,
 ὢ ὄρος, ὢ Ἑλικὼν οὐκέτι μοι παριτέ,
ἦ μεγάλ' ἀντ' ὀλίγων ἐπράξαο· δόρκας ὀλέςςας
 καὶ πρόκας οὐ πολλὰς φάεα παιδὸς ἔχεις.'
ἁ μὲν ⟨ἅμ'⟩ ἀμφοτέραιςι φίλον περὶ παῖδα λαβοῖςα
 μάτηρ μὲν γοερᾶν οἶτον ἀηδονίδων
ἆγε βαρὺ κλαίοιςα, θεὰ δ' ἐλέηςεν ἑταίραν.
 καί νιν Ἀθαναία πρὸς τόδ' ἔλεξεν ἔπος·
'δῖα γύναι, μετὰ πάντα βαλεῦ πάλιν ὅςςα δι' ὀργάν

75 sqq. Eust. 1665.45 Καλλίμαχος λέγει τὸν Τειρεςίαν ἰδόντα γυμνὴν λουομένην τὴν Ἄρτεμιν περί που τὴν Βοιωτίαν πηρωθῆναι.
83–4 Schol. BT *Il.* 22.452–3 νέρθε δὲ γοῦνα πήγνυται] Καλλίμαχος· 'ἐκόλληςαν γὰρ (γάρ μοι B) ἀνῖαι γούνατα (γόνατα T)'. 87 Cf. *Suda* et Zonar. p. 116 Tittmann (et Zonar. par. ap. Cramer, *AP* IV 106.30) s.v. ἄλαςτε· ἀνεπίληςτε. 'τέκνον ἐμὸν ἄλαςτον'.

75 μῶνος Ernesti: μοῦνος Ψ ἁμᾶι Ψ: ἁμᾶ Brunck 78 θεμιτὰ FE: θεμιτ e, θέμιδες γS^2, om. δʒ 81 χαλεπὰν Ernesti: χαλεπὴν Ψ
82 ἔλαβεν anon. in marg. Aldinae ap. Ernesti: ἔβαλεν Ψ 83 ἑςτάκη Buttmann: ἑςτάθη Ψ (ἐςτάθη FS) 84 ἀμαχανία Blomfield: ἀμηχανία Ψ
85 ἐβόαςε Ernesti: ἐβόηςε Ψ 87 τῶ Ernesti: τοῦ Ψ ἀφείλεο E marg., PolLa: ἀφείλετο Ψ 93 ἅμ' suppl. Schneider: ἁ μὲν ἀμφ. Ψ, ἆγε μέν . . . ⟨ἁ⟩ μάτηρ Wilamowitz λαβοῖςα PolLa: λαβοῦςα Ψ
94 γοερᾶν anon. in marg. Aldinae ap. Ernesti: γοερῶν Ψ 95 κλαίοιςα Ernesti: κλαίουςα Ψ 96 νιν Meineke: μιν Ψ

Tiresias quite alone together with his dogs, his beard
just darkening, had come to the sacred spot.
Thirsting quite unspeakably he came to the fountain's flow,
poor fool; he unwittingly saw what god's law forbids.
Although angered Athena addressed him nonetheless:
'You shall never more take back your eyes.
What fate, Eueres' child, brought you this hard way?'
She spoke, and night removed the boy's eyes.
He stood there, unable to speak, for anguish stuck fast
his limbs, and helplessness took his voice.
But Chariclo cried out: 'What have you done to my boy,
my lady? Is this the way you gods are friends?
It's my son's eyes you have taken. Oh you wretched child,
it was Athena's breast and loins that you saw,
but you shall not see the sun hereafter. O miserable me,
O mountain, O Helicon never more to be trod,
how great the payment you exacted for a little: you lost some deer
and a few roe, and it's my son's eyes you have.'
The mother threw both arms around her beloved son
and sustained the mournful nightingales' lament
wailing heavily; the goddess took pity on her companion.
And Athena declared to her the following words:
'Noble lady, reconsider all that you said in anger;

εἶπας· ἐγὼ δ᾽ οὔ τοι τέκνον ἔθηκ᾽ ἀλαόν.
οὐ γὰρ ᾽Αθαναίαι γλυκερὸν πέλει ὄμματα παιδῶν
ἁρπάζεν· Κρόνιοι δ᾽ ὧδε λέγοντι νόμοι·
ὅς κε τιν᾽ ἀθανάτων, ὅκα μὴ θεὸς αὐτὸς ἕληται,
ἀθρήσηι, μισθῶ τοῦτον ἰδεῖν μεγάλω.
δῖα γύναι, τὸ μὲν οὐ παλινάγρετον αὖθι γένοιτο
ἔργον, ἐπεὶ Μοιρᾶν ὧδ᾽ ἐπένησε λίνα,
ἁνίκα τὸ πρᾶτόν νιν ἐγείναο· νῦν δὲ κομίζευ,
ὦ Εὐηρείδα, τέλθος ὀφειλόμενον.
πόσσα μὲν ἁ Καδμηὶς ἐς ὕστερον ἔμπυρα καυσεῖ,
πόσσα δ᾽ ᾽Αρισταῖος, τὸν μόνον εὐχόμενοι
παῖδα, τὸν ἡβατὰν ᾽Ακταίονα, τυφλὸν ἰδέσθαι.
καὶ τῆνος μεγάλας σύνδρομος ᾽Αρτέμιδος
ἔσσεται· ἀλλ᾽ οὐκ αὐτὸν ὅ τε δρόμος αἵ τ᾽ ἐν ὄρεσσι
ῥυσεῦνται ξυναὶ τᾶμος ἑκαβολίαι,
ὁππόκα κ᾽ οὐκ ἐθέλων περ ἴδηι χαρίεντα λοετρά
δαίμονος· ἀλλ᾽ αὐταὶ τὸν πρὶν ἄνακτα κύνες
τουτάκι δειπνησεῦντι· τὰ δ᾽ υἱέος ὀστέα μάτηρ
λεξεῖται δρυμὼς πάντας ἐπερχομένα·
ὀλβίσταν δ᾽ ἐρέει σε καὶ εὐαίωνα γενέσθαι
ἐξ ὀρέων ἀλαὸν παῖδ᾽ ὑποδεξαμέναν.
ὦ ἑτάρα, τῶι μή τι μινύρεο· τῶιδε γὰρ ἄλλα
τεῦ χάριν ἐξ ἐμέθεν πολλὰ μενεῦντι γέρα,
μάντιν ἐπεὶ θησῶ νιν ἀοίδιμον ἐσσομένοισιν,
ἦ μέγα τῶν ἄλλων δή τι περισσότερον.
γνωσεῖται δ᾽ ὄρνιχας, ὃς αἴσιος οἵ τε πέτονται
ἄλιθα καὶ ποίων οὐκ ἀγαθαὶ πτέρυγες.

---

99 παιδῶν scripsi: παίδων Ψ 100 ἁρπάζεν scripsi: ἁρπάζειν Ψ 104 ἐπένησε Bentley: ἐπένευσε ψ 105 ἁνίκα La: ἡνίκα ψ πρᾶτον Brunck: πρῶτον Ψ κομίζευ La: κομίζου Ψ 107 πόσσα FLa: πάσσα eS, πᾶσσα Q, πᾶσα E, ὅσσα ΠPol, ss. S^2, om. ȝ καυσεῖ Ernesti: καύσει Ψ 108 πόσσα FΠLa: πολλὰ β, ὅσσα PolS^2, πάσσα Q^2, om. δȝ 109 ἡβατὰν scripsi: ἁβατὰν Ψ ἀκταίονα ηLa: ἀκταίωνα Ψ 112 ἑκαβολίαι La: ἑκη- Ψ 113 ὁππόκα κ᾽ οὐκ scripsi: ὁππόταν οὐκ Ψ, ὁππόκα κοὐκ Wilamowitz 117 δ᾽ E: om. Ψ 123 ὄρνιχας Ernesti: ὄρνιθας Ψ 124 ἄλιθα scripsi: ἤλιθα Ψ

it was not I who made your son blind.
It is not Athena's pleasure to snatch children's eyes.
This is how Cronos' laws ordain:
whosoever discerns an immortal, when the god himself does not choose,
this man sees the god at a great price.
Noble lady, this act is hereafter irrevocable,
for so spun the threads of the Fates
right at the time when you bore him; so now take,
Eueres' child, the payment due to you.
How many offerings Cadmus' daughter will later burn,
how many Aristaeus, making prayer
to see their only son, the young Actaeon, blind.
He too shall be co-hunter of the mighty
Artemis; yet neither their hunting nor archery
shared in the mountains shall then avail,
that time when unwitting he sees the beauteous bath
of the divinity. No then his very own hounds
shall dine on their former master, while a mother shall gather her son's
bones, going round all the thickets.
Happiest of women and blessed she shall call you,
since you received a blind son from the mountains.
So do not cry, my friend: for Tiresias besides
because of you there will await many gifts from me,
since I shall make him a prophet renowned in posterity,
and one who is much more eminent than the rest.
He will know the birds, the auspicious and those that fly
to no purpose and which have ill-omened wings.

πολλὰ δὲ Βοιωτοῖϲι θεοπρόπα, πολλὰ δὲ Κάδμωι
χρηϲεῖ, καὶ μεγάλοιϲ ὕϲτερα Λαβδακίδαιϲ.
δωϲῶ καὶ μέγα βάκτρον, ὅ οἱ πόδαϲ ἐϲ δέον ἀξεῖ,
δωϲῶ καὶ βιότω τέρμα πολυχρόνιον,
καὶ μόνοϲ, εὖτε θάνηι, πεπνυμένοϲ ἐν νεκύεϲϲι
φοιταϲεῖ, μεγάλωι τίμιοϲ Ἀγεϲίλαι.'
ὣϲ φαμένα κατένευϲε· τὸ δ' ἐντελέϲ, ὧι κ' ἐπινεύϲηι
Παλλάϲ, ἐπεὶ μώναι Ζεὺϲ τόγε θυγατέρων
δῶκεν Ἀθαναίαι πατρώϊα πάντα φέρεϲθαι.
λωτροχόοι, μάτηρ δ' οὔτιϲ ἔτικτε θεάν,
ἀλλὰ Διὸϲ κορυφά. κορυφὰ Διὸϲ οὐκ ἐπινεύει
ψεύδεα ... ἁ θυγάτηρ.

ἔρχετ' Ἀθαναία νῦν ἀτρεκέϲ· ἀλλὰ δέχεϲθε
τὰν θεόν, ὦ κῶραι, τὦργον ὅϲαιϲ μέλεται,
ϲύν τ' εὐαγορίαι ϲύν τ' εὔγμαϲι ϲύν τ' ὀλολυγαῖϲ.
χαῖρε, θεά, κάδευ δ' Ἄργεοϲ Ἰναχίω.
χαῖρε καὶ ἐξελάοιϲα, καὶ ἐϲ πάλιν αὖτιϲ ἐλάϲϲαιϲ
ἵππωϲ, καὶ Δαναῶν κλᾶρον ἅπαντα ϲάω.

---

130 *Et. Mag.* 8.32 s.v. Ἀγεϲίλαοϲ (deest in *Et. Gen.* B, de A non constat) ἐπώνυμον τοῦ Ἅιδου. Καλλίμαχοϲ· 'φοιτάϲει (sic D, φοιτῶϲι cett. codd.) μεγάλωι Ἀγεϲιλάωι'. εἴρηται δὲ παρὰ τὸ ἄγειν τοὺϲ λαούϲ. ἄρχει γὰρ τῶν θανόντων. οὕτω Μεθόδιοϲ.

---

127 ἀξεῖ La: ἄξει Ψ 128 δωϲῶ . . . τέρμα FγS^{2}Q^2: om. spatio relicto βδʒ καὶ FLa,S^2 corr., Q^2: δὲ ΠPolS^2, ss. Q^2 βιότω Ernesti: βιότου FPolLaS^{2}Q^2: βοιωτοῦ Π 129 εὖτε θάνηι FEγS: εὖ δὲ θάνη e, εὖ ἐθάνη Q, lacunam trium litt. inter εὐ et θάνη ʒ 130 φοιταϲεῖ La: φοιτάϲει Ψ 131 ὣϲ φαμένα FβγS^{2}Q^2: om. spatio relicto δ, φαμένα om. spatio relicto ʒ 136 ψεύδεα F: ψευ β ἁ θυγάτηρ F: αἱ θυγάτηρ Atη, θυγάτηρ γS^{2}Q^2, om. β. totum versum om. spatio relicto δʒ 137 ἔρχετ' PolLa: ἔρχεται Ψ 138 τὦργον Boissonade: τὦργοϲ Ψ 139 ὀλολυγαῖϲ om. δ (add. S^2, γαιϲ post spatium relictum Q^2), τ' ὀλολυγαῖϲ om. ʒ 140 Ἰναχίω Ernesti: ἰναχίου Ψ 142 ἵππωϲ Brunck: ἵππουϲ Ψ

Many a word from god to the Boeotians, and many to Cadmus
will he make, and later to Labdacus' mighty heirs.
And I shall give a great staff to guide his feet as he needs,
and I shall give a life's end that is long-delayed,
and he alone when he dies will be conscious among the dead
as he roams, honoured by mighty Hagesilas.'
So saying she nodded assent, and that to which Pallas consents
is fulfilled, since this Zeus gave Athena alone
of all his daughters, that she acquire her father's full powers.
Bathpourers, there was no mother that bore the goddess
but the head of Zeus, and Zeus' head does not consent
to lies . . . . daughter.

Athena really comes now, so make welcome
the goddess, girls, whose duty the task is,
with acclamation, with prayings, with joyous answering cries.
Hail, goddess, look after Inachian Argos.
Hail as you drive out, and as you drive back in again
your horses, and protect the whole Argive estate.

SCHOLIA

FEeΠLaQ Ἔν τινι ἡμέραι ὡριϲμένηι ἔθοϲ εἶχον αἱ Ἀργεῖαι γυναῖκεϲ λαμβάνειν τὸ ἄγαλμα τῆϲ Ἀθηνᾶϲ καὶ Διομήδουϲ καὶ ἄγειν ἐπὶ τὸν Ἴναχον ποταμὸν κἀκεῖϲε ἀπολούειν· ὃ δὴ καὶ λουτρὰ ὠνομάζετο τῆϲ Παλλάδοϲ.

FeLaQ 2. φρυαϲϲομενᾶν ἤτοι ποιὸν ἦχον ἀποτελουϲῶν.

FLaQ 4. ϲοῦϲθε: ὁρμᾶτε, ἀπὸ τοῦ ϲεύω.

eΠLaQ 5. ⟨πάχειϲ:⟩ ἀπὸ μέρουϲ τὸ ὅλον.

8. ⟨γαγενέων:⟩ τῶν γιγάντων.

eLaQ 11. ⟨ἐφοίβαϲεν:⟩ ἐκάθηρεν.

EeΠLAQ 13. ἀπὸ κοινοῦ τὸ οἴϲετε.

14. ⟨ϲυρίγγων:⟩ τῶν χοινικίδων.

eLaQ 15. ⟨ἀλαβάϲτρωϲ:⟩ τὰϲ μυροθήκαϲ.

eΠLaQ 24 a. ⟨παρ' Εὐρώται:⟩ ποταμὸϲ Λακεδαιμονίαϲ.

FeΠLaQ b. ⟨τοὶ Λακεδαιμόνιοι | ἀϲτέρεϲ:⟩ οἱ Διόϲκουροι.

FEeLAQ 25 a. ⟨ἐμπεράμωϲ:⟩ ἐμπείρωϲ.

FeΠLaQ b. λιτά: ἀϲκεύαϲτα, ἄμεικτα.

EeQ 28. ⟨ϲίβδαϲ:⟩ ῥοιᾶϲ.

FEeΠLaQ 29. ἄρϲεν ἤτοι καθαρόν, ἄμεικτον.

eQ 32. ⟨ϲμαϲαμένα:⟩ ϲμηξαμένη.

FEeΠLaQ 33. ἴλα: ἡ τῶν νυμφῶν φρατρία καὶ ἄθροιϲιϲ.

34. ⟨Ἀρεϲτοριδᾶν:⟩ Ἀρεϲτορίδαι φυλὴ ἐπίϲημοϲ ἐν Ἄργει.

37. ⟨Εὐμήδηϲ:⟩ ποτὲ τῶν Ἡρακλειδῶν ἐλθόντων κατὰ τῶν Ὀρεϲτειδῶν Εὐμήδηϲ, ἱερεὺϲ τῆϲ Ἀθηνᾶϲ, ὑπενοήθη ὑπὸ τῶν Ἀργείων ὡϲ βουλόμενοϲ προδοῦναι τὸ Παλλάδιον τοῖϲ Ἡρακλείδαιϲ· φοβηθεὶϲ οὖν ὁ Εὐμήδηϲ ἔλαβε τὸ Παλλάδιον καὶ παρεγένετο εἰϲ τὸ ὄροϲ τὸ καλούμενον Ἴφειον.

eΠLaQ 40. ⟨Κρεῖον:⟩ ὄροϲ Ἄργουϲ.

---

2 καὶ Διομήδουϲ Ψ: om. E, καὶ τὸ Διομήδουϲ La, καὶ τὸ Διομήδουϲ ϲάκοϲ Meineke 3 ποταμὸν F: om. cett. κἀκεῖϲε F: κἀκεῖ cett. ὃ δὴ . . . τῆϲ Παλλάδοϲ F: om. cett. 5 φρυαϲϲομενᾶν Meineke: φρυαϲϲομένων F, om. cett. ἤτοι F: om. cett. ἀποτελουϲῶν La: ἀποτελούντων cett. 6 ὁρμᾶτε solum LaQ 10 ad v. 17 E οἴϲετε E: οἴϲατε cett. 16, 18, 20 lemmata F: om. cett. 20 ἄθροιϲιϲ solum E 21 Ἀρεϲτορίδαι Valckenaer: ἀκεϲτορίδαι Ψ 27 εἰϲ τὸ ὄροϲ Ψ: εἰϲ τὸ ὄροϲ Ἄργουϲ E, εἰϲ ὄροϲ La 28 Ἴφειον Ψ: Κρεῖον E

41. ⟨ἀπορρώγεςςιν:⟩ ἐν πέτραις ἐρρηγμέναις.

FeΠLaQ 42. ⟨Παλλατίδες:⟩ οὕτω γὰρ καλοῦνται ἀπὸ τῆς Παλλάδος.

eΠQ 45. ⟨Ἄργος:⟩ τουτέςτιν ὦ Ἀργεῖοι.

FEeΠLaQ 47 sq. ⟨ἢ ’c Φυςάδειαν | ἢ ἐς Ἀμυμώναν:⟩ Φυςάδεια καὶ Ἀμυμώνη θυγατέρες Δαναοῦ, ὅθεν τὴν ὀνομαςίαν ἔςχον αἱ κρῆναι.

57. ⟨νύμφαν μίαν:⟩ τὴν Χαρικλώ, μητέρα Τειρεςίου τοῦ μάντεως.

(F)eΠLaQ 60–3. Θέςπεια, Κορώνεια, Ἁλίαρτος πόλεις Βοιωτίας.

eΠQ 64. ⟨Κουραλίωι:⟩ ποταμὸς Βοιωτίας.

FeΠLaQ 71. ⟨ἵππω ἐπὶ κράναι:⟩ οὕτω καλεῖται Ἵππου κρήνη ἐν Ἑλικῶνι, ἣν ὁ Πήγαςος τῆι ὁπλῆι πλήξας ἐποίηςεν.

eQ 72. ⟨λῶντο:⟩ ἐλούοντο.

FEeΠLaQ 76 a. περκάζων ἤτοι μελαινόμενος ὑπὸ τῆς ἐκφύςεως τῶν τριχῶν.

S [b.] μελανίζων.

FEeΠLaQ 81. ⟨ὦ Εὐηρείδα:⟩ Εὐήρους υἱὸς ὁ Τειρεςίας.

87. ⟨ἄλαςτε:⟩ ἤτοι ’νεπίληςτα ὑπομείνας.

FEeQ 90. ⟨παριτέ:⟩ παραβατέ, παροδεύςιμε.

eΠLaQ 97. ⟨μετὰ πάντα βαλεῦ:⟩ τὸ ἑξῆς· μεταβαλεῦ.

EeΠQ 106. ⟨τέλθος:⟩ χρέος.

FeΠLaQ 108–15. Ἀκταίων υἱὸς Ἀριςταίου καὶ Αὐτονόης. οὗτος ὑπὸ τῶν ἰδίων κυνῶν ἐςπαράχθη διὰ τὸ τὴν Ἄρτεμιν ἰδεῖν γυμνήν.

EeΠLaQ 109. ⟨ἡβατάν:⟩ ἡβητήν.

eΠLaQ 115. ⟨τουτάκι:⟩ τηνικαῦτα.

eΠQ 120 a. ⟨τεῦ:⟩ ςοῦ.

eΠLaQ b. ⟨μενεῦντι:⟩ μενοῦςι.

124. ⟨ἄλιθα:⟩ μάτην.

e 126. ⟨Λαβδακίδαις:⟩ τοῖς περὶ Οἰδίποδα καὶ Ἰοκάςτην.

F 130. ⟨Ἁγεςίλαι:⟩ τῶι Ἅιδηι, τῶι Πλούτωνι.

Π 139. ⟨ὀλολυγαῖς:⟩ εὐχαῖς.

ES 140. ⟨κάδευ:⟩ κήδου.

---

37 sic F: μητέρα τοῦ Τειρεςίου solum cett. 40 πόλεις αὗται τῆς Βοιωτίας F 42 ἣν . . . ἐποίηςεν F: ἴςως τοῦ Πηγάςου Π, om. cett. 44 περκάζων ἤτοι F: om. cett. μελαινόμενος solum E 47 ὁ F: om. cett. 48 ἤτοι ΠLa: ἤγουν eQ, om. FE 49 παραβατέ om. F παροδεύςιμε om. Q 52 Ἀριςταίου καὶ Αὐτονόης F: Αὐτονόης καὶ Ἀριςταίου cett. 54 γυμνήν F: λουομένην cett., om. Q

COMMENTARY

For purposes of comment I have divided the poem into the following sections and sub-sections.

1–32 The address to the celebrants
- 1–4 Preliminary invocation
- 5–12 Athena's first attribute: care for her horses (the Gigantomachia)
- 13–17 Second summons to the celebrants
- 18–28 Athena's second attribute: her beauty (the Judgement of Paris)
- 29–32 Final instructions to the celebrants

33–56 Invocation of Athena herself
- 33–4 Preliminary invocation
- 35–42 The ceremony I: the Shield of Diomedes
- 43–4 Second invocation
- 45–54 The ceremony II: warning to the profane
- 55–6 Third invocation and transition to the narrative

57–136 A cautionary story: the blinding of Tiresias
- 57–69 The friendship of Athena and Chariclo
- 70–84 Tiresias' intrusion and punishment
- 85–95 Chariclo's grief
- 96–106 Athena's response to Chariclo's grief
- 107–18 Actaeon's intrusion and punishment
- 119–36 Athena's gifts of friendship

137–42 The epiphany announced: final instructions to the celebrants and greetings to the goddess.

1–32 The first part of the poem is an extension of a common hymnal feature, an address to the celebrants.[1] The Argive women are called to the ceremony and instructed how to equip themselves; only after they have assembled (v. 33 πάρα τοι καταθύμιος ἴλα) is the goddess herself invoked directly. This long opening section is cleverly composed so as to approximate in tone as closely as possible to an actual cult hymn. Although formally comprising preliminary instructions to the participants, it incorporates much material which would also appear in a hymn addressed direct to the divinity: Athena's care for her horses (vv. 5–12) and her natural beauty (vv. 13–32), formally mentioned to explain certain ritual

[1] Usually three or four lines in length: cf. Aristoph. *Ran.* 372–385, Isyllus E (Powell, *CA* 133), the *Erythraean Paean* (Powell, *CA* 136ff.), Macedonius in Powell, *CA* 138f.

details, are both attributes which would be thoroughly in place in the aretalogical sections of a hymn, and the method of establishing the attributes by reference to mythological examples is also that of the prayer-hymn (Norden, *Agnostos Theos* (Berlin 1913) 143ff.).

1–4 A preliminary invocation to the celebrants, in three stages: (1) the initial summons for those with specific duties (λωτροχόοι) to assemble; (2) the reason, that the horses' behaviour presages the approach of the divinity; (3) the summons repeated, this time implicitly including all participants (Πελαςγιάδες). These three stages, and some of the stylistic details, are characteristic in Greek of invocations prefatory to any ritual or formal act: cf., e.g., the herald's summons to the official announcement of Phaethon's marriage at Eur. fr. 773.66ff. (*Phaethon* 99ff.) Ὠκεανοῦ πεδίων οἰκήτορες, | εὐφαμεῖτ' ὦ, | ἐκτόπιοί τε δόμων ἀπαείρετε· | ὦ ἴτε λαοί. | κηρύςςω . . . ἀλλὰ cῖγ' ἔcτω λεώς; C.'s epiphany hymn to Apollo opens with a similar prefatory address to the celebrants, which, after warning off the profane and announcing signs of the impending epiphany, culminates in vv. 7f. ὁ γὰρ θεὸc οὐκέτι μακρήν· | οἱ δὲ νέοι μολπήν τε καὶ ἐc χορὸν ἐντύναcθε.[1] Short sentences with asyndeton and changing subjects here give a sense of urgency and excitement.

1 The first line provides immediately all the information needed to identify the situation: a formal summons to Athena's bath-attendants (forcefully delivered in a line marked at beginning and end by assonant relative and antecedent ὅccαι . . . πᾶcαι).

ὅccαι The doubled c is Doric as well as Homeric (LSJ).

λωτροχόοι Those who will officiate at the ceremony: at the Athenian Plynteria two girls were deputed as 'bathers' (Λουτρίδες, Πλυντρίδες: L.Deubner, *Attische Feste* (Berlin 1932) 18), and the Argive festival too will have been the responsibility of particular officials.[2]

λουτροχόοc was a normal classical term (*Od.* 20.297, Xen. *Cyr.* 8.8.20 in a list of household officials, Athen. 12.518c), replaced, however, in the *koine* by παραχύτηc (see LSJ s.v. and R.Ginouvès, *Balaneutikè* (Paris 1962) 213); here therefore an apparently literary term.

The form λω̲τρ- is not attested elsewhere, but λωτήριον occurs in the Argolid (*IG* IV 1488.37 = Schwyzer, *DGEE* 108g 3) and *Tab. Ḥeracl.* 1.184

[1] Cf. also Pind. *P.* 11. 1–16, the parodies in Aristoph. *Thesm.* 39ff., *Ach.* 204ff. (invocation to the chase resulting in ritual celebration at 237ff.), and Cat. 61. 76ff. quoted below on 3 καὶ ἁ θεόc . . .

[2] See also on v. 138. At Didyma one of the officials of the Cabiri bore the title λουτροφόροc (A.Rehm, *Didyma: II Die Inschriften* (Berlin 1958) 330.4); a priestess of Aphrodite at Sicyon had the same title (Paus. 2.10.4).

(Schwyzer, *DGEE* 62 = Collitz, *GDI* 4629), and λωτρόν in Laconia (Hesych. s.v.). Cf. on v. 138 τῶργον.

τᾶϲ Παλλάδοϲ The choice of name establishes from the very beginning the religious identification of statue and goddess which is implicit throughout the Hymn: ἡ Παλλάϲ (with the article) is the term used in Athenian ephebic inscriptions of *the* Palladion which was ritually bathed each year at Phaleron (*IG* II² 469.10, 470.11, 471.11).[1] The name also sets the mood: as Palladia were always representatives of the goddess in arms, so Παλλάϲ is particularly used of Athena the warrior-goddess (cf. Wilamowitz, *GH* I 231, Nilsson, *GGR* I 348ff., 433ff., Roscher, *LM* III 1301ff.).[2] See Introduction pp. 14–16.

O. Weinreich, 'Pallas Athene', *Würzburger Jahrbücher* 2 (1947) 33–7 notes that C.'s use of the name in this hymn is 1 τᾶϲ Παλλάδοϲ, 15 τᾶι Παλλάδι, 53 τὰν Παλλάδα – the three oblique cases (in non-Homeric position and usage), except in the final instance at 132 Παλλάϲ (pentameter); W. suggests that this patterning of declination is specifically humorous.

ἔξιτε Taken by Cahen p. 219f. and Kleinknecht, *LP* 303 as 'aller en cortège, en procession solennelle', being a *terminus technicus* parallel to ἔξιθ' at v. 33. The interpretation of ἔξιτε depends on one's reconstruction of the ritual occasion, and several points which argue against Cahen and Kleinknecht should be noticed:

(1) the summons is followed immediately by a remark concerning the goddess' horses: topographical detail must not be pressed over-literally, but clearly the women are not in the same place as the horses, and the latter are presumably at or near the place where the procession will start;

(2) the instructions which follow the summons concern what equipment the women should bring, and are more appropriate to celebrants leaving their homes than to processors who have already assembled;

(3) when Athena herself is summoned at v. 33 she is told πάρα τοι καταθύμιοϲ ἴλα: the only possible interpretation of this is 'your celebrants are ready', not 'the procession has started', implying that up to that moment (i.e. in the course of vv. 1–32) the women have been in process of assembling in response to the opening summons.

---

[1] Cf. *Suda* and Photius s.v. οἱ Νομοφύλακεϲ . . . τῇι Παλλάδι τὴν πομπὴν ἐκόϲμουν, ὅτε κομίζοιτο τὸ ξόανον ἐπὶ τὴν θάλαϲϲαν: Παλλάϲ is not just an alternative name here since elsewhere it is never so used in prose. The article with the name of the god (τᾶϲ Παλλάδοϲ), though unusual in poetry, is normal in prose: Gildersleeve, *SCG* II § 541. Cf. Leonidas, *HE* 1988 Θῆριϲ ὁ δαιδαλόχειρ τᾶι Παλλάδι . . .

[2] Ancient etymologies of the name recognise this, in that they usually derive Παλλάϲ from battle-activity of some kind: Roscher, *LM* III 1335ff. Cf. on vv. 7f.

Best sense is obtained by taking ἕξιτε here as identical in meaning to Eur. fr. 773.68 (*Phaethon* 101: see above on vv. 1–4) ἐκτόπιοί τε δόμων ἀπαείρετε.[1] The Hymn starts at the very beginning of the ceremony when the officials are being called out; later Athena too will come out from her temple to join her companions.

2 ἔξιτε The repetition characteristic of prayers, invocations etc. (see Pfister, *RGR* 199f. and cf. vv. 13, 15 below).

τᾶν ἵππων ἄρτι φρυασσομενᾶν The notorious sensitivity of animals, which are often supposed to be the first to detect the presence of a god (cf. *Od.* 16.161f., II 5, Theocr. 2.35f. etc.). The line is parodied in an amatory epigram ascribed to Asclepiades or Posidippus, *HE* 977 ἑσπερινῶν πώλων ἄρτι φρυασσομένων (of a hetaira's customers), the incongruity deriving presumably from the ceremonial solemnity of C.'s line. The parody assists the dating of V only in that Asclepiades and Posidippus are known to have been still living, at any rate, in 276/5 and 263/2 respectively.[2]

The ceremony is restricted to women, and the horses which will draw the waggon are naturally mares.

The double articles τᾶν ἵππων . . . τᾶν ἱερᾶν are a non-epic feature (whether with noun + adjective or two separate nouns). Identical patterning recurs at v. 53 τὰν Παλλάδα τὰν πολιοῦχον and is characteristic of bucolic poetry; since double articles occur also at vv. 47, 51 and in II, and often in bucolic poetry and Herodas, but not in the narrative section of V or in the 'non-mimetic' I, III, or IV, they should undoubtedly be regarded as 'realistic' idiom.[3]

φρυασσομενᾶν *Suda*, *Et. Mag.* φρύαγμα· ἡ τῶν ἵππων καὶ ἡμιόνων διὰ μυκτήρων ἠχή, ἀγρίωι φυσήματι ἐκπίπτουσα. The whole group of cognates appears to be normal usage; the verb does not occur till Menander (fr. 1081), but thereafter is documented in various prose authors, including *LXX* and *N.T.* (for distribution see LSJ).

τᾶν . . . -ᾶν Feminine genitive plural in -αν (-αων) as universally in West Greek (Buck, *GD* 38). Ψ corrupted φρυασσομενᾶν but successfully preserved τᾶν here, ἱερᾶν in v. 3, and ἱππειᾶν at v. 6: Meineke's correction is therefore essential.

3 ἐσάκουσα A standard poeticism: εἰσακούειν in normal usage = 'listen

---

[1] Cf. also Eur. *Bacch.* 68–9 τίς μελάθροις; ἔκτοπος ἔστω as interpreted by J.Roux, *REG* 75 (1962) 67–9 and *Euripide: Les Bacchantes* (Paris 1972) II 264–6.

[2] Both poets were honoured at Delphi in 276/5 (*Fouilles de Delphes* III 3 no. 192; not mentioned by Gow–Page), and Posidippus at Thermon in 263/2 (see Gow–Page, *HE* II 481 and Fraser, *Ptolemaic Alexandria* II 796 n. 44). See Intro. p. 40f.

[3] More material in Svensson, *GBA* 62.

to', 'obey', but the tragedians used compound for simple 'hear', and Hellenistic poets continued the practice (A.R. 1.766, 3.696, 914, 4.624, Theocr. 4.46, 13.61, 24.34(?), Sotades fr. 3 (Powell, *CA* 238)). Absence of the temporal augment, here and at 95 ἐλέηcεν, accords with both (a) Homeric practice (Chantraine, *GH* I 482f.), and (b) contemporary Hellenistic Greek (Mayser, *GGP* I² 101f.) which not infrequently omitted the augment in compounds; C. omits or includes (e.g. 77 ἤλυθε) the augment, as Homer, according to metrical convenience. See also on 58 φίλατο for omission of the syllabic augment.

καὶ ἁ θεὸc εὔτυκοc ἕρπεν 'the goddess is ready to come'; anticipation, as frequently in the prelude to an epiphany. Exactly parallel is II 1–7 where, after a similar description of ominous signs, is remarked ὁ γὰρ θεὸc οὐκέτι μακρήν; cf. also Semus of Delos in Athen. 622B–C ἀνάγετ' . . . θέλει γὰρ ὁ θεόc . . . διὰ μέcου βαδίζειν, Mesomedes, *Hymn to Helios* (Heitsch, *Griech. Dichterfragmente* (Göttingen 1961) I 25) 5f. μέλλει γὰρ πορτ' ἡμᾶc βαίνειν | Φοῖβοc,[1] Cat. 61.76ff. *claustra pandite ianuae, | virgo adest. viden ut faces | splendidas quatiunt comas?* (the same three elements: orders of preparation to the celebrants, anticipation of the bride, ominous signs – the bride is finally led out at vv. 114ff.). Attempts to defend Ψ's ἕρπει (e.g. by Cahen), 'the goddess is ready and is coming', have failed to consider these parallels and the need on internal grounds for anticipation, not announcement, here: Athena is not even invoked until v. 33, and v. 137 ἔρχετ' Ἀθαναία νῦν ἀτρεκέc, the climax of the ceremony, precludes any such announcement earlier.

καί As indicated by Kleinknecht, *LP* 302, it is difficult to connect the verbs ἐcάκουcα and εὔτυκοc (ἐcτίν), which are not strictly parallel, by καί. Good sense is obtained by punctuating with a colon after ἐcάκουcα and making καὶ ἁ θεόc . . . an independent additional clause; καί = 'also' (Denniston, *GP* 293, 'ascending climax').[2] This construction of καί is also in harmony with the asyndeton of the whole passage and contributes to the general effect of urgency.

καῐ Correption of καί, always an exception to normal practice, occurs only at this position in v (35, 49, 59, 117, 141); cf. on v. 71 ἵππω.

ἁ θεόc For the feminine of ὁ θεόc Homer, most lyric poets and the tragedians used either ἡ θεόc or ἡ θεά,[3] but Ionic used exclusively ἡ θεόc, and in Attic θεά occurred only in antithetical phrases (Wackernagel, *Vermischte Beiträge* (Basel 1897) 60f. (= *Kleine Schriften* I 821f.), *VUS* II 25, Meisterhans, *GAI* 125.4). In the *koine*, however, ἡ θεά became the rule (Mayser, *GGP* I² 8f., Moulton, *GNT* II 125) and although ἡ θεόc is not

[1] An Aristophanic parody: *Thesm.* 49 μέλλει γὰρ ὁ καλλιεπὴc Ἀγάθων.

[2] Same usage again at v. 35 καὶ ἁ Διομήδεοc ἀcπίc.

[3] In Pindar, however, ἡ θεόc is the regular feminine.

uncommon in Hellenistic poetry it is a manifest poeticism, allowed as an alternative to the more common θεά only for reasons of metrical expediency.[1] Strict Hellenistic Doric would have θεύς (see on v. 97 βαλεῦ), but, quite apart from the fact that poetic Doric commonly admits uncontracted εο (see on v. 97), Argolic seems mostly to have avoided the contraction θευ-: see Bechtel, *GD* II 446f. Contrast VI 57 θεύς.

εὔτυκος A rare poeticism, before C. only in Pratin. *PMG* 709, Bacchyl. 9.4, Aesch. *Supp.* 974, 994; possibly revived from Aeschylus by C., who also uses the very rare εὐτυκάζειν (177.32: earlier only in Aeschylus). Also in Theocr. 24.88.

The unmetrical εὔτυκτος preserved in some MSS indicates that Ψ contained a variant with which the hyparchetypes dealt in different ways; only β, parent of E and e, preserved both words (as again at v. 14). εὔτυκτος crept in here perhaps as a familiar Homericism, but palaeographically the two words are close, and εὔτυκος appears as a variant (unsuitable) on εὔτυκτος at Hdt. 1.119, and at Aesch. *Supp.* 974 εὔτυκος was corrupted to εὔτυκτος. See on v. 14 ὑπαξόνιον.

ἕρπεν Not just a poeticism: it is a Doric, and especially Argolic, feature that ἕρπειν is used = ἔρχεσθαι (see Bechtel, *GD* II 282, 509; also 598, 785: also Buck, *GD* 126, Gautier, *LX* 27f.). Cf. the *Hymnus Curetum* (Powell, *CA* 160ff.) 6 ἕρπε καὶ γέγαθι μολπᾶι.

Ψ's ἕρπει must be corrected to an infinitive (see above on ἁ θεὸς εὔτυκος ἕρπεν), and Schneider's Doric ἕρπεν is preferable to Wilamowitz' ἕρπειν. The -εν infinitive of thematic verbs was used in many Doric areas including the Argolid: Thumb, *GD* I 99f. and Buck, *GD* 122. Again in C. at VI 10. At v. 100 ἁρπάζειν should be changed to ἁρπάζεν, and at VI 52 Blomfield's πέλεν should be accepted. Cf. Gow, *Theocritus* I lxxiv. The -εν infinitive could also appear in the mouth of a Doric speaker (a doctor) on the Attic stage: Men. *Asp.* 448 θάλπεν.

4 After the expression of anticipation comes another injunction to the celebrants, as at II 8 οἱ δὲ νεοί . . . ἐντύνασθε, Theocr. 2.35–6 Θεστυλί, ταὶ κύνες ἄμμιν ἀνὰ πτόλιν ὠρύονται. | ἁ θεὸς ἐν τριόδοισι· τὸ χαλκέον ὡς τάχος ἄχει.

σῶσθε The -ου- forms σοῦσθε, σοῦται etc. are of uncertain etymology but appear to be regular poeticisms, connoting haste away to or from a place.[2]

---

[1] θεά, on the other hand, is often used when θεός would be equally possible metrically. The only two Callimachean examples of ἡ θεός not metrically necessary occur in the *Ionic* iambic poems: 193.37, 200[a].1. A.R. mostly uses ἡ θεά.

[2] Commentators derive these forms variously from σεύομαι, σόομαι, σοέομαι etc.: see in particular W. Schulze, *Kleine Schriften* (Göttingen 1959) 378f. and my references in *CQ* 20 (1970) 272 n. 1. The etymology may well have

A notably frequent form is the imperative, often repeated as here: e.g. Aesch. *Supp.* 836, 842 coῦcθε, coῦcθ', Soph. *Aj.* 1414 coύcθω, βάτω, Aristoph. *Vesp.* 209 coῦ, coῦ, and again possibly in C. at 7.31f.

Ψ here has coῦcθε, but since elsewhere in v ο+ε contracted produces ω (see on v. 1 λωτροχόοι, v. 138 τῶργον) cῶcθε should probably be read, particularly in view of Hesychius' entries cῶμαι· ἕρπω Δωριεῖc and cῶται· ὁρμᾶται, ἔρχεται, πορεύεται (cf. Epilycus fr. 3 (Kock I 803) cώμαι).

ὦ ξανθαί The presence of ὦ, here and at v. 27, indicates a (not surprising) tone of familiarity: see on v. 81 ὦ Εὐηρεῖδα. The adjective is a standard compliment: fair hair was always prized among the Greeks, and many of Homer's gods, heroes, and heroines have the epithet ξανθόc. Hellenistic poets use the adjective regularly of any person(s) to be described in terms of enhancement. Full documentation in Pease on Virg. *Aen.* 4.590; cf. J. André, *Étude sur les termes de couleur dans la langue latine* (Paris 1949) 326f., Schmidt *SGS* III 34f.

Πελαcγιάδεc The final word of the introductory section locates the ceremony at last (the dialect has been manifestly Doric since the second word of the poem): we are in Argos. The belief that the Peloponnesian Argives were originally Pelasgians was at least as old as Aeschylus (*Supp.* 253ff.) and became a respectable historical theory (e.g. Hdt. 1.56–8, 146: cf. Pearson on Soph. fr. 270.4). 'Pelasgian' became a common poetic alternative to 'Argive' among the dramatists,[1] and C. follows this classical tradition even though in A.R., assiduously following his Homeric model, only Thessalian Argos is 'Pelasgian' (*Il.* 2.681). Πελαcγιάδεc = 'Αργεῖαι again at 66.9.

The ethnic suffix -ιc was from Homer on often replaced by the synonymous -ιαc, whose forms are metrically easier to handle in the oblique cases.[2] Πελαcγιάc occurs first in C.[3] who also coined, e.g., 'Ακτιάδεc (63.12), 'Ικιάδεc (185). Patronymics and ethnics in -ιc, -ιαc were particularly popular among early Hellenistic poets (see Bühler on Mosch. 2.44).

5–12 After the prologue, the first of Athena's attributes, as Athena Hippia, exemplified by reference to a myth. Nowhere in this section is any direct reference made to the celebrants or the ritual, and to the modern reader the passage seems ambiguous: the address to the celebrants seems to have finished and a hymnal account of the Πράξειc Θεοῦ to have begun (cf. Norden, *Agnostos Theos* 163ff.) – but then with v. 13 ὦ ἴτ' 'Αχαιιάδεc at the

---

been disputed already in the third century B.C.: A.R., e.g., uses the unique cωέcθαι.

[1] See Wilamowitz on Eur. *HF* 464, Gow on Theocr. 15.142 and Collard on Eur. *Supp.* 367–8; cf. *RE* XIX 251 s.v. Pelasgia.

[2] Cf. Risch, *WHS* 134f., Debrunner, *GW* 190f., Jebb on Soph. *Phil.* 1333.

[3] Whence in Nonn. *D.* 28.34, 47.534, 568.

beginning of the next section it becomes clear that vv. 5–12 also must have been spoken to the celebrants. Retrospectively the transition from v. 4 to vv. 5ff. looks abrupt, and the selection of Athena's care for her horses for particular mention is prima facie puzzling. We must assume that, quite apart from such care as the normal attribute of a good warrior, the bathing of the processional horses was an important first stage in the Argive ritual, even though no evidence for this survives (so, e.g., Wilamowitz, *HD* II 15f.): note that in Rome the ritual washing of the Magna Mater statue in the river Almo included the waggon (H.Hepding, *Attis* (Gieszen 1903) 174) and Ambrosius, *epistula* 18.30, referring to the event, says *currus suos simulato Almonis in flumine lavat Cybele*. Vv. 5–12 would have been easily understood in themselves as a paradigm to the celebrants for the ritual; the train of thought stems from mention of the ceremonial horses' restiveness in vv. 2–3.[1]

The construction of this section as a single expanding period is effective: vv. 5–6 briefly state the attribute with two clauses in matching lines (| οὔποκ' . . . | πρίν . . .); vv. 7–8, introducing a famous 'historical' example as illustration, comprise a single clause across the whole couplet; and finally assertion of the attribute from the historical example spills over from vv. 9–10 into the final couplet, which emphasises the point by the addition of a second, parallel, clause.

These lines provide the first impression of the divinity being celebrated: sharp details depict a vigorous and powerful (but just) warrior-goddess.

5–6 Cf. on vv. 9f.

5 οὔποκ' Stephanus' necessary correction of Ψ's οὔποτ' makes for consistency with vv. 57, 59.

'Αθαναία By the Hellenistic period the long form was a poeticism/archaism which had been replaced in the *koine* by 'Αθηνᾶ (Meisterhans, *GAI* 31f., Mayser, *GGP* I² 5, K–B, *GG* I 495f., cf. Björck, *AI* 133f.). However the Doric form 'Αθαναία[2] is well attested in Doric inscriptions even into the third century B.C. (see Schwyzer, *DGEE* Index s.v.); the shorter form also appears in V (35, 51, 79).

μεγάλως It is characteristic of epiphany hymns and descriptions to

---

[1] The next section, vv. 18–28, representing the second of Athena's attributes, is preceded by instructions to the celebrants, vv. 13–17, which make for a good introduction to the attribute; one misses a similar introduction here and it is tempting to posit a short lacuna. However, though simple, this solution is drastic, too drastic when one remembers how little we know about the Argive cult which forms the basis of the poem and which may have been well known to C.'s readers.

[2] A necessary correction by Politian in view of vv. 33, 43, 55 etc. Ψ Atticised the name again at v. 16.

represent the person or divinity concerned as being exceptional in both size and beauty (Pfister in *RE* Suppl. IV 314f.).[1] Athena's size is mentioned early, her beauty later in the extensive section 13–32. Rhea is similarly described at I 30 εἶπε καὶ ἀντανύcαcα θεὴ μέγαν ὑψόθι πῆχυν.

The masculine accusative plural -ωc used in most Peloponnesian Doric areas including Argos (Buck, *GD* 68, 86) is uniformly used in v (13, 15, 23, etc.).

ἀπενίψατο The verb is common in Homer and absent from fifth-century B.C. prose, but is none the less normal usage, not a poeticism. This is evidenced by instances in Aristophanes and other comic poets and a wide distribution in *koine* prose, including *LXX* and *N.T.*: thus, e.g., Theophr. *Char.* 16.2 ἀπονιψάμενοc τὰc χεῖραc καὶ περιρρανάμενοc ἀπὸ ἱεροῦ, Ditt. *Syll.*[3] 1168.63f. (Epidaurus: third century B.C.) ἀφελόμενον τὰν ταινίαν ἀπονίψαcθαι τὸ πρόcωπον ἀπὸ τᾶc κράναc.[2] λούειν and νίζειν (and compounds) are normally distinct, the former denoting the general action of bathing, the latter the more specific and careful act of cleansing, usually of particular parts of the body;[3] hence at v. 72 when Athena and Chariclo bathe in the spring the verb is λῶντο.

πάχειc The standard Doric form (very poorly documented in LSJ Suppl.): Pind. fr. 169.30, 344.6(?), Sim. *PMG* 519 fr. 92.6, Call. fr. 196.38, Theocr. 3.30, 7.67.

6 ἱππειᾶν The usual adjectival form in (hexameter) poetry: Hellenistic prose writers, like earlier authors, normally use ἱππικόc (cf. Debrunner, *GW* 197).

ἐξελάcαι 'drive away, banish': the verb always denotes vigorous action and must not be translated simply 'remove' – its use here indicates that even after battle Athena is energetic.[4]

λαγόνων Strictly used, λαγών denotes the lower abdomen (see on v. 88 λαγόναc where this usage is important), but the word is sometimes used

---

[1] Apparitions in dreams too are commonly notable for their size and beauty: see R.G.A.Van Lieshout, *Mnemosyne* 23 (1970) 228 n. 2. E.Cahen, *C* 545 mistakenly criticises C. for using the adjective μέγαc so often in this Hymn.

[2] See also LSJ s.v.

[3] Cf. LSJ s.v. λούω and R.Ginouvès, *Balaneutikè* (Paris 1962) 152ff.

[4] LSJ unnecessarily put this passage under a separate heading. What is unusual here is not so much the usage of the verb, but the representation of the action in energetic terms rather than, say, in terms of cleanliness; Plut. *Mor.* 654D, with which LSJ classify v. 6, is a separate figurative usage to be compared with, e.g., Gorgias, *Helen* 17, Aristot. *Eth. Nic.* 1154^b 13, Nic. *Ther.* 35. I can find no exact parallel for the Callimachean application of the verb to dirt etc., but ἐξελάcαι is easily understood even if it is a mild metaphor.

more vaguely of the flank:[1] here as, e.g., in A.R. 2.663f. (of oxen ploughing) πέρι δ' ἄσπετος ἱδρώς | εἴβεται ἐκ λαγόνων τε καὶ αὐχένος.

7–8 The battle against the Giants was one of Athena's most famous military victories; in Athens the ceremonial robe (πέπλος) which adorned the ξόανον of Athena was always embroidered with scenes from the Gigantomachia (see *RE* xviii³ 460f.): particularly explicit is Eur. *Hec.* 466ff. ἢ Παλλάδος ἐν πόλει τὰς καλλιδίφρους Ἀθαναίας ἐν κροκέωι πέπλωι ζεύξομαι ἆρα πώλους . . . ἢ Τιτάνων γενεάν . . . Possibly at the Argive festival too Athena Hippia and the war against the Giants were similarly depicted on one of the cult objects; indeed the specific mention in v. 70 πέπλων λυσαμένα περόνας might suggest that the Argive ritual involved the use of a ceremonial robe just as in the Panathenaea (? and Plynteria?: see Deubner, *Attische Feste* 19ff.).[2] Cf. Intro. pp. 11f. and Commentary on 70 πέπλων. Many ancient sources explain the name Pallas (v. 1) as having originated from the Gigantomachia (Roscher, *LM* iii 1335ff., F.Vian, *La Guerre des Géants* (Paris 1952) 198ff.: cf. on v. 1 τᾶς Παλλάδος). From *c.* 540 B.C. onwards Athena is often represented as having fought from her chariot: see in general Vian, *op. cit.* 63ff., 200. Athena's washing of her horses in the sea on that occasion is not recorded elsewhere and is presumably a Callimachean embellishment introduced to reflect the Argive ritual (see on vv. 5–12).

7 λύθρωι πεπαλαγμένα Epic phraseology and vocabulary: *Il.* 6.268, *Od.* 22.402 (and possibly 23.48) αἵματι καὶ λύθρωι πεπαλαγμένον. λύθρος is exclusively Homeric vocabulary, always dative with παλάσσεσθαι (two formulaic phrases: this one and *Il.* 11.169, 20.503 λύθρωι δὲ παλάσσετο χεῖρας). C. uses the Homeric dative (again at 328.2),[3] but other Hellenistic writers, to whom the Homeric term was a valuable poeticism, use all cases: λύθρωι Lyc. 491, Maiistas, *Aretalogy* 25 (Powell, *CA* 70), λύθρον Euphor. fr. 50P.2, Nic. fr. 74.7, λύθρος Antip. Sid. *HE* 582. In later prose λύθρος became normal usage: see LSJ[4] and Lampe, *PGL* s.v. παλάσσεσθαι is also exclusively epic (LSJ) and used by the Alexandrians strictly according to Homeric precedent, as an archaism: A.R. 3.1046 σάκος πεπαλαγμένον

---

[1] Homer and Ionic use κενεών or λαπάρα, but λαγών is the standard technical term in Attic from the fifth century B.C. onwards; the medical writers distinguish each of these three terms from one another (see, e.g., Hipp. *Morb.* 2.55, *Int.* 17).

[2] Argive Hera seems to have had a special garment woven for her by ritually pure girls, presumably to be worn at a similarly important ceremonial occasion: 66.2–4 οὐδὲ μὲν Ἥρης | ἁγνὸν ὑφαινέμεναι τῇσι μέμηλε πάτος | στῆναι [πὰ]ρ κανόνεσσι πάρος θέμις ἦ . . .

[3] This time with πλήθειν: imitated by Maiistas, *Aretalogy* 25 (Powell, *CA* 70).

[4] Hipp. *Epist.* 17 should be classified as later prose.

(echoing *Od.* 22.184), Theocr. (?) 25.225 πεπάλακτο φόνωι (cf. *Od.* 22.402).[1]

πάντα To be taken with λύθρωι πεπαλαγμένα (placed early for emphasis) rather than the delayed τεύχεα: 'her armour all spattered with gore'.

φέροιcα The participial forms in -οιcα found in Pindar, Theocritus, C. etc. are now recognised as genuine Doricisms (not Aeolicisms); they are only sporadically documented before the third century B.C. but are standard in Hellenistic literary Doric (cf. on v. 8 ἦνθ', v. 27 κῶραι, v. 97 βαλεῦ): see Magnien, 'Le syracusain littéraire et l'Idylle xv de Théocrite', *Mémoires de la Soc. de Ling. de Paris* 21 (1920) 65f., Monteil, *T* 35f., Dover, *Theocritus* xl–xli. Lascaris' correction of Ψ's -ουcα is necessary: elsewhere Ψ preserved the correct form (e.g. vv. 21, 25), though cf. vv. 25, 93 λαβοῖcα.

For the verb with τεύχεα cf. *Il.* 11.247, 18.137, 617.

8 τῶν ἀδίκων . . . ἀπὸ γαγενέων ὁ γηγενὴc cτρατὸc Γιγάντων (Soph. *Trach.* 1058) was symbolic of lawlessness from Homer onwards; the Giants were ὑπέρθυμοι (*Od.* 7.59) and ἄγρια φῦλα (7.206) and at Eur. *Bacch.* 995f. specifically τὸν ἄθεον ἄνομον ἄδικον Ἐχίονοc γόνον γηγενῆ.[2] Here the article and adjective give necessary definition distinguishing them from the ordinary earthborn men (e.g. Erechtheus) whom γηγενήc also sometimes denotes.[3] Athena's association with the cause of justice is established early in the poem.

ἦνθ' West Greek often has ντ, νθ, from λτ, λθ, and literary Doric commonly uses ἐνθεῖν: Buck, *GD* §72, Schwyzer, *GG* I 213, Monteil, *T* 36, also Thumb, *GD* I 79, 102, 211. Although originally restricted to certain Doric areas (notably the N.E. Peloponnese and Sicily) this phenomenon apparently came to be regarded by the Hellenistic writers as a general Doricism;[4] again at 197.46, 48, VI 74, 77 and often in Theocritus.

ἀπὸ γαγενέων With the wording cf. 119.3 Γιγαντείου δαίμονεc ἐκ πολέμου, and 75.24f. οὐδ' ἀπὸ θήρηc | ἔκλυζεν . . . Meineke's γαγενέων for

---

[1] Later in Antip. Thess. *GP* 623, Q. S. 12.410. In two Homeric passages the verb seems to mean 'determine by lot'. Ancient editors discussed them and some interpreted the verb as meaning 'shake': accordingly at *Il.* 7.171 Aristarchus emended to πεπάλαcθε and at *Od.* 9.331 to πεπαλάcθαι, deriving the verbs from πάλλειν, but both C. and A.R. attributed this meaning to παλάccειν and so used the verb at IV 78 and 1.358 respectively, again as an archaism (a gloss).

[2] A.R. 1.942 ὑβριcταί τε καὶ ἄγριοι continues the tradition.

[3] The Attic use of γηγενήc of the primeval men renders implausible Dover's suggestion (Aristoph. *Nub.* 853) that γηγενήc was a generally pejorative term suggesting 'sub-human'.

[4] Cf. the similar development over ευ: see on v. 97 βαλεῦ. Also cf. on v. 7 φέροιcα, v. 27 κῶραι.

Ψ's γηγ. is probable though not certain: the form is preserved only from Herodian in *Et. Gen. B* s.v. γηγενής (cf. Lentz in *Gramm. Graec.* III² 419.29). See Björck, *AI* 114ff.

9–12 Picked up by Nonn. *D.* 42.19ff. (of Dionysus) ἀπὸ βλοσυροῖο δὲ δίφρου | πόρδαλιν ἱδρώοντα Μάρων ἀνέλυσε λεπάδνων, | καὶ κόνιν ἐξετίναξε καὶ ἔκλυσεν ὕδατι πηγῆς | θερμὸν ἀναψύχων κεχαραγμένον (cf. v 7 πεπαλαγμένα) αὐχένα θηρῶν.

9–10 Ruhnken appropriately compared Prop. 2.18.9f. *illum saepe suis decedens fovit in ulnis | quam prius abiunctos sedula lavit equos.*

9 ἀλλὰ πολὺ πράτιστον Homeric phraseology: *Od.* 4.456 ἀλλ' ἦ τοι πρώτιστα, 14.220 ἀλλὰ πολὺ πρώτιστος, *Il.* 14.442 ἔνθα πολὺ πρώτιστος, *H.H.Ap.* 407 ἀλλ' ὡς τὰ πρώτιστα. In Attic and Ionic the 'double superlative' πρώτιστος occurs only in poetry and late prose,[1] and its use by C. in the non-Doric Hymns and *Aetia* is Homeric diction; here, however, it is also in context as a widely used Doricism (see Bechtel, *GD* II 540 [Thera], 583 [Cos], 736 [Crete] and add *SEG* 9 (1944) 72.55 [Cyrene] and *IG* XII.3.540 III, 1324 (Suppl.) [Thera]: cf. also Buck, *GD* § 114.1).

πρᾱτ- The standard West Greek form: Buck, *GD* 94 and LSJ s.v.

9–10 ὑφ' ἅρματος αὐχένας ἵππων | λυσαμένα Homeric phraseology: *Il.* 8.543, *Od.* 4.39 οἱ δ' ἵππους μὲν ἔλυσαν ὑπὸ ζυγοῦ ἱδρώοντας, 7.5f. οἵ ῥ' ὑπ' ἀπήνης | ἡμιόνους ἔλυον,[2] the reverse of *Od.* 3.475f. ἵππους | ζεύξαθ' ὑφ' ἅρματ' ἄγοντες (cf. 15.46f.). The periphrasis αὐχένας ἵππων is a typical Alexandrian variation on the Homeric ἵππους.

ὑπό = 'from under' is normal usage: Hdt. 4.8 τὰς δέ οἱ ἵππους ὑπὸ τοῦ ἅρματος νεμομένας . . . ἀφανισθῆναι, Xen. *An.* 6.4.25 λαβὼν βοῦν ὑπὸ ἁμάξης etc.

10 παγαῖς = 'waters', 'streams' is poetic usage, first in Homer (LSJ).[3] The 'streams of ocean' are poetic commonplace: Hes. *Theog.* 282, Pind. fr. 30.2, Eur. *IT* 1039, fr. 773.33N (*Phaethon* 77), though here the suspension of Ὠκεανῶ till the end of the line gives the phrase additional impact. On the Doric form, amply testified in Pindar and Theocritus, cf. Björck, *AI* 360.

ἔκλυσεν Homeric κλύζειν = 'wash [over]', 'drench', always of the sea or weather, but in post-Homeric normal usage (Xenophon, Aristotle, Hippocrates etc.) only 'wash [out]', 'clean thoroughly'. C. follows normal usage, here and at 75.25,[4] though A.R. and Aratus adhere strictly to the archaic Homeric usage.[5]

---

[1] See K–B, *GG* I 573 and cf. Mayser, *GGP* I² 61f., Moulton, *GNT* II 166.

[2] λύειν ὑπό with other cases (same context): *Il.* 18.244, 23.7, 24.576.

[3] Add *Il.* 23.148, delete Hdt. 1.189. Cf. Jebb on Soph. *Ant.* 803.

[4] So also Theocr. 1.27 and Nic. *Al.* 140 in technical senses, though Theocr. 1.140 also draws on Homeric usage.

[5] Also in Euphorion fr. 44.5 (by emendation), Numenius Her. in Athen.

Although the term is normal usage the syntax is poetic. The direct object of κλύζειν, νίζειν, λούειν etc. is normally the object or person cleansed; however poetic diction occasionally objectifies the dirt etc. removed (with κλύζειν again at Soph. fr. 854, Eur. *IT* 1193, Call. 75.25, and cf. LSJ s.v. νίζειν II).[1]

11 ἱδρῶ The Homeric accusative: Attic consistently has ἱδρῶτα (cf. Chantraine, *GH* I 54f., 211f., K–B *GG* I 509f.).[2] Again at A.R. 2.87, 4.656, Antip. Thess. *GP* 295.

ῥαθάμιγγας A rare poetic gloss (*Il.* 11.536, 20.501, 23.502, Hes. *Theog.* 183 and probably Pind. fr. 52g 9). Schmidt, *SGS* II 269 rightly insists that ῥαθάμιγξ denotes a particle (dislodged) of any substance, liquid or solid, and should not be translated 'drop' as it is by most lexica; here presumably the word denotes 'dust, grime' in contrast to ἱδρῶ: cf. Hesych. s.v.: ῥανίδες, σταγόνες· καὶ ὁ ἀπὸ τῶν ἵππων κονιορτός (cf. Photius, *Suda* s.v.).[3] Again as a rarity in Arat. 889 (rain) and Bion fr. 4.1G (water), and later in Oppian and Christodorus.

ἐφοίβασεν φοιβᾶν is a rare verb which is recorded before the Hellenistic period only at Eur. fr. 773N.13 (=*Phaethon* 57). Thereafter here, A.R. 2.302 and Theocr. 17.134;[4] other instances, now lost, must be presumed. Photius, Hesychius, and the collection of *Useful Oratorical Terms* in Bachmann, *Anecd. Graec.* (Leipzig 1828) I 407 (cf. *Et. Mag.* 797.1) have the entry φοιβᾶσθαι· καθαίρεσθαι.

12 χαλινοφάγων The adjective, only here in Greek, is of a common

---

7.304F (=*SH* 584) v. 5, and later in Philodemus, *GP* 3251. A.R. even coined ἀνακλύζειν in the Homeric sense.

[1] This poetic usage presumably derives from the similarly poetic practice of giving such verbs double objects (person cleansed + thing thereby removed: cf. Schwyzer, *GG* II 83, K–G, *GG* I 327): the 'additional' object remains, even though the 'direct' object is omitted.

[2] After Homer (who consistently avoids all -τ- forms) the declension of -ώς nouns (with or without -τ-) varied from noun to noun (see Schwyzer, *GG* I 514: Wackernagel, *SUH* 146f. is an oversimplification), but forms without -τ- were available for poetic usage even where prose normally avoided them.

[3] According to Eustathius 1313.10 ῥαθάμιγξ was customarily used of liquids, only rarely of solids.

[4] The reading φοιβήσετε at *LXX Deut.* 14.1 is both doubtful and obscure in sense. Lycophron three times uses φοιβάζειν as if it were φοιβᾶν (731, 875, 1166): interchange of -ᾶν and -άζειν suffixes is not uncommon in the *koine* (Mayser, *GGP* I² 118), and later Cyril, *Os.* 99 (3.131D) uses φοιβᾶν for φοιβάζειν. (Cf. also Alexandrian use of (περι-)τροχᾶν for Attic τροχάζειν: IV 28, Arat. 227, 815, 1105, Posidippus, *HE* 3156.)

type: -φαγος compounds are coined in all periods of Greek (Risch, *WHS* 186, Buck and Petersen, *Reverse Index* (Chicago 1945) 624f.). The word-order is important: χαλ. standing away from its own noun is juxtaposed between two words for which it also gives the reason, παγέντα . . . ἀφρόν, making the line particularly compact.

Verbally similar is A.R.4.1607f. ἀργινόεντα δ' ἐπὶ στομάτεσσι χαλινά | ἀμφὶς ὀδακτάζοντι . . . Cf. also A.R. 3.1352f. ἀμφὶ δὲ πολλός | ἀφρὸς ἀπὸ στόματος χαμάδις ῥέε (neither C. nor A.R. seem to be directly dependent on each other in these two passages).

13–17 A second summons, like vv. 1–4 (cf. in particular notes on v. 14 and vv. 15–16), unequivocally addressed to the celebrants. This time, after an opening formulaic summons, details of the ceremony. But what appear superficially to be instructions for preparation turn out for the moment to be non-instructions and a vehicle for conveying another of Athena's attributes, her beauty (cf. on v. 5 μεγάλως); the passage leads directly into a second mythological *exemplum*, parallel to the first (vv. 7–12), and only after this are positive instructions given (vv. 29–32). With this passage the pace quickens (see detailed notes below); in general, note that completion of the syntactical structure begun in v. 13 is delayed by interruptions and repetitions until v. 17.

This second *exemplum* relates, like the first (see n. on vv. 5–12), directly to a part of the ritual: after being bathed the statue was doubtless decked out in new finery (see Intro. pp. 11f. and n. on vv. 7f.).

13 ὦ ἴτ' Ἀχαιιάδες An established mode of urgent appeal, usually ceremonial (but also in other circumstances): Eur. *Hec.* 1091ff. ἰὼ Ἀχαιοί . . . ὦ ἴτε, μόλετε . . . ('au secours'), *Bacch.* 152 ὦ ἴτε Βάκχαι, fr. 773.69N (*Phaethon* 112) ὦ ἴτε λαοί, Antagoras, *HE* 164 ὦ ἴτε Δήμητρος πρὸς ἀνάκτορον, ὦ ἴτε, μύσται, A.R. 4.1414 ἴτ' ὦ νύμφαι,[1] cf. Aristoph. *Pax* 298 δεῦρ' ἴτ', ὦ πάντες λεῴ, Plut. *Thes.* 25.1. For other aspects of the idiom ὦ + imperative see Fraenkel on Aesch. *Ag.* 22.

Hiatus after vocative or exclamatory ὦ is standard: again at vv. 81, 89, 90, 106, 119.

Ἀχαιιάδες The use of this ethnic to denote Argives may here be academic irony. The Homeric phrase Ἄργος Ἀχαιικόν was interpreted by some Alexandrian scholars[2] as a deliberate antithesis to Πελασγικὸν Ἄργος: scholia to *Il.* 9.141 τὴν Πελοπόννησον Ἀχαιικὸν Ἄργος λέγει . . . Πελασγικὸν δὲ Ἄργος τὴν Θεσσαλίαν (cf. scholia to 19.115). With the close succession of v. 4 Πελασγιάδες and v. 13 Ἀχαιιάδες, both synonymously of

---

[1] Incorrectly obelised by Fränkel: see G.Giangrande, *CQ* 18 (1968) 54.
[2] K.Lehrs, *De Aristarchi Studiis Homericis* (Leipzig 1882[3]) 224, L.Friedländer, *Aristonicus* (1853) 157.

Argives, C. flagrantly ignores this distinction which was carefully followed by A.R. (see on v. 4).

μὴ μύρα μηδ' ἀλαβάcτρωc The terms and the objects themselves are entirely unexceptional: Promethion writes to Zenon (*PSI* 333.6ff.) κομίζει δὲ νυνὶ μύρου ἴνια ῑ ἐν [ἀλ]αβάcτροιc κᾱ, οἵ εἰcιν ἐcφραγιcμένοι τῶι ἐμῶι δακτυλίωι. Unguents, contained in jars, were regularly and normally used when washing on occasions of every kind (cf. Gow on Theocr. 15.114), though the use of perfumes was not always approved of (see on v. 16).

Similar phraseology (perhaps by reminiscence) in the anonymous epigram *AP* 11.8 μὴ μύρα μὴ cτεφάνουc λιθίναιc cτήλαιcι χαρίζου.

14 Like the first summons, the second also is given added urgency by parenthetical reference to the processional chariot; earlier the horses were restive (vv. 2–3), this time the waggon seems actually to be moving (or being loaded up). The Argive waggon here is like Diomedes' chariot, which also creaked as Athena stepped aboard, at *Il.* 5.837–9 ἡ δ' ἐc δίφρον ἔβαινε παραὶ Διομήδεα δῖον | ἐμμεμαυῖα θεά· μέγα δ' ἔβραχε φήγινοc ἄξων | βριθοcύνηι· δεινὴν γὰρ ἄγεν θεὸν ἄνδρα τ' ἄριcτον.

The same descriptive detail is used for a similar effect of vivid actuality by Parmenides in the preface describing his chariot-ride to the Truth: 28 B 1.6–8 ἄξων δ' ἐν χνοίηιcιν ἵει cύριγγοc ἀυτήν | αἰθόμενοc (δοιοῖc γὰρ ἐπείγετο δινωτοῖcιν | κύκλοιc ἀμφοτέρωθεν) . . . Cf. Aesch. *Sept.* 151ff. ὄτοβον ἁρμάτων ἀμφὶ πόλιν κλύω· ὦ πότνι' Ἥρα· ἔλακον ἀξόνων βριθομένων χνόαι, *Supp.* 180f. ὁρῶ κόνιν, ἄναυδον ἄγγελον cτρατοῦ· | cύριγγεc οὐ cιγῶcιν ἀξονήλατοι.

cυρίγγων Pollux, *Onom.* 1.144 τὸ δὲ κενὸν τοῦ τροχοῦ τὸ ἐναρμοζόμενον τῶι ἄξονι cῦριγξ, i.e. the nave. LSJ (followed by Gow on Theocr. 24. 120) wrongly translate 'the hole in the nave of a wheel', and the Supplement only partially corrects the entry: in all of the passages cited by LSJ cῦριγξ must mean 'nave'.[1]

ἀίω Developing v. 3 ἐcάκουcα.

φθόγγον The masculine is the ordinary form of φθογγ- (prose and poetry: only here in C.): A.R. uses only the poetic φθογγή (four times: never in C.), which otherwise appears only in Rhianus, *HE* 3255 in the Hellenistic period.

ὑπαξόνιον The division of MSS between -ιον and -ιων and the recording in some of both readings suggests, as Pfeiffer remarks, that Ψ had a fully recorded variant.[2] Only -ιον gives good sense: it is not the naves that

[1] The most vivid illustration of cῦριγξ is Eur. *Hipp.* 1234f. cύριγγέc τ' ἄνω | τροχῶν ἐπήδων ἀξόνων τ' ἐνήλατα: as Barrett remarks 'holes do not fly in the air'. LSJ's mistaken translation seems to derive from the muddled entry in the *Suda*.

[2] In contrast, e.g., to v. 3 where one might conclude from the simple

are best described as 'under the axle' (-ίων), but the sound which comes from contact of axle on nave when weighed down from above.[1]

ὑπαξόνιος here and its opposite ἐπαξόνιος at Theocr. (?)25. 249 are both ἀπ. λεγ.: one of the pair was perhaps formed in imitation of the other.[2]

15–16 The repetition, verbal, rhythmic, and syntactic, between this and previous couplets creates a religious urgency and solemnity (cf. on v. 2 ἔξιτε). The whole of v. 15 is repetitious: the anaphora μὴ μύρα is of a common type not infrequently religious in purpose (cf. Lapp, *TF* 57ff.); λωτροχόοι τᾶι Παλλάδι provides a strong link with v. 1, binding the two summons sections together and, along with other details of repetition, contributing to a kind of sub-refrain effect which characterises the whole of vv. 1–56 (cf. on vv. 2, 4, 14, 18, 33); the epiphora μηδ' ἀλαβάστρως, much rarer than anaphora, is used by C. almost solely in religious contexts – e.g. VI 12–16 οὐ πίες οὔτ' ἄρ' ἔδες τῆνον χρόνον οὐδὲ λοέσσα | . . . καὶ οὐ φάγες οὐδὲ λοέσσα (cf. Lapp, *TF* 60 for other examples); the use of the pentameter again for a parenthesis, albeit of a different kind to v. 14, also contributes to the refrain effect.

16 A favourite Callimachean device for creating tension: an explanatory parenthesis (negative as often) interrupting the syntactical construction of the main sentence. Cf., e.g., III 1f. Ἄρτεμιν (οὐ γὰρ ἐλαφρὸν ἀειδόντεσσι λαθέσθαι) | ὑμνέομεν and see Lapp, *TF* 53 for other examples.

χρίματα μεικτά On the use and effect of scents and the production of perfumed unguents by compounding oil and fragrance(s) see Theophr. *de odor.* 7ff. When χρῖμα, which denotes simply 'unguent' whether plain or treated, is used specifically of μύρον (properly 'scent', but most often of perfumed oil) the fact that it is a compounded product is normally made explicit as here (similarly Xenophanes 3.6 ἀσκητοῖς' . . . χρίμασι).

Scented oils were usually considered effeminate by Greeks: Solon

---

division of MSS between εὔτυκτος and εὔτυκος without note of a variant that the alternative reading may have been recorded simply by the insertion (or deletion) of a single letter which scribes either accepted or ignored (ΕΥΤΥΚ^{T}ΟΣ or ΕΥΤΥΚΤ̸ΟΣ).

[1] Furthermore a locative epithet with συρίγγων would be superfluous, whereas with (and after) φθόγγον it adds precision. Nineteenth-century editors also objected to -ίων and proposed various unsuitable readings (see Schneider) but virtually ignored -ιον since its status as an ancient variant had not yet been established.

[2] Otherwise ἀξόνιος generates only the rare παραξόνιος (Aristoph. *Ran.* 819 and later Greek). Similarly C. and Theocr. coin the locative ὑποκόλπιος (IV 86 and 14.37) on a previously not very generative stem (ἐγκόλπιος: Heraclitus, παρακόλπιον: Theophrastus and Menander). ὑπαξόνιος later at Σ Eur. *Or.* 1384 ἔνιοι δὲ ἁρμάτειον τὸ ὀξύφωνον ἀπὸ τῶν ὑπαξονίων ἤχων.

legislated against male perfume-sellers (Athen. 612A), Pherecrates fr. 64 (Kock I 162) made fun of them, the Spartans expelled perfume manufacturers (Seneca, *nat. quaest.* 4.13.9, Athen. 686F), Socrates in Xen. *Symp.* 2.3 denounces inappropriate use of perfumes (cf. Seneca, *de benef.* 7.25.1), Xenophon's troops in Armenia used simple oils even though scented ones were also available (*An.* 4.4.13),[1] and Plutarch, *Alex.* 40 instancing the lax living of Alexander's companions describes them as μύρωι δὲ χρωμένους ἰέναι πρὸς ἄλειμμα καὶ λουτρὸν ὅσους οὐδὲ ἐλαίωι. Conversely Athena's use of untreated natural oil was a clear sign of manliness (Xen. *Symp.* 2.3 ὀσμὴ ἄλλη μὲν ἀνδρί, ἄλλη δὲ γυναικὶ πρέπει).

χρίματα The spelling offered by Ψ (Attic: ?literary?), contrary to the current χρῖσμα (fourth century B.C. on), is confirmed by the papyrus at 194.45, 76.

μεικτά Ψ has μικτά, and at A.R. 4.677 MSS have μικτοῖσιν; the -ι- forms of μειγ- are documented as early as the fifth century B.C. and eventually predominated, but inscriptions and papyri show that the -ει- forms were still apparently more common in the third century B.C.: see LSJ s.vv. μείγνυμι, μικτός,[2] Meisterhans, *GAI* 36, 48ff. and esp. 181, Mayser, *GGP* I^1 60ff., esp. 62 A.4, I^2 187.

17 οἴσετε The rare forms of sigmatic aorist with thematic conjugation οἶσε, οἰσέτω etc. are a feature of both Homer and Attic popular speech (Aristoph. *Ach.* 1099, 1101, 1122, *Ran.* 482: add to LSJ Alexis fr. 120 (Kock II 340), ? Herodas 7.19). Here and at vv. 31, 48, VI 136, 278.2, *SH* 283.3(?), Theocr. 24.48 their use is perhaps as poeticisms rather than colloquialisms: their status is indicated by Antimachus fr. 19.2 οἰσόντων which is a manifest imitation of *Od.* 8.254, and Theocr. 24.48, a reminiscence of *Il.* 15.718. Moeris s.v. remarks οἶσε Ἀττικοί· φέρε Ἑλληνικὸν καὶ κοινόν.[3]

---

[1] Note the antithesis χρῖσμα – μύρον. Several commentators misinterpret this passage; the novelty of the unguents lay not in their effeminacy but in their abundance to soldiers on a long march. All that the troops used were untreated oil extracts: Xenophon notes in passing that they also found perfumes available, but the men clearly regarded them as of little use to themselves.

[2] Aristoph. *Thesm.* 1114 quoted by LSJ for μικτός should be excluded: the Scythian archer's Greek was far from reliable.

[3] The occurrence of οἶσε in Herodas 7.19 (if sound: Headlam's reading has not been accepted by later editors) is evidence not for Hellenistic idiom but only for earlier Attic and Ionic. On the forms generally see Chantraine, *GH* I 416–19, K–B, *GG* II 103, Schwyzer, *GG* I 788. C.L.Prince, 'Some "Mixed Aorists" in Homer', *Glotta* 48 (1970) 155–63 discusses the origin of these forms: the examples in fourth-century B.C. comedy and Moeris' note must indicate that the Aristophanic instances cannot be 'parody of the grand style'.

ἀεὶ καλὸν ὄμμα τὸ τήνας Reverential statements like this occur elsewhere in C.'s Hymns, always as generalised summaries confirming or explaining what precedes and/or follows: e.g. II 68 ἀεὶ δ' εὔορκος Ἀπόλλων, III 258 Ἐφέσου γὰρ ἀεὶ τεὰ τόξα πρόκειται, IV 26 θεὸς δ' ἀεὶ ἀστυφέλικτος. (Cf. the address to Apollo at A.R. 2.708–9 αἰεί τοι, ἄναξ, ἄτμητοι ἔθειραι, | αἰὲν ἀδήλητοι and to Hestia at Delphi in *H.H.* 24.3; similar is fr. 7.12 (of the Graces) ἀπ' ὀστλίγγων δ' αἰὲν ἄλειφα ῥέει.) Thus ὄμμα here means not 'face', as translated by most editors,[1] but 'look', 'aspect'; for ὄμμα extended from the source of the impression to the impression itself cf. Soph. *El.* 903 ἐμπαίει τί μοι | ψυχῆι σύνηθες ὄμμα (where the scholiast glosses with ὅραμα), *Aj.* 1004 (when Ajax's corpse is uncovered) ὦ δυσθέατον ὄμμα, and cf. Eur. *Ion* 1261 ὦ ταυρόμορφον ὄμμα. (M.T.Smiley, *CQ* 14 (1920) 65 objected that 'a mirror could not have aided Athena to improve her eye if it had been unsightly' and proposed accepting δ's ἔνδυμα: however mention of clothing hardly coheres with what precedes, and, as Pfeiffer pointed out, ἔνδυμα is probably a gloss on ἔμμα mistakenly written for ὄμμα. In any case, make-up can be used to enhance the appearance of the eye.)

McKay's suggestion (*PP* 64ff.) that ἀεὶ καλὸν ὄμμα here alludes to a notorious demerit in the colour of Athena's eyes is unconvincing, and it is difficult to see precisely how a sinister reference to Athena Ὀξυδερκής would be relevant at this point in the poem. Prop. 2.28.9–12, Luc. *dial. deor.* 8, 20.10, and Hygin. *fab.* 165.2 are evidence only that Athena's grey eyes were occasionally the object of a cheap insult: the passages collected by D.R.Shackleton Bailey, *Propertiana* (Cambridge 1956) 119 (cf. Pease on Cic. *de nat. deor.* 1.83) in fact indicate that Athena was generally regarded as a

---

[1] ὄμμα never really denotes the face. In all the passages normally referred to for this meaning (see, for example, LSJ s.v. and Jebb on Soph. *Aj.* 977) ὄμμα either (1) means 'eye' plain and simple, or (2) as the most important single part of the body symbolises a thing or person especially precious or dear, or (3) is the source of impressions made on other people (not only are emotions evident in the eye, but also love, desire etc. are often described as originating in the eyes of the beloved). See the excellent discussion of ὄμμα in Schmidt, *SGS* I 371ff., and see further the passages discussed by Blaydes on Aristoph. *Ach.* 1184 ('pro eo quod animo voluptatem affert'), Di Benedetto on Eur. *Or.* 1082 and Barrett on Eur. *Hipp.* 246, p. 207.

Fraenkel felt compelled to remark in passing on Aesch. *Ag.* 1428 (p. 672 n. 1) that LSJ's 'face' for ὄμμα is incorrect, and refers to Kaibel on Soph. *El.* 903. A passage like Eur. *Hipp.* 86 κλύων μὲν αὐδῆς, ὄμμα δ' οὐχ ὁρῶν τὸ σόν is explained by *Il.* 23.66 where the features by which Achilles recognises Patroclus are size, voice, eyes, and clothes; as Eustath. 866.8 remarks τὰ ὄμματα ὡς ἀναγκαιότατον μέρος ἐπὶ τοῦ ὅλου προσώπου.

beautiful exception to the Greek dislike of grey eyes (cf. Theocr. 28.1, 20.25).

καλόν Standard terminology in hymnal descriptions of divine beauty (cf. on v. 5 μεγάλωϲ): I 55 καλὰ μὲν ἠέξευ, καλὰ δ' ἔτραφεϲ, οὐράνιε Ζεῦ, II 36 καὶ μὲν ἀεὶ καλὸϲ καὶ ἀεὶ νέοϲ . . . (Apollo).

τήναϲ Lexica and grammars are only partially correct in describing τῆνοϲ as the Doric equivalent of (ἐ)κεῖνοϲ: Ahrens, *DD* 267ff. and esp. 269e 'saepissime τῆνοϲ ad ea spectat, quae paullo ante commemorata sunt, ut Latinum is . . . Graecitas vulgaris hanc in sententiam αὐτόϲ adhibet, ubi nulla pronominis vis est, οὗτοϲ et rarius ἐκεῖνοϲ, ubi pronomini aliquid ponderis tribuitur.'

18–28 Exemplification of the second attribute by reference to another famous myth: this section is parallel to vv. 7–12, and οὐδ' ὄκα provides a formal 'refrain' link with v. 7. In addition to exemplifying an attribute of Athena this myth, like te first (see on vv. 5–12), also validates parts of the Argive ritual (vv. 29–32; see also Intro. p. 11).

Choice of the Judgement of Paris to illustrate Athena's beauty seems odd at first sight, since it was Aphrodite whom Paris chose as the most beautiful goddess. This oddity, however, turns out to be a deliberate Callimachean puzzle. In vv. 23–8 C. subsequently uses Theocritus' *Epithalamion to Helen* (see below on vv. 23ff.) to suggest that Athena is in fact identical in beauty with the exquisite Theocritean Helen (a pure Spartan athlete who habitually sang of the two virgin goddesses Artemis and Athena: Theocr. 18.35–7). Long before the Hellenistic period the Contest had come to be interpreted as rivalry between the different kinds of prowess represented by the three goddesses: in particular, masculine Athena and feminine Aphrodite were contrasted with one another.[1] C. maintains the traditional polarity, but by the rather academic artifice of the allusion to Theocritus suggests that Athena might well have been able to rival Aphrodite with an Artemisian kind of feminine beauty. Later in the narrative Athena has various other 'Artemisian' characteristics too (see Intro. pp. 19, 23 and on vv. 107–18), and indeed the effectiveness of the Tiresias story depends on Athena's credibility as a goddess with powerfully feminine qualities: the establishment of Athena early on in this section as a strong competitor in the Contest (against a rival who anyway won by deceit) is therefore important to the success of the poem as a whole.

18 τὰν Ἴδαι Ψ's Ἴδαν is impossible since the ethnic is not Ἴδοϲ but Ἰδαῖοϲ. The correction made independently by Stanley (see F.Wrangham in *Classical Journal* (London) 17 (1818) 361) and Bentley is essential. The

---

[1] See, e.g., Soph. frr. 360f., Eur. *IA*. 1304ff., *Tro*. 924ff., Isocr. *Hel*. 41ff., Chrysippus *apud* scholia to Eur. *Andr*. 277. For similar characterisation in vase-painting see C.Clairmont, *Das Parisurteil in der antiken Kunst* (Zürich 1951) *passim*.

simple locative dative is an almost entirely poetic (and mostly epic) feature: K–G, *GG* I 441ff., Schwyzer, *GG* II 154ff. Parallel in C. are 59.9 ἀγωνιστάς . . . τοὺς Ἐφύρηι, 67.6 τὴν Δήλωι . . . βουφονίην.

Φρύξ Allusion by 'antonomasia', especially with proper names, is common in C.: Lapp, *TF* 25ff. Cf. *E.* 27.3 ὁ Σολεύς = Aratus, *E.* 59.3 ὁ Φωκεύς = Pylades, where again the context provides enough clues for the person to be identified without difficulty.

Reference to Paris here as simply Φρύξ may conceivably have overtones of contempt: the Phrygian was proverbial in Greece as a worthless barbarian (*Suda* s.v. Φρύξ· Φρὺξ ἀνὴρ πληγεὶς ἀμείνων καὶ διακονέστερος, Men. *Asp.* 241f. Waiter: ποταπός π̣[οτ' εἶ;] | Daos: Φρύξ. W.: οὐδὲν ἱερόν· ἀνδρόγυνος; see also Headlam on Herodas 2.37 and 5.13). A nuance of this kind here would suggest at the outset that Paris' judgement was not too respectable ('a Phrygian') and would prepare the way for the diminution of Aphrodite in vv. 21ff. and the corresponding magnification of Athena.

ἐδίκαζεν Note the imperfect of duration.

ἔριν The Contest was traditionally so called: Eur. *IA* 183 ἔριν μορφᾶς, 1308 ἔριν καλλονᾶς. ἔρις of a competition not necessarily involving hostility (the ἀγαθὴ Ἔρις of Hes. *Op.* 24) is normal usage, not just 'in later poets' (LSJ): e.g. Hdt. 6.129, Thuc. 2.54, Xen. *Lac.* 4.2.

19–20 A couplet of typically Callimachean formulation: dicolon with something common to both cola expressed in only one. See Lapp, *TF* 38 and especially III 8f. οὔ σε φαρέτρην | οὐδ' αἰτέω μέγα τόξον, V 125f., 194.60f. Here as in vv. 125f. the delaying of the crucial verb until the second colon in the pentameter gives the couplet rapidity of movement.

19 οὔτ' . . . οὔτε Schneider's attempted defence of Ψ's οὐδέ (imported from 18 οὐδ' ὅκα . . .) was misplaced: the effect of double οὐδέ is to stress the first of the two objects negatived at the expense of the second (K–G, *GG* II 294: 'not even into a mirror, nor water'), whereas equal weight must be given to each ('not even when . . . did the goddess look either . . . or . . .').

ὀρείχαλκον A legendary substance of great beauty and value mentioned in the early poets (LSJ): Plato, *Crit.* 114E τὸ νῦν ὀνομαζόμενον μόνον τότε δὲ πλέον ὀνόματος ἦν τὸ γένος ἐκ γῆς ὀρυττόμενον ὀρειχάλκου . . . πλὴν χρυσοῦ τιμιώτατον ἐν τοῖς τότε ὄν (cf. Aristot. *An. Post.* 92b 22 where ὀρείχαλκος = 'a patently non-existent substance'). Ancient authors speculated ignorantly on its nature and occasionally even identified it with certain products, but without agreement or conviction[1] (cf. scholiast to A.R. 4.973).

[1] *Pace* H. Michell, *CR* 69 (1955) 21f. In Roman times some writers may have had a particular type of metal or alloy in mind, though often its association with gold (and silver) is no more than a rhetorical *topos*: see the passages quoted by Allen–Halliday–Sikes on *H.H.* 6.9.

The metonymy here of a mirror is unique[1] and comprises a kind of literary puzzle whose solution is first adumbrated in v. 19 (the second element of the compound was often used metonymically by poets, even though nowhere of a mirror: see on v. 21) and then confirmed in v. 21 by διαυγέα χαλκόν.

μεγάλα θεός The adjective is functional, magnifying Athena when her rival is about to be denigrated. Cf. also on v. 5 μεγάλως.

Cιμοῦντος The Simoeis flows into the Scamander north of Troy over 60 kilometres away from Mt Ida. Like the Scamander, however, the Simoeis came to symbolise the whole Trojan area (cf. Aesch. *Ag.* 696, Eur. *IA* 751, *Tro.* 810, Aristoph. *Thesm.* 110), and C. may have assumed that the Simoeis flowed close by, if not from, Ida because of *Il.* 4.474f. Cιμοείcιον, ὅν ποτε μήτηρ | Ἴδηθεν κατιοῦcα παρ' ὄχθηcιν Cιμόεντοc | γείνατ' (Cahen simply remarks that C. made a geographical error).

The name is usually uncontracted but cf. Hes. *Theog.* 342 θεῖόν τε Cιμοῦντα |.[2] Doric Cιμῶντοc should perhaps be read here (see on v. 1 λωτροχόοι, v. 4 cῶcθε, v. 138 τὦργον), although it is not attested elsewhere.

20 ἔβλεψεν βλέπειν was normal usage in Attic (LSJ) and the *koine* (e.g. A. Mauersberger, *Polybios-Lexikon* (Berlin 1956–), Mayser, *GGP* I² 171),[3] but being un-Homeric (except for *Batr.* 67) was avoided by A.R., Aratus, Nicander etc., though frequent in C., Theocr., Herodas, *AP* etc. Ψ's ἔβλεψαν is an elementary mistake possibly encouraged by the other -αν endings in v. 20.

δίναν The surface would need to be smooth for use as a looking-glass: in poetic diction δίνη ('eddy') commonly conveys little more than 'water' (e.g. Eur. *Tro.* 210 δίναν Εὐρώτα, *Or.* 1310). In Euphorion (?) fr. 175P Eutelides looks at himself δίνῃ ἐν ποταμοῦ.

Verbally similar is Eur. *IA* 751 Cιμόεντα καὶ δίναc ἀργυροειδεῖc.

διαφαινομέναν 'transparent': normal usage, though the use of the participle (stressing verbal activity) instead of διαφανήc is poetic. The analysis in LSJ, who quote the relevant testimony, can be clarified:

---

[1] The fact that the *Suda*, Photius, and the glossography at L.Bachmann, *Anecdota Graeca* (Leipzig 1828) I 320.5 gloss ὀρείχαλκοc with ὁ διαυγὴc χαλκόc, the very periphrasis used in v. 21 for a mirror, suggests that this was the metonymy's only occurrence known to the lexicographical tradition.

[2] Cιμουντίc: Eur. *Hec.* 641, Aristoph. *Thesm.* 110, Posidippus, *SH* 700.2; Cιμούντιοι: Eur. *Hel.* 250, *IA* 767, *Or.* 809.

[3] On the use of βλέπειν generally in classical and *koine* Greek see F.Thordarson, *Symb. Osl.* 46 (1971) 108–30.

transitive διαφαίνειν 'let a thing show through', gives rise to (a) passive διαφαίνεϲθαι 'appear through', (b) middle διαφαίνεϲθαι 'show something through in respect to oneself', i.e. 'be transparent'; διαφαίνεϲθαι (b) coincides almost exactly with intransitive διαφαίνειν as the verb of διαφανήϲ.

The word may have been suggested by (and pointed to) Theocr. 18.26 καλὸν διέφανε πρόϲωπον (see on 23–8 below).

21 οὐδ' Ἥρα Although only a subsidiary in this account of the Contest Hera is mentioned not just for completeness but also as a goddess of great importance to Argos. Ψ's Ionic ἥρη (Ἥρα Ernesti) infiltrated from Homeric usage (often in C. outside the Doric hymns).

21–2 Aphrodite's coquettishness and mirror were an early feature of the traditional account of the Contest and are represented in vase-painting and sculpture: see, e.g., C.Clairmont, *Das Parisurteil in der antiken Kunst* (Zürich 1951) 45, 48, 61 (twice), 63, 109. Literary references on vv. 18–28 above; in particular cf. Athen. 687c (=Soph. fr. 361) τὴν μὲν Ἀφροδίτην ἡδονήν τινα οὖϲαν δαίμονα (δαίμονα om. Kaibel, δαιμονίαν Pearson) μύρωι τε ἀλειφομένην παράγει καὶ κατοπτριζομένην, τὴν δὲ Ἀθηνᾶν φρόνηϲιν οὖϲαν καὶ νοῦν ἔτι δ' ἀρετὴν ἐλαίωι χριομένην καὶ γυμναζομένην.[1]

21 διαυγέα χαλκόν A striking periphrasis. διαυγήϲ, 'brilliant, radiant, translucent', normal usage but newly formed (first in Theophr. *H.P.* 3.7.5, fr. 1 (*de sens.*) 73, 77)[2], was popular amongst Hellenistic poets: A.R. 1.221, 2.1104, 4.1575, Nic. *Ther.* 726, ep. anon. *HE* 3800. χαλκόϲ is not otherwise used metonymically of a mirror.[3] The recurrence, therefore, of the phrase in Philetas, *HE* 3024f., a dedication on retirement by a hetaira of her equipment to Aphrodite (τὸν δὲ διαυγῆ | χαλκόν) suggests that C. may here be alluding to Philetas[4] and slightingly comparing Aphrodite to a human prostitute.

---

[1] Wilamowitz, *HD* II 16f. suggests that C. was drawing specifically on Sophocles' satyr-play; the combination of all the literary and artistic references, fragmentary though they are, indicates to my mind that the features which Sophocles and C. have in common were part of the general traditional account of the famous Judgement of Paris.

[2] Omitted by LSJ, whose reference to pseudo-Aristotle is of little significance. -αυγ- was a favourite with Hellenistic writers who coined many new derivatives: αὐγήειϲ, ἀπαυγάζειν, ἀπαυγή, διαυγάζειν, ἐν-, κατ-, ὑπ-.

[3] LSJ erroneously cite as parallels Aesch. fr. 670M and Theophr. *de ign.* 73: in neither is χαλκόϲ metonymical since in the former κάτοπτρον is expressed, and in the latter the material is expressly described as τρόπον τινα ἐργαϲθέντων.

[4] The epigram is early but the authorship is not certain since P heads the poem Φιλιτᾶ Ϲαμίου. There is no reason why this should not be the

The noteworthiness of the periphrasis is indicated by its repetition from C. by Nonn. *D.* 5.594, 42.79.

χαλκὸν ἑλοῖcα Homeric rhythm: χαλκὸν ἑλόντε *Il.* 23.803, χαλκὸν ἔλαccεν (-αι) *Il.* 13.388, 607 etc.

22 A typical gesture: Aphrodite with one hand adjusting her hair became a favourite motif in Hellenistic art after Apelles' famous portrait of Aphrodite Anadyomene (see Dümmler, *RE* I 2785f.). Here the goddess fussily attends several times to the same lock:[1] an anonymous scholar quoted by Ernesti aptly compared Tib. 1.8.10 *saepeque mutatas disposuisse comas*. Cf. also Nonn. *D.* 32.12f. πολλάκι δ' ἰcάζουcα καθειμένον ἄχρι μετώπου | πλαζομένηc ἔcτηcε μετήλυδα βότρυν ἐθείρηc.

μετέθηκε Normal usage mostly avoided by poetic diction.[2]

κόμαν The singular κόμη is almost always collective ('head of hair') like the plural, but of a single lock of hair is rare. This passage appears to be the only clear instance in the major authors of the specific singular, but it is a natural development in antithesis to the collective plural (θρίξ is similarly so used, as well as being collective, in antithesis to τρίχεc); Latin *coma* also occasionally denotes a single lock (Cat. 66.93, Mart. 5.68.1, Sen. *Phaedr.* 1182).

23–8 These lines contain a progressive and carefully marked echo of Theocritus 18.22–32 in which Helen's friends extol the beauty of Helen as compared with themselves (points of immediate verbal contact are underlined):

ἄμμεc δ' αἱ πᾶcαι cυνομάλικεc, αἷc δρόμοc ωὑτόc
χριcαμέναιc ἀνδριcτὶ παρ' Εὐρώταο λοετροῖc,
τετράκιc ἑξήκοντα κόραι, θῆλυc νεολαία,
τᾶν οὐδ' ἅτιc ἄμωμοc ἐπεί χ' Ἑλέναι παριcωθῆι.
Ἀὼc ἀντέλλοιcα καλὸν διέφανε πρόcωπον,
πότνια Νύξ, τό τε λευκὸν ἔαρ χειμῶνοc ἀνέντοc·
ὧδε καὶ ἁ χρυcέα Ἑλένα διεφαίνετ' ἐν ἁμῖν.
πιείραι μεγάλα ἅτ' ἀνέδραμε κόcμοc ἀρούραι
ἢ κάπωι κυπάριccοc, ἢ ἅρματι Θεccαλὸc ἵπποc,
ὧδε καὶ ἁ ῥοδόχρωc Ἑλένα Λακεδαίμονι κόcμοc· . . .
οὐ μὰν οὐδὲ λύραν τιc ἐπίcταται ὧδε κροτῆcαι
Ἄρτεμιν ἀείδοιcα καὶ εὐρύcτερνον Ἀθάναν
ὡc Ἑλένα, . . .

---

famous Philetas, but there may possibly have been two authors with the same name: see the discussion by Gow and Page in *HE* II 476.

[1] Curiously some editors have failed to see the point of this line and have argued that δίc . . . αὐτάν is intolerable repetition; most recently P. Maas who suggested ἁβράν for αὐτάν (*SJ*).

[2] Once in Homer (*Od.* 18.402: a problematic passage) and never in other epic writers or C.'s contemporaries.

The form which the echo takes is coincidence of detail in vv. 23–6, a link in v. 27, and finally climax in v. 28 which reveals the purpose of the quotation to be magnification of Athena: she is identified with the pure and exquisite kind of beauty represented by Helen, who combined femininity with very masculine Spartan athletics. Finally the echo is confirmed in v. 29.[1] There are many subsidiary points of contact betwen the two passages: both Athena and Helen are accompanied by a group of companions; in vv. 35ff. Helen sings not only of Artemis, divine symbol of Helen's pure beauty, but also of Athena; and the two poems have generally a number of linguistic details in common. Once the echo has been recognised extended mention of the Contest in a Hymn to Athena is seen to be a deliberate eccentricity, and Aphrodite's victory over her rivals is adequately countered by Athena's superior kind of beauty (especially after depiction in vv. 21f. of Aphrodite as vain and vulgar). When the warrior-goddess later punishes Tiresias for violation of her femininity her action is credible since she has already been represented as possessing unusual feminine qualities.

The passage is significant for evaluation of C.'s poetic technique: crucial to the poem is the establishment of Athena as a particularly feminine goddess and yet its success largely depends on recognition of diffuse quotation from another poem which has no intrinsic connection with Hymn v.

23–4 Introduction to the echo: the couplet picks up most of Theocr. 18.22–4. Note the key-word in Theocr. v. 23 λοετροῖϲ.

23 δὶϲ ἑξήκοντα Theocr. v. 24 τετράκιϲ ἑξήκοντα. F.Altheim, *Epochen der römischen Geschichte* II (Frankfurt 1935) 133 pertinently notes that the phraseology here makes for a pointed contrast with Aphrodite in v. 22 δὶϲ μετέθηκε κόμαν. As Spanheim remarked, the distance run by Athena was exceptional, being four times that run by Plato's hoplite in *Leg.* 833B ἑξήκοντα μὲν ϲταδίων μῆκοϲ. However, the number should probably not be interpreted as accurate measurement: ἑξήκοντα often expressed no more than an undefined large number (e.g. III 13, VI 130, Nic. fr. 74.13, Cleobulus in Diehl, *Anth. Lyr. Gr.* I 129). For other examples of gods' accomplishments on a characteristically enormous scale see Kleinknecht, *LP* 321 n. 5.

διαθρέξαϲα διαύλωϲ Theocr. v. 22 αἷϲ δρόμοϲ ωὑτόϲ.

διαθρέξαϲα A literary archaism (like ἔθρεξαν in 383.8 and θρέξειϲ at Lyc. 108). The suppletive -θρεξ- forms of τρέχειν which featured in Ionic (Homer) and colloquial Attic (often in comedy) gave way early to -δραμ-

---

[1] There is no external evidence to confirm that Theocritus' *Epithalamion* antedates v, only the internal, but adequate, indicator that whereas a reference by C. to T. has point within v, a reminiscence by T. of C. would be entirely gratuitous.

forms and were obsolete by the third century B.C. (Cf. Mayser, *GGP* I² 198f. etc.: instances listed in Veitch, *GV* 648f., K–B, *GG* II 554f.; most grammars incorrectly describe the suppletive forms as 'poetic'.)

24–5 The comparison with Castor and Polydeuces firmly establishes the reference to Theocritus. Although the Dioscuri were famous Doric representatives and patrons of athletic achievement, Athena was herself renowned for athletic prowess and physical strength and stands to gain nothing from a comparison with them as a runner.[1] Mention of the Dioscuri does, however, establish the presence of the person most closely connected with them, their sister Helen;[2] hence too the emphasis on their nationality (Λακεδαιμόνιοι, suspended at end of v. 24 before | ἀϲτέρεϲ), unnecessary to v but suggestive for Helen Λακεδαίμονι κόϲμοϲ (Theocr. v. 31).

24 παρ' Εὐρώται Theocr. v. 23 παρ' Εὐρώταο λοετροῖϲ. Mention of the Eurotas in association with the Dioscuri was something of a poetic formula: e.g. Theogn. 1087f. Κάϲτορ καὶ Πολύδευκεϲ, οἳ ἐν Λακεδαίμονι δίηι | ναίετ' ἐπ' Εὐρώτα καλλιρόωι ποταμῶι, Pind. *I.* 5.33 Κάϲτοροϲ δ' αἰχμὰ Πολυδεύκεόϲ τ' ἐπ' Εὐρώτα ῥεέθροιϲ, Aristoph. *Lys.* 1301f. Τυνδαρίδαϲ τ' ἀγαϲώϲ, | τοὶ δὴ πὰρ Εὐρώταν ψιάδδοντι. (Reference to the river to indicate locality is a traditional poetic formulation: e.g. Bacch. 3.6f. παρ' εὐρυδίναν ['Αλφεόν, 5.38 'Αλφεὸν παρ' εὐρυδίναν, Pind. *O.* 1.20 ὅτε παρ' 'Αλφεῶι: so later Virgil, *Aen.* 1.498 *qualis in Eurotae ripis* adapting *Od.* 6.103 ἢ κατὰ Τηΰγετον . . .)

τοί Doric as well as Homeric (Buck, *GD* 100).

25 ἀϲτέρεϲ Significant at two levels: the Dioscuri were not only illustrious persons (a common metaphorical denotation of ἀϲτήρ[3]), they

---

[1] Thus Kleinknecht, *LP* 309 felt impelled to remark: 'Im übrigen sind derlei überraschende und kurze, meist mythologische Andeutungen, die den Zusammenhang gelegentlich fast zu unterbrechen scheinen, bei K. geradezu Stil. (In unserem Gedicht sei nur an die Einführung der Λακεδαιμόνιοι ἀϲτέρεϲ in Vers 24/25 erinnert.)' Kleinknecht's solution ('Stil') was wrong, but he was right to discern a problem.

[2] It is worth noting that in Ptolemaic Egypt, where the cult of the Dioscuri was, as elsewhere in the Hellenistic world, very popular, Helen was particularly closely associated with her brothers: see C.E.Visser, *Götter und Kulte im ptolemäischen Alexandrien* (Amsterdam 1938) 19f., H.C.Youtie, *ZPE* 16 (1975) 272 and literature there cited, and F.Chapouthier, *Les Dioscures au service d'une déesse* (Paris 1935). For the indigenous Pisidian type representing two horsemen on either side of a goddess see L.Robert, *BCH* 107 (1983) 553–79.

[3] LSJ and Supplement s.v. are woefully inadequate: add Aristoph. *Ran.* 342, Plato, *Epigr.* 4.5D, Simias, *HE* 3281, Call. 67.8. Outstanding people are compared with stars early in similes: *Il.* 6.401, 11.62, 22.26, Alcm.

were also considered actually to manifest themselves as stars and the star is one of the symbols which accompanies and characterises them on monuments and coins.[1] (Is reference to the Dioscuri's astral existence complementary to Theocritus' comparison of Helen in vv. 26–8 to Dawn rising out of Night?)

ἐμπεράμως Emphatically placed at the beginning of its colon. The word is a new variant on ἔμπειρος, possibly a Callimachean coinage (here and I 71), used only in poetry (full citations in LSJ), and its mode of formation is obscure: the only other examples of -αμος as an adjectival suffix being ἰταμός, a doublet of ἴτης, and κάδαμος (Hesych., Salaminian for τυφλός). The origins of nouns in -αμος are also mostly obscure or non-Hellenic (Chantraine, *FN* 132ff.).

The normal ἐμπείραμος (Lyc. 1196: C., not Lyc., deviates from the norm, *pace* Schmitt, *NDK* 98) is here shortened for metrical reasons: this is an uncommon reversal of the more usual Homeric practice of lengthening short syllables (cf. Chantraine, *GH* I 98ff.);[2] parallel is Soph. fr. 464 ἐμπἔρής (= ἔμπειρος).[3]

25–6 ἐνετρίψατο . . . χρίματα Theocr. v. 23 χρισαμέναις ἀνδριστί.

25 ἐνετρίψατο Ψ's ἐτρίψατο was corrected by Meineke (p. 245): 'aliud est τρίβειν χρῖμα vel μύρον, aliud ἐντρίβεσθαι, illud est terere, macerare, subigere, alterum inungui. itaque ἐτρίψατο non minus inepte dictum est, quam si quis vel latine "trivit sibi unguentum" diceret pro "intrivit", vel nostra lingua "reiben" pro "einreiben".' Similarly M. corrected Antiphanes fr. 148 (Kock II 71f.) σμῆται, κτενίζετ', ἐκβέβηκε, τρίβεται to ἐκβέβηκ', ἐντρίβεται. Unless Meineke's corrections are accepted these are the only two examples of simple τρίβεσθαι = 'rub *in*, *on*': τρίβειν and ἐντρίβειν (particularly common with cosmetics) are both well documented. The evidence quoted by Pfeiffer in support of ἐτρίψατο in his app. crit. (rather muddled at this point) is unconvincing: (a) Ap. Dysc. *Gramm. Graec.* II 2.296.4ff. discussing the middle voice uses as an example 'ἐτριψάμην'. The word could mean anything, and the editor Uhlig suggested '"detritus" vel "detersus sum mea ipsius opera" quod fortasse in palaestris audiebatur' (mistakenly quoted by Pfeiffer as a scholion): even if Uhlig were correct this would be evidence only for second century A.D.; (b) to support his

---

PMG 3 fr. 3.66, Soph. *El.* 66, Aristoph. *Av.* 1710, A.R. 1.774, 2.40–2 (Polydeuces), Theocr. (?) 25.140.

[1] F.Chapouthier, *Les Dioscures* 114f., 141ff. The earliest unambiguous literary testimony for the belief that they appeared as actual stars is in Euripides: *El.* 990f., *Hel.* 140, 1495ff., *Or.* 1636, *Tro.* 1000f.; for later evidence see *RE* V 1096f.

[2] ει is commonly shortened to ε but only before vowels: K–B, *GG* I 137f.

[3] Cf. also αἴγερος for αἴγειρος and κύπερος for κύπειρος.

suggestion Uhlig referred to part of Heliodorus' commentary on Dion. Thrax, *Gramm. Graec.* I 3.401.26ff. (*sic*). In discussing the middle and passive Heliodorus uses as examples ἐτριψάμην ἠλειψάμην: the examples are Heliodorus' own (not Dionysius': see *Gramm. Graec.* I 1.48f.) so that even were the meaning of ἐτριψάμην inferable from this passage it would be valid only for the Byzantine period.

The correption ἐνĕτρ. is rare in C. but can be paralleled: in elegiacs at 18.10, 43.60, *E.* 11.1 and possibly 1.44, and in a Doric context at VI 35. Cf. Pfeiffer on 544.

λιτά A very common adjective which developed in the fourth century B.C.[1] in normal usage: hence although common in C. and epigrammatists it is avoided by A.R.[2] Again at 110.78 of unguents.

λαβοῖcα Ψ seems to have had a variant here. Pfeiffer accepts βαλοῖcα, and Wilamowitz read βαλοῖcα in his third edition but changed to λαβοῖcα in his fourth. βαλοῖcα is difficult for the same reason as ἐτρίψατο: more precise indication of locality is needed, and simple βάλλειν, 'put', cannot be used like προcβάλλειν without supporting clarification from the context. ἐνετρίψατο might just make βαλοῖcα possible, but λαβοῖcα still seems preferable.[3]

26 τᾶc ἰδίαc ἔκγονα φυταλιᾶc The oil from Athena's olive-tree. The expression is not gratuitously periphrastic or allusive by Greek criteria; poetic idiom commonly describes an object by reference to the divinity in whose provenance it comes: e.g. Theocr. 2.120f. μᾶλα μὲν ἐν κόλποιcι Διωνύcοιο φυλάccων, | κρατὶ δ' ἔχων λεύκαν, Ἡρακλέοc ἱερὸν ἔρνοc.

τᾶc ἰδίαc ὁ ἴδιοc reflexive = 'οὐκ ἀλλότριοc' is rare in the classical period (see LSJ: usually = 'οὐ κοινόc', 'private') but normal usage in the *koine* (Mayser, *GGP* II$^{2.1}$ 73f.: 231 instances are recorded in Polybius). For this reason, doubtless, it is avoided almost entirely by poetic writers, occurring only in C. and [Theocr.] 23.54 (a late Hellenistic work). The article, mostly omitted elsewhere in V, is unnecessary in poetic diction[4] and emphasises the ordinariness of ἰδίαc.

---

[1] The fragmentary Alcaeus 121]ε λίτωc is probably from λιτόc = 'supplicatory, supplicated'.

[2] Not in bucolic poetry; Aratus 824.

[3] LSJ s.v. B.II cite two references for βάλλεcθαι 'dash oneself, bathe', but neither is relevant here: in *H.H.Dem.* 50 expression of χρόα and in Eur. *Or.* 303 of ἐπὶ χροόc (Triclinius: ἐπὶ χροΐ codd.) gives the verb greater precision than in C. (cf. V. Di Benedetto and W. Biehl on *Or.* 303). Jebb on Soph. *Phil.* 67 cites a number of Sophoclean passages where βάλλειν stands for ἐμ- or προc-: each instance has a locative dative to clarify the verb.

[4] Cf., e.g., 55.2 ἴδιόν περ ἑὸν λάχοc; with article at *E.* 56.2.

ἔκγονα 'offspring'. Usually of humans or animals, ἔκγονον of inanimates is uncommon; Soph. *OT* 171 ἔκγονα κλυτᾶς χθονός is apparently live metaphor, but frequent use in Plato of ἔκγονον of abstracts (e.g. *Hipp. Mai.* 297B τὸ ἔργον αὐτῶν καὶ τὸ ἔκγονον . . . τὸ ἀγαθόν) is confirmed as normal by Hipp. *Flat.* 5 τὰ νοσήματα τούτου [πνεύματος] ἔκγονα.[1] χρίματα . . . ἔκγονα φυταλιᾶς is thus hardly metaphorical even if an unusual expression.[2] Critias fr. 2.12 Diels uses the noun similarly at the climax to an aetiological list: τὸν δὲ τροχὸν γαίας τε καμίνου τ' ἔκγονον ηὗρεν | κλεινότατον κέραμον . . .

φυταλιᾶς A rare and probably poetic word, favoured by Hellenistic poets, apparently = 'growth', 'plant(ing)'. Previously in literature φυτ. appears only in the Homeric formula τέμενος . . . | καλὸν φυταλιῆς καὶ ἀρούρης (*Il.* 6.195, 12.314, 20.185), but the Hellenistic writers do not use it as a Homeric archaism even though it may have been a purely literary word. The wide range of usage and its occurrence in two widely separated inscriptions suggest that it had a more complex history than now appears from the surviving evidence (fifth century B.C. Crete: *Inscr. Cret.* 4.43Ba 2; third century B.C. Delos: *IG* XI[2] 161 A 14). φυταλιά should probably be understood as a broadly used abstract collective:[3] 'garden, orchard (plantation)' in Homer[4], A.R. 3.1400, (?) anon. third-century B.C. elegy in *P. Hamb.* Inv. 381 (Powell, *CA* 131 = Page, *GLP* 110 = *SH* 958) 4, 'bed', 'growth' in anon. *HE* 3885, 'growth', 'growing', 'planting' in Leonidas, *HE* 2542, A.R. 2.1002f.,[5] and finally of individual 'growth', 'tree' here and Arat. 333 (φυταλιαί . . . ἀναλδέα φυλλιόωσαι).

MS C (and its copy B) has only φυται here, and at v. 83 only ἀνῖ (for ἀνῖαι): perhaps an ancestor with 28 or 29 lines to each side had a mark or damage which extended through two pages (in *CQ* 15 (1921) 116 n. 1 Smiley suggests that hyparchetype ʒ had 30 lines to the side).

27–8 The cool description of Athena's exquisite beauty even (or

---

[1] And in later writers this usage is common: see, e.g., Leisegang's *Index* to Philo Alex., Lampe, *PGL* etc.

[2] The expression is eased by the associative field of ἔκγονος: γόνος, γέν(ν)ημα, τέκος, τεκνοῦσθαι etc. are often used of inanimates.

[3] See Chantraine, *FN* 82 who suggests that most -ιά nouns may be collectives.

[4] Cf. Eustath. 907.37 κατὰ τοὺς παλαιοὺς χωρίον δενδρόφυτον (cf. 636. 17) and Hesych. and *Suda* s.v. (κῆπος etc.).

[5] Commentators remark on the strangeness of A.R.'s use of φυταλιά for the *activity* of planting, but cf. the unique usage in Hipp. *Hebd.* 4 of the season of planting: Greek abstract nouns are often used without firm distinction between active and passive. σπορητός has exactly the same range of usages: 'sown corn' Aesch. *Ag.* 1392, 'sowing of corn' Xen. *HG* 4.6.13, 'time of sowing' Hipp. *Hebd.* 4, 11.

especially) after such immense exertions has a wry humour reminiscent of Polydeuces fighting Amycus in Theocr. 22.113f. ὁ δ' αἰεὶ πάccονα γυῖα | αὔξομένου φορέεcκε πόνου καὶ χροιῆι ἀμείνω.

27 ὦ κῶραι The vocative is almost exclamatory as the description of Athena's beauty nears its climax, and, like λωτροχόοι at v. 134, reintroduces the girls when they have been unmentioned for ten lines but are about to receive instructions again.

Reference to the celebrants here may be additionally significant. V. 27 prepares for the climax in v. 28 of the reminiscence from Theocr. (cf. on v. 27 ἀνέδραμε), and ὦ κῶραι could be an initial pointer: Athena's band of girl attendants in the cult procession (and later the nymphs who accompany her in the narrative) are parallel to Helen's κόραι, θῆλυc νεολαία (v. 24).

Loss of post-consonantal ϝ in the combinations νϝ, ρϝ, λϝ was accompanied by a lengthening of the preceding vowel in some Ionic and Doric areas: thus κόρϝα (Corinth, Messenia) became κώρα in Crete, in contrast to Attic κόρα. Only Argolic on the Doric mainland featured this compensatory lengthening,[1] and C. uses it throughout v; however, κώρα, μῶνοc etc. occur also in VI and throughout Theocritus' Doric poems and would appear to have been regarded (incorrectly) by the Hellenistic writers as a general Doric feature, though Theocritus also uses the unlengthened forms as alternatives.[2] See Monteil, *T* 33; cf. on v. 7 φέροιcα, v. 8 ἦνθ', v. 97 βαλεῦ.

τὸ δ' ἔρευθοc ἀνέδραμε The fresh flush of youthful beauty. Cf. the descriptions of the beautiful Eros: A.R. 3.121f. γλυκερὸν δέ οἱ ἀμφὶ παρειάc | χροιῆc θάλλεν ἔρευθοc; and Jason, when joyously taking the fleece, compared to a young girl: A.R. 4.172f. καί οἱ ἐπὶ ξανθῆιcι παρηίcιν ἠδὲ μετώπωι | μαρμαρυγῆι ληνέων φλογὶ εἴκελον ἶζεν ἔρευθοc. Cf. Pollux, *Onom.* 2.87 καὶ ἀνθοῦcαι παρειαί, καὶ εὐανθεῖc, καὶ ἐρυθαινόμεναι, λάμπουcαι, cτίλβουcαι, ἐρυθριῶcαι etc. Cf. the rather overwritten description of a beautiful woman in Chaeremon fr. 1 Snell (*TGF* I 71) 3–4 αἰδὼc δ' ἐπερρύθμιζεν ἠπιώτατον | ἐρύθημα λαμπρῶι προcτιθεῖcα χρώματι.

ἔρευθοc An uncommon literary form. The *koine* used only ἐρυθ- forms almost without exception,[3] the noun being ἐρύθημα (fifth century B.C. on: often in Hippocrates, Aristotle etc.); Hellenistic literary vocabulary has not only the *koine* forms but also ἐρευθ- forms, apparently for metrical convenience (ἐρεύθεcθαι is doublet to ἐρύθειν, ἐρυθαίνειν). ἔρευθοc is rare before the Alexandrians (A.R., Arat., [Mosch.]) but its occurrence in

---

[1] Bechtel, *GD* II 445, Thumb, *GD* I 115, Buck, *GD* 54f.

[2] Ψ's κόραι was clearly an attempt to 'normalise' the Doric κῶραι (correctly restored by Stephanus).

[3] See indices to *LXX*, *N.T.*, Polybius, papyri etc. Hesychius glosses ἔρευθοc with ἐρύθημα. Before the Hellenistic period ἐρευθ- forms seem to be restricted largely to Ionic (prose and poetry).

Hipp. *Epid.* 1.26 case 5 and later in Philo Alex. I 210.7 etc. suggests that it was not a restricted poeticism.

ἀνέδραμε Theocr. v. 29 ἀνέδραμε. The shared verb is the introductory point of contact between vv. 27f. and Theocr. vv. 29–31, linking Athena to Helen. The contexts for the verb are similar: the growth of plants, denoted by the verb in Theocritus, is picked up by C. in the ensuing simile.

The verb is in each case normal usage, though lexica are not very helpful. Of plants: Hdt. 8.55, Theophr. *C.P.* 1.12.2, 3.23.3; similarly ἀναδρομή in Theophr. *C.P.* 4.5.1, 4.11.3, Hesych. Of flushes, coloration etc. ἀνατρέχειν, questioned by Meineke p. 245f., is not common (*Il.* 23. 717, Hipp. *Epid.* 7.110) but the prose instance indicates normal rather than poetic usage, and similar use of other compounds supports this: ἀμφιτρέχειν: Pind. *P.* 3.39, ἐπιτρέχειν: *Od.* 6.45, Hipp. *Prorrh.* 2.40, Arat. 80, 834 (ἔρευθος), A.R. 2.670, ξυντρέχειν: Hipp. *Acut. Sp.* 7, ὑποτρέχειν: Sappho fr. 31.10, Hipp. *Fract.* 27 (ἔρευθος). Cf. Numenius of Heracleia in Σ Nic. *Ther.* 237 ὑπόχλωρόν ⟨γε⟩ μὲν ἕλκος | κοιλαίνει· τὸ δὲ πολλὸν ἀνέδραμεν αὐτόθεν οἶδος (*SH* 590).

27–8 The allusion to Theocritus reaches a climax in these lines, and after the initial reference ἀνέδραμε, πρώϊον οἵαν prepares the way. Although the beginning of a new subordinate clause after the bucolic diaeresis is regular, the lack of indication as to how the syntactical structure will develop is not: πρώϊον οἵαν as a phrase leaves in suspense the nouns which each word might qualify and their relationship to one another in the overall syntactical structure.[1] This 'syntactical tension' concentrates attention on two words in v. 28, ῥόδον and χροϊάν. (The delaying of the crucial χροϊάν to the end of v. 28 increases the concentration.) The allusion focuses on Theocr. v. 31 ὧδε καὶ ἁ ῥοδόχρως Ἑλένα: Athena at her moment of beauty suggests the incomparable Helen.

The objects of comparison in v. 28 support the allusion to Theocritus: each is symbolic of Helen's patroness Aphrodite (see below), and the two passages are structurally similar, each containing a comparison (οἵαν – ἅτε) and a set of alternatives (ἤ . . . ἤ . . .). At the climax of the heightened description C. expropriates even the symbols of the rival Aphrodite to enhance Athena's beauty.

27–8 πρώϊον . . . ῥόδον The force of the adjective is not completely

---

[1] IV 125f. οἷος ἔφεδρος | οὔρεος ἐξ ὑπάτου σκοπιὴν ἔχει exemplifies regular practice: the clausula of v. 125 is a syntactically complete element for which a predicate can be expected in v. 126. The delaying of relative οἵαν so as to conceal the syntactical construction as long as possible (instead of οἵαν πρώϊον) is also rare: there seems to be no exact parallel for this sixth-foot relative (in Mosch. 2.80, 82 the delay has the very different effect of supporting the anaphoric patterning).

clear. πρώϊος can mean either 'early in the day' or 'early in the year'; here it has presumably the latter meaning, the rose by its earliness symbolising spring freshness: cf. *LXX* Sirach 50.8 where the exalted Simon is compared (ὡς ἀστὴρ ἑωθινός . . .) ὡς ἄνθος ῥόδων ἐν ἡμέραις νέων, Rhianus, *HE* 3206f. τόσσον δ' Ἐμπεδοκλῆς φανερώτερος ὅσσον ἐν ἄλλοις | ἄνθεσιν εἰαρινοῖς καλὸν ἔλαμψε ῥόδον.[1] (Theocr. 20.15f. uses a similar image to describe anger and embarrassment sympathetically: ἐμοὶ δ' ἄφαρ ἔζεσεν αἷμα, | καὶ χρόα φοινίχθην ὑπὸ τὤλγεος ὡς ῥόδον ἔρσαι.)

27 οἵαν οἷον Ψ by assimilation to πρώϊον. Stephanus' Doric οἵαν is preferable to Lascaris' Epic/Ionic οἵην.

28 σίβδας κόκκος As the fruit ripens pomegranate seeds go from red through green to red again: [Aristot.] *de color.* 799ª 9ff. τὸ μὲν γὰρ ἐξ ἀρχῆς οἱ κόκκοι [ῥοιᾶς] γίνονται φοινικοῖ . . .[2]

The Doric form σιβδ- (Attic σιδ-) is attested only here, but Hesychius has an entry σίβδαι· ῥοιαί, and Steph. Byz. notes a Carian city Σίβδη; cf. Frisk, *EW* s.v. Ernesti's -ας (-ης: Ψ) completes the Doricisation.

Both rose and pomegranate were sacred to Aphrodite from the earliest recorded times and appear in cult practice, literature, and visual representations:[3] here they bring extra validification to the description of Athena's female beauty.

---

[1] Those who interpret πρώϊον as 'early in the day' may find mild (and late) support in [Virg.] *de rosis nascentibus* 15ff. *ambigeres raperetne rosis Aurora ruborem | an daret et flores tingeret orta dies. | ros unus, color unus, et unum mane duorum* (where, however, the context is explicit: the author takes an early morning walk in the garden), in the *Pervigilium Ven.* VI *en pudorem florulentae praediderunt purpurae | . . . ut recenti mane nudae virgines nubant rosae*, and in Heliodorus, *Aeth.* 5.13.3 ἡ μὲν γὰρ ἀδρανεῖ τῶι ἄνθει φοινίσσεται καὶ ῥόδωι προσέοικεν ἐκ καλύκων ἄρτι πρὸς πέταλα σχιζομένωι καὶ πρῶτον ἡλιακαῖς ἀκτῖσιν ἐρευθομένωι.

For the rose as the proverbial sign of spring cf. Cic. *Verr.* 2.5.27 *cum rosam viderat, tum incipere ver arbitrabatur*, Colum. 12.28.3, Plin. *N.H.* 21.38.1 (repeating Theophr. *H.P.* 6.8.2). In Egypt the rose appeared even two months earlier than in mainland Greece: Theophr. *H.P.* 6.8.5 προτερεῖν δέ φασι τῶν ἐνταῦθα καὶ ῥόδα καὶ ἴα καὶ τὰ ἄλλα ἄνθη καὶ διμήνωι.

[2] Cahen's strictures on C.'s disregard for accuracy are thus unnecessary.

[3] The rose needs little illustration: see C.Boetticher, *Der Baumkultus der Hellenen* (Berlin 1856) 456–60, J.Murr, *Die Pflanzenwelt in der griech. Mythologie* (Innsbruck 1890) 78–83, V.Hehn, *Kulturpflanzen und Hausthiere* (Berlin 1902⁷) 247ff., C.Joret, *La Rose dans l'antiquité* (Paris 1892) 45–87. For the pomegranate (often called simply μῆλον) see Murr, *op. cit.* 50–5. Representations in statues and painting of Aphrodite with pomegranate: Roscher, *LM* I 411, *RE* I 2767, 2779–87, Farnell, *CGS* II 670ff. See also F.Muthmann, *Der Granatapfel* (Schriften der Abegg-Stiftung Bern VI:

(οἷαν . . . ῥόδον) . . . ἔχει χροϊάν The phraseology is normal: Theophr. *H.P.* 1.13.1 καὶ ὅcα δή φαcιν ἐν τῆι ἔξω θαλάττηι ῥόδων ἔχειν τὴν χρόαν.

χροϊάν The final word of the simile provides a link back to the main point of comparison: χροιά denotes not only 'surface-appearance, colour', but also 'skin' and particularly its complexion (LSJ).

The diaeresis, although not recorded elsewhere for χροιά, is consistent with general poetic practice (K–B, *GG* I 243ff.). Commonest in Homer is Τροΐη, but poetic diaeresis is applied generally to -οια nouns: III 230 ἀπλοΐη is another Callimachean innovation.[1]

Ψ's χροιήν is an elementary corruption to the Epic/Ionic form.

29–32 The long first part of the poem closes, as it began, with four lines addressed to the celebrants, this time containing instructions deriving directly from the preceding mythological *exemplum*. The point has been demonstrated that Athena need not, by being unfeminine, be any less beautiful than masculine Helen, and vv. 29f. give it final and forceful expression. The comb for her hair is doubtless no extravagance: it presumably featured in the actual Argive ritual.

29 τῶι καὶ νῦν Homeric in tone: for τῶι καί – see Ebeling, *LH* II 353, as also for the common τῶι νῦν (or τῶι – νῦν) which is a regular Homeric introduction to an imperative. Again at *E.* 44.5.

ἄρcεν τι Theocr. v. 23 χριcαμέναιc ἀνδριcτί: in conclusion C. refers back to the early part of the Theocritus passage.

Bergk's τι is much preferable to Ψ's τε which has to be linked with v. 31 καί in the face of οἴcετε.

κομίccατε There are strong arguments for Schneider's κομίξατε since in West Greek -ζειν verbs had ξ in the aorist forms (Buck, *GD* § 142) and Theocritus uses them almost without exception in his Doric poems (Monteil, *T* 46).[2] However, caution is advisable here because VI 101 ἐκτερέϊξαν, the only certain example of a ξ aorist in C., is probably a Homericism (LSJ): elsewhere in C. MSS have the sigmatic forms (V 10, 40, VI 4, 35, fr. 228.48) and although the two examples in V might be explained as conforming to Argolic practice, which avoids ξ after a preceding guttural, the same cannot be true of the other instances. -ξ- may be correct, but it can be read only on the assumption that the MSS have normalised

---

Bern 1982) and especially pp. 39–52 for Aphrodite (plentifully illustrated). The fruit has the same associations in Semitic belief, to which much of the Greek Aphrodite is owed (W.W.G.Baudissin, *Studien zur semitischen Religionsgesch.* (Leipzig 1878) II 207–9).

[1] On the etymology of χροιά (χρο-ιά) see Frisk, *EW* s.v. Schmitt, *NDK* 43 suggests that perhaps *Il.* 14.164 χροιῆι should also be resolved to χροϊῆι.

[2] 2.84 ἐφραcάμην (and possibly 24 καππυρίcαcα) seems to be the only non-ξ form, admitted presumably for metrical reasons.

every instance with a consistency which they apply to the normalisation of no other Doric form.

μῶνον Ahrens, *DD* 162 and K–B, *GG* I 130 suspect μῶνος of being a hyper-Dorism created by poetic analogy. However, it is probably the result of dialectal compensatory lengthening following lost post-consonantal ϝ, as κῶραι in v. 27 (see note): none of the areas which exhibit such lengthening (the Argolid is one) have yet provided any inscriptional evidence for any form of μόνος, but μῶνος is testified again in v. 132, VI 8, 112 (whence Ernesti correctly emended Ψ's μουν- to μων- here and at v. 75 and VI 93) and Theocr. 2.64, 20.45 (also correctly restored by Wilamowitz at 18.18). μόνος is also admitted for metrical reasons: vv. 108, 129, *E.* 46.5, 59.4.

30 A 'trick' line. The first half is shaped as if for an exact doublet, and the heavy anaphora ᾧι . . . ᾧι (verb delayed) with the καί in the second colon strengthening the parallelism, suggests that Castor must be accompanied, as in the preceding myth (vv. 24f.), so here (τῶι καὶ νῦν), by his brother: but the extravagant preparation instead furnishes a surprise riddle – Heracles. Polydeuces, already implied in vv. 24f., is here referred to only elliptically through mention of his brother.[1]

καί Protreptic, linking Castor with Heracles. Placing of a protreptic before the pentameter diaeresis to heighten anticipation became something of a stylistic affectation among the early Hellenistic writers, especially with the definite article: see Gow–Page on Asclepiades, *HE* 913, Leonidas, *HE* 2119f., Meleager, *HE* 4095, and cf. on v. 103 οὐ παλινάγρετον. καί is apparently similarly placed at fr. 31e (Addenda II).

χρίεται Theocr. v. 23 χρισαμέναις. The correption is unusual at this point in the line. Cf. on v. 89 ὄψεαι.

Ἡρακλέης Like Castor Heracles symbolises (masculine) athletic prowess. It was he who introduced, at Olympia, the wild olive (Pind. *O.* 3), which was regarded by the Greeks, incorrectly, as male (ἄρσεν τι . . . ἔλαιον).[2] Heracles fits easily into the context of the Hymn: Argos was the city with which he was most closely associated (*RE* Suppl. III 910f.), and in so far as he had a patroness it was Athena (*RE* Suppl. III 1096f.).

-έης The poetic form, Attic and the *koine* contracting to Ἡρακλῆς (see Zwicker in *RE* VIII 517f.).

31–2 Cf. A.R. 3.45ff. (Aphrodite) κόμας . . . κόσμει χρυσείηι διὰ κερκίδι,

---

[1] Kleinknecht, *LP* 322 n. 2 points out that it was something of a feature of Hellenistic style to refer to a well-known pair by mentioning only one of the two: cf. Prop. 2.1.23, 4.11.21. Again in C. at 64.11 οὐδ' ὑμέας, Πολύδευκες, ὑπέτρεσεν . . .

[2] In contrast to the female domestic olive: see Arthur Platt, *CQ* 4 (1910) 164–6 explaining Soph. *Trach.* 1196 ἄρσενα . . . ἄγριον ἔλαιον.

μέλλε δὲ μακρούς | πλέξαςθαι πλοκάμους; like C., A.R. draws on *Il.* 14.175ff. (see below).

31 οἱ The only word before which 'unsoftened' hiatus is permitted in v (again at vv. 38, 63, 127; see on v. 71 κράναι Ἑλ.): like other Alexandrians C. admits hiatus before originally digammated words (see Gow on Theocritus 8.14f., Mooney, *The Argonautica* (London 1912) pp. 419f.).

παγχρύςεον It has not been generally remarked that Attic (and subsequently the *koine*) uses suffix -εος for adjectives of material which are *un*compounded, but for *compounds* only the suffix -ος, in spite of many Homeric compounds in -εος. Homeric χάλκεος becomes Attic χαλκοῦς, but Homeric παγχάλκεος is transformed by Attic into πάγχαλκος.[1] Pindar, Sophocles and Euripides use only πάγχρυσος: here as in A.R. 4.120, 1397, 1434 -εον is specifically Homeric.

31–2 ὡς . . . πλόκαμον This section alludes ironically to *Il.* 14.175ff. where Hera prepares herself to seduce Zeus: τῶι ῥ' ἥ γε χρόα καλὸν ἀλειψαμένη ἰδὲ χαίτας | πεξαμένη, χερσὶ πλοκάμους ἔπλεξε φαεινούς | καλοὺς ἀμβροσίους ἐκ κράατος ἀθανάτοιο. (Hera then puts on a dress woven for her by Athena and borrows a girdle from Aphrodite.) The point of contact between the two passages is, typically, a lexical one. πέκειν, πέκεσθαι, which normally = 'shear', 'cut',[2] is used only by Homer = 'comb': C. ignores later usage and picks up the Homeric term, repeating the same collocation of words and metrical arrangement (χαίτ- | πεξ-), and echoing the ordinary details of the rest of the passage. Allusion to the Homeric episode gives a witty bite to the final instructions to the celebrants, a final reminder, after the play with the Judgement of Paris, that Athena can be as potently seductive as Homeric Hera once was.

31 ὡς P.Maas, *SJ* suggested reading ὧι κ' ἀπό; the relative is perhaps more concise than final ὡς (cf. the parallels quoted on vv. 31f.), but that is not sufficient ground to diagnose a corruption.

ἀπό In Theodoridas, *HE* 3506f., the only other instance of ἀποπέκεσθαι and possibly a verbal reminiscence of this passage, the verb is used as normally = 'cut off': [κόμαι] . . . ἃς ἀπὸ Φοίβωι | πέξατο.[3] In C. the prefix cannot denote separation and is perhaps occasioned by the Homeric ἐκ κράατος (see above), 'down', 'out', though it could, as often, be an intensive = 'thoroughly' (see Schwyzer, *GG* II 445).[4] The expression

---

[1] Hence at the much-disputed Eur. *Or.* 1457 ἀμφιπορφυρέων is almost certainly impossible by virtue of its form alone. On -εος adjectives of material generally see Chantraine, *FN* 50ff., Debrunner, *GW* 149f.

[2] See LSJ, who misclassify Euphorion, *HE* 1801 where ἔπεξε means 'shear'.

[3] Cf. Hesychius ἀποπέπεκται· ἀποκέκαρται.

[4] The parallel A.R. 3.45f. which also makes use of the *Iliad* passage (see above) supports ἀπό = 'down', 'out': κόμας . . . | κόσμει χρυσείηι διὰ

ἀπό . . . πέξηται should at any rate be seen as a literary puzzle, starting from the impossibility of Athena cutting off her hair, and solvable only once the Homeric reference has been spotted.

31–2 ὡς ἀπὸ χαίταν | πέξηται The rhythm is something of a Hellenistic cliché: e.g. A.R. 4.985f. ὧι ἀπὸ πατρός | μήδεα νηλειῶς ἔταμε, Anyte, *HE* 684f. ἅς ἐπὶ πολλοί | νυμφίοι ἱέμενοι, Mnasalces, *HE* 2639f. ἅς ἄπο φαιδράν | ἔκλασας etc.

32 λιπαρόν . . . πλόκαμον Athena is εὐπλόκαμος at *Od.* 7.41, ἠύκομος at *Il.* 6.92, 273, 303, and ξανθά at Pind. *N.* 10.7, fr. 34, Bacch. 5.92 (cf. also Tib. 1.4.26, Ovid, *Am.* 1.1.7). Radiant hair was traditionally a mark of special beauty: in addition to *Il.* 14.176 (above on vv. 31f.) cf., e.g., Pind. fr. 33c λιπαροπλοκάμου . . . Λατοῦς, Antigenes fr. 1.4D λιπαρὰν ἔθειραν, Theocr. 5.91 (the beautiful Cratidas) λιπαρὰ δὲ παρ' αὐχένα σείετ' ἔθειρα.

σμασαμένα The later Atticists claimed to be able to distinguish between Attic σμᾶν and non-Attic σμήχειν (Phrynichus § 224 Fischer σμῆγμα καὶ σμῆξαι καὶ ταῦτα ἀναττικά· τὸ γὰρ ἀττικὸν σμῆμα καὶ σμῆσαι . . . , Moeris σμώμενος Ἀττικοί, σμηχόμενος Ἕλληνες etc.), and such a distinction does seem to be valid: K–B, *GG* II 538, Meisterhans, *GAI* 175, W.G.Rutherford, *The New Phrynichus* (London 1881) 321ff., Frisk, *EW* s.v. Ptolemaic papyri, *LXX* and *N.T.* use mostly the guttural forms;[1] σμασαμένα here seems therefore to be a literary form, as is Theocr. 15.30 σμᾶμα.[2] C. seems to have used σμήχω, or a compound thereof: *SH* 260A 6]ϲ̣μήξας.

33–56 After the summons and instructions of vv. 1–32 the celebrants have now assembled (v. 33), and the next twenty-four lines are devoted to invocation of the goddess herself. This second part of the poem is identical in construction with the first part, though shorter in length and, giving a balance, emotionally more intense: three sections (parallel to vv. 1–4, 13–17, 29–32) of direct invocation of the goddess form the framework (beginning, central pause, ending) and contain two expository passages (parallel to vv. 5–12, 18–28). Just as the two expositions in the first part of the poem exemplified attributes of the divinity being celebrated, these two relate to the ceremony itself, being an aetiology and a final warning to the profane.

33–4 Announcement that the celebrants are ready (cf. on v. 1 ἔξιτε)

κερκίδι. Schneider was rightly worried by ἀπό but failed to find a convincing explanation; Meineke's ἄρα (p. 247) was better, but emendation is not necessary.

[1] The Callimachean scholiast translates σμασαμένα into σμηξαμένη (and G has σμαξαμένα which Meineke adopted), and Hesychius felt the need to gloss σμᾶν with σμήχειν.

[2] Hermann's conjecture seems now to have been confirmed by a papyrus: see Gow ad loc.

and the first direct invocation of Athena. The opening words, as well as providing a link with the first part of the poem (the imperative provides a 'sub-refrain' link with vv. 1f. ἔξιτε), are the first in a series of repeated vocatives creating an atmosphere of increasing religious fervour (v. 35 ὠθάνα, v. 41 δαῖμον, v. 55 πότνι' Ἀθαναία), and the whole phrase becomes a regular refrain which marks the beginning of each invocatory section: v. 43 ἔξιθ', Ἀθαναία, v. 55 cὺ μὲν ἔξιθι.

For the reassurance in the invocation that eager celebrants await the divinity cf. *Pind. N.* 3.1–5 ὦ πότνια Μοῖcα, μᾶτερ ἁμετέρα, λίccομαι | . . . | ἵκεο . . . Αἴγιναν· ὕδατι γὰρ | μένοντ' ἐπ' Ἀcωπίωι μελιγαρύων τέκτονες | κώμων νεανίαι, cέθεν ὄπα μαιόμενοι.

33 πάρα = πάρεcτι, a common poeticism (Schwyzer, *GG* II 423): for phraseology cf., e.g., *Od.* 3.324 εἰ δ' ἐθέλειc πεζόc, πάρα τοι δίφροc τε καὶ ἵπποι.

Cf. the similar phraseology in the Adonis festival address to Aphrodite at Theocr. 15.112ff.: πὰρ μέν οἱ ὥρια κεῖται . . . | πὰρ δ' ἁπαλοὶ κᾶποι . . . | . . . ἀλάβαcτρα, | εἴδατά θ' . . . | . . . | ὅccα τ' . . . | πάντ' αὐτῶι πετεηνὰ καὶ ἑρπετὰ τεῖδε πάρεcτι.

καταθύμιοc A literary word, perhaps of poetic status outside Ionic prose until the first century A.D.[1] Although in Homeric vocabulary καταθύμιοc = 'in the mind', post-Homeric usage resolved the duplication with synonymous ἐνθύμιοc by differentiating καταθύμιοc into an antonym of ἀποθύμιοc, 'according to one's mind', 'pleasing' (the more usual usage of the prefix); there is therefore no question of Homeric usage here or at v. 69.[2] καταθύμιοc again in the Hellenistic period at Parthenius, Ἐρ. Παθ. 15.1, again of a devotee (of Artemis: possibly a poeticism), and in two heightened prophetic passages in *LXX* (Mic. 7.3 and Isai. 44.9); then in poetry of the first century A.D. (Antiphilus, *GP* 1073 and anon. lyric in Powell, *CA* 183 v. 16) and late prose (Dio Cass. 37.56 and the patristic writers: Lampe, *PGL* s.v.).

---

[1] Comprehensive list of passages in LSJ (add Theogn. 1238, 1283, Antiphilus, *GP* 1073, Diog. Laert. 2.5, and patristic writers): in the only non-Ionic prose instance Antiphon Soph. fr. 49 a poetic word would not be out of place. The 'letter of Anaximenes' reported by Diog. Laert. 2.5 is full of poeticisms and usually regarded as a late forgery. A stock phrase or term might be responsible for many of the prose instances: Hdt. 5.39, Musonius 14 p. 74H γυνὴ καταθύμιοc, Democr. fr. 277 κ. παῖc, – ?like English 'beloved'?

[2] The argument of F. de Ian, *De Call. Homeri interprete* (Diss. Strasbourg 1893) 33, that the Homeric meaning of κ. was disputed in Alexandria and C. is here 'interpreting' Homer, is unconvincing guesswork (cf. Cahen, *C* 529).

ἴλα 'band', 'company'. ἴλη denotes an organised group, usually military though in poetic diction sometimes a ritual group: Pind. *N.* 5.38 ἔνθα μιν εὔφρονες ἶλαι cὺν καλάμοιο βοᾶι θεὸν δέκονται.[1]

34 παρθενικαί A poetic alternative to παρθένοc in all periods (LSJ: add A.R. and bucolics *passim*). The whole line is formulated according to standard modes of expression: παρθενική stands not uncommonly in apposition with other nouns (e.g. *Od.* 7.20 παρθενικῆι εἰκυῖα νεήνιδι, Eur. *Ep.* 2 Bergk παρθενικήν τε κόρην: cf. LSJ s.v. παρθένοc); so too does παῖc (e.g. *Il.* 21.282 παῖδα cυφορβόν, Aristoph. *Lys.* 595 παῖδα κόρην, IV 298f. παῖδεc . . . ἄρcενεc); and παρθένοc + genitive = 'daughter' is a regular poeticism: see Pfeiffer, *Callimachus* II 103 on the similarly phrased pentameter fr. 2ª.25 Περμήccου παρθένοc Ἀονίου. The word does not necessarily imply, therefore, that only unmarried women were permitted to celebrate (at VI 118 παρθενικαί, καὶ ἐπιφθέγξαcθε, τεκοῖcαι the sense 'virgin' is made explicit by the antithesis). See Intro. pp. 10f.

μεγάλων Not gratuitous. V. 34 is aimed at encouraging Athena's epiphany: the line emphasises first that the company is all feminine (παρθενικαί), then that they are descended from an important family of long standing. For the phraseology of this line cf. 64.14 ὤλιcθεν μεγάλουc οἶκοc ἐπὶ Cκοπάδαc, and V 126 καὶ μεγάλοιc ὕcτερα Λαβδακίδαιc.

παῖδεc For the shaping of the line cf. fr. 33 τετράενον Δαμάcου παῖδα Τελεcτορίδην.

Ἀρεcτοριδᾶν Here and in the scholiast's note Ψ had Ἀ<u>κ</u>εcτ. Valckenaer's correction seems certain: whereas an Acestor is nowhere else associated with Argos,[2] Arestor was an Argive national hero, son-in-law of Inachus, father of Argos (hence A.R. 1.112, 325 Ἄργοc Ἀρεcτορίδηc); for full references see *RE* II 668. Textual mistakes are notoriously common with names and this one was again corrupted at A.R. 1.112 to Ἀλεκτορίδηc.[3] Ἀρεcτορίδαι = 'Argives' is parallel to the poetic Ἐρεχθεῖδαι, Κεκροπίδαι etc. of Athenians (cf. Wilamowitz, *Aristoteles und Athen* (Berlin 1893) II 180–5).

35–42 The first of the two sections concerning the ceremony: announcement of the Shield of Diomedes and (as generally with important

---

[1] Where the scholiast remarks: ἶλαι αἱ τάξειc καὶ αἱ cυcτροφαὶ τῶν νέων αἱ ἐν τῶι χορῶι γινόμεναι. The Callimachean scholiast glosses v. 33 ἴλα with ἡ τῶν νυμφῶν φρατρία καὶ ἄθροιcιc. Cf. Soph. *Aj.* 1407f. μία δ' ἐκ κλιcίαc ἀνδρῶν ἴλη τὸν ὑπαcπίδιον κόcμον φερέτω.

[2] Except as an unknown historical person in two third-century B.C. inscriptions from the Argolid, *IG* IV 729.5 (Hermione), 772.3 (Trozen).

[3] Cf. *P.Colon.* 929 (*ZPE* I (1967) 113ff.) for the text of A.R. 1.325: Ἄκαcτοc for ὁ καλήν after Ἀρεcτορίδηc earlier in the line. Mair's note that Hesychius records ἀκέcαcθαι as an equivalent of ἀρέcαcθαι (and that therefore Ἀ<u>κ</u>εcτ. is an etymological variant for Ἀ<u>ρ</u>εcτ.) is incorrect.

ritual acts) an aetiological explanation of its presence. Right at the start the invocation of Athena is accompanied by a reassurance that the ritual will be seriously and properly carried out: Diomedes' Shield is being carried in the procession. Although the Shield was manifestly of great symbolic importance in the ceremony, we have no other relevant evidence outside this Hymn, and the reason for the Shield's presence is obscure to the modern reader. The association of the Argive hero with Athena was renowned and is well-documented, and it was Diomedes who brought back the Palladion from Troy to Argos where he founded a temple to the goddess (see Intro. pp. 14–16); however, the preservation of his shield as a relic, even though entirely in accord with Greek practice,[1] is known only from C.,[2] and the Eumedes story does not explicitly connect Palladion and Shield. This has led some editors to suppose that our text is incomplete, and Wilamowitz posited a lacuna after v. 36 (*HD* II 18), Ziehen after v. 36 or v. 42 or both (*RE* XVIII[3] 175), but this approach is unnecessarily drastic.[3] In such an habitually allusive writer as C. failure to mention directly the role of the Shield when Eumedes removed the Palladion should not be surprising; for such an important feature of the ceremony the aetiological myth was doubtless well-known and recorded, and it is probably due to chance that the modern reader lacks the information which C. could take for granted in his own audience.

The story can be reconstructed in general with some probability. That Eumedes' action was to be approved is clear both from v. 37 κεχαριcμένος and from the scholiast who notes that Eumedes was planning to join the returning Heracleidai. In Doric mythology the Heracleidai re-entered the Peloponnese to reclaim the kingdoms from which they had been wrongly

---

[1] See, e.g., Nilsson, *GGR* I 208f., and for shield-relics see Frazer's Index to *Pausanias* s.v. 'Shields'. One of the most famous relics was the shield of Euphorbos at Argos by which Pythagoras proved that he had lived before: Hor. *Od.* 1.28.11ff. (see Nisbet and Hubbard ad loc.).

[2] McKay's statement (*PP* 28) 'according to tradition Diomedes' shield was preserved in this temple [the temple of Athena dedicated by Diomedes]' is not supported by any evidence, though one might wish to *infer* from C. that Shield and Palladion were housed in the same temple. It is worth noting that shields had always been prominent in Argive tradition, especially in association with Hera: see I. R. Arnold, 'The Shield of Argos', *AJA* 41 (1937) 436–40.

[3] Kleinknecht's much more extravagant suggestion, *LP* 306–15, that Palladion and Shield were one and the same object, has found no support; the theory was adequately shown to be impossible by L. Ziehen, *Hermes* 76 (1941) 426–9. One might add that the Eumedes story becomes even less explicable on K.'s interpretation when it has to be an *aition* of the whole purification ceremony.

ejected by the Argive Eurystheus, so that what Eumedes' plan involved was the returning of the city's talisman to its rightful owners.[1] It would be reasonable to infer that at this crucial moment the Argive national hero, long since become divine (Roscher, *LM* I 1024), assisted the loyal priest, whether by appearing in person or protecting Eumedes and the Palladion from the agitated populace through the charmed medium of his shield. Callimachus' Ptolemaic patrons may have had a particular interest in the Heraclid connections with Argos, and this may be behind the extensive Eumedes aetion here (see Intro. pp. 12f.).

The reassurance given to Athena is thus substantial: the Shield probably represents protection for the Palladion when it moves away from its temple as on the earlier critical occasion when the Heracleidai reclaimed their lost Argive territories. (Whether or not the ritual purification was also believed to have orginated from Eumedes' action, as Wilamowitz suggested for his lacuna after v. 36 (see below) is completely unascertainable.) Cf. the similar explanation (and implicit assurance) given in the invocation to Zeus in the *Hymnus Curetum* (Powell, *CA* 160ff.) 16ff. ἕρπε καὶ γέγαθι μολπᾶι. | ἔνθα γὰρ cέ, παῖδ' ἄμβροτον, | ἀcπιδ[ηφόροι τροφῆες] | παρ 'Ρέας λαβόντες πόδα | κ[ρούοντες ἀντάχον].

35 φέρεται An implicit contrast with ἔξιθ', strengthening the illusion that the Palladion *is* the goddess (the Shield has to be carried, whereas the Palladion is spoken of as a person moving: so again at v. 141 the latter 'drives' from and to the city).

---

[1] The scholiast on v. 37 describes the Heracleidai as coming κατὰ τῶν 'Ορεcτειδῶν: the Oresteidai are otherwise unknown, though according to Paus. 1.41.2 Orestes was ruler of Argos at the time of the unsuccessful first attempt by Heracles' son Hyllus to regain the Peloponnese (at 8.5.1 Pausanias corrects himself and places this invasion in the reign of Echemus, not Orestes). A similar account to that of the scholiast is noted in Plut. *Quaest. Gr.* 48: Temenos, a leading Heraclid who took over Argos after the invasion (see in general Roscher, *LM* v 355–8), is said to have persuaded Ergiaios, a descendant of Diomedes, to steal the Palladion from Argos; as Halliday remarks ad loc. 'before the Heraclid Temenos could capture Argos it was necessary for him to get hold of the Palladium'. Ergiaios is otherwise unknown, and the Callimachean Eumedes may likewise have been a descendant of Diomedes.

McKay's assumption (*PP* 67) that the scholiast follows a different tradition from C., in which emphasis was on the treachery of Eumedes, and that C. has edited his material (or even invented it himself), is overbold and makes much less coherent sense of the various pieces of evidence. On the return of the Heracleidai generally see E.N.Tigerstedt, *The Legend of Sparta in Classical Antiquity* I (Stockholm 1965) 28–36 and the full list of references on pp. 322–31.

καί To be taken with the whole clause (Denniston, *GP* 305) which gives a reassurance to Athena in addition to the reason already given in vv. 33f. why she can now appear (that a pleasing group of celebrants awaits her).

καῒ ἁ See on v. 3 καὶ ἁ.

36 The line as given by Ψ (Ἀργείων . . . παλαιότερον) is difficult. The main problem is Ἀργείων, which, if dependent on ἔθος, is redundant, and if on παλαιότερον ('older than the Argives') makes poor sense. The best solution seems to be that of the unknown humanist who in Jean Courtier's MS, now at Berne, conjectured Ἀργείως along with παλαιοτέρως (R.Reitzenstein, *Hermes* 26 (1891) 313).[1] Ἀργείως goes excellently as object of ἐδίδαξε, and although παλαιότερον could still be read the adjective fits well with Ἀργείως, giving it greater definition and providing the internal rhyme common in the pentameters of this Hymn (cf. also the parallel in Clearchus of Soloi cited below on v. 36 παλαιοτέρως). Ψ often corrupts Doric inflections (-ως again at vv. 62, 142): παλαιοτέρως will presumably have been first assimilated to τοῦτο and Ἀργείως then corrected to go with ἔθος. The double conjecture is supported by Tibullus' Callimachean mock-festival poem, 2.1.2 *ritus ut a prisco traditus extat avo.* Wilamowitz retained the text of Ψ and marked a lacuna after v. 36 in which 'narrabatur quo modo Eumedes postquam rediit sacrum lavandi Palladii ritum instituisset.'

παλαιοτέρως The suffix denotes not a direct comparison, but an implicit contrast (with present-day Argives), a usage which is idiomatic to Greek (in English an ordinary positive would suffice). This 'contrastive' comparative occurs usually where the contrast is explicit, often in pair-phrases and particularly with adjectives of age: Theogn. 935f. νέοι . . . παλαιότεροι, Pind. *P.* 10.58f. ἐν καὶ παλαιτέροις, νέαισίν τε . . . , *N.* 3.72f., Aesch. *Eum.* 721, Timoth. *PMG* 791.211 etc;[2] but the idiom also extends to the solitary comparative where the contrast is implicit: e.g. *Il.* 1.32, 21.101, 24.52, *Od.* 3.69, 4.292, 16.147, 17.176, 23.262, Hdt. 6.107.3. The 'contrastive' comparative was a particularly common feature in the *koine*, where the superlative was gradually disappearing and the comparative developing into a strong form of the positive.[3] παλαιότεροι again at

---

[1] Ernesti reported that Ἀργείως was recorded also by an anonymous sixteenth-century German scholar in the margin of his Aldine edition.

[2] Shakespeare, *A Winter's Tale* III 2, Paulina: 'What old or newer torture / Must I receive?' Fullest treatments of this usage are O.Schwab, *Syntax der griech. Komparation* (Würzburg 1893–4) I 53ff. and M.Wittwer, *Glotta* 47 (1969) 54–110. Cf. also K–G, *GG* I 24 A.2.

[3] Mayser, *GGP* II[1] 46–54, Moulton, *GNT* I[3] 77ff., Blass–Debrunner–Rehkopf, *GNG* §§ 60, 244, C.F.D.Moule, *Idiom Book of N.T. Greek* (Cambridge 1953) 97f. The gradual disappearance of the superlative also involved

117.8, in the epigram by Clearchus of Soloi inscribed at Aï-Khanoum (L.Robert, *CRAI* (1968) 416–57), v. 1 ἀνδρῶν τοι coφὰ ταῦτα παλαιοτέρων ἀνάκει[τα]ι | ῥήματ' ἀριγνώτων, and at Rhianus fr. 25.1P.

37 τεΐν This rare dative form which occurs 5 times in Homer was noted and explained by ancient Homeric commentators as a Doricism (Σ to *Il.* 11.201, cf. Σ to *Od.* 4.619), as also by Ap. Dysc. *de pron.* 105B (*Gramm. Graec.* II[1] 82). C. too seems to have regarded it as such since he uses the form only here. Ahrens, *DD* 252 argued that since τεΐν is absent from Pindar, Theocr., inscriptions etc., the ancient explanation was a theoretical one based on analogy with τιν (Buck, *GD* 98); but its probable use in Aristoph. *Av.* 930, a parody of a Doricising dithyramb (cf. Σ ad loc.), suggests that it was a feature of at least literary Doric.[1]

κεχαριcμένοc = '*gratus*', normal usage: the perfect participle is used in all periods, and especially in Attic and Hellenistic prose, almost as an independent adjective, often with a dative as here (LSJ).

ἱρεύc The contraction ἱρ- is a Homericism (Ionicism) foreign to Doric inscriptions (which have ἱαρ-, or ἱερ- from the *koine*), but though avoided by Theocritus it is found occasionally in Pindar (*P.* 4.6, *O.* 3.30, fr. 123.11, 189). Cf. ἱρόν v. 39, VI 24.

38 A good example of C.'s intricate style. Apart from a few details (οἱ, delaying of γνούc) the diction is unexceptional (cf. on βωλευτόν) and the sense seems to have been completed by the end of the couplet at θάνατον: in the *koine* -τοc verbal adjectives were commonly used as perfect passives, often equivalent to a participle (Mayser, *GGP* II[1] 357ff.), and βωλευτόν . . . θάνατον could well be the full object of γνούc, εἶναι being omitted as often with verbal adjectives (cf. C.E.Bishop, *AJP* 20 (1899) 248–53, C.Guiraud, *La Phrase nominale en grec* (Paris 1962) 21ff.). However, the beginning of the new hexameter 39 δᾶμον ἑτοιμάζοντα, sends the reader back to reassess the previous line and the whole syntactical structure has to be recast.

---

confusion of comparative and superlative in use (O.Schwab, *op. cit.* II 172ff., Mayser, *GGP* II[1] 46ff.: cf. ὕcτερον in C. III 109, IV 172 and see Gillies on A.R. 3.91) and also led to their confusion in MSS (see Gow on Theocr. 12.32 (and cf. 15.139, 145, 17.4), Wilamowitz, *Textgesch. der griech. Bukoliker* (Berlin 1906) 50 n., M.L.West, *CR* 13 (1963) 10 suggesting πικρότερον for πικρότατον in A.R. 2.222, and M.Campbell, *CQ* 21 (1971) 403 proposing ὁπλότατοc for ὁπλότεροc in A.R. 1.43).

[1] Otherwise only in two Homericising oracles in Hdt. 5.60, 61 and Boeotian: Corinna, *PMG* 654 iv 20 and (?) ii 30. Cf. Chantraine, *GH* I 265. Aristoph. *Av.* 930 must remain textually doubtful but I am not convinced by M.L.West *CR* 18 (1968) 7–8 that ἐμὶν τεΐν must be excised; as L.P.E.Parker, *CQ* 18 (1968) 250 points out, the passage reads like a metrically incomplete quotation (whence the humorous effect).

βωλευτόν . . . ἐπί οἱ θάνατον Normal usage: e.g. Hdt. 3.122.3 ἐμοὶ γὰρ βασιλεὺς Καμβύσης ἐπιβουλεύει θάνατον, Andoc. 4.15 λαθραῖον θάνατον ἐπεβούλευσε Καλλίαι.[1] (The indirect object of uncompounded βουλεύειν normally appears in the simple dative and not with a preposition: ἐπί here, though strictly not in tmesis, is generated naturally in this context from ἐπιβουλεύειν.)[2]

ποκα βωλευτόν Ψ 'normalised' the whole phrase: Meineke's ποκα gives consistency with vv. 57, 59 (cf. on v. 5 οὔποκ'); βωλευτόν (first proposed by Degner, *DUC* 30ff.), conforming to common West Greek practice (Buck, *GD* §§ 25, 75),[3] is supported by VI 32 βωλά and similar compensatory lengthening elsewhere in V (κώρα, μῶνος etc.).

39 ἑτοιμάζοντα Normal usage (particularly common in *LXX*, Polybius etc.). The verb appears to reduplicate βωλευτόν and Ernesti seems to have suggested that the latter had its technical sense here 'decreed' ('decretam . . . mortem populum parare'), but some degree of tautology is normal in phrases of this kind: cf., e.g., Dinarch. *Dem.* 30 βουλεύσας μετ' ἐκείνου τὸν Νικοδήμωι θάνατον κατασκευασθέντα.

φυγᾶι The word is positioned so as to give maximum prominence to the logical development of the situation, being juxtaposed between ἑτοιμάζοντα, the cause of Eumedes' distress, and τεὸν ἱρὸν ἄγαλμα, the resulting hostage, the sacred object least given to violent movement.

τεόν An epicism common in all Hellenistic poetry; also Doric (LSJ).

ἱρὸν ἄγαλμα IV 307 ἱρὸν ἄγαλμα, also of a ξόανον.

40 ᾤχετ' ἔχων Not a weighty phrase: οἴχεσθαι + participle, 'away', 'off', was common in prose and verse of all periods (K–G, *GG* II 63f., Schwyzer, *GG* II 392: cf. La Roche on *Il.* 2.71).[4] The lightness of the phrase gives a pause in the forward movement of this long sentence and allows Κρεῖον δ' etc. to introduce yet another point in the story without undue strain to the overall cohesion.

Κρεῖον δ' εἰς ὄρος The name of the mountain (or hill) is recorded only here and nothing can be deduced about its identity. Editors of Strabo compare 8.376 ἐπὶ τῆι ὁδῶι ἐκ Τεγέας εἰς Ἄργος διὰ τοῦ Παρθενίου ὄρους καὶ τοῦ Κρεοπώλου, but Wilamowitz (*HD* II 18) rightly argued against

---

[1] Meineke doubted βωλευτὸν θάνατον (p. 248), and was followed by Bergk, *Opuscula philologica* (Halle 1886) II 191 who extravagantly suggested ὅς ποκ' ἔβα λευστόν; C.'s phraseology is perfectly acceptable.

[2] Cf. Aesch. *Cho.* 494 βουλευτοῖσιν where, as the scholiast points out, ἐπιβ. would be expected in prose.

[3] Cf. Thumb, *GD* I 114 (Argos), 129, 152 etc.

[4] Some Hellenistic examples: Theocr. 2.7 (| ᾤχετ' ἔχων), 4.6, 13.56, 22.167, 24.101, A.R. 4.1435, Anyte, *HE* 745 (ᾤχετ' ἔχων), Herodas 2.37 (see Headlam ad loc.).

such tenuous association.[1] The name Κρεῖος is otherwise used only of a Titan in Hes. *Theog.* 134, 375.[2] The situation is complicated by the fact that the scholion to v. 37 remarks that the mountain to which Eumedes withdrew was called Ἰφεῖον, another unique name;[3] C. was perhaps using a rare (?antiquarian?) secondary name (cf. on v. 41 Κρεῖον). Cf. *RE* xi[2] 1705.

ᾠκίcατο οἰκίζειν always denotes either settlement or intended permanancy of occupation and here implies at the very least that Eumedes was threatening to establish Athena elsewhere, and may suggest that the site remained that of Athena's temple down to historical times. The verb is often used in the middle (*Thes. Graec.* s.v.) and εἰc is the normal preposition: e.g. Eur. *Ion* 915 παῖδ' εἰc οἴκουc οἰκίζειc, [Plato] *Axioch.* 371c εἰc τὸν τῶν εὐcεβῶν χῶρον οἰκίζονται. The form is well suited to the end of the pentameter: 75.19, 178.34 ἐcωικίcατο, 617 ᾠκίcατε, *E.* 24.4 παρῳκίcατο.

41 Κρεῖον ὄροc The repetition may be insistence. As Wilamowitz suggested (*HD* ii 18) C. was perhaps following an unusual tradition (the scholion to v. 37 gives the name of the mountain as Ἰφεῖον); the purpose may have been to link the πέτραι Παλλατίδεc with the Palladion.[4] The explanation that such repetition is a standard feature of epic diction[5] is less satisfactory. We should not exclude the possibility of corruption arising from damage in Ψ's exemplar (which had 24 lines on each page side) which may also have affected the end of 17 in the corresponding place on the other side of the page (see Intro. pp. 71f.). Cf. also P.Maas, *SJ*.

cὲ δέ, δαῖμον Athena is referred to, appropriately in this context, as a somewhat abstract power to be reckoned with rather than as a goddess with

[1] The Parthenion mountain might be the same as the Ἀθηναῖον ὄροc mentioned in [Plut.] *de fluv.* 18.12 as the site of a temple to Athena founded by Diomedes on his return from Troy. Perhaps both are identical with the well-known Larisa hill (which is on the inland route to Tegea) on which, W.Vollgraff argues, was the temple housing the Palladion in historical times (see Intro. p. 15).

[2] One might also compare Κριόc, the name of a Spartan seer who, according to Paus. 3.13.3, betrayed Sparta to the Dorians, just as Eumedes deserted to the Heracleidai.

[3] A good Argive one, though: Iphis, son of Alector ([Apollod.] 3.6.2), ruled Argos two generations before Orestes (Paus. 2.18.5).

[4] McKay's suggestion (*PP* 67f.) that C. was 'tampering with the facts' ('the Pallatides were too useful to be wasted') seems rather simplistic: the 'popular etymology' Παλλάc/Παλλατίδεc was doubtless well-documented even if not universally accepted.

[5] See Schneider. As a stylistic feature this kind of repetition invariably involves an extension of the sentence so as to give additional information (e.g. through a relative clause) and not just bald insistence. 'Epic' repetition is common in C. too: Lapp. *TF* 54ff.

a personality (θεά): see on vv. 80f. τίς . . . δαίμων, 86 δαίμονες. The vocative again with similar respectful overtones at 384.9, I 44 (also an aetiology), III 86, 173.

The non-Doric cέ here and at vv. 80, 117, and cύ at v. 55 are problematic since elsewhere in V Ψ gives Doric τεῦ, τοι and τεΐν. Theocritus uses uniformly τύ and τε in his Doric poems (cf. Monteil, *T* 41), but the Callimachean MSS show no trace of the Doric nominative or accusative; since the Pindaric poems also have a mixture of Doric and non-Doric forms (W.J.Slater, *Lexicon to Pindar* (Berlin 1969) s.v. cύ, E. Des Places, *Le Pronom chez Pindare* (Paris 1947) 12f.), Ψ's forms are probably best left unchanged failing more evidence.

41–2 ἀπορρώγεccιν . . . | ἐν πέτραιc Standard phraseology (*pace* Pfeiffer on fr. 309): πέτρα ἀπορρώξ in Xen. *An.* 6.4.3, Aristot. *HA* 611ª 21, Polyb. 10.48.5, *LXX* 2 Macc. 14.45, πέτραι ἀπορρῶγεc in Polyb. 5.59.6, and ἀπορρώξ as a noun ('cliff') in Polyb. 7.6.3 etc.[1] Cf. the similar formulation at fr. 309.2–3 πᾶcα δ' ἀπορρώξ | πέτρη ἔην. A.R. 4.637 and Arat. 45 also use ἀπορρώξ, not, like C., as in normal usage, but as a Homeric archaism = ἀπορροή (*Il.* 2.755, *Od.* 9.359, 10.514).

42 αἷc C. usually has Homeric/Ionic feminine dative plural forms -ηιc, -ηιcι(ν) (Pfeiffer, *Proleg.* lxxxix), but V and VI consistently have the Doric forms -αιc, -αιcι(ν) (cf. Buck, *GD* 86, Monteil, *T* 38).[2]

οὔνομα The Homeric form. ὤνομα, proposed by Degner, *DUC* 31f. and discussed by Schneider, is a false Doricism: Doric has ὄνυμα (LSJ and Buck, *GD* 27), and οὔνομα is the result of metrical lengthening of a naturally short vowel (cf. Frisk, *EW* II 396). οὔνομα again in Doric poetic texts at Theocr. 7.13, [Theocr.] 27.40, 41.

Παλλατίδεc The name is otherwise unknown. P.Charneux, *BCH* 82 (1958) 13f. drew attention to the existence of an Argive κώμη called Παλλάc (*SEG* 17 (1960) 144.4: third century B.C.), but the location of the district is unknown and there is no known reason why it should be associated with the Παλλατίδεc.[3]

43–4 The second section of direct invocation, beginning with what

---

[1] Although ἀπορρώξ is used with other nouns too it is most frequently associated with πέτρα; cf. Schmidt, *SGS* III 121. Similarly the cognates: Soph. *Phil.* 937 καταρρῶγεc πέτραι, A.R. 1.995 πέτραc ἀμφιρρῶγαc, Polyb. 9.27.4 πέτρα περιρρώξ, Theocr. 24.95 ῥωγάδαc ἐc πέτραc, A.R. 4.1448 ῥωγάδοc ἐκ πέτρηc, Nic. *Ther.* 644 ῥωγάδι πέτρηι.

[2] This is the only non-Homeric form of the relative in C.: again in the Doric Theocr. 18.22. A.R. uses only Homeric ᾗιcι(ν). (The only Homeric instance of αἷc seems to be *H.H.Aphr.* 249.)

[3] Meineke p. 248f. suggested reading Παλλαδίαιc or Παλλαcίδεc, but too little is known for Ψ's Παλλατίδεc to be suspected reasonably.

now becomes a ritual refrain, ἔξιθ', Ἀθαναία (v. 33), and continuing with similarly ritualistic epicletic epithets. Although many of the nuances of the preceding aetiological section are obscure to the modern reader, it is clear that the invocation continues the mood of conflict and possibly open battle from the Eumedes story. (V. 44 σακέων . . . πατάγωι seems to support the possibility that Diomedes' shield helped Eumedes by defending the Palladion from armed attack.)

43 περσέπτολι A rare poetic epithet, earlier applied to Athena by Lamprocles, *PMG* 735 Παλλάδα περσέπολιν[1] (parodied by Aristoph. *Nub.* 967 and Phrynichus fr. 72 (Kock I 388)).[2] περσέπτολις is the counter-aspect of ἐρυσίπτολις by which Athena is also described at *Il.* 6.305, *H.H.* 28.3, and which is later referred to in v. 53 τὰν Παλλάδα τὰν πολιοῦχον; both aspects appear side by side in *H.H.* 11.1ff. Παλλάδ' Ἀθηναίην ἐρυσίπτολιν ἄρχομ' ἀείδειν | δεινήν, ἧι σὺν Ἄρηϊ μέλει πολεμήϊα ἔργα | περθόμεναί τε πόληες ἀυτή τε πτόλεμοί τε.

χρυσεοπήληξ The epithet otherwise only of Ares in the Hellenistic *H.H.* 8.1.[3] Cf. Anacreon, *PMG* 346 fr. 11+3+6.18 χρυσολόφου⟦c⟧ Παλλάδ[ος, Aristoph. *Lys.* 344f. ὦ χρυσολόφα . . . πολιοῦχε . . . Τριτογένει', Leonidas, *HE* 2525 εὐπήληκος Ἀθηναίης. At *Il.* 5.743f. amongst Athena's armour is ἀμφίφαλον κυνέην τετραφάληρον χρυσείην. (Again of Athena in Procl. *H.* 7.4.) F.H.Sandbach suggests that the Argive Palladion may have had a gilded helmet, like the statue of Athena in the Partheneion.

44 *Il.* 12.338ff. ἀυτὴ δ' οὐρανὸν ἷκε, | βαλλομένων σακέων τε καὶ ἱπποκόμων τρυφαλειῶν | καὶ πυλέων. Wilamowitz' suggestion (*HD* II 18) that the Argive procession might have been accompanied by a shield ceremony is attractive and the invocation here may indeed have been grounded in some such aspect of the ritual (cf. Intro. p. 11); however the reference at Zenob. 2.3 (quoted by W.) which mentions an Argive shield procession, could equally be to a celebration in the cult of Hera (see I.R.Arnold, 'The Shield of Argos', *AJA* 41 (1937) 440).

σακέων An epic/poetic word (LSJ)[4] common in Hellenistic poetry.

---

[1] Or even Stesichorus perhaps: *PMG* 274 (see Page's notes on *PMG* 735).

[2] The fact that Aesch. *Pers.* 65f. πεπέρακεν μὲν ὁ περσέπτολις ἤδη βασίλειος στρατός was parodied by Eupolis fr. 192 (Kock I 311) πεπέρακεν μὲν ὁ περσέπτολις ἤδη Μαρικᾶς suggests that the adjective was highly poetic in tone. Cf. the satirical *AP* 5.2 (anon.) τὴν καταφλεξίπολιν Σθενελαΐδα, τὴν βαρύμισθον . . .

[3] χρυσοπήληξ also of Ares in Aesch. *Sept.* 106, of the Sparti in Eur. *Phoen.* 939. The only other compound generated by πήληξ other than εὐπήληξ (above) is τινακτοπήληξ (Hesychius).

[4] Hdt. 1.52 is a unique prose-instance (LSJ's 'etc.' is misleading); this

πατάγωι A poetic/Ionic (and hence literary-*koine*) word (LSJ). Of the crashing of armour πάταγος is unexceptional: Aesch. *Sept.* 103, Soph. *Trach.* 517, Eur. *Hcld.* 832 (ἀςπίδων), Aristoph. *Ach.* 539 (ἀςπίδων); of horses π. is not otherwise used, but this is only a variation on the common Homeric κτύπος ἵππων[1], referring to the rumbling ἐρίγδουποι πόδες ἵππων (*Il.* 11.152).

45–54 The second expository section: *procul o procul este profani*, II 2 ἑκὰς ἑκὰς ὅςτις ἀλιτρός; Hipp. *Lex* 5 τὰ δὲ ἱερὰ ἐόντα πρήγματα ἱεροῖςιν ἀνθρώποιςι δείκνυται· βεβήλοιςι δὲ οὐ θέμις, πρὶν ἢ τελεςθῶςιν ὀργίοιςιν ἐπιςτήμης. The warning extends over four couplets in which an atmosphere of urgency and religious fervour is created by an abrupt imperative (not aposiopesis) and refrain-like repetitions (ςάμερον . . . ςάμερον . . . ςάμερον, ἢ 'ς . . . ἢ ἐς); the last couplet forcefully spells out the punishment for intrusion into the sacred territory.[2]

45 ςάμερον Attic τήμερον had been completely superseded in the *koine* by the sigmatic form (Mayser, *GGP* I[1] 198).

ὑδροφόροι Not just the slaves, who are referred to in the next couplet, but any women, perhaps, who are not initiates: see Intro. pp. 10f. and cf. VI 3ff. where similar instructions are given to the βέβαλοι in similar language (μήδ' ἀπὸ τῶ τέγεος μήδ' ὑψόθεν αὐγάςςηςθε . . .).

μὴ βάπτετε 'Do not draw water': a general instruction of which πίνετ' ἀπὸ κρανᾶν is a consequence and not just a repetition (see below on vv. 45f.). The sense is complete (no aposiopesis): βάπτειν usually means 'dip', but the occasional usage developed in Hellenistic literary Greek 'draw by dipping'. Cf. Theocr. 5.127 ἁ παῖς ἀνθ' ὕδατος τᾶι κάλπιδι κηρία βάψαι, A.R. 4.157, Nic. *Al.* 171, 516, Eratosthenes *ap.* Athen. 11.482B. Antiphanes fr. 25 (Kock II 19), Eur. *Hec.* 610 and *Hipp.* 123, where the verb is ambiguous between 'dip' and 'draw', illustrate well how the sense developed: see W.G.Rutherford, *Babrius* (London 1883) 68f.[3]

45–6 ςάμερον, Ἄργος . . . is an expansion of the brief μὴ βάπτετε: if the source of flowing river water is prohibited the inhabitants will have to use

testimony may indicate an Ionicism, but since the passage is describing a dedication by Croesus H. may be echoing the language of the dedicatory inscription.

[1] Cf. Aesch. *Sept.* 100 where the question ἀκούετ' ἢ οὐκ ἀκούετ' ἀςπίδων κτύπον; is answered in v. 103 by κτύπον δέδορκα· πάταγος οὐχ ἑνὸς δορός.

[2] P.Maas, *SJ* saw vv. 45f. as two amongst many interpolated verses in this Hymn.

[3] Cf. also ἀποβάπτειν: *LXX* 2 Macc. 1.20 ὕδωρ . . . ἀποβάψαντας φέρειν; ἀπόβαμμα in *IG* IV 1607 (fourth century B.C.: Argolis) = 'water drawn from a spring'.

instead the constructed fountains in or near the city (on the distinction between πηγή = 'natural source' and κρήνη = 'place where spring water is made artificially available' see R.E.Wycherley, *CR* 51 (1937) 2f.). Schneider and Cahen were curiously embarrassed by μηδέ, linking it with μὴ βάπτετε: the conjunction has its usual sense 'and not' following a preceding positive clause (K–G, *GG* II 293f.) – 'today, Argos, drink from fountains and not from the river.' The construction is clear once the meaning of βάπτετε has been recognised.

45 Ἄργος The city for the inhabitants, as often: e.g. Eur. fr. 713N (= Aristoph. *Eq.* 813) ὦ πόλις Ἄργους, κλύεθ' οἷα λέγει; *Suppl.* 808 ὦ πόλις Ἀργεία, τὸν ἐμὸν πότμον οὐκ ἐσορᾶτε;

46 πίνετ' A collective singular (Ἄργος) commonly has a plural verb: K–G, *GG* I 53.

κρανᾶν The Doric form is well attested in inscriptions (LSJ) and in Pindar and Theocritus.

τῶ ποταμῶ Ψ 'normalised' to τῶν ποταμῶν: the correction made by the anonymous humanist in Anon. Bern. (cf. on v. 36) is an obvious one, since only the Inachus is involved (vv. 49f.). Ψ corrects the Doric genitive singular also at vv. 87, 128, 140, and in v. 3 again 'normalises' at the cost of the sense.

47–8 Lines which expand with variations the injunction of the preceding couplet. The naming of two specific springs has partly the effect of increased realism,[1] but it also emphasises the seriousness of the ban on Inachus: although the whereabouts of Physadeia is unknown, Amymone, one of the most important sources of water for the proverbially dry Argos, was situated at Lerna near modern Mýli, nearly eight kilometres from the city. (On Argos and its water supplies see A.Philippson, *Die griech. Landschaften* III[1] (Frankfurt 1959) 139ff. and R.A.Tomlinson, *Argos and the Argolid* (London 1972) 8–11.)

47 αἱ δῶλαι Not the same as v. 45 ὑδροφόροι in spite of the anaphora linking the two hexameters: the article defines *the class* δῶλαι, 'those who are slaves', and, where simple δῶλαι might have been in apposition to ὑδροφόροι, distinguishes a new group of addressees.

δωλ- is the standard Doric form (Buck, *GD* 28ff.); again at VI 95 and Theocr. 2.94 (where a papyrus corrects the 'normalising' MSS), 5.5.

τὰς κάλπιδας On the 'familiar' double article αἱ . . . τάς see on v. 2 τᾶν ἵππων. κάλπις, restricted to literary and mostly poetic texts, seems to have

[1] Cf. the naming of names to similar effect in *Il.* 6.456f. καί κεν ἐν Ἄργει ἐοῦσα πρὸς ἄλλης ἱστὸν ὑφαίνοις, | καί κεν ὕδωρ φορέοις Μεσσηίδος ἢ Ὑπερείης. One wonders whether the first few generations of Greeks in Alexandria had romantic feelings about place-names in mainland Greece.

denoted the same vessel as ὑδρία, a more current prose term.[1] Some Hellenistic writers use κάλπις of the funerary urn and other containers, but C., like Theocr. 5.127 and A.R. 1.1207, 1234, uses it in the Homeric and Classical sense of a water-pitcher. Cf. Daremberg–Saglio, *DA* s.v., Brommer, *Hermes* 77 (1942) 358, 365.

ἢ 'ϲ In his Index Verborum Pfeiffer suggests that 'ϲ should perhaps be deleted. Aphaeresis, an un-Homeric and mostly dramatic phenomenon, is very rare with ἐϲ;[2] however, 194.32 κἠγὼ μὲν ἢ 'πὶ δαῖταϲ ἢ 'ϲ χορὸν φοιτέω has firm papyrological support, and the MSS here are unanimous. Elsewhere in C. aphaeresis seems restricted to the iambic poems (cf. Lapp, *TF* 144), but its recurrence at v. 63 ἢ 'πί indicates that for whatever reason it was a permissible licence in this Hymn.[3] On aphaeresis in general see K–B, *GG* I 240–3 (elsewhere in Hellenistic poetry apparently only in Theocritus' Aeolic 30.6, 12).

Φυϲάδειαν The name is little mentioned in ancient authors (outside C. only in Antimachus fr. 179 Wyss, Euphorion fr. 23.3P, and probably Σ to Eur. *Phoen.* 188), but 66.7 πότνι' 'Αμυμώνη καὶ Φυϲάδεια φίλη suggests that Physadeia was, along with Amymone, one of the most important Argive springs even though its location is now unknown. Cf. below on v. 48 'Αμυμώναν: here as at frr. 65–6 C.'s source was doubtless Agias and Dercylos.

48 ἢ ἐϲ C. allows hiatus only between a longum and a disyllabic biceps, even though Homer has frequent and unregulated hiatus: Maas, *GM* § 141.[4] See Pfeiffer on fr. 287 and cf. on v. 65 ἑῶ.

'Αμυμώναν In Eur. *Phoen.* 182ff. Antigone, reporting Capaneus, describes the women's slavery, which the victorious Argive army will impose, in terms of their being sent as water-carriers Λερναίαι

---

[1] See references in LSJ s.v. κάλπιϲ (add Polyb. 15.25.6); unlike ὑδρία, κάλπιϲ is conspicuously absent from inscriptional and papyrological texts.

[2] The only pre-Callimachean examples seem to be Aesch. *Sept.* 208 μὴ 'ϲ (where however R.D.Dawe, *Collation and Investigation of Manuscripts of Aeschylus* (Cambridge 1964) 90 argues that the correct reading is γ' εἰϲ), Eur. *Ion* 1562 (by emendation) and three, perhaps four, in comedy: see M.Platnauer, 'Prodelision in Greek drama', *CQ* 10 (1960) 140–4.

[3] The unplaced elegiac fr. 493.2 may also have aphaeresis (see Pfeiffer), but synaloepha (μὴ‿ἐξ) may be more appropriate: see on v. 52 μὴ οὐκ.

[4] The only two exceptions to Maas' observation are 260.55 and IV 30 (both ἤ): in each case a reminiscence of Homer is involved (*Il.* 21.111 and *H.H.Ap.* 25). At 326 the hiatus makes Bentley's ἢ ὕϲτατον very dangerous. A.R. was much more free in his use of hiatus (Mooney, *The Argonautica* 421ff.); Theocritus was also somewhat more free (see Gow on 15.67, 22.174).

τε . . . τριαίναι Ποcειδανίοιc Ἀμυμωνίοιc ὕδαcι. 'After passing the source of the Pontinus and traversing in a few minutes the village of Lerna we come to the springs of the Amymone, which rise beside the road at the southern end of the village, a few yards to the north of a white-washed chapel of St. John' (Frazer, *Pausanias's Description of Greece* (London 1898) v 604); the Amymone and the river Erasinos, which rises five kilometres south-west of Argos (modern Kephalári), are the only reliable sources of water in the vicinity of Argos if Inachus is ruled out (A.Philippson, *Griech. Landschaften* III[1] (Frankfurt 1959) 139f.).[1]

τὰν Δαναῶ Paus. 2.37.1 Ἀμυμώνη δὲ ἀπὸ τῆc Δαναοῦ θυγατρὸc ὄνομα τῶι ποταμῶι. A reference to the famous Argive myth that when Poseidon dried up the rivers of Argos in anger, Danaos sent out his fifty daughters to search for water: several of them were successful, but the most famous was Amymone who, having given herself to Poseidon, was rewarded with the spring at Lerna (Roscher, *LM* I 949–52).[2] The meeting of Poseidon and Amymone was widely celebrated both in literature and in painting (Roscher, *LM* I 327f.).

Maas' suggestion τὰc Δαναῶ (*SJ*) is attractive logically but is unnecessary: Amymone was individually the most famous Danaid 'spring-nymph', and C. characteristically gives an adjective to only the second of a pair of nouns (Lapp, *TF* 126).

49–51 Miraculous events in the natural world often accompanied the advent of a Greek god: frequently it was brilliancy of light and wonderful fragrance (*RE* Suppl. IV 315f.), but general movement through the whole of nature was not uncommon (cf. *H.H.Ap.* 135ff., Theogn. 8ff., II 1ff., IV 249ff., A.R. 1.1141ff., 2.679f.).[3] Gold, the divine metal, often pervades such occasions: *H.H.Ap.* 135f. (birth of Apollo) χρυcῶι δ' ἄρα Δῆλοc

---

[1] It is tempting to suggest that ancient Physadeia should be identified with the source of the Erasinos. Pfeiffer argues in his notes to fr. 66, which deals with Amymone, that the four springs Amymone, Physadeia, Hippe, and Automate were situated inside the city of Argos; the argument rests entirely on Strabo 8.371 who says that the city possessed wells (φρέατα) ascribed to the daughters of Danaus: since the wells are unnamed and Strabo is anyway notoriously unreliable on Argos, it seems better to follow the overwhelming body of evidence which places Amymone outside the city in Lerna (see Roscher, *LM* I 327f. and references quoted above).

[2] Cf. frr. 65–6 (*Fontes Argivi*): the four successful daughters were Amymone, Physadeia, Hippe, and Automate. Hes. fr. 128 Ἄργοc ἄνυδρον ἐὸν Δαναοὶ θέcαν Ἄργοc ἔνυδρον: see Strabo 8.371 who quotes the fragment.

[3] Cf. also O.Weinreich, 'Türöffnung im Wunder-, Prodigien- und Zauberglauben der Antike, des Judentums und Christentums', in *Genethliakon Wilhelm Schmid* (Stuttgart 1929) 200ff. and esp. 207ff.

ἅπαcα | ἥνθηc', ὡc ὅτε τε ῥίον οὔρεοc ἄνθεcιν ὕληc, Pind. *O.* 7.34 (birth of Athena) βρέχε θεῶν βαcιλεὺc ὁ μέγαc χρυcέαιc νιφάδεccι πόλιν, IV 260–4 (birth of Apollo) including 261 χρυcῷι δὲ τροχόεccα πανήμεροc ἔρρεε λίμνη . . . 263 χρυcῷι δὲ πλήμυρε βαθὺc Ἰνωπὸc ἑλιχθείc.

49 καὶ γὰρ δή A rare collocation of particles. Denniston, *GP* 244 leaves the combination undiscussed, but it seems mostly to be used when defining more closely and emphasising a point already made: cf., for example, Hdt. 1.135, Xen. *HG* 6.5.41, 52, Plato, *Theaet.* 203B. Today the river's waters are for Athena and no-one else.

χρυcῷι τε καὶ ἄνθεcιν Homeric rhythm: *Il.* 10.438, 17.52, *Od.* 23.200 χρυcῷι τε καὶ ἀργύρωι, *H.H.Dem.* 472 πᾶcα δὲ φύλλοιcίν τε καὶ ἄνθεcιν εὐρεῖα χθὼν | ἔβριc'.

ὕδατα Ψ's ὕδατι was a simple corruption by assimilation to the preceding datives.

μείξαc 'mingling'. Ψ's μίξαc is almost certainly post-Callimachean spelling: see on v. 16 μεικτά.

50 ἠξεῖ The Doric contract future (from -cέω) found in most West Greek areas (Buck, *GD* 115) and widely used in literary Doric (in general see Boisacq, *DD* 192ff.; for Theocritus see Monteil, *T* 45). The form is often differentiated, as here, by the accent alone, which is not always preserved in MSS, but treatment of the vowels is sometimes a test of Doric inflection: v. 112 ῥυcεῦντι and v. 120 δειπνηcεῦντι indicate Doric future forms in v,[1] and here and at 128 the MSS are unanimous in giving Doric accentuation (at 127 Ψ had ἄξει). The papyrus at 228.65 and Ψ at VI 123 also preserve the accentuation ἠξεῖ.

φορβαίων The usual interpretation 'pastoral' is not satisfactory and Pfeiffer was tempted to follow Meineke and others and look for a proper name.[2] However φορβαίων can probably be retained: although -αιοc adjectives are often analysed as locatives or associatives based on the cognate noun ('having to do with . . .'),[3] K.Zacher, *De Nominibus Graecis in* αιοc, αια, αιον (Halle 1877) 186ff. pointed out that some -αιοc adjectives seem to be more closely connected with the verb than with the substantive, having the force of a Nomen Agentis (e.g. πομπαῖοc, τροπαῖοc, κλοπαῖοc).[4] If φορβαῖοc is so interpreted as a direct associate of φέρβειν rather than φορβή, then more appropriate than the otiose 'giving pasture' (LSJ) would

---

[1] On the mixing of Doric and non-Doric future forms in the same poem see on v. 111 ἔccεται.

[2] Thus the Venetian edition of 1555 has φωκαίων from which Meineke extracted Φωκιακῶν or Φωκείων; Schneider offered Λυρκείων. Schneider also proposed φορβαδίων and φορβάμων.

[3] Debrunner, *GW* 143; cf. Frisk, *EW* s.v. φέρβω.

[4] Cf. also G.Sandsjoe, *Die Adjektiva auf* -αιοc (Diss. Uppsala 1918) 7f., 15.

be 'nourishing'[1] – viz. Inachus which φορβαίων immediately precedes: the Inachus is a dry river except after substantial rainfall when the mountains west of Argos, where it has its sources, supply torrential waters (A.Philippson, *Griech. Landschaften* III[1] (Frankfurt 1959) 139). In this context φορβαίων implies more than nourishment with water: it suggests that the gold and flowers of v. 49 result from the natural opulence of the Argive mountains.

Ἴναχος The name of the river is given for the first time, having been withheld from the negative injunctions of vv. 45–8 until the positive religious description of vv. 49–51.

51 τἀθάναι Emphatically placed at the beginning of the line: 'it is for *Athena* that . . .'

τὸ λοετρόν 'her bath'; for the idiomatic double article see on v. 2 τᾶν ἵππων. Uncontracted λοε- is Homeric: Doric generally has λωτρόν (cf. Hesych. s.v. and see on v. 1 λωτροχόοι, v. 72 λῶντο), but λοετρά is attested in the Doric prose of Agias and Dercylus' *Argolica* (on which see Intro. pp. 16f.) *FGrHist* 3B 305 F4 (cited by Pfeiffer on fr. 65). Cf. on v. 97 βαλεῦ for the mixture of forms.

ἄγων The participial phrase follows naturally after v. 50 ἡξεῖ: ἥκειν in particular commonly so combines with a 'completive' participle (K–G, *GG* II 60f.; for tragedy see G.W.Bond on Eur. *Hyps.* fr. 60.39 and T.C.W.Stinton, *Proc. Cam. Phil. Soc.* 21 (1975) 84f.). Cf. on v. 40 ὤιχετ' ἔχων.

καλόν The final word of the sentence, summarising the description of the previous two lines, is also suggestive of what is later at v. 113 described as χαρίεντα λοετρά (see note), and provides a suitable transition to the following ban on male observers.

51–4 Finally the warning away of the profane turns to the most important class of people, males, who will violate the sanctuary by virtue of their sex alone. [Plut.] *Parall. Min.* 17A, B (= *Mor.* 309E–310A) records that Ilus and Metellus were blinded on separate occasions after trying to steal the Palladion; see Intro. p. 23, and cf. Kleinknecht, *LP* 316.

Πελασγέ A specifically masculine ending, picked up in the next line by ἐθέλων. The contrast is with v. 4 Πελασγιάδες (see note). Use of the ethnic to address someone gives a rather oracular tone.

52 φράζεο μή Imperative of φράζεσθαι + μή + subjunctive is common from Homer on (K–G, *GG* II 390, cf. Ebeling, *LH* II 446: LSJ s.v. very misleadingly imply that v. 52 is a rare instance). For φράζεο μή in this position cf. *Il.* 16.446, Theocr. 6.13.

μὴ οὐκ Although C. allows hiatus after ἤ, μή almost always has

[1] Unlike φορβή and φορβάς which refer mainly to animal pasturage, the verb has a wide range of meaning and seems to be used of any kind of nourishment (LSJ).

synaloepha (Lapp, *TF* 144).[1] Ψ's μ' οὐκ probably originated from an earlier false crasis μοὐκ (at *E*. 8.5 MSS incorrectly give μηνδικα for μὴ ἔνδικα).

οὐκ ἐθέλων As is forcefully demonstrated in the Tiresias narrative intrusion on divine privacy is no less a crime because it is unintentional: the issue is one of a mortal encountering an overwhelming immortal force, not one of morality (v. 78, v. 113 οὐκ ἐθέλων: cf. v. 101f.).

τὰν βαcίλειαν The warning is expressed in its starkest terms: βαcίλεια denotes Athena's sacral authority, her absolute power within the province of the Argive cult, which any outsider crosses at his peril.[2] On the religious use of βαcιλεύc, βαcίλεια see H. Usener, *Götternamen* (Bonn 1896) 226–31, and cf. *RE* XI 2131.

53–4 The final general warning is expressed in a rather legal manner: cf. on vv. 101f. where Athena herself picks up these lines and makes an explicit legal pronouncement.

53 τὰν Παλλάδα As the whole invocatory section comes to a close the ambiguous terminology of v. 1 returns, reinforcing the identification of goddess and Palladion (see on v. 1 τᾶc Παλλάδοc).

τὰν πολιοῦχον The adjective indicates the implications of intrusion by the profane: the safety of the community is at stake as well as the goddess's personal privacy. The epithet, commonly applied to a city's guardian deity, is regularly used of Athena (see LSJ, the citations in Farnell, *CGS* I 398 n. 38, and Preller–Robert, *LM* I 219f.). The article is normal: in the combination God's Name + Epithet either both have the article or neither has it (Gildersleeve, *SCG* II 235f.), and here the article with Παλλάδα is necessary for the religious ambiguity (see on v. 1 τᾶc Παλλάδοc).

Doric regularly has πολιᾶχοc (-ᾱ-οχοc) where Attic has πολιοῦχοc (-ο-οχοc) and Meineke proposed πολιᾶχον here which Pfeiffer was tempted to accept.[3] However, πολιοῦχοc is testified in the Epidaurian Isyllus (Powell, *CA* 133) 16 and in the third-century B.C. Cretan

---

[1] 493.2 μὴ ἐξ is usually interpreted as aphaeresis, but synaloepha may be preferable not only because μή nowhere else causes aphaeresis but also because of the elegiac context: see on v. 47 ἢ 'c.

[2] Thus when at [Theocr.] 27.30 Daphnis speaks of τεὴ βαcίλεια . . . Ἄρτεμιc he is referring to the goddess in the same terms as did the girl he woos (vv. 16ff.) – as a power to which to devote oneself, like Hippolytus. The fact that neither Athena nor Artemis is called βαcίλεια before these two passages is of no significance: there is no question of any cult title here (cf. Wilamowitz, *HD* II 19), only a description of religious power such as was possessed by all Greek divinities.

[3] For the various dialectal forms see LSJ, Schwyzer, *GG* I 439 n. 5, and Frisk, *EW* s.v. The different forms cause confusion in the MSS of the tragedians: e.g. at Aesch. *Sept*. 109.

inscription, Schwyzer, *DGEE* 193.23 τὰν ᾿Αθαναίαν τὰν πολιοῦχον; although both instances may have been influenced by the *koine*, Ψ's text is best left unchanged here failing more evidence.

54 τὤργος τὸ Ἄργος: the article, well in place after τὰν Παλλάδα τὰν πολιοῦχον to which it forms an antithesis, is protreptic to τοῦτο, 'this his city of Argos' (cf. Gildersleeve, *SCG* II 243f.). The juxtaposition of πολιοῦχον and Ἄργος expresses the punishment in its most forceful terms: Athena is the city's guardian, but intrusion on her privacy results in the reversal of her patronage for the intruder (the double aspect of her nature has been referred to earlier, e.g. in v. 43 περσέπτολι contrasting with πολιοῦχον here).[1]

The crasis ο+α=ω is normal for Doric: K–B, *GG* I 224 (cf. *E.* 46.6 τὠγαθόν, *E.* 59.1 ὡρχαῖος).

τοῦτο πανυστάτιον For similar phraseology with demonstrative and ὑστατ- cf. A.R. 2.65f. οὐδέ τι ᾔδειν | νήπιοι ὕστατα κεῖνα κακῆι δήσαντες ἐπ' αἴσηι.

πανυστάτιον A Callimachean coinage: earlier usage had only πανύστατος (LSJ), but C. was following Homeric precedent which already allowed ὑστάτιος (*Il.* 8.353, 15.634, *Od.* 9.14, whence in later poets). On -ιος/-ος doublets see Risch, *WHS* 104.

55–6 The last of the three invocatory sections, which is also the point of transition to the narrative. The refrain ἔξιθ', ᾿Αθαναία is here slightly varied (πότνι') and extended (σὺ μέν), with the effect of relaxing the tension a little and easing the digression from the ritual.

The disclaimer in v. 56 serves two purposes: it relieves the narrator of any supposed moral responsibility, in case the story might incur Athena's displeasure (a protestation of this kind was a stylistic topos in Hellenistic poetry: e.g. Arat. 637 Ἄρτεμις ἱλήκοι· προτέρων λόγος . . . , A.R. 4.984f. ἵλατε Μοῦσαι, | οὐκ ἐθέλων ἐνέπω προτέρων ἔπος);[2] it also provides the source-credentials which are a feature of C.'s poetry (612 ἀμάρτυρον οὐδὲν

---

[1] M.L.West, *Philologus* 110 (1966) 158 mistakenly proposed τὤργον (τὸ ἔργον) for τὤργος. ('The article with Ἄργος is out of place *in this style*; and it does not seem very good sense to say "whoever sees Pallas naked, this will be his last sight of Argos"' (my italics): the first statement is incorrect and the lack of good sense is in West's misleading translation, not the Greek.)

[2] E.Maass, *Aratea* (Berlin 1892) 259 points out that the form of such disclaimers was standard: cf. Eur. *Hel.* 513 λόγος γάρ ἐστιν οὐκ ἐμός, σοφῶν δ' ἔπος, fr. 484 κοὐκ ἐμὸς ὁ μῦθος, ἀλλ' ἐμῆς μητρὸς πάρα, ὡς οὐρανός τε γαῖά τ' ἦν μορφὴ μία. For further references and discussion cf. R.Kannicht on Eur. *Hel.* 513 (Heidelberg 1969), Nauck on Eur. fr. 484 (who draws attention to the parody in Plato, *Symp.* 177A οὐ γὰρ ἐμὸς ὁ

ἀείδω): here the ἕτεροι are teasingly left unidentified, and although the plural may be a generalising one it may indicate that C.'s source was the *Argolica* of Agias and Dercylus (see Intro. p. 17).

For the general shape of the expression cf. Pind. *N.* 3.10f. ἄρχε . . . , θύγατερ [the Muse], δόκιμον ὕμνον. ἐγὼ δὲ κείνων [the chorus] τέ νιν ὀάροις λύραι τε κοινάσομαι, III 186 εἰπέ, θεή, σὺ μὲν ἄμμιν, ἐγὼ δ' ἑτέροισιν ἀείσω and the related Theocr. 22.116f. εἰπέ, θεά, σὺ γὰρ οἶσθα· ἐγὼ δ' ἑτέρων ὑποφήτης | φθέγξομαι (see Gow ad loc.).

The phraseology is picked up by Tib. 2.1.35f. *huc ades aspiraque mihi dum carmine nostra | redditur agricolis gratia caelitibus* (cf. on 36 above).

55 πότνι' A term of careful respect (cf. on v. 86 πότνια) which follows directly from v. 52 βασίλειαν. At *Il.* 6.305 Theano begins her prayer to Athena with the address πότνι' Ἀθηναίη ἐρυσίπτολι. Athena is πότνια again at 238.12 and 260.36.

σύ On the non-Doric form (Meineke proposed τύ which Wilamowitz accepted) see on v. 41 σέ.

μέστα μέσφα was epic/poetic vocabulary, revived by the Hellenistic poets from *Il.* 8.508 (see citations in LSJ); however it was normal usage in Arcadian, Thessalian, and some Doric areas (Crete and Cyrene),[1] and may therefore have appeared less exceptional in a Doric poem.[2] Elsewhere μέσφα is always a preposition or a conjunction ('*dum*'), and is adverbial ('meanwhile') only here; a Homeric touch since ἄχρις is also uniquely adverbial in *Il.* 4.522, 16.324, 17.599.[3]

Although Ψ had μέσφα, μέστα (Pfeiffer) is almost certainly correct: this is the form attested in two Hellenistic Doric inscriptions (LSJ),[4] and at VI 92, 111 where Ψ also had the more 'normal' μέσφα *P. Oxy.* 2226 preserves μέστα.[5] (For the reading of hyparchetype η, μέγα δέ σφ' ἐγώ τι, see Smiley, *CQ* 15 (1921) 67.)

μῦθος, ἀλλὰ Φαίδρου τοῦδε), Kleinknecht, *LP* 323 n. 1, and T.C.W.Stinton, 'Si credere dignum est', *Proc. Cam. Phil. Soc.* 22 (1976) 60–89.

[1] Buck, *GD* 104; citations and passages in Schwyzer, *GG* II 658. Cf. also Frisk, *EW* s.v. μέσφα and E.Hermann, *Griechische Forschungen: I Die Nebensätze in den griech. Dialektinschriften* (Berlin 1912) 302f.

[2] μέστα occurs three times in VI; however, the word was something of a favourite in C., who uses it at least ten times.

[3] Cf. Schwyzer, *GG* II 549, Chantraine, *GH* II 148, and Schwyzer's discussion of the 'adverbial origins' of many prepositions/conjunctions at *GG* II 419ff.

[4] The τ is also evident in Arcadian μέστε and Gortynian μέττα (LSJ). μέστα seems also to be testified in the last line of a papyrus fragment of undated lyric (?choral?), *P. Oxy.* 2880 (=*SLG* S459) 11 μ̣εστεπαυ̣[.

[5] The same papyrus shows the process of 'normalisation' actually taking place, for at VI 128 it too has μέσφα.

57–136 For the cautionary tale, the unusual story of the blinding of Tiresias, see Intro. pp. 17–25.

The narrative can be analysed as dividing into six sections expressively organised in 'ring' form:

the friendship	(57–69)	(119–36)	the gifts, as a mark of friendship
Tiresias' intrusion and punishment	(70–84)	(107–18)	Actaeon's intrusion and punishment
Chariclo's grief	(85–95)	(96–106)	Athena's response to Chariclo's grief

The central issue is Chariclo's grief, and it is around the apparent contradiction between the punishment and the friendship that the narrative develops.

57–69 The friendship between Athena and Chariclo. Although this was treated by Pherecydes too ([Apollod.] 3.6.7 οὖcαν γὰρ τὴν Χαρικλὼ προcφιλῆ τῆι Ἀθηνᾶι) it is characteristic of C. that Chariclo is presented as a *favourite* of Athena: elsewhere Artemis has Britomartis (III 189), Cyrene (III 206), Procris (III 209) and Anticleia (III 210f.), and Demeter has Enna (VI 29f.).[1] The narrative remarks on the intimacy between Athena and Chariclo very emphatically (v. 58 πουλύ τι καὶ περὶ δή, v. 59 οὔποκα χωρίc, v. 65 πολλάκις, v. 69 καταθύμιον), but in fact representation of the friendship is limited almost entirely to externals: there is little suggestion of how either of them was affected by their friendship.[2]

This studied detachment is increased further by the geographical information provided in vv. 60–4: nominally these lines are an illustration of v. 59 οὔποκα χωρὶc ἔγεντο, but the quantity of information inevitably distracts from the topic of friendship. Furthermore the places mentioned do not really concern Chariclo at all: it is Athena whose cult centres they are. Nominally this section concerns Chariclo as well as Athena, but in fact its

---

[1] A rare example of a goddess having a favourite in pre-Hellenistic poetry is Sappho fr. 142 Λάτω καὶ Νιόβα μάλα μὲν φίλαι ἦcαν ἔταιραι; this is probably not part of a narrative but a mythological model to a personal experience: cf. Denys Page, *Sappho and Alcaeus* 129f.

[2] In v. 67 ἁδεῖαι is an orthodox epithet of little expressive value: see note ad loc. Inseparability of two friends travelling together is also a standard motif (see on vv. 60ff.) and C.'s treatment does not especially illuminate the friendship (by way of contrast Theocr. 13.10ff. describing Heracles' love for Hylas – χωρὶc δ' οὐδέποκ' ἦc – manages to express through a brief reference to a mother hen with her chicks the fussiness with which he cared for the boy).

main effect is to continue the detailed representation of the goddess already described in vv. 1–56.

What tension there is is largely formal: the language is extensively 'epic' and more highly coloured than the first part of the poem; from v. 65 onwards the main syntactical breaks conflict with the couplet form, coming at the end of three successive hexameters instead of pentameters, and the result is a cumulative underlying agitation, a suitable prelude to the tense atmosphere of the first section of the story proper at vv. 70ff.

57 Ἀθαναία The first word, contrasting with the less specific νύμφαν μίαν, gives immediate prominence to the protagonist as often at the opening of a narrative: cf., e.g., 230 Ἀκταίη τις, Theocr. 24 Ἡρακλέα δεκάμηνον ἐόντα, Mosch. 2 Εὐρώπηι.

ἔν ποκα Θήβαις As an introductory particle ποτε is often attracted to a locative phrase for which it may be delayed as here from its normal place with the first word-element: cf. 230 Ἐρεχθέος ἔν ποτε γουνῶι|, III 238 ἔν κοτε παρραλίηι Ἐφέσωι, Philodamus Scarph. *Paean* 6 (Powell, *CA* 165ff.) [ὃ]ν Θήβαις ποτ' ἐν εὐίαις, Leonidas, *HE* 2161 ἔν ποτ' ἀλωῆι.

The tmesis of preposition and noun is poetic: prose allows only a conjunctive particle to intervene (see K–G, *GG* I 552f. and add Pind. *P.* 2.33 ἔν ποτε θαλάμοις, *N.* 8.18 ποντίαι ἔν ποτε Κύπρωι). Cf. Wackernagel, *IF* I (1892) 370 (= *Kleine Schriften* I 38).

Verbally similar is the line-ending at Theocr. 16.105 ἀπεχθόμενόν ποτε Θήβαις.

58 πουλύ τι Intensive adverbial τι with quantitative adverbs was a standard idiom mostly avoided in poetry,[1] but with qualitative neuter adjectives used adverbially (ἡδύ τι, καλόν τι etc.) was a mannerism in C. and Theocritus,[2] and its use here with πουλύ is made more unusual by the reinforcing περὶ δή. Again in Meleager, *HE* 4608 πουλύ τι κείνης| πικρότερον . . . κῦμα.

Reduplication of intensive adverbs is a feature of Hellenistic poetry: e.g.

---

[1] σχεδόν τι, in Soph. *OT* 736, *Ant.* 470, *El.* 609 and Eur. *Hel.* 112, is exceptional. For adverbial τι in prose see K–G, *GG* I 663f., Stein on Hdt. 5.33.9, Classen on Thuc. 1.138, and Mayser, *GGP* II² 85; it is not uncommon in Aristophanes. When intensive τις had disappeared from the spoken language the Atticists carefully revived it, and especially this use of adverbial τι: Schmid, *Atticismus* (Stuttgart 1887) I 136f., 293, II 157f., III 68f.

[2] For the Alexandrian extension to qualitative adverbs cf.: ἡδύ τι in II 4, Theocr. 1.1, 5.89, 20.21 (cf. 8.82, 11.3), ὀϊζυρόν τι in II 24, ἔκπαγλόν τι in IV 247, ἄφατόν τι in V 77, VI 57, and καλόν τι in Theocr. 5.135 (cf. 15.23). The phrase μέγα δή τι is also especially common in C.: 228.56, IV 60, 189, V 122, *E.* 43.5; A.R. too favours the expression (1.253, 3.637, 891, 4.1255), but it is otherwise not common (*pace* Bühler on Mosch. 2.146).

IV 60 cπερχομένη μέγα δή τι καὶ οὐ φατόν, A.R. 4.1383 ὦ περὶ δὴ μέγα φέρτατοι, Theocr. 5.135 καλόν τι με κάρτ' ἐφίλησεν.

περὶ δή περί of superiority or advantage (adverb or preposition) is an archaic epic usage[1] common in A.R. but otherwise rare in Hellenistic poetry: Theocr. (?) 25.119 (cf. *Il.* 1.287 etc.), Arat. 237. Only here for certain in C.[2]

περί was taken as a preposition governing τᾶν ἑταρᾶν until Stephanus read it as an adverb, and since then only Spanheim, Schneider and Mair have defended the preposition. An adverb is certainly preferable: τᾶν ἑταρᾶν is best dependent on μίαν ('one nymph out of her friends': Chariclo *is* a ἑτάρα) rather than on περί, from which it is separated ('one nymph more than her friends'); that πουλύ and περί should be taken closely together is indicated not only by the diaeresis after περὶ δή, but also by the almost identical phraseology at 75.52 (φῦλον) πουλύ τι καὶ περίτιμον Ἰουλίδι ναιετάουcιν. (The close association between περί and πουλύ is well illustrated by A.R. 1.152 where the coinage περιθαρcής replaces the usual Homeric πολυθαρcής.)

Most editors anastrophise περί to πέρι when it is adverbial, but although the accentuation of such 'prepositional' adverbs was a point of discussion for ancient commentators, the most authoritative ancient grammarians are unanimous against anastrophe and all reliable evidence points to περι = περιccῶc being oxytone: see the full and excellent discussion in B.Laum, *Das Alexandrinische Akzentuationssystem* (Paderborn 1928) 195–201.[3] (For what it is worth Ψ read περὶ.)

φίλατο Epic in form and meaning. The abbreviated φιλα- aorist middle forms of φιλεῖν (with compensatory lengthening of ι) are used only by Homer and Hesiod, always of divine love for mortals.[4] Hellenistic poets revive the archaic epic usage: Posidippus (?), '*Seal*' (*SH* 705, H.Lloyd-Jones, *JHS* 83 (1963) 75–99) 9, C. fr. 43.53, III 185, 189, A.R. 3.66 (middle

---

[1] Cf. Chantraine, *GH* II 129, Schwyzer, *GG* II 423f., 501f.; outside Homer and Hesiod the only pre-Hellenistic instance seems to be Pind. *O.* 6.50 περὶ θνατῶν δ' ἔcεcθαι . . . ἔξοχον (an explicitly Homeric passage).

[2] *Hecale* 238.12 may be another example; for 202.82 see Barber, *CR* 5 (1955) 242; 186.28 is too fragmentary to allow any conclusions.

[3] Cf. also Erbse on Σ to *Il.* 1.46, 2.831, K–B, *GG* I 335, H.W.Chandler, *Greek Accentuation* (Oxford 1881[2]) 258f.

[4] Cf. Ebeling, *LH* II 431. On the form and other λ, ρ verbs which drop the aorist sigma see Chantraine, *GH* I 172f. and Schwyzer, *GG* I 718. *H.H.Dem.* 117, where φίλωνται is apparently used of human love, is no exception: the object is Demeter in disguise and the verb ironically plays on the reversal of normal circumstances as yet unappreciated by the speaker.

form, passive sense), 1002, 4.990, Lyc. 274, 518, Leonidas, *HE* 2088 (of human love for a cicada!).

The syllabic augment is commonly omitted by C., as in Homer, in narratives of clearly past tense (Chantraine, *GH* I 483f.): metrical convenience seems to have been the sole criterion since MSS generally offer the augment when either form would be possible (68 πόλλ' ἔμενε, 85, 96). Such forms were not pure poeticisms: contemporary Hellenistic Greek not infrequently omitted the syllabic augment, though usually in compounds (Mayser, *GGP* I^2 98). Again at 72, 73, 133; see also on 3 ἐcάκουcα for omission of the temporal augment.

τᾶν ἑταρᾶν ἑτάρα for ἑταίρα is an apparently unique Homeric form occurring only at *Il.* 4.441;[1] revived by C. here, v. 119 and I 46, and otherwise only in Mosch. 2.102. The form is rare enough to be glossed by Hesychius with φίλη ἑταίρα, cυνεργόc (? from Mosch. 2.102 ἑτάραι φιλίαι?).

59 **ματέρα Τειρεcίαο** The significant information is given early in the narrative before the Tiresias story begins. Athena's companion is described first in the terms in which she will be involved in the subsequent action, as mother of her son: her actual identity, irrelevant in this respect, is not given until the end of v. 67 when it is delivered with the force of freshness (cf. the same device in v. 50 with Ἴναχοc). The periphrasis here also has the effect of posing a puzzle whose solution is delayed for nine lines: Chariclo is very rarely mentioned in ancient literature and her identity can be considered a semi-erudite point (cf. Roscher, *LM* I 872: to make the puzzle more difficult there were two other Chariclos, both better known than this one).

Τειρεcίαο The epic genitive, contrary to all Doric dialects which have -ᾱ (Schwyzer, *GG* I 560 γ), Monteil, *T* 37: Theocritus too uses the epic form as an alternative). Cf. on v. 97 βαλεῦ.

οὔποκα χωρὶc ἔγεντο Theocr. 13.10, of Heracles and Hylas, χωρὶc δ' οὐδέποκ' ἦc.

ἔγεντο On this much-discussed form see A.Morpurgo Davies, *Glotta* 42 (1964) 150f. and references. It features widely in post-Homeric

[1] MSS give ἑτάραc at Sappho fr. 126, but dialect and metre almost certainly require ἑταίραc: see Denys Page, *Sappho and Alcaeus* 139 n. 4 and *Lyrica Graeca Selecta* (OCT) no. 236. W.Schulze, *Quaestiones Epicae* (Gütersloh 1892) 82 first explained the variety of forms: ἕταροc had the feminine *ἕταρjα which became ἑταίρη and itself generated the analogous masculine ἑταῖροc; ἑτάρη is a later analogy to ἕταροc completing the symmetry: cf. Risch, *WHS* 153, Frisk, *EW* I 579, Chantraine, *DE* 380f. It is worth considering whether ἑτάρη may not have been coined precisely for *Il.* 4.441: κacιγνήτη ἑτάρη τε may be a direct formulaic extension of *Il.* 24.793 κacίγνητοί θ' ἕταροί τε.

non-dramatic poetry,[1] and although often explained as a Doricism it was certainly not so regarded by the Hellenistic poets, who use it frequently as an alternative to ἐγένετο (C. 63.6, 270, I 50, IV 147, A.R. 1.1141, 3.1321, 4.1427, Theocr. 1.88, 13.2 etc.).

60–5 Cf. Sappho fr. 94.24ff. recollecting places visited together to illustrate inseparability in friendship: κωὔτε τις[ ]. . τι | ἶρον οὐδυ[ ] | ἔπλετ' ὄππ[οθεν ἄμ]μες ἀπέσκομεν, | οὐκ ἄλσος.

The listing of alternative places gives the passage a tone of religious formalism: the need to be as comprehensive as possible when addressing a god naturally applied also to the localisation (when given), and prayers often list the main places where the divinity might be found.[2] Thence the cautious listing of places is adopted as here in narratives about the gods: e.g. *Od.* 6.102f, A.R. 1.307ff., 536ff., 3.876ff., 1240ff.[3] The variation in phraseology is typical of Hellenistic diction: cf. III 170ff. ἀγχόθι πηγάων . . . ἢ Πιτάνηι . . . ἢ ἐνί . . . ἢ ἵνα . . . , A.R. 1.536ff. ἢ ἐνί . . . ἤ που ἐν . . . ἢ ἐφ', and contrast, e.g., *H.H.Ap.* 210ff. Ἴσχυ' ἅμ' ἀντιθέωι . . . | ἢ ἅμα . . . ἢ ἅμ' . . . | ἢ ἅμα . . .

The worship of Athena was of great antiquity and importance round Lake Copais (*RE* II 1947–9), and Alalcomenae near Haliartos was claimed by Boeotians to be her birthplace. The three towns mentioned here were the main settlements in the foothills round the Boeotian part of Mt Helicon, the setting of the Tiresias story (v. 71): good descriptions of the locality and the situation of each town in Frazer, *Pausanias* V 140–2 (Thespiae), 164–6 (Haliartos), 170 (Coroneia).[4] (Full survey of the evidence in A.Schachter, *Cults of Boiotia* (*BICS* Suppl. 38.1: London 1981) 111–35.)

60 ἀρχαιᾶν The adjective has an unusual meaning = 'ancient', 'of antiquity', and not the normal 'ancient', 'original'. Thespiae was an early

---

[1] Parmenides, Empedocles, Theognis etc.: full list of instances in Wackernagel, *SUH* 173 (add Sappho fr. 61.1, Pindar fr. 33b, C. 63.6, 270, A.R. 3.1321).

[2] E.g. *H.H.Ap.* 179ff., *Il.* 1.37f., Sappho fr. 35, Ananius fr. 4D, Aristoph. *Ran.* 659, Theocr. 1.67, 123ff., C. III 170ff., IV 47ff. etc.; cf. F.Schwenn, *Gebet und Opfer* (Heidelberg 1927) 60, H.Kleinknecht, *Die Gebetsparodie in der Antike* (Berlin 1937) 19, 24f., 88f.

[3] Also with features other than places: *H.H.Ap.* 209ff. lists a variety of Apollo's companions; Pind. *I.* 7.1–15 uses the listing of alternatives to create an atmosphere of religious intensity. Of course Greek does lend itself to this form of expression: cf. E.Kemmer, *Die polare Ausdrucksweise in der griech. Literatur* (Würzburg 1903) esp. 166ff.

[4] See also A.Philippson, *Die griech. Landschaften* I (Frankfurt 1950) 463–6 ('Das Helikon-Gebiet'), 466–90 ('Das Kopais-Becken'), and P.W.Wallace, 'Hesiod and the valley of the Muses', *GRBS* 15 (1974) 5–24 (with maps and photographs).

foundation, built by Thespius descendant of Erechtheus,[1] but it was younger than Haliartos and Coroneia, which were founded by grandsons of Sisyphus, and the relative antiquity of Thespiae is anyway of no significance here. Rather, ἀρχαιᾶν is like v. 57 ποκα = 'in the olden days', 'of old', with a general emotive value, setting the story firmly in the past in relation to the supposed occasion of the Hymn (hence the adjective's position at the front of its long clause, before even εὖτε). C. uses ἀρχαῖος = πρότερος (LSJ s.v. A.II) elsewhere too: IV 308 ἄγαλμα | Κυπρίδος ἀρχαίης ἀριήκοον, ἥν ποτε Θησεύς | εἵσατο, *E.* 59.1 ὡρχαῖος 'Ορέστας, 75.54 ἀρχαίου Ξενομήδεος and possibly 7.26 ἀρχαίην ... Αἱμονίην (a similarly phrased pentameter); the usage is rare in other authors but cf. Bacch. 5.150 ἀρχαίαν πόλιν Πλευρῶνα, Soph. *Aj.* 1292 ἀρχαῖον ... Πέλοπα, Theocr. 11.8 ὡρχαῖος Πολύφαμος, Rhianus fr. 25.2P Πύρρης ... ἀρχαίης, Nic. *Ther.* 487 ἀρχαίη Μετάνειρα.[2]

The Doric genitive plural (feminine) restored by Meineke makes for consistency with Ψ's text elsewhere at vv. 2, 3, 6; Θεσπιέων is the (feminine) name of the city, not a masculine ethnic (see on v. 60 Θεσπιέων).

εὖτ' An epic conjunction (occasionally in lyric and tragic poets by Homeric influence) extensively used by C. and A.R. (but very rare in bucolics and avoided by Aratus): see Monteil, *PR* 286ff., Schwyzer, *GG* II 660f. For the characteristic delaying of the conjunction to second position see on v. 121 ἐπεί.

Θεσπιέων The only evidence connecting historical Thespiae with Athena is Paus. 9.26.8 who notes in a lacunose passage the existence of a statue of Worker Athena ('Αθηνᾶν τὴν 'Εργάνην); Athena is notably absent from the fairly extensive evidence surviving of the cults practised in Thespiae (*RE* VI^a 44–51), but this could be due solely to chance (cf. on v. 61 'Αλίαρτον).

C. uses the contemporary form of the city's name and not the Homeric one: from *Il.* 2.498 until the fourth century B.C. the name was singular Θέσπεια (citations in Pape–Benseler, *Wörterbuch der griech. Eigennamen* (Braunschweig 1884) s.v.), but from the fourth century B.C. plural Θεσπιαί was generally used. However, C. does inflect with the epic Ionic genitive

---

1 Thespius' fifty daughters produced, through one of Heracles' multiple sexual exploits, the family which in historical times still had sufficient standing and power to rule the city: cf. Diod. Sic. 4.29, and variations in Paus. 9.27, Steph. Byz. s.v.

2 Also perhaps Arat. 98f. ὅν ῥά τέ φασιν | ἄστρων ἀρχαῖον πατέρ' ἔμμεναι, where Friesemann's suggested ἀρχαῖοι is unnecessary if the Callimachean sense is admitted.

plural (-έων for -άων),[1] which is foreign to Doric (see Chantraine, *GH* I 69):[2] similarly A.R. 1.106 Θεςπιέων.

61 The first half of this line is textually problematic: all MSS, except the ʒ branch which omits vv. 61f. completely,[3] have ἤ 'πὶ Κορωνείας which is intolerable for four reasons:

(1) the masculine caesura after Κορωνείας in v. 61 requires a secondary caesura either after the seventh element (proclitic εἰς) or after the eighth element ('Αλι-) or both (Maas, *GM* §93). There are in C. only nine exceptions to this practice of secondary caesura (in *c.* 1,700 hexameters), and none occur in elegiacs;[4]

(2) ἤ before εἰς 'Αλίαρτον should almost certainly be correpted to a short syllable (see on v. 48 ἤ ἐς), requiring Κορωνείας [˘];

(3) the epanaphora with v. 63 ἤ 'πὶ Κορωνείας is inelegant, making vv. 61f. ἤ εἰς 'Αλίαρτον . . . an awkward interruption;

(4) if such a phrase is repeated the disjunctive ἤ should be omitted the second time (i.e. at v. 63): see O.Danielsson, *Eranos* 4 (1900–2) 106.

A subsidiary point is that the three cities mentioned are most naturally listed with Haliartos in the middle as they are situated on the road (Paus. 9.32.5 travelling inland from the Corinthian Gulf gives Thespiae, Haliartos, Coroneia).

---

[1] Pape–Benseler s.v. Θεςπιαί and T.Bergk, *Opuscula philologica* (Halle 1886) II 187 interpret Θεςπιέων here as a genitive of the ethnic Θεςπιεύς, as if Θεςπιεῖς were interchangeable with Θεςπιαί; this is impossible, and in Appian, *Mithr.* 29, cited as another example of ethnic for place, Θεςπιέων can be only ethnic, as is indicated by the preceding 'Αχαιοὶ καὶ Λάκωνες.

[2] The Ionic genitive plural is almost always metrically monosyllabic in Homer, although there are a few disyllabic exceptions after ι (Chantraine, *GH* I 64f., K–B, *GG* I 376). Alexandrian interest in the Ionic genitive is evidenced at *Il.* 5.818, 15.656, where Aristarchus read -έων instead of -ῶν.

[3] Presumably by haplography. It is worth noting that in the *editio princeps* of this hymn in 1489 Politian's Florentine printer made the same error: the couplet is omitted in the Greek text without gap, but it appears in the Latin version and Politian notes the erratum in his prefatory list of '*emendationes*'. 'The transference of 63 to follow straight on 61 probably arose from the feeling that it belonged there, ἤ 'πὶ Κορωνείας in the former following naturally after ἐπὶ Θεςπιέων in the latter. The lacuna would appear to have been indicated before 63 was transposed, a shrewd scribe noticing the lack of a principal verb in 60 + 63 + 64 as they stood when he found them' (M.T.Smiley, *CQ* 15 (1921) 119).

[4] Six are in VI (vv. 5, 11, 72, 91, 109, 118); the remaining three occur at I 36, 58, III 262. For a similarly phrased but metrically correct line cf. VI 86 ἤ 'ἔπες' ἐξ ἵππων', ἤ 'ἐν "Οθρυϊ . . .'

Ernesti, followed by Cahen and P.Maas, *SJ*, transposed vv. 61f. after vv. 63f., resolving the difficulty of the awkward interruption, but leaving the other difficulties untouched. P.B.Marzolla, *Stud. It.* 26 (1952) 211f. (followed by E.Howald and E.Staiger, *Callimachi Poemata* (Zürich 1955) and McKay, *PP* 4) replaced v. 61 ἢ 'πὶ Κορωνείας with ἢ 'πὶ Πλαταιάων taken from Nonn. *D.* 4.335f., 13.70 where Thespiae and Haliartos are mentioned together with Plataea, but this too still leaves the metrical difficulties unresolved: quite apart from which, Plataea is geographically inappropriate in C. since it is situated well away from Helicon on the northern slopes of Mt Cithaeron.[1]

The only satisfactory approach seems to be that of Wilamowitz: excision of the whole phrase from v. 61 and the positing of a lacuna pending further evidence.[2]

Ἁλίαρτον No ancient source records any association of Athena with Haliartos,[3] but in 1931 a sanctuary discovered earlier on the acropolis containing a temple and other buildings (R.P.Austin, *ABSA* 27 (1925–6) 81ff., 268f.; 28 (1926–7) 128ff.) was shown from an inscribed fragment of pottery to belong to Athena (*ABSA* 32 (1931–2) 180ff.). The sanctuary was in use from mid-sixth century B.C. until Hellenistic times, probably until the destruction of Haliartos by the Romans in 171 B.C.

61–2 ἐλαύνοι | ἵππως With the same attention to detail A.R. describes the travels to cult centres by Artemis in 3.878ff. χρυσείοις Λητωὶς ἐφ' ἅρμασιν ἑστηυῖα | ὠκείαις κεμάδεσσι διεξελάῃσι κολώνας, | τηλόθεν ἀντιόωσα πολυκνίσου ἑκατόμβης, and by Poseidon in 3.1240ff. Ἴσθμιον εἶσι Ποσειδάων ἐς ἀγῶνα, | ἅρμασιν ἐμβεβαώς, ἢ Ταίναρον ἢ ὅγε Λέρνης | ὕδωρ ἠὲ καὶ ἄλσος Ὑαντίου Ὀγχηστοῖο, | καί τε Καλαύρειαν μετὰ δὴ θαμὰ νίσσεται ἵπποις.

61 ἐλαύνοι The iterative optative with historic tense main verb was almost obsolete in the *koine*, but the poets follow Classical usage and show no sign of influence by contemporary idiom:[4] e.g. III 61, VI 68, A.R. 3.954f., 2.471, Theocr. 13.10ff., 17.14, 24.32, 25.134ff.

---

[1] In Nonnus Plataea is appropriate since both passages are concerned with a more general survey of Boeotia; Nonnus is in any case probably indebted not to C. but to *Il.* 2.503f. οἵ τε Κορώνειαν καὶ ποιήενθ' Ἁλίαρτον | οἵ τε Πλάταιαν ἔχον.

[2] ἢ 'πὶ Κορωνείας may conceal another name, but no place in the area seems suitable.

[3] Though close by Haliartos was Mt Tilphosion which may have been associated with Athena (*RE* II 1948f.), and the Tilphusa spring by which tradition placed Tiresias' grave (Paus. 9.33.1).

[4] Mayser, *GGP* II[1] 295f., Moulton, *GNT* III 124f.: the iterative optative survived only in stereotype formulae and official communications, being replaced elsewhere either by the simple indicative or, later, by indicative

62 ἵππως Ernesti's correction of Ψ's 'normalised' ἵππους is necessary: elsewhere Ψ has -ως accusative plural (vv. 5, 13, 15 etc.). Corrupted again at v. 142.

ἔργα 'works'. In the rural sense of worked land ἔργα is notably epic (LSJ), whence occasionally in other archaic writers (Tyrt. 4.7, Sol. 1.21, Bacch. 10.44), and especially with an accompanying genitive as here (αἰζηῶν, ἀνδρῶν etc.). However, its sporadic appearance in prose authors suggests that it was probably a feature of literary *koine* also (?from Ionic? – almost undocumented in LSJ): Hdt. 1.36.1,2 [Xen.] *Cyn.* 4.9, 5.12, 15, 34, 8.2, 9.11, ?Aristot. *HA* 552a 13?, Theophr. *Sign.* 3.9, *SEG* 15 (1958) 517 II 29 (third century B.C. Paros: *Vita Archilochi*), *LXX* Exod. 23.16, Jer. 14.4, *P. Petr.* (third century B.C.) 2.4 frr. 3.5, 37.1b 8, *P. Teb.* 47.4 (second century B.C.), *P. Baden* 40.5 (second century A.D.); cf. Pollux, *Onom.* 5.35 ἐν πᾶσι τόποις . . . ἔργοις, πεδίοις, ὄρεσιν . . .[1] (cf. τὰ ἐργάσιμα in Xen. *Cyr.* 1.4.16, *Cyn.* 5.15 etc.). In the Hellenistic poets, here, III 125, 156, Theocr. 22.42, Arat. 1126 (cf. Theophr. *Sign.* 3.9); not in A.R.

ἔργα διερχομένα Vaguely reminiscent of Homeric phraseology: the common | ἔργον ἐποίχεσθαι ('set about the task': *Od.* 1.358, 17.227 etc.) produces *Od.* 16.314 | ἔργα μετερχόμενος of Odysseus going round his farmsteads (thence Arat. 1126 | ἔργα κατέρχηται of the wolf coming down to the farmlands).

63 ἤ 'πὶ Κορωνείας The participial phrase in v. 62 turns out not to have been a summarising clausula at the end of the list of places, but only a pause before mention of the most important centre of all, to which a whole couplet is devoted. In the plain before the city of Coroneia was the ancient sanctuary of Itonian Athena where every year the Pan-Boeotian festival with military contests was held: see *RE* XI 1425ff. ('Koroneia'), IX 2375f. ('Itonia'), and P.Roesch, *Thespies et la confédération béotienne* (Paris 1965) 107 and *Études béotiennes* (Paris 1982) 220–4.[2]

For aphaeresis of ἐπί see on v. 47 ἤ 'ς.

ἵνα οἱ τεθυωμένον ἄλσος The whole phrase is heavily epic: τεθυωμένον is an isolated perfect participle form on root θυ-[3] previously used only in epic;

---

with ἄν. The occasional use by Xenophon of the indicative in this construction represents an earlier stage of this development: cf. K–G, *GG* II 451 A.5, Monteil, *PR* 284f.

[1] Cf. Hesychius s.v. ἔργα· ποτὲ μὲν τὰ περὶ τὴν ταλασιουργίαν· ποτὲ δὲ τὰ κατὰ τὴν γεωργίαν.

[2] Cf. also Preller–Robert, *GM* I 214f., 220, Farnell, *CGS* I 301.

[3] Cf. Frisk, *EW* I 694f., Chantraine, *DE* 448. Hedylus, *HE* 1839 θυωθέν is the only other form generated (no doubt as a variant on τεθυωμένον); it should be noted that the words preceding θυωθέν are corrupt (see Gow and Page ad loc.).

cf. especially *Il.* 14.172, *H.H.Aphr.* 63 (of oil) τό ῥά οἱ τεθυωμένον ἦεν.[1] In addition cf. the similar syntactical shape at *Il.* 8.48, *Od.* 8.363 ἔνθα δέ οἱ τέμενος βωμός τε θυήεις (*Il.* 23.148 ὅθι τοι . . . , *H.H.Aphr.* 59 . . . θυώδης). Finally, epithet + ἄλcoc | is standard epic idiom (e.g. *Il.* 2.506 ἀγλαὸν ἄλcoc | , *H.H.Herm.* 186 πολυήρατον ἄλcoc etc.).

ἵνα οἱ See on v. 31 οἱ.

64 Sappho fr. 2.2ff. χάριεν μὲν ἄλcoc | μαλί[αν], βῶμοι δὲ τεθυμιάμε|νοι [λι]βανώτωι, III 38 'Αρτέμιδος βωμοί τε καὶ ἄλcεα.

κεῖντ' Elision of middle and passive ending -αι, common in epic, lyric and comedy (K–B, *GG* I 237–9, Maas, *GM* 74), is not unusual in C.: see Pfeiffer on fr. 535.

ἐπί + dative = 'by', 'near' is common in epic (Ebeling, *LH* I 444f.), and also in early prose (though the lexica and grammars give little indication of this).[2] In the *koine*, however, local ἐπί + dative is very rare,[3] and its frequent appearance in C. is as a poeticism. Like Homer C. uses ἐπί + dative particularly with rivers:[4] e.g. 43.46 οἶδα Γέλα ποταμοῦ κεφαλῆι ἔπι κείμενον ἄcτυ.

Κουραλίωι The river is earlier mentioned by Alcaeus 325 in a similar context:[5] ἄναcc' 'Αθάναα πτολε[μάδοκοc | ἅ ποι Κορωνήαc μεδ[έοιc' | ναύω πάροιθεν ἀμφι[| Κωραλίω ποτάμω πὰρ ὄχθαιc. The name is not otherwise documented, and Strabo 9.411f. calls the river Κουάριοc (again at 9.435 and, following Strabo, Eustathius 268.22) remarking that Alcaeus had changed the form.[6] Κουραλίωι may therefore be either a poetic or a cult form. The MSS are unanimous in reading Κουρ-, but this may be due to 'normalisation' of Κωρ- (Schneider), and certainly so if Preller–Robert, *GM* I 187 (cf. Farnell, *CGS* I 265) are correct in interpreting the name as 'brook of the maiden' (vv. 27, 138 κῶραι).

65 πολλάκιc An iterative (in form or tense) main verb is occasionally replaced by an aorist when the iteration is expressed by an accompanying

---

[1] Otherwise only at *H.H.Ap.* 184 (by emendation), *Cypria* fr. 3.8K (εἵματα) . . . τεθυωμένα. The cognates θυώδηc and θύωμα, by contrast, are normal usage (LSJ).

[2] See e.g., R.Helbing, *Die Präpositionen bei Herodot* (Würzburg 1904) 61f.

[3] Cf. Mayser, *GGP* II² 471f., Moulton, *GNT* III 271f., F.Krebs, *Die Präpositionen bei Polybios* (Würzburg 1882) 84–6.

[4] See Ebeling, *LH* I 445 and cf. Σ to *Il.* 21.87 'ἐπὶ' τοῖc ποταμοῖc φαμὲν κεῖcθαι τὰc πόλειc.

[5] The text derives from Strabo 9.411 now supplemented by a Vatican palimpsest, on which see W.Aly and F.Sbordone, *De Strabonis Codice Rescripto* (Studi e Testi 188: Vatican City 1956) 34, 277–8, and cf. H.Lloyd-Jones, *CR* 19 (1969) 21.

[6] On the form Κουάριοc see Bechtel, *GD* I 148.

adjective or adverb (K–G, *GG* II 450, Schwyzer, *GG* II 335f.): cf. *Il.* 3.232 πολλάκι μιν ξείνισσεν . . . , A.R. 3.954 ἦ θαμὰ δὴ ἐάγη.

ἁ δαίμων The article, rare in this generally 'epic' narrative section, reasserts the subject of the main period after the long intervening subordinate clause from v. 60, as again at v. 85 ἁ νύμφα the article re-presents Chariclo (cf. Chantraine, *GH* II 162).

νιν Meineke's correction here and at v. 96 of Ψ's μιν gives the Doric form consistent with Ψ's νιν at vv. 105 and 121. Cf. Gow on Theocr. 1.48.

ἑῶ ἐπεβάσατο δίφρω Epic rhythm of expression (e.g. *Od.* 5.76, 7.134 etc. ἑῷι —το θυμῷι |, *Il.* 9.148 ἑῆι ἐπέδωκε θυγατρί, *H.H.Dem.* 466 ἑῷι δ' ἐπένευσε κάρητι: again in C. at II 90 ἑῆι δ' ἐπεδείξατο νύμφηι) and epic phraseology: *Il.* 8.44, 13.26 ἑοῦ δ' ἐπιβήσετο δίφρου | (cf. *Il.* 24.322 ξεστοῦ ἐπ., *Il.* 5.109 καταβήσεο δίφρου |, *Od.* 3.481 περικαλλέα βήσετο δίφρον |).[1]

ἑῶ ἐπ. Hiatus in C. commonly occurs in the pattern Noun + Preposition: see Pfeiffer on 43.46 κεφαλῆι ἔπι and Bühler on Mosch. 2.87 (here ἐπ- governs ἑῶ . . . δίφρω).[2] After a longum, hiatus is permitted only when two short syllables follow (see on v. 48 ἦ ἐς). Cf. on v. 71.

ἐπεβάσατο Within the orthodox epic phraseology the *transitive* use of the middle is a unique Callimachean variation (again at *Orph. Arg.* 1195 κούρην ἐπεβήσατο), and the voice may emphasise the closeness of Athena and Chariclo (Athena acts with her own interest in view). On the interchangeability in Hellenistic poetry of active and middle see G.Boesch, *De Apollonii Rhodii Elocutione* (Diss. Göttingen 1908) 16ff. and on middle for active 21f. and Schneider on I 80; other examples in C. are 228.68, II 98, III 42, 50, 166 (cf. *H.H.Dem.* 170), 234.[3]

The ending -ατο is also non-Homeric. Epic diction possessed a number of irregular verbs which combined aorist -σ- with thematic inflections, e.g. βήσετο, δύσετο (G. Curtius, *The Greek Verb* (London 1880) 460ff., Chantraine, *GH* I 416ff.). Although the Alexandrian Homeric commentators preserved these mixed aorists against normalisation[4] the Hellenistic poets themselves seem always to have used the normal -α- endings: Philetas

---

[1] A.R. also imitates this cluster of Homeric formulae: 3.869, 1152 θοῆς ἐπεβήσατ' ἀπήνης; cf. 4.288 ἐπιβήσεται οὔρους, 458 ἱερῆς ἐπεβήσετο νήσου.

[2] For hiatus at this position in the line in Theocritus see Gow on 5.148: of the eleven examples quoted five are of the type Noun + Preposition/Preverb.

[3] This interchangeability is part of the more general process which involved the confused use and eventual obsolescence of the middle voice in the *koine*: Mayser, *GGP* II[1] 109–16, Moulton, *GNT* III 53–7.

[4] See Σ to *Il.* 2.35, 3.262, 10.513, 14.229; Aristarchus was uncertain about the form, preferring -ε- but keeping -α- in his text (cf. A.Ludwich, *Aristarchs homerische Textkritik* II (Leipzig 1885) 123).

fr. 18K (Powell, *CA* 94 fr. 22), A.R. 1.382, 3.869, 889, 1152, 1237, 4.775, 865, 1663, Nic. *Al.* 302, *Ther.* 31. Only at A.R. 1.63 do the MSS unanimously read ἐδύϲετο, and at 4.458, 1176 they divide between -ετο and -ατο. The possibility of 'normalisation' on an extensive scale in the MSS of Hellenistic authors cannot therefore be excluded, but the -ε- readings in A.R. may equally be due to 'Homericisation',[1] and it should be noted that developments in the *koine*, where weak aorist -α- endings were encroaching on the non-sigmatic strong aorist endings,[2] made the Homeric mixed forms even more unusual.

66–7 Cf. the description of Artemis at *Od.* 6.105f. τῆι δέ θ' ἅμα νύμφαι, κοῦραι Διὸϲ αἰγιόχοιο, | ἀγρονόμοι παίζουϲι, III 170ff. ἡνίκα δ' αἱ νύμφαι ϲε χορῶι ἔνι κυκλώϲονται . . . (cf. A.R. 3.881ff.). Similarly Delos leads the Aegean islands at IV 16–18 ἀλλά οἱ οὐ νεμεϲητὸν ἐνὶ πρώτηιϲι λέγεϲθαι, | ὁππότ' ἐϲ Ὠκεανόν . . . | νῆϲοι ἀολλίζονται, ἀεὶ δ' ἔξαρχοϲ ὁδεύει.

66 ὄαροι ὄαροϲ and cognates belong to epic vocabulary and have the same spread of meaning as English 'association', 'intercourse';[3] Mair's 'dalliance' is very good. By the fourth century B.C. ὀαρ- words seem to have become obscure, since Plato quoting *Od.* 19.179 at *Min.* 319E explains the meaning of ὀαριϲτήϲ (οἱ γὰρ ὄαροι λόγοι εἰϲίν, καὶ ὀαριϲτὴϲ ϲυνουϲιαϲτήϲ ἐϲτιν ἐν λόγοιϲ), but some early Hellenistic poets revived them as rare archaisms: Timon, *SH* 831.2, A.R. 3.1102, C. fr. 401.3, 500.2. After this brief revival ὀαρ- words disappear until the end of the first century B.C., after which they appear regularly in poetic diction, especially in the context of love.[4]

χοροϲταϲίαι A rare noun, apparently a Hellenistic coinage formed from the common expression χορὸν ἱϲτάναι (LSJ s.v. χορόϲ: of the dancer, the accompanying musician, or the institutor of the dance). The immediate cognates seem to be standard usage (χοροϲτάτιϲ Alcm. *PMG* 1.84, χοροϲτατήϲ *IG* XII^2 645.36 (fourth century B.C. Nesos), χοροϲτατεῖν *IG*

---

[1] G.Marxer, *Die Sprache des A.R. in ihren Beziehungen zu Homer* (Diss. Zürich 1935) 29f. is also undecided about these forms.

[2] Mayser, *GGP* I^2 143ff., Crönert, *MGH* 210, 231ff., Moulton, *GNT* II 208ff. Cf. also on v. 98 εἶπαϲ, and for other -α- endings in C. see Pfeiffer on 384.41.

[3] Cf. Hesych. s.v. and Eustathius 932.39. For the etymology see Frisk, *EW* 343f. and cf. R.R.Dyer, *Glotta* 42 (1964) 129–31. Outside Homer and Hesiod only Pindar, Empedocles and Ariphron use ὀαρ- (to citations in LSJ add Ariphron (Page, *PMG* 813) 9).

[4] Antip. Thess., *GP* 112, thence *AP* 16.202, Q.S. 7.316, Opp. *Cyn.* 4.23, Lucian, *Alex.* 54.258 (verse), *de parasit.* 43.868 (a very heightened ironical prose passage), *Orph. Arg.* 1327, Mus. 132, 230, *AP* 9.358, 362, 381, 10.68, 16.272.

Rom. 1.562), but χοροστασία itself is poetic, first in Hermesianax fr. 7.58 and here, thence Antip. Sid., *HE* 593 etc. as a weighty alternative to χορός.[1] C. seems also to have coined the adjective χοροστάς (fr. 305).

67 ἀδεῖαι The adjective has even less weight than might be supposed. The dance, as an expression of joy, often has a conventional epithet in epic regardless of the context: e.g. καλός *Od.* 12.318, *H.H.Aphr.* 261, *H.H.* 27.15, ἱμερόεις *Il.* 18.603, *Od.* 18.194, *H.H.Herm.* 481, *H.H.* 6.13 etc.[2]

τελέθεσκον τελέθειν, epic diction, refers to the result or issue of an action = 'come about', 'become', 'happen to be' (hence also in statements of a generalising nature: Chantraine, *GH* II 6, cf. K–G, *GG* I 42, Schwyzer, *GG* II 624). So occasionally in Hellenistic poetry as an epicism: II 50, A.R. 4.1576, Theocr. 5.18, 10.49, 16.69, 24.100, 26.21, Arat. 79, 1144, Nic. *Ther.* 213, 369, Theodotus, *SH* 759.8, anon. in *SH* 1025. Here τελέθεσκον is doubly in place since τελέθειν seems to have been normal usage in Doric: *Tab. Heracl.* 1.111 (Schwyzer, *DGEE* 62.111: fourth century B.C.), *SEG* 23 (1968) 474.7 (Dodona: fourth to third century B.C.), Epicharmus fr. 170.17, frequently in Pindar and tragic lyrics,[3] 'Εφημ. 'Αρχ. 1907.209ff. 10.4 (Rhodes: undated verse), anon. in *PMG* 1019.6, Hagemon of Rhodes in *ZPE* 15 (1974) 223 v. 8, Theocritus (see above), and three Doric epigrams, Erinna, *HE* 1784, Nossis, *HE* 2804, Antip. Thess., *GP* 208.

The rare iterative -εσκον[4] adds a further fine shade of meaning: in English perhaps 'nor did . . . *ever* come about . . .'

ὅκ' οὐχ ἁγεῖτο Χαρικλώ George of Crete as evidenced in MSS B and C

[1] There is no reason to conclude, as does Schmitt, *NDK* 39, that χοροστασία is a '*terminus technicus*'. LSJ's documentation is poor: in addition to the three Hellenistic examples cited above, later instances include Diodorus, *GP* 2165, *IG* XIV 1389 i 58 (second century A.D.), Dion. Per. 842, Nonn. *D.* 46.165, Leontius, *AP* 16.284. In Christian literature the noun is commonly used of 'the choir of the blessed' (which supports interpreting it as a poeticism in C.): see Lampe, *PGL* s.v. and add Greg. Naz. *AP* 8.2, 144, Diogenes, *AP* 7.613.

[2] ἀδεῖαι is attributive, not predicative. McKay, *PP* 5 translates 'nor were the conversations . . . agreeable to her unless Chariklo . . .': τελέθεσκον, however, is intransitive (see note ad loc.), and the parallelism of structure with vv. 60ff. suggests that a statement of the type 'on such occasions Chariclo led' is required to maintain the balance.

[3] Not in Soph.: several times in Aeschylean lyrics (though *Ag.* 100 is an epicism), and Eur. *Andr.* 782, *Med.* 1096. τελεθεῖν at Xen. *An.* 3.2.3, 6.6.36, *Lac.* 13.5 may be a Doricism if sound (see Kühner on *An.* 6.6.36 and Gautier *LX* 26f.), but the three instances in Hipp. *Morb.* 2.5, 20, 74 suggest that the verb may have been idiosyncratic to Ionic too.

[4] *H.H.Dem.* 241 appears to be the only other example of the iterative suffix with this verb.

suggested, or adopted, ἀγοῖτο for ἀγεῖτο, and Schneider received this emendation into his text with the explanation, which was no doubt George's too, that the parallel with v. 61 ἐλαύνοι makes the optative necessary here also. However the construction is not what it seems: the chiasmic clauses εὖτ' . . . ἐλαύνοι . . . ἐπεβάcατο – τελέθεcκον, ὅκ' . . . ἀγεῖτο are parallel only in rhetorical appearance. The logic of the sense of vv. 66f. is the inverse of the syntactical structure, namely 'when there were dances, then C. was the leader': ἀγ- must be iterative imperfect indicative as it would be if the proposition were expressed in its positive form.[1] This neatly articulated inversion brings the long exposition of vv. 60–7 to a well-rounded close, and provides for the sentence to end on Χαρικλώ, who is here mentioned by name for the first time.

The leader of the χορόc was by right the most honoured member, and the god himself was often χορηγέτηc: *H.H.* 27.17f. (Artemis) ἡγεῖται . . . | ἐξάρχουcα χορούc, Pind. *N.* 5.23f. Μοιcᾶν ὁ κάλλιcτοc χορόc, ἐν δὲ μέcαιc . . . Ἀπόλλων . . . ἀγεῖτο.

ὅκ' Wilamowitz' emendation for MSS' ὅθ' or ὅτ' makes for consistency with the Doric form in vv. 7, 18.

68–9 Expression of foreboding at an early point to effect a contrast between apparent calm and imminent disaster was a common device in Greek narrative poetry of all periods: cf., e.g., *Il.* 12.113ff., *Od.* 7.270ff., 10.26f., *H.H.* 7.8, A.R. 3.1133ff., Mosch. 2.72f. (where see Bühler).

68 ἀλλ' ἔτι Common epic phraseology in this position (*LfgrE* 506.29ff.); ἀλλ' ἔτι καί again at the pentameter-beginning at 178.16.

τήναν '*illam*': see on v. 17 τήναc.

ἔμενε Transitive μένειν of events in post-Homeric poets often expresses the inevitability of something unwelcome;[2] similarly in the Hellenistic writers: e.g. Mnasalces, *HE* 2658 ἐπεί cε μένει καὶ κατόπιν δάκρυα, A.R. 1.6 μοῖρα μένει cτυγερή, 1.681f., Lyc. 666, 1075f. Conversely at v. 120 Athena uses the word to assure Chariclo that Tiresias will be compensated for his blinding (πολλὰ μενεῦντι γέρα).

69 Ἀθαναίαι Emphatic early positioning: 'even though she was *Athena*'s beloved companion.'

---

[1] This construction is very rare in Greek but common in Latin: cf. Kühner–Stegmann–Thierfelder, *Lat. Gramm.* (Leverkusen 1955[3]) II 338ff. on *cum 'inversum'*. In the negative form of 'when A then B' propositions, protasis and apodosis change places but the modal relationship between the two clauses is unchanged.

[2] Hence often in Aeschylus of a family curse or suffering: see Fraenkel on *Ag.* 1563, where Groeneboom aptly translates μίμνει by '*ratum est*'; in addition to the passages cited by Fraenkel cf. Pind. *I.* 7.48 and Eur. *Ion* 1246f.

καταθύμιον A rare word: see on v. 33 καταθύμιος ἴλα. The repetition links Athena's mythical attendants here with her actual ones in the cult procession.

ἔσσαν The very little evidence surviving for this form (Attic οὖσαν) is almost entirely Doric. Appropriately the only inscriptional evidence comes from the Argolid: *IG* IV 952.2 ἔσσας (Epidaurus: *c*. 320 B.C.), *IG* IV 757 B 21 ἔσσαν (Trozen: third century B.C.); literary evidence: Philolaus (from Croton or Tarentum) fr. 6D ἔσσα, Hellenistic Doricising [Archytas] Περὶ ἀρχῶν in Stob. *Ecl.* 1.41.2W ἔσσα.[1] The lengthened form ἦσσαν is testified once in Cyrene (*SEG* 9 (1944) 11.17: fourth century B.C.).[2] Politian and Lascaris emended to the form more familiar from Theocritus (2.76, 5.26) εὖσαν.

70–84 The narrative proper begins: the midday bath, Tiresias' intrusion, and his punishment. The account opens quietly on the pentameter. The passage consists almost entirely in the creation of atmosphere with a minimum of movement and action, and Tiresias' appearance is expressed simply and neutrally (v. 76 ἀνεστρέφετο, v. 77 ἤλυθε). This confining of the dramatic action to a minimum and the concentration on atmosphere and individual reactions is typical of Callimachus and many of the later Hellenistic writers influenced by him. The tension is built up by formal means: first, in the order of presentation which places the naked bathing unemotionally (with emphasis on geographical detail) at the beginning, separate from the description of the menacing stillness, which follows in a second stage acting as atmospheric preparation for the third stage, the intrusion; secondly, in the expression, which enacts the monotony of the sultriness, vv. 73f. restating v. 72, with slight variants extending each point: λῶντο → <u>ἀμφότεραι</u> λώ<u>ο</u>ντο, μεσαμβρινά → μεσαμβριναί . . . <u>ἔσαν ὧραι</u>, εἶχ' → <u>κατ</u>εῖχεν, ὄρος → <u>τῆνο</u> . . . ὄρος, ἁσυχία → <u>πολλά</u> . . . ἁσυχία.[3] The static effect is reinforced too by the return of rhythmic regularity, colon-end coinciding once again with

[1] = H.Thesleff, *Pythagorean Texts of the Hellenistic Period* (Åbo 1965) 20.

[2] ἔσσα may also have been a Lesbian feature: in Sappho fr. 121.2 MSS' ἔσσα, which some editors emend to ἔοισα, is supported by Theocr. 28.16 ἔσσαν.

[3] For a more general discussion of 'expressive repetition' and stillness enacted by verbal lingering see L.P.Wilkinson, *Golden Latin Artistry* (Cambridge 1963) 66–8 (who thinks that Tennyson had this passage of C. in mind when he wrote in *Oenone* 'For the noonday quiet holds the hill: / The grasshopper is silent in the grass . . .'). It is surprising how many distinguished scholars have thought vv. 73f. to be unnecessarily repetitive and even interpolated: Hemsterhuys, Ruhnken, Ernesti, Blomfield, Bergk and P.Maas are among them. As Ernesti remarked, 'vide quam differant hominum sensus.'

pentameter-end, in contrast to the preceding couplets (see on vv. 57–69). Most important of all, the scene is not *interpreted* until the moment when Tiresias appears, and then as economically as possible (v. 76 ἱερόν, v. 78 τὰ μὴ θεμιτά). Even the blinding is presented in terms which are spectatorial (vv. 80f.) and neutrally 'factual' (v. 82); the tension is not released until vv. 85ff. with a cry of protest, not from Tiresias but from Chariclo. The fatal event itself is momentary: the central issue is the wider repercussions of the punishment.

70 δή ποκα γάρ Here as at v. 5 Ψ's normalised form should be replaced by the Doric ποκα (Meineke: cf. vv. 57, 59). δή ποτε (sometimes written as one word) regularly = '*olim*', 'once upon a time', mostly in poetry (Denniston, *GP* 213).[1] Only here in C.: its frequent use by A.R. suggests that it is a phrase of some solemnity (2.477, 3.997 (opening the sentence as here),[2] 1095, 4.988, 1131).

For the word sequence cf. III 202 | δή τότε γὰρ πέπλοισιν.

πέπλων The πέπλος, a garment which was fastened by a pin on each shoulder (see M.Bieber, *Griechische Kleidung* (Berlin 1928) 11f. for diagrams, explained on pp. 17f., and illustrations I–VI),[3] was still worn by women in the Hellenistic period, though it was slowly being replaced by the περονατρίς which had no pins (*RE* III 2311ff., M.Bieber, *Entwicklungsgesch. der griech. Tracht* (1967^2) 35f.). Cf. on vv. 7f.: the Argive ritual may have involved a ceremonial πέπλος.

λυσαμένα The dual form is read by all MSS; although obsolete in the spoken language by the third century B.C.,[4] it was still standard poetic usage. The mixture of dual and third person plural verb is found in all writers from Homer onwards (K–G, *GG* I 70, Schwyzer, *GG* II 50): again in C. at IV 64f. . . . ἵππω | . . . ηὐλίζοντο.

71 The spring created by Pegasus,[5] now called Kyropegadi, is situated just under the summit of Helicon (full description in Frazer, *Pausanias* V 158); it is reached by leaving the road between Thespiae and Haliartos (vv. 60f.) at Ascra and climbing up to the west (for a full discussion of the area see P.W.Wallace, 'Hesiod and the valley of the Muses', *GRBS* 15 (1974) 5–24, and for Hippocrene pp. 14–18). Hes. *Theog.* 6 represents the spring as

---

[1] In *Od.* 6.162 (LSJ) δή probably belongs to preceding Δήλωι: there is no other example of this δή ποτε in Homer.

[2] Denniston, *GP* 228: 'Homer never opens a sentence or clause with δή, except when it precedes a temporal adverb or γάρ . . .'

[3] More illustrations in R.Horn, *Stehende weibl. Gewandstatuen in der hellenistischen Plastik* (Munich 1931).

[4] See K–B, *GG* I 362 and references, Schwyzer, *GG* II 47.

[5] The *aetion* is first mentioned by Arat. 216–24; further references in Pfeiffer on frr. 2.1,4; 546, and *RE* VIII 1854f.

being used for bathing by the Muses (who had a shrine lower down the hill: see Frazer on Paus. 9.29.5).[1]

ἵππῳ ἐπί Epic correption is very rare in elegiacs at this position between the shorts of a dactyl (in C. only here and *E.* 62.2).[2] However the narrative section of v is epic in tone in spite of the elegiac form, and for correption at this position in, e.g., the *Hecale* see 274.2, 278.2, 284, 309.3.

κράναι Ἑλικωνίδι This and v. 65 are the only examples in v of true hiatus (excepting after ὦ, ὤ, and ἤ and before dative οἱ): as at v. 65 the collision of vowels is 'softened', here by the intervention of the caesura.[3]

καλὰ ῥεοίcαι Epic in tone: cf. καλὰ ῥέεθρα | *Il.* 21.238, 244 etc., εὐρὺ ῥέοντοc | *Il.* 2.849, 16.288 etc., and the common Homeric epithet καλλίρ(ρ)οοc of springs (LSJ). For a similar variation of the traditional formulaic phraseology cf. A.R. 4.1300 ἢ ὅτε καλὰ νάοντοc ἐπ' ὀφρύcι Πακτωλοῖο.

72 λῶντο Cf. Attic/Ionic λοῦται, λοῦνται etc. (LSJ). Inscriptional evidence from most Doric areas is of λου-forms,[4] but λωcάμενοc is testified in Cyrene (*Berl. Sitzb* (1927) 157 = *SEG* 9 (1944) 72.13; fourth century B.C.), λωτηρίωι in the Argolid (see on v. 1 λωτροχόοι), and λωτρόν in Laconia (Hesych. s.v.).

μεcαμβρινά In ancient Greece and Rome, as still in many countries today, the period around noon was a critical time, when gods might appear and when to encounter or disturb them would mean severe danger.[5] It was

---

[1] Wilamowitz, *HD* II 20 'Man kann auch gar nicht in ihr baden' is too contentious: contrast Frazer loc. cit.

[2] See Pfeiffer on 535. Correption is also severely restricted in late Hellenistic contributors to the *Anthology*: for Meleager see Gow–Page, *HE* II 645 and for later poets *GP* I xxxix–xl. When it occurs correption is commoner after a diphthong than a single vowel (cf., e.g., Mooney, *The Argonautica* 421ff.) but there are many examples in A.R. of correption of -ω in this position: M.Campbell, 'Notes on Apollonius Rhodius, *Argonautica* II', *Revue de Philologie* 47 (1973) 84.

[3] For a similar 'softening' of hiatus by the main caesura in Theocr. see Gow on 2.145.

[4] Bechtel, *GD* II 452 (Argolid), 626 (Rhodes), *IG* IV[1] 1390.107 = Ditt. *Syll.*[3] 736 (Messenia: first century B.C.).

[5] See Roscher, *LM* II 2832ff. s.v. 'Meridianus daimon' and Frazer on Paus. 9.3.9. Midday is also a time for poetic inspiration: cf. A.Kambylis, *Die Dichterweihe und ihre Symbolik* (Heidelberg 1965) 59–61. Cf. also Kleinknecht, *LP* 328f. T.G. Rosenmeyer, *The Green Cabinet* (California 1969) 89 pertinently cites Petrarch, *de vita solitaria* 1.2.5 who remarks that noon is a time for devotion and prayer. In an autobiographical essay written when he was eighteen Wilamowitz remarked that he was born as midday struck 'so dass ich Geister sehen kann' (*GRBS* 12 (1971) 564: W.M.Calder III ad

when the sun had reached the middle of the heavens that Proteus came out of the sea for Menelaus to challenge (*Od.* 4.400, 450): Jason sees the Libyan nymphs at midday (A.R. 4.1312ff.) and averts his eyes; at Theocr. 1.15ff. the goatherd warns against disturbing Pan at midday (to avoid an epiphany); C. VI 38 refers to the nymphs' midday games; in Ovid, *Met.* 3.144ff. (echoing C.?) it was at midday that Actaeon saw Artemis bathing and was torn apart by his hounds.

The temporal suffix -ινος usually has short ι, and the ι is long in μεσαμβρινός here for the first time.[1] In this rare metrical variation C. follows Homeric precedent: ὀπωρινός in Homer always has long ι (but short ι subsequently in Attic),[2] and, like C., Posidippus, *HE* 3145, Arat. 948, A.R. fr. 5.1 use ὀρθρινός for the first time with long ι (although Meleager reverts to ῐ). Cf. Arcadius' epitome of Herodian p. 195.9 (*Gramm. Graec.* III[1] 528.26 *app. crit.*) τὰ διὰ τοῦ ινος ὑπὲρ δύο συλλαβὰς ὀξύτονα παρὰ καιροῦ συντιθέμενα συστέλλει τὸ ῑ· ἐαρινός, νυκτερινός, θερινός. οἱ δὲ ποιηταὶ πολλάκις ἐκτείνουσι.

εἶχ' The simple verb is unusual of 'natural' phenomena, for which κατέχειν is normally used.[3] Rare parallels, which suggest that εἶχ' is poetic, are *Od.* 13.245 αἰεὶ δ' ὄμβρος ἔχει τεθαλυῖά τ' ἐέρση and A.R. 3.750 σιγὴ δὲ μελαινομένην ἔχεν ὄρφνην; the effect is perhaps emotive, suggesting that the stillness was almost a personal state or condition (the usual connotation of ἔχειν with abstract subject: φόβος μ' ἔχει φρένας etc.).[4] V. 74 picks up εἶχ'

loc. refers to E. Hoffmann-Krayer and Hanns Bächtold-Stäubli, *Handwörterbuch des deutschen Aberglaubens* 6 (Berlin–Leipzig 1934–5) 398ff. s.v. 'Mittag').

[1] Not again until Oppian, *Cyn.* 1.299, 2.17 and Synesius' epigram on an astrolabe: N. Terzaghi, *Synesii Cyrenensis Opuscula* (Rome 1944) 142 = Migne, *Patrologia Graeca* 66.1588; other Hellenistic poets retain short ι: Asclepiades, *HE* 1018, A.R. 4.1505, Theocr. 1.15, 10.48, Nic. *Ther.* 401.

[2] Hesiod uses both ῑ (*Op.* 677) and ῐ (*Op.* 674); the Hellenistic poets scrupulously follow Homeric usage: Arat. 417, Nic. *Al.* 517, Oppian *passim.*

[3] E.g. *Od.* 13.269 νύξ . . . δνοφερὴ κάτεχ' οὐρανόν, Cratin. fr. 138 τίνες αὖ πόντον κατέχους' αὖραι; Hermipp. fr. 82 ὀσμή . . . κατὰ πᾶν δ' ἔχει δῶ, *Od.* 9.145 σελήνη . . . κατείχετο . . . νεφέεσσιν; cf. Aesch. *Pers.* 387, Aristoph. *Nub.* 572 (see Starkie on v. 328), and also *Il.* 17.368, 644, Alcaeus, *P. Colon.* Inv. 2021.15 (Page, *Lyrica Graeca Selecta* p. 76), Aesch. *Pers.* 427. LSJ's 'spread', 'cover' without specification of natural phenomena is highly misleading and has resulted in inadequate citations. Apollonius' use of κατέχειν with σιγή and γαλήνη in 2.740, 4.1249 are unexceptional normal usage.

[4] Hdt. 6.135.2 ὥς σφεας ἡσυχίη τῆς πολιορκίης ἔσχε is to be explained in this way: 'rest from the siege' was a personal state, not a natural phenomenon.

with the verb which prompted it, κατεῖχεν; for expressive variation using the same verb, but with competitive, not lingering, effect, see Soph. *OT* 566f. Oed.: ἀλλ' οὐκ ἔρευναν τοῦ θανόντος ἔςχετε; | Cr.: παρέςχομεν . . . (cf. *Ant.* 32–4, and cf. also F.Vian, *REA* 75 (1973) 83f. on a number of possible Hellenistic instances of simple for compound).

ἁcυχία 'Stillness is the traditional response of nature to a divine epiphany': Dodds, on Eur. *Bacch.* 1084f., who compares Aristoph. *Av.* 777f., *Thesm.* 42ff., Limenius (Powell, *CA* 149) 8ff., Mesomedes, *Hymn* 2.1ff. The ἁ- forms, also in Theocritus' Doric poems, were until recently regarded as hyper-Dorisms (Frisk, *EW*, Chantraine, *DE* s.v. ἥcυχος), but are now established as true Doric: B.Forssman, *Untersuchungen zur Sprache Pindars* (Klassisch-philologische Studien 33: Wiesbaden 1966) 48–55.

73 ἀμφότεραι This addition to v. 72 λῶντο is important: by stressing the closeness between Chariclo and Athena it isolates Tiresias, who is, explicitly, 'quite alone' (v. 75 ἔτι μῶνος) and thus vulnerable. Chariclo, linked with Athena, is powerless to defend him.

Verbally similar is Theocr. 24.3 | ἀμφοτέρους λούςαςα.

ἔςαν An epic form (ἦςαν without the augment: Chantraine, *GH* I 289) foreign to Doric, which had ἦν. C. has ἔςαν again in VI 27, but Theocr. uses only the true Doric form (ἔςαν only in the dubious *Idyll* 25: vv. 117, 128, 130).

ὧραι The plural is unusual and probably poetic: in expressions specifying a particular moment or a part of the day ὥρα is almost always singular, and the only parallels to this passage seem to be the much later *Anacreont.* 33.1 μεςονυκτίοις ποθ' ὥραις, and Leonidas of Alexandria (first century A.D.) in *AP* 6.321.1, 9.355.1 γενεθλιακαῖςιν ἐν ὥραις. μεςημβρία, like English 'midday', generally denoted a period rather than a precise time,[1] and the plural emphasises duration extending over several smaller units of time. A similar plural is normal in the phrase μέςαι νύκτες (see LSJ).

74 τῆνο The demonstrative (weaker than κεῖνο)[2] gives the stillness even more significance and menace by making it particular almost to Helicon. (Bentley insensitively emended to τηνικάδ' εἶχεν ὄρος on the grounds that other mountains too were silent in the midday heat: C. does not suggest that they were not, only that the silence is specially significant on Helicon.) In the next line, immediately after this concentration on the scene, Tiresias enters.

κατεῖχεν See on v. 72 εἶχεν.

75 Τειρεςίας δ' ἔτι μῶνος The pace quickens: in contrast to his mother

[1] Cf. G.Bilfinger, *Die antiken Stundenangaben* (Stuttgart 1888) 19, 38.

[2] Another example of τῆνος in narrative with weak demonstrative force, = 'the one which I have just mentioned', is Theocr. 2.84 οὐκέτι πομπᾶς | τήνας ἐφραςάμαν. Cf. Aesch. *Pers.* 395 πάντ' ἐκεῖνα.

Chariclo earlier, Tiresias is identified specifically by name at the moment of his entry.[1] The phraseology seems to be reminiscent of *Il.* 2.212 Θερσίτης δ' ἔτι μοῦνος ἀμετροεπὴς ἐκολῴα, though Tiresias and Thersites have little in common.

'Tiresias quite alone . . .':[2] cf. *E.* 30.3 ὀστέα τοι καὶ μοῦνον ἔτι τρίχες 'you are *nothing but* . . .' (cf. Theocr. 2.89f.), fr. 43.17 ἔτι μοι μοῦνα πάρεστι τάδε 'the only things I still have left'.

ἁμᾶι (ἅμα) here, signifying accompaniment, is seemingly Homeric (in Homer 'ἅμα gibt die Zusammengehörigkeit von Personen (Dingen u.a.) an, die . . . *in dem Verhältnis von Führendem und Folgendem zueinander stehen*' (*LfgrE* 595f.)). In the *koine* ἅμα had become a general equivalent of σύν, denoting simply attachment of any sort;[3] the didactic and bucolic poets use ἅμα in this contemporary sense (Mommsen, *Beiträge* 187ff.), but A.R., like C. here, frequently has it with its more restricted Homeric application.

The Doric form with long final syllable is attested in Pindar and Aristophanes (LSJ), and in the Hellenistic period at Theocr. 9.4, 11.39.[4] The spelling of ἁμᾶι, along with its origin (cf. Schwyzer, *GG* I 622f.), is uncertain. In most instances MSS read ἁμᾶ, and this form is testified in Doric inscriptions (Bechtel, *GD* II 357f.); however, here and in Theocritus, and occasionally elsewhere, the MSS read ἁμᾷ, and since this is mentioned as a possible spelling by Herodian (Σ to Pind. *P.* 3.36)[5] there seems no reason to emend (Pfeiffer accepts Brunck's ἁμᾶ).

ἁμᾶι κυσίν The detail, apparently superfluous at this stage of the narrative, will be important when Athena makes out her case that Tiresias could have been punished like Actaeon: see on v. 114 ἀλλ' αὐταί . . . κύνες. Young men do sometimes have dogs with them, and Tiresias' approach is somewhat reminiscent of Telemachus' entry to the Ithacan assembly at *Od.*

---

[1] Cf. L.P. Wilkinson, *The Georgics of Virgil* (Cambridge 1969) 218f. who sees a considerable similarity in treatment between this passage and *Georg.* 4.425ff., where again an extensive passage creating the atmosphere of noontide heat precedes the dramatic entrance of Proteus, announced with his name at the beginning of v. 429.

[2] McKay's 'still an only child' (*PP* 39 referring to vv. 108f. τὸν μόνον . . . παῖδα) is not acceptable.

[3] Mayser, *GGP* II² 527. In general see Tycho Mommsen, *Beiträge zu der Lehre von den griech. Präpositionen* (Berlin 1895²); ἅμα usually implies simultaneity and outside Homer and Herodotus is rarely used of people. Cf. also Schwyzer, *GG* II 534f.

[4] The Callimachean passage is the only example of ἁμᾶι as a preposition, but that is doubtless due to the chance that so few examples of the Doric form have survived (*pace* Schwyzer, *GG* II 534 n. 3).

[5] *Gramm. Graec.* III¹ 489.18; cf. Ahrens, *DD* 34, 372. The related Delphic form ἁμεῖ is further support for Doric ἁμᾶι (Bechtel, *GD* II 140).

2.11 οὐκ οἶος, ἅμα τῶι γε κύνες πόδας ἄργοι ἕποντο (Athena's role here was different: 12 θεσπεσίην δ' ἄρα τῶι γε χάριν κατέχευεν 'Αθήνη).

75–6 ἄρτι γένεια | περκάζων Here, as often on such occasions in Greek, the promise of Tiresias' age contrasts pathetically with what he is about to suffer: cf., e.g., *Od.* 11.318ff. (Otus and Ephialtes) ἀλλ' ὄλεσεν Διὸς υἱὸς . . . | ἀμφοτέρω, πρίν σφωϊν ὑπὸ κροτάφοισιν ἰούλους | ἀνθῆσαι πυκάσαι τε γένυς εὐανθέι λάχνηι. The detail of the newly darkening beard to indicate early manhood is a poetic commonplace: *Od.* 11.319f., Aesch. *Sept.* 534, Pind. *O.* 1.67f., *N.* 5.6, Eur. *Cret.* 82.15 (Austin, *Nova Fragmenta Euripidea* (Berlin 1968)), Call. fr. 274, 1 56, Theocr. 11.9, 15.85, A.R. 1.972, 2. 3, 779, Herodas 1.52, Antip. Thess., *GP*, 633f.[1]

The expression too appears at first to be unexceptional: cf. Xen. *Cyr.* 4.6.5 ἄρτι γενειάσκοντα τὸν ἄριστον παῖδα, Theocr. 11.9 ἄρτι γενειάσδων περὶ τὸ στόμα (cf. Aesch. *Sept.* 534, Xen. *Symp.* 4.23). However, the first word of the pentameter unexpectedly converts an ordinary expression into an impressive one. περκάζειν normally refers specifically to fruit (usually grapes, occasionally olives) changing in colour from light to dark as they reach maturity.[2] Such a comparison of the swarthiness of the first beard with the darkening grape is in itself not new: Eur. *Cret.* 82.15 (Austin) παρ' ὀμμάτων σέλας | οἰνωπὸν ἐξέλαμπε περ[καί]νων γένυν, Chaeremon trag. fr. 12 (Snell *TGF* I 71 F 12) πολλὴν ὀπώραν Κύπριδος εἰσορᾶν παρῆν | ἄκραισι περκάζουσαν οἰνάνθαις χρόνου (cf. Pind. *N.* 5.6 οὔπω γένυσι φαίνων τέρειναν ματέρ' οἰνάνθας ὀπώραν). However, in both tragic passages the image is established gradually, the verb being prepared in Eur. by οἰνωπόν, in Chaer. by ὀπώραν:[3] in C. the verb alone carries the image, forcefully expressed and prominently placed at the beginning of the line.

75 γένεια 'beard'. γένειον normally = 'chin', but the plural is generally

---

[1] Xen. *Cyr.* 4.6.5 ἄρτι γενειάσκοντα τὸν ἄριστον παῖδα, and *Symp.* 4.23 τούτωι μὲν παρὰ τὰ ὦτα ἄρτι ἴουλος καθέρπει are probably poetic, the tone in the former passage being of pathos, in the latter of irony.

[2] The evidence is much more decisive than lexica indicate: *Od.* 7.126 ὄμφακες . . . ὑποπερκάζουσι, Soph. fr. 255.6 κἀποπερκοῦται βότρυς, Theophr. *H.P.* 2.7.5, 3.4.4 (βότρυς), 9.11.7 (σταφυλή), *C.P.* 3.16.3 (βότρυς), *LXX* Amos 9.13, Sirach 51.15 (σταφυλή), *IG* XII[5] 739.168 (first century B.C.: *coni.* ὄμφαξ), *Geopon.* 9.19.2, 9.32.1 (ἐλαία), 9.33.1 (κολυμβάς).

[3] In Pind. *N.* 5.6 too the image is less abrupt, being more diffuse: preparation in τέρειναν and 'spread' across οἰνάνθας and ὀπώραν. When the verb is next so used after C., in Philip, *GP* 3031 ὡς δ' ἐπιπερκάζεις μιαρῆι τριχί, the epigram is based on the metaphor, with preparation and continuation.

used by Hellenistic writers = 'beard' (*Thes. Graec.*, LSJ).[1] Again at Theocr. 6.36.

76 ἱερόν The first explicit indication in the narrative of the situation: if he goes to the stream T. will violate a place which has become sacrosanct.

ἱερὸν χῶρον ἀνεστρέφετο The expression has an epic tone even though the vocabulary in itself is neutral. ἀναστρέφεσθαι in Classical and Hellenistic prose = 'turn up and stay in', 'arrive at and pay a visit', 'sojourn' and generally 'be in a place'; the verb is intransitive and constructed with a locative phrase (preposition or simple dative).[2] 178.6 ξεῖνον ὃς Α[ἰ]γύπτωι καινὸς ἀνεστρέφετο 'was in Egypt on a visit'. However, the direct accusative ἱερὸν χῶρον is most unusual and paralleled only by *Od.* 13.325f. ἀλλά τιν' ἄλλην | γαῖαν ἀναστρέφομαι, which is doubtless the 'authority' for the Callimachean expression.

The imperfect, as in 178.6, is the narrative equivalent of Odysseus' words above, 'was there having arrived': perhaps best translated as 'had come to'.[3]

77 ἄφατόν τι The tone heightens: the uncommon ἄφατος = 'unspeakable'[4] as a general superlative (= 'awful', 'terrible') is restricted before the Hellenistic period almost entirely to lyric in passages of some considerable solemnity (serious or mock): Bacch. 18.18, 64.23, Pind. *N.* 1.47, Soph. *OT* 1314, *OC* 1464, Eur. *Ion* 782, Aristoph. *Av.* 428, Anaxander fr. 41.63 (Kock II 153), Epicrates fr. 11.12 (Kock II 287).[5] ἄφατος features occasionally in the literary *koine* (?from Ionic?), but rarely, and as a heightened word: (Hdt. 7.190), Antig. Car. 148 (= Call. fr. 407.74), Polyb. 15.28.1, Philod. *D.* 3.14, Antonin. Lib. 17.4, 30.3, Plut. *Marius* 45.1, Numenius *ap.* Euseb. *PE* 543C, Hermog. *Inv.* 1.4. The adverbial use appears to have been a Callimachean mannerism: IV 60, VI 57 (the entry in Hesychius is of the adverb, glossed by ἀμήχανον, πολύ, ἄρρητον, ἀμέτρητον, δεινόν).

---

[1] Cf. Eustath. 1257.56f. περὶ δὲ γενείου γράφει Αἴλιος Διονύσιος (second century A.D.) ὅτι γένεια αἱ τρίχες, γένειον δὲ ὁ τόπος.

[2] See LSJ and Supplement s.v., Arndt–Gingrich, *GNT* s.v.

[3] 'Ranged . . . the holy place' (Mair) and 'was ranging . . . the holy place' (McKay) are thus wrong. There is no suggestion of movement ('ranged', 'wandered' would require <u>ἐπ</u>εστρέφετο): the tense is imperfect only to indicate continuity of presence.

[4] The other usage = 'unspoken' is also rare: Hes. *Op.* 3, Timon, *SH* 783.2 (after Hesiod).

[5] It appears also to have been a feature of Laconian: Aristoph. *Lys.* 198, 1080, 1148 suggest that the effect to Athenian ears was of quaintness. οὐ φατός and οὔ τι φατει- are used almost entirely in the same way: Hes. *Theog.* 310, *Scut.* 144, 161, 230, Pind. *I.* 7.37, Aristoph. *Av.* 1189, 1714, Plut. *Mor.* 383A. Cf. Blaydes on Aristoph. *Lys.* 1148. (οὐ φατός does also occasionally = 'unspoken'.)

Adverbial τι is also a poetic mannerism particular to C. and Theocritus: see on v. 58 πουλύ τι.

ποτὶ ῥόον ἤλυθε κράνας Epic phraseology: ῥόος in Homer is often accompanied by the name of a river in the genitive case (e.g. *Il.* 16. 151 παρὰ ῥόον Ὠκεανοῖο), and the prepositional phrase shaped ⏑ – ῥόον in this position is also common (e.g. *Il.* 17.264 ποτὶ ῥόον).[1]

ποτί Doric as well as Homeric (Buck, *GD* 107f.) and the only form of the preposition used by C. in v and vi. The lengthening of final -ι is a general poeticism (Maas, *GM* § 130 'Initial ρ may always count as a double consonant').

78 σχέτλιος Ambiguous in this kind of context since the adjective denotes not only 'qui alios non curat, audax' but also 'qui tolerat, patiens, perseverans, qui se ipse non curat' (Ebeling, *LH* s.v.): hence after Homer 'miserable, wretched'. In any case σχέτλιος here implies that the person described is, factually even if not morally, responsible for what he suffers,[2] and C. uses the word elsewhere of sinners punished by a god;[3] but the word suggests sympathy too (cf. English 'wretch'), and the sympathy is here supported by οὐκ ἐθέλων (extending διψάσας).

Nominative σχέτλιος always in this position in Homer; the phraseology too is Homeric: *Il.* 23.88 | νήπιος, οὐκ ἐθέλων . . . (of Patroclus when he unintentionally killed the son of Amphidamas).

δ' Effectively second element, not delayed, since οὐκ ἐθέλων is a common Homeric periphrasis = ἀεκών (Ebeling, *LH* I 344.2).

εἶδε τὰ μὴ θεμιτά The fateful moment. The description is brief and in terms not of the action itself (details only later in v. 88) but solely of its legality and hence the inevitable implications: we are brought immediately to the moment of the punishment. Contrast Ovid's description of Actaeon's intrusion on Diana's bath, *Met.* 3.177ff., which attempts to depict an actual scene in detail, even down to Diana's blush; Callimachus' economy achieves a very powerful effect, making the event and the subsequent punishment awful and convincing, and by contrast Ovid is merely pretty. This economy is made possible by the fact that Athena's femininity and beauty have already been established in vv. 18–28 (see note ad loc.).

θεμιτά Cf. Plato, *Epigr.* 23.4f. (Aphrodite:) 'ποῦ γυμνὴν εἶδέ με

---

[1] For both phenomena see Ebeling, *LH* II 266 s.v. ῥόος.

[2] Thus Σ to *Il.* 18.13 σχέτλιος· ὁ ἑαυτῶι κακῶν αἴτιος, ὁ τλήμων.

[3] Of Erysichthon at a similar point in the poem after the description of his crime when he is about to be punished (vi 68), and of ἄδικοι punished by Artemis (III 124): the latter are σχέτλιοι because they have incurred Artemis' χαλεπήν . . . ὀργήν, just as the path taken by Tiresias was χαλεπάν (v. 81).

Πραξιτέλης;' | Πραξιτέλης οὐκ εἶδεν ἃ μὴ θέμιc . . .[1] and Oedipus' instructions to his daughters before his transfiguration at Colonus, Soph. *OC* 1640–2 χρή . . . μηδ' ἃ μὴ θέμιc | λεύccειν δικαιοῦν, μηδὲ φωνούντων κλύειν.

θέμιc (*fas*) is the unwritten, eternal natural law: no more fundamental code or order of things could be infringed; see Schmidt, *SGS* I 348ff., K. Latte *Kleine Schriften* 140ff. (= *RE* v[a] 1626ff.). Cf. Aristoph. *Thesm.* 1150f. ἀνδράcιν οὐ θέμιc εἰcορᾶν ὄργια cεμνὰ θεοῖν: 'the expressions οὐ θέμιc and οὐ θεμιτόν are particularly used of divulging secrets to those who have not gone through rites of initiation or do not belong to a given sex, family or nationality' (Dover on Aristoph. *Nub.* 140). At Theocr. 1.15f. the goatherd uses the same terminology to warn Thyrsis against disturbing Pan at midday: οὐ θέμιc, ὦ ποιμήν, τὸ μεcαμβρινὸν οὐ θέμιc ἄμμιν | cυρίcδεν.

For the euphemistic periphrasis of negative and positive word to avoid the outright expression of a term of misfortune (ἀθέμιcτον) cf. Theocr. 7.127 τὰ μὴ καλά and the Platonic epigram cited above; Candaules' wife was similarly discreet when instructing Gyges at Hdt. 1.10 ὡc ἂν μή . . . ἴδηιc τὰ μή cε δεῖ. Heliodorus may have had C. in mind at *Aeth.* 4.19.3 ἐξ οὗπερ εἰc τὸ ἄδυτον ἀωρὶ παρελθὼν εἶδον ὀφθαλμοῖc ἃ μὴ θέμιc, ὁ θεόc μοι προεῖπεν ἀνθ' ὧν οὐ προcηκόντωc εἶδον τῆc τῶν φιλτάτων ὄψεωc cτερήcεcθαι (at 19.8 Charicles specifically refers to Charicleia as τῶν ἐμῶν ὀφθαλμῶν).

The MSS report θεμιτά in different degrees of completeness. The verse was the last line of a recto page, and the damage at the end of v. 78 corresponds to the damage at the beginning of vv. 107f. (for a description of the archetype see Intro. pp. 68f.); the different readings probably indicate that Ψ was difficult to read and in process of deteriorating, but possibly only θεμιτ was legible and scribes dealt with the problem in different ways.

79 A line epic in structure: *Il.* 3.413, 6.205, 24.55 τήν/τόν} δὲ χολωcαμένη προcεφ- + name of god (cf. *Il.* 23.482, *Od.* 18.25) is only one example of the common Homeric line-type τήν/τόν} δέ + participle + προcεφ- + subject (cf. Schmidt, *PH* 206f., 208, 212f., 215f.).

χολωcαμένα χολοῦcθαι is epic/poetic vocabulary and used mostly in participial form (LSJ: Hdt. 8.31 seems to be the only prose instance before the late Hellenistic period).

περ ὅμωc Equivalent to Homeric περ ἔμπηc. Only here in C., but several times in A.R. in this position: 1.99, 896, 4.1148; perhaps derived from Hes. *Op.* 20, the only pre-Hellenistic example of the phrase.[2]

---

[1] For the Hellenistic date of the Plato epigrams see D.L. Page, *Further Greek Epigrams* (Cambridge 1981) 125ff.

[2] Some editors emend the Hesiodic and Apollonian passages to read ὁμῶc; this is unnecessary since the combination περ + ὅμωc is guaranteed by Ap. Dysc. *Gramm. Graec.* II[1] 257.12–15 who, commenting on περ, remarks also on the concessive force of περ ὅμωc. Although strictly speaking ὅμωc

προσέφασεν The line's Homeric phraseology (see above) is the more striking since epic προσφάναι appears nowhere else in the major Hellenistic poets except at Theocr. (?) 25.42. The Homeric form is always προσέφη: προσέφασεν is the Doric (and Hellenistic)[1] form (evidence for the Doric form is slight but sufficient: Pind. *N.* 1.66 φᾶσε (suspected by some editors), Sim. *PMG* 521 φάσηις).

80–1 Athena begins on the pentameter. She speaks in the terms of standard Greek thought, though the diction is fairly poetic. From Homeric times on δαίμων was equivalent almost to πότμος or τύχη, and in particular denoted whatever power might be responsible for an unexpected or unpleasant event, illness, accident etc.[2] Hence, e.g., *Od.* 17.446 τίς δαίμων τόδε πῆμα προσήγαγε; *H.H.Ap.* 473 ἀλλά τις ἀθανάτων δεῦρ' ἤγαγεν οὐκ ἐθέλοντας, Pind. *N.* 5.15f. πῶς δὴ λίπον εὐκλέα νᾶσον, καὶ τίς ἄνδρας ἀλκίμους δαίμων ἀπ' Οἰνώνας ἔλασεν; Eur. *Hel.* 669 τίς ⟨γάρ⟩ σε δαίμων ἢ πότμος συλᾶι πάτρας;

The terminology is meaningful at two levels. T. has actually moved, or 'been brought', to the spring by a particular route, but the vocabulary is normal also of Fate or external circumstance which not only 'takes' (ἄγει) people from one place to another (*Od.* 7.248, 14.386, 16.370, 24.149, *H.H.Ap.* 473, Timoth. *PMG* 791.187f. etc.: cf. Headlam on Herodas 1.8), but also brings them metaphorically to critical moments in their lives: Soph. *Ant.* 623f. ὅτωι φρένας θεὸς ἄγει πρὸς ἄταν, A.R. 1.236 εὖτ' ἂν ἄγηι χρέος ἄνδρας ὑπεὶρ ἅλα ναυτίλλεσθαι. The sequence of events leading to such a critical moment can be described as the 'way' by which a person has come: cf. the same double use of ὁδός at, e.g., Soph. *Aj.* 994–5 ὁδὸς θ' ὁδῶν πασῶν ἀνιάσασα δὴ | μάλιστα τοὐμὸν σπλάγχνον, ἣν δὴ νῦν ἔβην, *Ant.* 1212f. ἆρα δυστυχεστάτην | κέλευθον ἕρπω τῶν παρελθουσῶν ὁδῶν; Call. IV 184f. ἀσπίδας, αἳ Γαλάτηισι κακὴν ὁδὸν . . . | στήσονται.[3] Finally, χαλεπός, 'hard', describes both the ruggedness of a traveller's path and the severity of a person's misfortune: cf. Plato, *Rep.* 328E δοκεῖ γάρ μοι χρῆναι παρ' αὐτῶν

---

belongs to the apodosis, in practice it is often closely attached in this way to the protasis (see LSJ s.v. II), like Homeric ἔμπης.

[1] In the simple verb, ἔφησα developed as an alternative to the strong aorist ἔφην in the Classical period (Schwyzer, *GG* I 673, LSJ) and superseded it in the *koine* (Mayser, *GGP* I^2 200, Crönert, *MGH* 281), although ἔφην continued to be used in literary Greek (see Arndt–Gingrich, *GNT*).

[2] *RE* Suppl. III 285ff., Nilsson, *GGR* II 219ff., Schmidt, *SGS* IV 2ff., Fraenkel on Aesch. *Ag.* 1341f.; also H.Nowak, *Zur Entwicklungsgeschichte des Begriffes* δαίμων (Diss. Bonn 1960) and F.A.Wilford, 'δαίμων in Homer', *Numen* 12 (1965) 217–32. Cf. Kleinknecht, *LP* 343ff.

[3] For more examples see O.Becker, *Das Bild des Weges* (*Hermes* Einzelschr. 4, 1937) 195ff., 202ff.

[τῶν cφόδρα πρεcβυτῶν] πυνθάνεcθαι, ὥcπερ τινα ὁδὸν προεληλυθότων, ἣν καὶ ἡμᾶc ἴcωc δεήcαι πορεύεcθαι, ποία τίc ἐcτιν, τραχεῖα καὶ χαλεπή, ἢ ῥαιδία καὶ εὔποροc.

C.'s couplet may have influenced the phraseology and articulation of Alcaeus, *HE* 122f. τίc cε τὸν οὐχ ὁcίωc ἠγρευμένον ὧδε πεδήcαc | θήκατο; See also on v. 87 ἀφείλεο.

80 τὸν ὀφθαλμὼc οὐκέτ' ἀποιcόμενον Phrases in apposition to a personal pronoun normally have the article (K–G, *GG* I 602 A.2, Gildersleeve, *SGG* II § 606); this sentence is analogous to, e.g., *Od.* 7.248 ἀλλ' ἐμὲ τὸν δύcτηνον ἐφέcτιον ἤγαγε δαίμων. Athena is abrupt and coldly precise, speaking as if Tiresias' eyes are a separable possession, like his tunic or sandals; she goes straight into Tiresias' punishment, with not a word of explicit pity or sympathy. Only χαλεπάν in the following line gives any indication of what the blinding might *mean* to Tiresias.

ἀποιcόμενον A colourless word: ἀποφέρεcθαι 'take back' is normal usage – e.g. Hdt. 1.132f. ἀποφέρεται ὁ θύcαc τὰ κρέα.

81 ὦ Εὐηρείδα Tiresias is similarly addressed at Theocr. 24.71 | μάντι Εὐηρείδα. T.'s father is always reported as Eueres,[1] but nothing more is known about him; he seems to be simply a convenient means of providing T. with a patronymic.

The use of the patronymic and not T.'s own name gives to Athena's address a tone of gravity, which is strengthened by the fact that ὦ Εὐηρείδα fills the whole of the first half of the line up to the caesura without a break.[2] Athena is angry as well as grave, and this is expressed by the interjection ὦ: in Callimachus as in Homer the presence of ὦ indicates a throwing off of reserve in some way, in familiarity, sympathy or anger.[3] Here the rare combination of the interjection and the patronymic has the same effect as when Philoetius angrily addresses Ctesippus at *Od.* 22.287 ὦ

---

[1] By Pherecydes, *FGrHist* I 3.92 and Hyginus *passim*; cf. Phlegon, *mir.* 4.

[2] It is not correct to suggest, as does Pfeiffer on fr. 21.4 (cf. *Addenda II*), that such words of 'semiquinarial' length are abnormal. Metrical practice requires that one consider phrases such as καὶ-τὸν-ἀεθλοφόρον (VI 109) as a single metrical unit, equal to one 'word', and there are many such 'semiquinarial' units in C., as in other writers (cf. H.Fränkel, 'Der homerische und der kallimachische Hexameter', *Wege und Formen frühgriechischen Denkens* (Munich 1960^2) 132f.).

[3] The effect of the presence or absence of ὦ has been well studied: for Homer and Hesiod, the lyric poets, dramatists, Herodotus and Plato by J.A.Scott, *AJP* 24 (1903) 192–6, 25 (1904) 81–4, 26 (1905) 32–43, for A.R. and C.'s *Hymns* I–IV by G.Giangrande, *CQ* 18 (1968) 52–9, and for Theocritus by F.Williams, *Eranos* 71 (1973) 52–67. See also Wackernagel, *VUS* I 310ff., and Sandbach on Menander, *Dysc.* 823.

Πολυθερσεΐδη.[1] Contrast Chariclo's respectful πότνια (without interjection) at v. 86 when addressing Athena.

(F.H.Sandbach suggests the possibility of scanning Εὐηρεΐδα, though the heaviness of the spondaic line up to the masculine caesura, the only instance in this poem, might be thought expressive.)

χαλεπάν See on vv. 80f. above. The adjective does not necessarily imply any criticism of the god responsible for T.'s misfortune: cf. III 124 cχέτλιοι (as at V 78), οἷc τύνη (Artemis) χαλεπὴν ἐμμάξεαι ὀργήν.

ὁδόν ὁδόν often so in the 'internal accusative' as verbal abstract to verbs of movement (especially ἰέναι, ἐλθεῖν): Schwyzer, *GG* II 74ff.

82 ἁ μὲν ἔφα, παιδὸς δ' μέν . . . , δ' . . . : Athena and the blinding are *separate*. This is important when Athena later (v. 98) claims ἐγὼ δ' οὔ τοι τέκνον ἔθηκ' ἀλαόν: Athena is not in fact represented as actually blinding Tiresias, though a reader might be forgiven for assuming in v. 82 that she is none the less responsible. C. seems to have reduced the savagery of the earlier version, since according to [Apollodorus] in Pherecydes Athena blinded T. ταῖc χερcὶ τοὺc ὀφθαλμοὺc αὐτοῦ καταλαβομένην (3.6.7 = *FGrHist* I 3.92a).[2] But although the syntactical structure separates Athena and the blinding, the rhythm binds them: παιδὸc δ' is followed by a pause at the caesura and is thus emphatically juxtaposed with the preceding ἁ μὲν ἔφα.

The tone is epic: ἁ μὲν ἔφα has no exact Homeric precedent,[3] but it is evocative of common formulae such as ἡ μὲν ἄρ' ὣc εἰποῦc', and the syntactical shape ὣc [part of φημί]· . . . δέ is common in Homer (Ebeling, *LH* II 419f.).

παιδός The insistence here and at v. 85 τὸν κῶρον, v. 87 τῶ παιδόc on Tiresias' youth makes for pathos. Cf. on vv. 75f. ἄρτι γένεια | περκάζων.

ὄμματα νὺξ ἔλαβεν This concise description is dramatic and powerful. Three factors especially combine to emphasise the gravity of the blinding:

---

[1] This and *Od.* 24.517 are the only examples in Homer of ὦ added directly to a patronymic. Use of the patronymic normally conveys a tone of respect.

[2] Cf. Paul's blinding of the magician Elymas in Acts 13.11 καὶ νῦν ἰδοὺ χεὶρ κυρίου ἐπὶ cέ, καὶ ἔcῃ τυφλὸc μὴ βλέπων τὸν ἥλιον ἄχρι καιροῦ. παραχρῆμα δὲ ἔπεcεν ἐπ' αὐτὸν ἀχλὺc καὶ cκότοc. Phlegon, *Mir.* 4 also describes Hera's blinding of T. with the words κατανύξαι αὐτοῦ τοὺc ὀφθαλμούc; the other sources for the same story are much milder (cited in Merkelbach–West, *Fragm. Hesiodea* 275).

[3] A.R. on the other hand uses *only* the Homeric ὣc ἄρ' ἔφη.

(1) the expression is reminiscent of common Homeric descriptions of the type . . . ὄσσε κελαινὴ νὺξ ἐκάλυψεν[1] used always to describe death;

(2) although σκότος not infrequently denotes blindness (temporary or permanent),[2] νύξ seems not to be so used before C.; metaphorically applied, 'night' is something more extensive and more final than vague 'darkness', it is the night of death or near death;[3]

(3) the verb ἔλαβεν, an apparently unusual verb to describe the onset of blindness,[4] is particularly appropriate of a force taking control or possession of a person, and in this context is reminiscent of *Il.* 5.82f., 16.333f., 20.476f . . . τὸν δὲ κατ' ὄσσε | ἔλλαβε . . . θάνατος καὶ μοῖρα.

This passage may have inspired Ovid, *Met.* 1.721 *centumque oculos nox occupat una* (of Argus).

ὄμματα The 'Aeolic' form ὄθμ- (see Pfeiffer on fr. 1.37) seems to be restricted in C. to the Ionic *Aetia*; Hymns v and vi have only ὄμμ-.

ἔλαβεν All MSS, except I before correction (ἔλαβε I^{ac}, ἔβαλε I^{pc}), read ἔβαλε(ν), 'hit', 'struck'. Ernesti tried to defend ἔβαλεν by comparing the phrase οὔατα βάλλειν of sound (the verb is used also of smell: see LSJ s.v.); however blinding is not an *impression on* the sensation (to reproduce the metaphor in English), but a *removal of* it, and the easy correction ἔλαβεν makes much better sense.

83–4 Tiresias is stunned. His sensations (loss of voice, inability to move) are typical in Greek poetry for one dazed either by shock or by love. Metaneira's reaction to the epiphany of Demeter at *H.H.Dem.* 281f. is described in similar terms: τῆς δ' αὐτίκα γούνατ' ἔλυντο, | δηρὸν δ' ἄφθογγος γένετο χρόνον; and the Callimachean passage is also reminiscent (in general as well as in some details of phraseology: see below) of a Homeric formulaic context which is fullest at *Od.* 4.703ff. (Penelope learns of Telemachus' danger) ὣς φάτο, τῆς δ' αὐτοῦ λύτο γούνατα καὶ φίλον

---

1 *Il.* 5.310 etc. (see Concordances to *Iliad* and *Odyssey* s.vv. ἐκάλυψε and κάλυψε) and after Homer in tragedy *passim*.

2 E.g. Soph. *OT* 419, 1273, 1313, Eur. *Bacch.* 510, *Phoen.* 377, 1534 and in the medical writers of dizziness.

3 Of death: *Il.* 5.659, 13.425, 580, *Od.* 20.351, Soph. *Aj.* 660, *OC* 1684, Eur. *Alc.* 269, *HF* 1071, *Ion* 1466. At *Il.* 5.310, 11.356, 14.439, Aeneas and Hector are overcome in battle and almost die, and at 22.466 Andromache falls into a dead faint on seeing Hector dragged by Achilles: in each case the accompanying terminology is that of death.

The only other example I can find of νύξ expressing blindness is in the later visionary passage *LXX* Micah 3.6 διὰ τοῦτο νὺξ ὑμῖν ἔσται ἐξ ὁράσεως, καὶ σκοτία ὑμῖν ἔσται ἐκ μαντείας, καὶ δύσεται ὁ ἥλιος ἐπὶ τοὺς προφήτας, καὶ συσκοτάσει ἐπ' αὐτοὺς ἡ ἡμέρα.

4 A rare example is Hipp. *VC* 14 τὸν ἄνθρωπον ὅτι δῖνός τε ἔλαβε καὶ σκότος.

ἦτορ, | δὴν δέ μιν ἀμφασίη ἐπέων λάβε· τὼ δέ οἱ ὄσσε | δακρυόφι πλῆσθεν, θαλερὴ δέ οἱ ἔσχετο φωνή. (Similarly the last two lines at *Il.* 17.695f. and, in more abbreviated form, *Il.* 23.396f., *Od.* 19.471f.) Theocritus and A.R. describe the sensation of love in a similar way (see below on v. 83 ἐκόλλασαν), and at A.R. 3.422f. Jason is likewise bewildered by Aietes' challenge: ὣς ἄρ' ἔφη· ὁ δὲ σῖγα ποδῶν πάρος ὄμματα πήξας, | ἧστ' αὔτως ἄφθογγος, ἀμηχανέων κακότητι: the same characteristics once again, inability to move,[1] loss of voice and general bewilderment (cf. also Lucretius 3.152–8 on the symptoms of fear).[2] Cf. Men. *Sam.* 105 ἀπόπληχθ', ἕστηκας ἐμβλέπων ἐμοί; and also Bühler on Mosch. 2.48 ἕστασαν.

83 ἐστάκη δ' ἄφθογγος Ψ's ἐστάθη is senseless. MSS F and S changed the breathing to read ἑστάθη, but this solution requires the addition of a long syllable, of which no indication remains in the MSS, before ἄφθογγος to shorten -η by correption: Schneider supplemented ἑστάθη, ἆ, ἄφθογγος and suggested an allusion to Aesch. *Pers.* 206 φόβωι δ' ἄφθογγος ἑστάθην, φίλοι, but this reading has found favour with no subsequent editor.[3] G.Giangrande *CQ* 12 (1962) 212f. (and again in *Maia* 26 (1974) 227f.) similarly proposed ἑστάθη ὧδ' ἄφθογγος which, although superior to Schneider's text, still involves the difficulties of asyndeton and an almost redundant word in an otherwise concise passage (ὧδ' would mean 'like that', 'just as he was', referring, presumably, to his blindness).[4]

---

[1] ἧστ' αὔτως: see below on v. 83 ἐστάκη.

[2] G.Giangrande, *CQ* 12 (1962) 212f. argues of A.R. 3.422f. and v 82–4 'that one poet is echoing the other appears doubtless, as the lexical coincidences show'. There are some superficial verbal similarities (cf. C.'s ἃ μὲν ἔφα, ὄμματα, ἐστάκη, ἄφθογγος, ἀμαχανία) but no particular effect is achieved in either passage by reference to the other: the lexical coincidences arise directly from the use of stock material; indeed A.R.'s description of Jason is more closely related to that of Demeter at *H.H.Dem.* 194ff.: 194 κατ' ὄμματα καλὰ βαλοῦσα, 197 ἔνθα καθεζομένη, 198 δηρὸν δ' ἄφθογγος τετιημένη ἧστ'.

[3] The 'allusion' to Aeschylus is unconvincing: the only link between the two passages is that two common (and neutral) words recur in descriptions of a not uncommon sensation (as elsewhere too: cf. *H.H.Dem.* 198, Soph. *Aj.* 311, A.R. 3.423).

[4] Giangrande suggests that ὧδε (and also αὔτως) had come to mean 'so very' = μάλα, πάνυ (ὧδ' ἄφθογγος = 'very speechless') but this is not substantiable. ὧδε + adjective is either directly correlative ('so speechless . . . that . . .') or emphasises the permanence of the state (Rumpel, *Lex. Theocr.* s.v. αὔτως 2). In A.R. 3.423 ἧστ' αὔτως ἄφθογγος, which G. ingeniously adduces in support of his conjecture, αὔτως qualifies ἧστ' and = 'like that', i.e. ποδῶν πάρος ὄμματα πήξας (v. 422). One might

Redivision of the letters has also failed to produce a satisfactory emendation (ἔστα δήν Hecker, ἔστα θήν Meineke, ἔστα δ' ὧδ' Bergk). Only P.Buttmann has suggested a really convincing solution: ἑστάκη (*Ausführliche griechische Sprachlehre* II[1] (Berlin 1825) 159 n. 3). One letter is changed and the unusual Doric form (see below) explains Ψ's attempted 'correction' to a more normal form of the verb. (For ἕστηκα = 'stand motionless' see LSJ s.v. ἵστημι B II, Headlam on Herodas 5.40, and cf. Pollux, *Onom.* 3.89 ἕστηκεν, ἡσυχάζει, μένει, ἀτρεμεῖ etc.)[1]

ἑστάκη = Attic ἑστήκει: for Doric ᾱ cf. Pind. *P.* 8.71 παρέστακε, Aesch. *Sept.* 956 ἕστακε, Soph. *Aj.* 200 ἕστακεν etc. (for inscriptions see Peek, *GVI* 8, 67). The third singular ending -η is testified only once inscriptionally, at *Tab. Heracl.* 1.39 (Schwyzer, *DGEE* 62) ἀπολώλη, but it appears also as a variant in some MSS at Theocr. 10.38 ἐλελάθη and 13.40 πεφύκη, where it should probably be retained.[2]

The absence of the augment is regular. Already omitted often in poetry and Ionic, it is absent frequently in papyri and usually in *N.T.* Greek.[3] Pluperfect ἑστήκειν is anyway an exceptional verb and unaugmented in all periods (LSJ s.v. ἵστημι, Veitch, *GV* 339) but particularly in the *koine* (Schwyzer, *GG* I 652, Mayser, *GGP* I² 103).[4]

---

note that no additional word like ὧδ' appears in the imitative Nonn. *D.* 35.199 | ἱσταμένη δ' ἄφθογγος where, in a similar situation, Chalcomede watches Morrheus bathe (cf. also *D.* 46.273).

[1] P.Maas, *SJ* was so offended by ἑστᾶθη that he proposed deleting the whole of vv. 83f. as an interpolation. The objection to ἑστάκη by G.R.McLennan, *CQ* 21 (1971) 425, on the grounds that the resulting pattern of spondees and dactyls (SSDSD) would be unique in the Fifth Hymn, has no substance: by the same criterion v. 41 would have to be considered corrupt since DDDSD is equally unique in the Hymn. Both patterns can be paralleled in the *Aetia* and that is sufficient metrical support.

[2] Gow reads -ει in both places. Schwyzer, *GG* I 776, 778 notes -η as a Doric ending, but refers only to *Tab. Heracl.* 1.39. -η in the Homeric third singular ἠ(ε)ίδη may be compared: cf. Curtius, *The Greek Verb* 431f. and Chantraine, *GH* I 438. Third singular pluperfect -η also features in *koine* papyri (especially third-century B.C.), though -ει is commoner: Mayser, *GGP* I² 82.

[3] For a good general summary see Blass–Debrunner–Rehkopf, *GNG* §§ 66f.; cf. K–B, *GG* II 16ff., H.St.J.Thackeray, *Grammar of the Old Testament* (Cambridge 1909) 198ff. For papyri see Mayser, *GGP* I² 101–3, and for the *N.T.* see Moulton, *GNT* II 190.

[4] Homeric MSS offer both augmented and unaugmented forms, but Aristarchus read the unaugmented form: see Σ to *Il.* 4.329 and passages cited by Erbse ad loc. (The second-century B.C. papyrus *Lit. Lond.* 251

83–4 After the dramatic summary of the effect on Tiresias (ἑcτάκη δ' ἄφθογγοc), comes a more detailed description of his sensations: ἑcτάκη → ἐκόλλαcαν . . . , ἄφθογγοc → φώναν . . .

ἐκόλλαcαν γὰρ ἀνῖαι | γώνατα A common poetic metaphor, originating from Homer, in which the verb is usually πήγνυμι: *Il.* 22.452f. (where ΣBT quote Callimachus) νέρθε δὲ γοῦνα | πήγνυται (Andromache, frightened for Hector, is unable to move), Eur. *HF* 1394f. Theseus: ἀνίcταc', ὦ δύcτηνε· δακρύων δ' ἅλιc. | Heracles: οὐκ ἂν δυναίμην· ἄρθρα γὰρ πέπηγέ μου, Theocr. 2.110 (Simaetha in love) ἀλλ' ἐπάγην δαγῦδι . . . ἶcα (v. 108 οὐδέ τι φωνῆcαι δυνάμαν), A.R. 3.962ff. (Medea in love) ὄμματα δ' αὔτωc | ἤχλυcαν . . . | γούνατα δ' οὔτ' ὀπίcω οὔτε προπάροιθεν ἀεῖραι | ἔcθενεν, ἀλλ' ὑπένερθε πάγη πόδαc.[1] C.'s change of verb revitalises the metaphor, and this passage is probably behind Rhianus, *HE* 3214ff. (=fr. 71 Powell) ἦν δ' ἐπὶ Λεπτινέω cτρέψηιc δέμαc οὐκέτι γυῖα | κινήcειc ἀλύτωι δ' ὡc ἀδάμαντι μενεῖc | ἴχνια κολληθείc (though the metaphor with κολλᾶν may possibly have been more current in Hellenistic literature than now appears from the extant fragments: cf. *LXX* Job 29.10 γλῶccα αὐτῶν τῶι λάρυγγι αὐτῶν ἐκολλήθη and similarly Psalm 21.16, 136.6, Lam. 4.4).

ἀνῖαι See on v. 26 φυταλιᾶι.

84 γώνατα So all MSS except G and I which read γούνατα. γων- is unique to this passage (Alcman, Tyrtaeus, Pindar and Theocritus always use γουν- for the long form) and must remain suspect as a possible hyper-Dorism of an over-zealous scribe.[2] However, the reading of Ψ should be retained since Doric γων- is theoretically possible by analogy with *μόνϝοc → Attic μόνοc, Ionic μοῦνοc, Doric μῶνοc.[3] Cf. also related γωνία (all dialects) and the probably related γουνόc which may in the Argolid have been γωνόc (Collitz, *GDI* 3321: Nemea). Cf. Frisk, *EW* I 322 s.v. γουνόc, 337 s.v. γωνία, Chantraine, *DE* 244 s.v. γωνία.

φωνὰν ἔcχεν ἀμαχανία Reminiscent of the Homeric θαλερὴ δέ οἱ ἔcχετο φωνή (see above on vv. 83f.),[4] and similar in phraseology to the only Homeric instance of ἀμηχανία, *Od.* 9.295 ἀμηχανίη δ' ἔχε θυμόν; however, ἀμηχανία is normal usage in Hellenistic literary vocabulary (Xenophon, Polybius, Josephus, *passim*) and the phraseology is not unusual: cf. Xen. *Oec.* 1.21 ἀμηχανίαιc cυνέχονται, Joseph. *B.* 6.180 ἐπέcχε . . . τοὺc

---

gives ἑcτήκει for *Il.* 12.446: see S. West, *The Ptolemaic Papyri of Homer* (Köln 1967) 121.)

[1] Note Cobet's suggestion πέπαγε at Sappho fr. 31.9, the *locus classicus* for these sensations in love.

[2] A unique hyper-Dorism is prima facie unlikely to have originated with the Cyrenaean Callimachus.

[3] See Buck, *GD* § 54 and notes on v. 27 κῶραι, v. 29 μῶνον.

[4] Cf. A.R. 3.811 | ἔcχετο δ' ἀμφαcίηι, cf. 3.284 τὴν δ' ἀμφαcίη λάβε θυμόν.

περιcχεθέντας ἀμηχανία, and A.R. 1.638f. ἀμηχανίῃ δ' ἔcχοντο [Fränkel after a suggestion of Wilamowitz: ἐχέοντο MSS] | ἄφθογγοι.

Ψ had Attic ἀμηχ-: Pindar and Bacchylides use only ἀμαχ-,[1] and Blomfield's suggestion should therefore be accepted here, and ἀμάχανος restored to the thoroughly Doric Theocr. 1.85.

85–95 Chariclo's grief. Tiresias is a κωφὸν πρόcωπον, and the reaction to his punishment comes entirely from Chariclo. In eight lines she reacts vehemently, but it is important not to misunderstand what she says: although she immediately rounds on Athena as a friend betrayed, she is not in fact questioning the basis of the punishment. She knows what has happened, that Tiresias has intruded on a goddess's privacy (vv. 88f.: see notes): it is only the magnitude of the punishment, not its logic, that horrifies her (see on v. 87 ὄμματα). She addresses Tiresias in words of despair, not sympathy (see on v. 87 ἄλαcτε), and her impassioned denunciation of Helicon is an attempt to objectify her rage and despair, to make sense of an event which is nonsensical emotionally (cf. on vv. 91f. δόρκας . . . ἔχεις): she does not attempt to defend Tiresias' intrusion. She speaks with passion and with dignity (see on vv. 89f. ὦ ἐμέ . . . , ἦ μεγάλ', etc.), and the narrative consistently describes her in terms of high tragic pathos (see on vv. 93–5, 94f.). When Athena speaks the goddess claims that she can justify the apparent severity of the punishment; but although C. describes Athena as pitying Chariclo (v. 95 ἐλέηcεν) the ἔλεος of a Greek god is always the reaction of a detached observer, not the emotional and practical involvement of the Christian deity, and the impact of Chariclo's grief is undiminished. See Intro. pp. 47ff.

85 ἁ νύμφα The article is necessary to re-emphasise Chariclo, who has not been mentioned since v. 73, and to contrast her with the silent Tiresias for whom she speaks ('but *Chariclo* cried out'); see on v. 65.

δ' Commonly delayed in poetry and prose following an article and substantive (Denniston, *GP* 186), as again in C. with the same syntactical rhythm at III 51 αἱ νύμφαι δ' ἔδδειcαν, and at fr. 1.12, 24.

ἐβόαcε the usual verb for crying aloud in anguish or for help when threatened: cf. Eur. *HF* 975 βοᾷ δὲ μήτηρ· ὦ τεκών, τί δρᾷς; τέκνα | κτείνεις; etc. See Schmidt, *SGS* I 127f.

ἐβόαcε is Politian's correction of Ψ's ἐβόηcε. This is the only place in V and VI where Ψ corrupted original ᾱ in contract verbs to Attic η: cf. V 11, 65, 83, 130, VI 137.

τὸν κῶρον Here and at v. 87 τῶ παιδός the article is possessive,

[1] Also at adesp. *PMG* 1019.7 and by emendation (surely correct) at Stesich. *PMG* 244.1; the more restricted Doric of tragedy has ἀμηχ-: see Björck, *AI* 178f.

reinforcing μοι and expressing Chariclo's particularly heartfelt emotions at this point for her son.[1] For the form see on v. 27 κῶραι.

ἔρεξας Prose would have ἔρρεξας, but poetic licence occasionally allows single ρ after the syllabic augment in epic and tragic lyric (Maas, *GM* § 130). The major Hellenistic writers are stricter than Homer and allow this licence only with ῥέζειν.[2]

86 Chariclo's bewilderment at what has happened is strongly expressed, but it is not outrageous: cf. Bacch. 3.38 πο]ῦ θεῶν ἐςτι[ν] χάρις; (Croesus), Hdt. 1.90.4 ταῦτά τε ἐπειρωτᾶν [Croesus' messengers] καὶ εἰ ἀχαρίςτοιςι νόμος εἶναι τοῖςι Ἑλληνικοῖςι θεοῖςι. At Eur. *Hipp.* 1441 Hippolytus remarks to Artemis μακρὰν δὲ λείπειc ῥαιδίως ὁμιλίαν.

πότνια 'mistress, my lady'. The tone is explicitly reverent and respectful:[3] the main reason for Chariclo's bewilderment is that Athena's action seems to be in direct contradiction to her position as divine patroness of Chariclo. πότνι' Ἀθαναία (v. 55) seems senselessly to have become an evil δαίμων.

δαίμονες For the moment Chariclo regards Athena not simply as a goddess (θεός), but as the irrational force responsible for the disaster which has just befallen Tiresias (see on vv. 80f. τίς . . . δαίμων).

φίλαι Cf. on v. 58 φίλατο.

87 **ὄμματά μοι τῶ παιδὸς ἀφείλεο** The answer to v. 85 τί μοι τὸν κῶρον ἔρεξας; The repeated syntactical shape sustains the anguish of the rhetorical question.

Ariston of Chius, a Stoic near-contemporary of Callimachus, is said by Diog. Laert. 7.163 to have replied to an Academic, who claimed to be so sceptical that he did not even think he could see the man sitting next to him: τίς ⟨δέ⟩ ς' ἐτύφλωςεν, τίς ἀφείλετο λαμπάδος αὐγάς; (= *SH* 205). Ariston is generally considered to have been taunting the Academic with a quotation; perhaps he had in mind C.'s hymn and what happened to Tiresias and ironically combined Athena's question at v. 80 with Chariclo's statement here.

ὄμματα First word in the sentence, contrary to syntactical requirements, because of its priority of emphasis: 'it's my son's *eyes* you've taken' (emphasis also on 'my': see on v. 85 τὸν κῶρον).

τῶ Ernesti's correction of Ψ makes for consistency with the Doric article elsewhere in v. Cf. corruption of τῶ to τῶν at v. 46.

---

[1] Cf. e.g. *Il.* 19.331 ὡς ἄν μοι τὸν παῖδα . . . This 'genitival' μοι is common with close relatives in Greek: see especially Wackernagel, *VUS* II 77f.

[2] The only exception appears to be [Mosch.] 3.32 ἔριψε.

[3] Apollonius Soph. *Lex. Hom.* πότνια· ςεβαςτὴ καὶ ἔνδοξος. ὁ δὲ Ἀπίων δέςποινα, τιμία (cf. Hesych. s.v. πότνα, *Suda* etc. s.v. πότνια). Note too the absence of the interjection ὦ (see on v. 81 ὦ Εὐηρείδα).

ἀφείλεο It is important to recognise the normality of ἀφείλεο, for much depends on the tone at this particular point. ἀφαιρεῖν (-εῖcθαι) is a common neutral verb (probably for this reason, rare in Hellenistic poetry);[1] typical, e.g., is Xen. *Mem.* 1.5.3 οἱ πλεονέκται τῶν ἄλλων ἀφαιρούμενοι χρήματα ἑαυτοὺc δοκοῦcι πλουτίζειν. Chariclo does *not* say that Athena 'snatched away' Tiresias' eyes (McKay, *PP* 35).

Chariclo's syntax, as well as her vocabulary, is simple and direct. τῶ παιδόc, ambiguously placed, is both possessive with ὄμματα and separative with ἀφείλεο;[2] Classical ἀφαιρεῖcθαι most commonly has a double accusative (τι τινα) or accusative *rei* + preposition (ἀπό, πρόc etc. τινοc), but τι τινοc, occasionally found in earlier periods,[3] was the normal construction in the *koine*: Mayser, *GGP* II² 232, Mauersberger, *Polybios-Lexikon* s.v. (2) b.[4]

Ψ's ἀφείλετο cannot be defended; ἀφείλεο, written into the margin of E, is essential.

τέκνον ἄλαcτε The precise meaning of ἄλαcτε, if it has one, is unclear, but assessment of its tone is important for the understanding of Chariclo's whole speech. In this kind of context the word seems to have a mainly emotive value; poetical, used mostly of grief, misfortune etc. or their cause (πένθοc, ἄχοc, ἔργα etc.), ἄλαcτοc = something like 'terrible', 'insufferable',[5] but of people the adjective is very rare: before C. only *Il.* 22.261 Ἕκτορ, μή μοι, ἄλαcτε, cυνημοcύναc ἀγόρευε and Soph. *OC* 1482 ἄλαcτον ἄνδρ' ἰδών.[6] Jebb's explanation is very plausible: 'the epithet of the *act* . . . is transferred to the *agent*, – the doer of ἄλαcτα being called ἄλαcτοc in the general sense of "wretch", "accursed one"'. What appears to be the only other direct testimony, a passage of second-century A.D. mime in *P. Oxy.* 413.60 (= Page, *GLP* 76.66) βάcκ', ἄλαcτε (derogatory: 'away, wretch'),[7] seems to support Jebb, as do some of the explanations of ancient

---

[1] Once in A.R. 4.1040, never in Aratus, bucolics, Nicander. In C. again at 714.2 and III 236 (a similar construction: θυμὸν ἀπ' ἄγριον εἵλεο παίδων). For the expression cf. Peek, *GVI* 1747 cάρκαc μὲν πῦρ ὄμματ' ἀφείλετο τῆ[ι]δε 'Ονηcῶc, | ὄcτεα δ' . . .

[2] This kind of ambiguity is typical of Greek; again with ἀφαιρεῖcθαι at Eur. *Andr.* 522 καὶ φόβον οἴκων ἀφελέcθαι.

[3] See *Thes. Graec.* s.v. 2603. In general see R.Kühner on Xen. *Mem.* 1.5.3.

[4] Later Greek replaces the genitive of separation generally by prepositional phrases and uses only τι ἀπό τινοc: see Blass–Debrunner–Rehkopf, *GNG* § 155.4, Moulton, *GNT* III 235.

[5] Etymologically ἄλαcτοc probably = 'not to be forgotten', as suggested by most of the ancient lexicographers: see Chantraine, *DE* s.v. ἀλάcτωρ. However, see also Barrett on Eur. *Hipp.* 877–80.

[6] Cf. 1672 πατρόc . . . ἄλαcτον αἷμα: in these two passages the emphasis seems to be entirely on the *pollution* of Oedipus.

[7] ἄλαcτε is still highly poetical, as is shown by βάcκ': the tone is

lexicographers and commentators: ΣBT to *Il.* 22.261 ἄλαστόν φησι τὸν ἀνεπίληστα κακὰ δεδρακότα, *Et. Mag.* ἀλαστὸς [*sic*] λέγεται ὁ λήθης ἄξια ποιῶν, διὰ τὴν κακοπραξίαν, Hesych. σχέτλιε, ἁμαρτωλέ.[1]

Chariclo's exclamation may thus be translated 'wretched child': these are words *not* of sympathy pure and simple, but of *despair* that Tiresias must be punished for what he has done – what follows immediately in the next line is an explanation of what his ἄλαστα consist in.

The adjective takes on a masculine ending, according to the person designated, contrary to strict syntax which would require ἄλαστον agreeing with τέκνον. This kind of 'attraction' is common in Greek: see Schwyzer, *GG* II 602f. amongst whose many examples are *Il.* 22.84 φίλε τέκνον and Eur. *Tro.* 740 ὦ φίλτατ, ὦ περισσὰ τιμηθεὶς τέκνον. Again in C. at VI 47 τέκνον πολύθεστε.

The quotation illustrating ἄλαστος in the *Suda* and the *Lexicon* of Zonaras[2] ἄλαστε· ἀνεπίληστε. 'τέκνον ἐμὸν ἄλαστον' appears to be a misquotation, or corruption, of v. 87 τέκνον ἄλαστε.

88 Ἀθαναίας In an emphatic position, placed early in the sentence juxtaposed with εἶδες, before στήθεα καὶ λαγόνας on which it is syntactically dependent: 'you saw *Athena's* breast and loins'. Had it been a mortal woman whom he had seen, the consequences would have been less severe.

στήθεα καὶ λαγόνας The two most feminine and intimate parts of the Greek female body. At Eur. *Hec.* 558ff. Polyxena about to be sacrificed dies as a free woman and exposes her virgin body to Neoptolemus' sword with a symbolic gesture: λαβοῦσα πέπλους ἐξ ἄκρας ἐπωμίδος | ἔρρηξε λαγόνας ἐς μέσας παρ' ὀμφαλόν | μαστούς τ' ἔδειξε στέρνα θ' ὡς ἀγάλματος | κάλλιστα . . . At Chaeremon trag. fr. 14.1ff. (Snell, *TGF* I 71 F 14) Oineus

---

mock-pompous. LSJ s.v. ἄλαστος refer also to Demophilus, *Sent.* 13 where however the text is τὸ ἄλαστον = 'the terribleness' (of the ever-watching deity: a reference to δαίμων ἀλάστωρ).

[1] Cf. ΣD to *Il.* 22.261 ἀλάθητε· δεινὰ καὶ ἀνεπίληστα εἰργασμένε, Eustath. 1268.55 ἄλαστον εἰπεῖν τὸν Ἕκτορα ὡς ἀλάθητα λυπήσαντα, *Suda* ἄλαστον· ἀνεπίληστε, Ap. Soph. *Lex. Hom.* 22.29 ἄλαστον· χαλεπόν, ἀνεπίληστον; and on cognate words: Hesych. ἀλάστορες· παλαμναῖοι. οἱ μιάσμασιν ἐνεχόμενοι. ἢ οἱ μεγάλα ἁμαρτάνοντες, Hesych. ἀλαστόρων· ἀσεβῶν . . . , *Suda*, Harpocration, *Et. Gud.*, Photius s.v. ἀλάστωρ etc. The paraphrase of the Callimachean scholia to this passage, ἤτοι ἀνεπίληστα ὑπομείνας (interpreting ἄλαστος as meaning 'about to suffer ἄλαστα'), is found nowhere else and is implausible in view of the other evidence. ἄλαστος of people does not so much describe them as record an emotional reaction to what they have done.

[2] J.A.H.Tittmann, *Zonarae Lexicon* (Leipzig 1808) I col. 116, and in the closely related lexicon of Paris Codex 2669 published by J.A.Cramer, *Anecd. Paris.* (Oxford 1839–41) IV 106.30.

describes a group of girls resting, their usual inhibitions forgotten in sleep after dancing: ἔκειτο δ' ἡ μὲν λευκὸν εἰς σεληνόφως | φαίνουσα μαστὸν λελυμένης ἐπωμίδος, | τῆς δ' αὖ χορεία λαγόνα τὴν ἀριστερὰν | ἔλυσε . . .

στήθεα 'breast', 'bosom', not 'breasts'. Plural στήθεα is normal prose usage[1] to denote the general area of the chest (male or female) and never denotes specifically the two breasts of the bosom or chest,[2] for which the Greek is μαστοί. The distinction made at Hipp. *Gland.* 16 ἀλλὰ καὶ ἀδένες ἐν τοῖσι στήθεσι μαζοὶ καλέονται is consistently maintained in all authors.

The term στήθεα is not unusual in epic representations of female beauty: e.g. *Il.* 3.396f. θεᾶς περικαλλέα δειρὴν | στήθεα θ' ἱμερόεντα (of Aphrodite), A.R. 4.432f. καλὰ μεμαρπὼς | στήθεα παρθενικῆς, cf. Theocr. 15.135 στήθεσι φαινομένοις. (On στήθεα as 'poetic plural' in Homer see K.Witte, *Glotta* 1 (1909) 132–7.)

λαγόνας λαγών is usually interpreted by lexica and commentaries as 'flank', but flanks are inappropriate here, being of little sexual significance. In fact, λαγών when used with precision denotes that part of the body which extends *from* the hollow between the ribs and hip down the side of the abdomen as far as the groin; some key passages make this definition quite clear: Aristot. *HA* 1.493a17ff. μετὰ δὲ τὸν θώρακα ἐν τοῖς προσθίοις γαστήρ, καὶ ταύτης ῥίζα ὀμφαλός· ὑπόρριζον δὲ τὸ μὲν διφυὲς λαγών . . . , Eur. *Hec.* 558ff. (quoted above).[3] This use of λαγόνες to refer implicitly to the sexual parts is paralleled by *LXX* Sirach 47.19 παρανέκλινας τὰς λαγόνας σου γυναιξὶν καὶ ἐνεξουσιάσθης ἐν τῶι σώματί σου.

89 ἀλλ' οὐκ ἀέλιον πάλιν ὄψεαι As earlier the narrative described T.'s blinding in the grave terms of death (see on v. 82 ὄμματα νὺξ ἔλαβεν), and later will describe Chariclo's lamentation as that of a mother whose child has been killed (see on vv. 94f.), so here Chariclo herself uses an expression, 'look on the sun', which is a common periphrasis for 'live' (*Il.* 18.61 ὄφρα δέ μοι ζώει καὶ ὁρᾶι φάος ἠελίοιο etc.). The arrangement is Homeric: *Il.* 24.462

---

[1] Hdt., Thuc., Xen., Plato, Aristot., Hipp. etc.

[2] LSJ quote Hipp. *Mul.* 2.133 for στήθεα = 'breasts', but there too στήθεα refers only to the general area of the bosom. Theocr.(?) 25.237 μεσσηγὺς δ' ἔβαλον στηθέων = 'in the middle of the chest': a lion can scarcely be said to have breasts.

[3] Also cf. Eur. *El.* 826, Aristot. *HA* 7.583b 1, *Physiogn.* 5.810a 5; from this usage developed the later application λαγών = 'belly', 'womb', 'bowels' (see LSJ and Lampe, *PGL*). λαγών is sometimes used vaguely of the 'flank', 'side of the body', as at Eur. *IT* 298, and especially of animals as at [Xen.] *Cyn.* 4.1, 6.1, Call. v 6 (see note), A.R. 2.664, but the flank as such is normally designated by κενεών or λαπάρα. Cf. L.Dindorf on [Xen.] *Cyn.* 4.1 (Oxford 1866).

ἀλλ' ἤτοι μὲν ἐγὼ πάλιν εἴcομαι· cf. 1.380 . . . πάλιν ᾤχετο, 21.468 . . . πάλιν ἐτράπετ'· (same metrical position).[1]

ἀέλιον Inscriptional evidence shows the true Doric form as ἅλιος (ἅ-)[2] but literary convention commonly allowed a 'Doricised' form of the Homeric uncontracted ἠέλιος; hence ἀέλιος in Pindar, Bacchylides and other lyric poets, and occasionally in tragic lyrics.[3] Again in C. at VI 91; Theocritus however uses only the true Doric ἅλιος in his Doric poems.

πάλιν In Homer πάλιν is always local (cf. K.Lehrs. *De Aristarchi Stud. Hom.* (Leipzig 1882³) 91f.), but thereafter commonly has a temporal sense.

ὄψεαι Doric contracts second person singular middle and passive -εαι to -ηι, as often in Theocritus' Doric poems (Monteil, *T* 28). Uncontracted -εαι is epic/Ionic (Attic, and thereafter the *koine*, contract to -ηι and -ει).[4] Cf. on v. 91 ἐπράξαο and v. 97 βαλεῦ.

The correption at the bucolic diaeresis is in no way exceptional: even those authors who only rarely allow correption do commonly permit it at this point in the line (cf. Gow–Page, *HE* II 645, *GP* I xxxix). Again in V at v. 99. Cf. on v. 71 ἵππῶ͜ ἐπί.

89–90 ὢ ἐμὲ δειλάν, | ὢ ὄρος, ὢ Ἑλικών . . . Chariclo's outburst is powerfully expressed: at such moments of tension Greek, like many languages, often reinforces the emotion through repetition, and the repetition commonly takes the form of an expanding tricolon. Thus, e.g., alarm in A.R. 3.674f.: ὤ μοι ἐγώ, Μήδεια, τί δὴ τάδε δάκρυα λείβεις; | τίπτ' ἔπαθες; τί τοι αἰνὸν ὑπὸ φρένας ἵκετο πένθος; admiration in Theocr. 15.123f., ὢ ἔβενος, ὢ χρυcός, ὢ ἐκ λευκῶ ἐλέφαντος | αἰετοὶ οἰνοχόον Κρονίδαι Διὶ παῖδα φέροντες, and formal lament again in Theocr. 1.115 ὢ λύκοι, ὢ θῶες, ὢ ἀν' ὤρεα φωλάδες ἄρκτοι. This figure is an especially Hellenistic feature and other notable examples in C., all with repeated lead-words, are: 203.31f., 384.13, I 22–5, III 172ff., IV 276f., V 45–8, (cf. also on vv. 108f., repeated τόν).

The repetition here has significance beyond the formal sentence structure: the third colon not only repeats the sense of the second, it also expands and suggests a reason for the outburst (οὐκέτι . . .). At such moments of dramatic exclamation or interjection this kind of expansion is typically Greek (cf., e.g., Aesch. *Eum.* 754 ὢ Παλλάς, ὢ cώcαcα . . .

---

[1] Cf. A.R. 3.1212 . . . πάλιν ἔcτιχεν· (same metrical position).

[2] See indexes in Collitz, *GDI* IV and cf. Buck, *GD* § 41.3.

[3] See indexes and Björck, *AI* 165.

[4] For Homer see J.Van Leeuwen, *Enchiridium Dictionis Epicae* (Leiden 1894) § 117, Chantraine, *GH* I 57, 474f.; in general see K–B, *GG* II 68, Mayser, *GGP* I² 90f. Uncontracted -εαι in correption at the bucolic diaeresis at Theocr. 1.82, 5.31.

δόμους)[1] and is again a feature which became a standard rhetorical device in the Hellenistic period: e.g. 191.47 ὦ παῖδες, ὦ ἐμαὶ τὠπιόντος ἄγκυραι, and Theocr. 16.104f. ὦ Ἐτεόκλειοι Χάριτες θεαί, ὦ Μινύειον | Ὀρχομενὸν φιλέοισαι ἀπεχθόμενόν ποτε Θήβαις.[2]

The seriousness of Chariclo's outburst is emphasised by another feature: in exclamations such as ὢ ἐμὲ δειλάν the case accompanying ὤ is usually the nominative, sometimes the genitive, but only very rarely the accusative. Normal in construction is, e.g., Thetis' lament on Achilles' behalf at *Il.* 18.54 ὤ μοι ἐγὼ δειλή, ὤ μοι δυσαριστοτόκεια.[3] The accusative is restricted entirely to exclamations of lament, usually of a ritual nature (ὢ τὸν Ἄδωνιν etc.). Examples before the Hellenistic period are few:[4] Sappho fr. 168, perhaps Alcaeus A 10 (B) 1 (where ἔμε δειλάν might be governed by a verb now lost), Aesch. *Ag.* 1146, Aristoph. *Lys.* 393; the Hellenistic writers offer slightly more examples: Asclepiades, *HE* 966, Duris, *HE* 1778, Bion, *Adonis* 28 etc. (refrain), 31, 32, Peek, *GVI* 1680.7f. (Egypt third to second century B.C.), Meleager, *HE* 4695f., Philip, *GP* 2815, Antip. Thess., *GP* 713.

The status of the repeated interjection need give no trouble. ὦ was used equally as an exclamation of surprise, joy, pain etc., and as a mode of address (with vocatives, imperatives etc.); the ancient grammarians attempted to distinguish between these two uses and accented the former ὤ, the latter ὦ (references in LSJ s.v.). Such a distinction is useless in this kind of passage,[5] but since an accent has to be printed one should perhaps argue as follows: the first ὤ is clearly exclamatory, but although the second and third ὦ accompany vocatives and are technically particles of address, ὢ ὄρος, ὢ Ἑλικών . . . has the function much more of an exclamation than of an address, in spite of παριτέ; Wilamowitz's ὢ then seems more appropriate than the traditional ὦ. (For the juxtaposition of exclamatory accusative and exclamatory vocative cf. Meleager, *HE* 4695f. αἰαῖ τὰς . . . χάριτας . . . ἰὼ κακοπάρθενε Μοῖρα.)

90 οὐκέτι μοι παριτέ After this Chariclo will find even going near

---

[1] Often in Sophocles: see F.Ellendt, *Lexicon Sophocleum* (Berlin 1872) s.v. ὦ p. 796.

[2] Again at Theocr. 18.38, 22.23f.; cf. A.R. 4.445ff.

[3] Cf. *Od.* 5.299, Theogn. 1107, 1318[a].

[4] See Fraenkel on Aesch. *Ag.* 1146 and Gow–Page, *HE* II 139. The remarks by Denniston–Page p. 174 on Aesch. *Ag.* 1146 are unnecessarily severe, and ἐμὲ δειλάν here is certainly not governed by ἐπράξαο in v. 91 as they suggest.

[5] Another passage where attempts to distinguish between ὦ and ὤ are fruitless is discussed by K.J.Dover on Aristoph. *Nub.* 219. See also Fraenkel on Aesch. *Ag.* 22 and Jebb on Soph. *Aj.* 373.

Helicon too painful.[1] Cf. Agave at Eur. *Bacch.* 1383ff. ἔλθοιμι δ' ὅπου | μήτε Κιθαιρὼν ⟨ἔμ' ἴδοι⟩ μιαρὸς | μήτε Κιθαιρῶν' ὄςςοιςιν ἐγώ, | μήθ' ὅθι θύρςου μνῆμ' ἀνάκειται.

The simple verbal adjective παριτός, which occurs nowhere else but here, is of regular formation and obvious meaning. For the formation of -τος verbal adjectives, which are usually equivalent to Latin *-tus* (past participle, active or passive) or *-bilis*, see K–B, *GG* II 288f., Schwyzer, *GG* I 501f., II 150.[2] παριτός itself is foreshadowed in Xen. *An.* 4.1.25 δυςπάριτον χωρίον, and the form is paralleled in other compounds of εἶμι: thus in a similar expression Hes. *Theog.* 732 (of the Titans buried in the roots of the earth) τοῖς οὐκ ἐξιτόν ἐςτι, and cf. Eur. *IA* 345 δυςπρόςιτος, Polyb. 3.49.7 ἀπρόςιτος.

91 ἦ μεγάλ' . . . Simple and ordinary diction which is given formal dignity by a Homeric cast of phrase. In Homer affirmative ἦ, which expresses 'subjective certainty',[3] often affirms a quantitative statement and is often preceded by a vocative/exclamation: e.g. *Od.* 20.112f. Ζεῦ πάτερ, . . . | ἦ μεγάλ' ἐβρόντηςας, 14.37 ὦ γέρον, ἦ ὀλίγου cε . . .[4]

ἐπράξαο πράττειν (-εςθαι) = 'exact payment', 'make a charge for something' is standard usage both in the literal financial sense and in the metaphorical sense of punishment (LSJ).[5]

Uncontracted -αο is an epicism. The second person middle ending was normally left uncontracted in Homer (Chantraine, *GH* I 54), but Doric always contracted to -ᾱ (Buck, *GD* §41).[6] Theocritus uses the Doric contraction (4.28 accepting the reading of K²QW, 5.6), but also admits uncontracted -αο as a useful metrical variation (e.g. 4.27). C. uses only the epic form (again at vv. 105, VI 15, 83). Cf. on vv. 59 Τειρεςίαο, 89 ὄψεαι, and 97 βαλεῦ.

91–2 δόρκας . . . ἔχεις The articulation is important: it is δόρκας and φάεα, each standing at the beginning of a colon and immediately after a strong metrical pause, which are directly contrasted. The comparison is essentially a qualitative one, and οὐ πολλάς is merely an additional consideration (one might almost translate 'and not many at that').

---

[1] Schneider's περιτέ is unnecessary. παριέναι + acc. = simply 'pass by', 'go close to' a place *en route* is normal usage (LSJ).

[2] In all instances except ἀπρόϊτος, -τος verbal adjectives from ἰέναι always denote possibility.

[3] Denniston, *GP* 279f.

[4] Cf. *Il.* 5.800, 19.270, and for the common ὢ πόποι, ἦ μέγα . . . see Ebeling, *LH* I 528f. In general on ἦ see Denniston, *GP* 279–81.

[5] ἀντί = 'in return for' is also normal usage: K–G, *GG* I 453f., Mayser, *GGP* II² 374f.

[6] Cf. also Thumb, *GD* I 71, 83, 115, 138, 150, Monteil, *T* § 15.

The contrast between δόρκας and φάεα may conceivably be reinforced by an etymological pun. Some post-Hellenistic writers connect δορκ- with δέρκομαι,[1] and modern philology explains ζορκ- as the original form from which δορκ- is derived by popular etymology with δέρκομαι etc.[2] Elsewhere C. usually has the ζ- form, and the δ- here may be an explicit pointer to δέρκομαι δέδορκα: Chariclo points to the disparity between Helicon's loss and Tiresias' punishment, but bitterly suggests that there may be some grotesque logic to the blinding.

δόρκας . . . | καὶ πρόκας The exact meanings of δορκ- and πρόξ are now obscure and by Hellenistic writers the two terms were probably regarded as literary alternatives. Both were certainly species of deer (ἔλαφος), and δορκ-, which probably denoted the non-Greek gazelle, may also have denoted the roe-deer.[3] πρόξ was a rare term,[4] possibly even obsolete by the third century B.C., and the authority for Hellenistic authors seems to be *Od.* 17.295 αἶγας ἐπ' ἀγροτέρας ἠδὲ πρόκας ἠδὲ λαγωούς: thence πρόξ become part of the Hellenistic poetic language (III 154f. πρόκες . . . λαγωοί, A.R. 2.279 ἢ αἶγας . . . ἠὲ πρόκας, Nic. *Ther.* 578, *Al.* 324) even though scholarly opinion on the meaning of the word varied: Σ to A.R. 2.279 πρόκας· ζῷόν τι ὅμοιον ἐλάφωι, ὁ λεγόμενος νεβρός. Διονύσιος δέ φησιν ὁ Ἀθηναῖος ἐν ταῖς Κτίσεσι τὰς ἐλάφους οὕτω λέγεσθαι πρόκας . . . Φιλητὰς δέ φησι πρόκας λέγεσθαι ἐλάφους τάς πρώτως τικτομένας, οἷον πρωτοτόκους (cf. *Et. Gen.* AB πρόκας, *Et. Mag.* 698.24, Zonaras, *Lex.* s.v. πρόκας), Apollonius Soph. *Lex. Hom.* 135.19f. πρόκας· οἱ μὲν ἐλάφους, οἱ δὲ ἕτερόν τι ζώιου εἶδος ὅμοιον λαγωῶι ὃ καλεῖται δορκάς (cf. Σ to *Od.* 17.295, Σ to Nic. *Ther.* 578, and *Al.* 324, and Aristophanes of Byzantium in M.E.Miller, *Mélanges de littérature grecque* (Paris 1868) 431[5]).

91 δόρκας A poetic form. The normal form is δορκάς, -άδος,[6] and the contracted form δόρξ, -κος appears in C. for the first time (here and 676.1,

---

[1] E.g. Basil the Great, *hom. in Prov. 6.4: ne dederis* (Migne, *Patrologia Graeca* 31.1500C) ἡ δορκὰς ζῷόν ἐστιν ὀξυδερκές, ἐπώνυμον τῆι ἑαυτοῦ ὀξυδορκίαι, *hom. in Deut. 15.9: attende* (Migne, *Patrologia Graeca* 31.201D), Greg. Nyss. *hom. 5 in cantica cant.* (Migne, *Patrologia Graeca* 44.861A–B), *Et. Mag.* 284.9ff., Eustath. 1259.60. There seems to be no direct evidence that this popular etymology was current earlier in the Hellenistic period.

[2] See Frisk, *EW* I 410, Chantraine, *FN* 3, *DE* 293f.

[3] For citations of evidence and discussion on δορκ- and πρόξ see: Gossen in *RE* IA s.v. 'Reh', O.Keller, *Thiere des Classischen Alterthums* (Innsbruck 1887) 77ff., 102ff., and cf. Orth in *RE* VIII 1936ff. s.v. 'Hirsch'.

[4] A few instances in Aristotle and one reported by Eustath. 711.40ff. in Archilochus (fr. 280 West).

[5] Reported in Aelian, *NA* 7.47.

[6] Hdt., Eur., Xen., *LXX*, *N.T.*, papyri etc.

III 97).[1] The formation was doubtless based on Homeric πρόξ: Homer has both πρόξ (see above on vv. 91–2) and προκάς, -άδος (*H.H.Aphr.* 71), and with δόρξ C. similarly completes the doublet δόρξ/δορκάς.

δ̲ορκ- is the normal spelling, but C. uses it only here: elsewhere he has the uncommon ʒ̲ορκ- (no doubt solely for its rarity) as does Nicander (*Ther.* 42, 142).[2] See above on vv. 91f. δόρκας . . . ἔχεις.

92 φάεα = 'eyes', a very rare metonymy of direct Homeric origin. The only previous such usage of the plural is in a recurrent formulaic line in the *Odyssey*, used each time in a context as here of emotional greeting: 16.15, 17.39, 19.417 κύσσε δέ μιν κεφαλήν τε καὶ ἄμφω φάεα καλά.[3] The distinctiveness of φάεα as Homeric diction prepares the way for an explicit reminiscence of *Od.* 17.38ff. in the following lines (see on vv. 93–5).

As a rare poeticism φάεα was taken up by the Hellenistic poets: in C.'s very Homeric Hymn III 53, 71, 211, and thereafter Mosch. 2.4, [Mosch.] 4.9 (cf. III 211), Nic. *Al.* 24, 84, *Ther.* 720.[4]

93–5 A reminiscence of Penelope's tearful greeting of Telemachus returned from the mainland at *Od.* 17.38ff. with which v. 92 φάεα = 'eyes'

---

[1] Whence *Et. Mag.* 284.9 δόρξ· ὄνομα ʒώιου· ἔνθεν δορκάς. Nic. *Ther.* 42,142 uses the Callimachean contract in the form ʒόρξ. The only examples of δόρξ in prose seem to be Lucian, *amor.* 16 which is easily emended to δορκάδος, and Aelian, *NA* 7.19 ʒόρκες where the initial ʒ is unusual as well as the contract form (elsewhere Aelian uses δορκάς): the whole phrase looks like a quotation in view of the obsolete πρόκες alongside ʒόρκες (?from Aristophanes of Byzantium?). At Eur. *HF* 376, where Dindorf and Wilamowitz read δόρκα, δόρκαν is more comfortable metrically.

[2] ʒ- is otherwise testified only at Hdt. 4.192 and Aelian, *NA* 7.19, 47 (quoting Aristoph. Byz.) and hence in commentators and lexicographers: Aristoph. Byz. in Miller, *Mélanges* (quoted above on vv. 91f.), Hesych., Eustath. 1259.61. On the two forms see G.Meyer, *Griech. Gramm.* (Leipzig 1896[3]) 270, Chantraine, *FN* 3, *DE* 293f., Frisk, *EW* I 410, Schmitt, *NDK* 7.

[3] The only other use of this Homeric metonymy before C. seems to be the singular in the Odyssean Eur. *Cycl.* 633 ἐκκαίειν τὸ φῶς | Κύκλωπος. Phrases such as φάος ὀμμάτων (Pind. *N.* 10.40, A.R. 2.184, Apollonides, *GP* 1191) may indicate the basis of the metonymy, but W.F.Wyatt Jr, *Metrical Lengthening in Homer* (Rome 1969) 100 suggests that even in Homer φᾱεα = 'eyes' may be an archaism, distinct from φᾰος = 'light' (though etymologically the two words must be related).

[4] φάεα was rare enough to be glossed specifically in the ancient Homeric commentaries (by ὀφθαλμοί etc.): cf. Meletius on *Od.* 16.15 in Cramer, *Anecd. Oxon.* III (Oxford 1836) 68.12, and the lexicographers *Et. Mag.* 786.35, *Et. Gud.* 547.31, *Et. Or.* 159.22, Hesychius, *Lex. Cyrill.* 63 (in Schmidt Hesych. app. crit. to φάεα).

(see note) formed a preparatory link: ἀμφὶ δὲ παιδὶ φίλωι βάλε πήχεε δακρύσασα, | κύσσε δέ μιν κεφαλήν τε καὶ ἄμφω φάεα καλά | καί ῥ' ὀλοφυρομένη . . . The reminiscence invests the description of Chariclo's embrace of her son with a formal epic dignity which is 'backed up' by some characteristically 'Homeric' features in v. 93 (see on ⟨ἅμ'⟩, ἀμφοτέραισι, φίλον . . .).[1] Chariclo's 'epic' reaction is that of Jason's mother also: A.R. 1.268 μήτηρ δ' ὡς τὰ πρῶτ' ἐπεχεύατο πήχεε παιδί, | ὧς ἔχετο κλαίουσ' ἀδινώτερον (cf. Aphrodite protecting her son Aeneas at *Il.* 5.311ff.).

93–4 Verbally similar are Theocr. 26.20 μάτηρ μὲν κεφαλὰν μυκήσατο παιδὸς ἑλοῖσα (Agave about to tear her son Pentheus to pieces), and A.R. 4.695 (Medea in Circe's house) ἡ μὲν ἐπ' ἀμφοτέραις θεμένη χείρεσσι μέτωπα.

93 ἁ μέν See on v. 94 μάτηρ μέν.

⟨ἅμ'⟩ Ψ's ἁ μὲν ἀμφοτέραισι is deficient by one short syllable. Many emendations have been proposed (see Schneider, *Callimachea* I 56f.), but only that of O.Schneider is really convincing:[2] ⟨ἅμ'⟩ both restores the metre and explains the corruption (haplography). ἅμα in this context, adverbial rather than prepositional,[3] is Homeric: e.g. *H.H.Herm.* 39 ὣς ἄρ' ἔφη· καὶ χερσὶν ἅμ' ἀμφοτέρῃσιν ἀείρας.[4] Homeric ἅμα is otherwise rare in the Hellenistic writers except A.R., but cf. Theocr. 22.130 ἀμφοτέρας ἅμα χεῖρας.[5]

ἀμφοτέραισι Ellipse of the noun is Homeric. In referring to parts of the body which go in pairs the noun is not uncommonly omitted with ἀμφότερος: for ellipse of χερσί cf. *Od.* 10.264 αὐτὰρ ὅ γ' ἀμφοτέρῃσι λαβὼν ἐλλίσσετο γούνων, and *Od.* 11.594, 17.356, 18.28, *Il.* 5.416; whence in the Hellenistic period A.R. 1.472, 1130, 3.146, 4.82, Theocr. 7.157, 22.96: cf. Gow on Theocr. 10.35 and 6.22.

φίλον . . . λαβοῖσα Homeric phraseology: cf., e.g., *Il.* 16.82 φίλον δ'

---

[1] It is the general situation and the circumstantial detail that C. evokes: there is no suggestion of a close analogy between Penelope/Telemachus and Chariclo/Tiresias in themselves.

[2] *Callimachea* I 355ff. The only other emendation worth considering is that of Wilamowitz (*HD* II 21): ἅ⟨γε⟩ μὲν ἀμφ. . . . /⟨ἁ⟩ μάτηρ [μέν]. Though neat this suggestion is unsatisfactory since (1) the text is further from Ψ and Ψ's corruption is less easily explained, (2) the article with μάτηρ is unwelcome (see on v. 65 ἁ δαίμων), whereas in v. 93 ἁ μέν is acceptable as a demonstrative (see below). P.Maas, *SJ* actually suggested excising the whole couplet.

[3] In Homer ἅμα reinforces ἄμφω in the nominative as well as the dative: *LfgrE* 601.

[4] Cf. also *Il.* 7.255, 23.686, *H.H.Dem.* 15 χερσὶν ἅμ' ἄμφω.

[5] For the different Hellenistic use of ἅμα see on v. 75 ἁμᾶι κυσίν.

ἀπὸ νόστον ἕλωνται, 19.209 φίλον κατὰ λαιμὸν ἱείη, *Od.* 14.405 φίλον τ' ἀπὸ θυμὸν ἑλοίμην.

περί . . . λαβοῖcα A verb of normal usage (LSJ) in poetic tmesis and Homeric context: so again at A.R. 1.1197 ἀμφοτέρηιcι περὶ cτύπος ἔλλαβε χερcίν. See on v. 97 μετά . . . βαλεῦ.

λαβοῖcα Politian: λαβοῦcα Ψ; see on v. 7 φεροῖcα.

94 μάτηρ μέν Repeated μέν is not common, but it occurs in a wide variety of authors (Denniston, *GP* 384–6): there is no parallel in C., but Ida Kapp, *Philologus* 84 (1929) 173 compared A.R. 1.1226f. αἱ μέν, ὅcαι . . . | αἵ γε μὲν ὑλήωροι (cf. the citations in Fränkel's app. crit.; but γε μέν might mark a new category as again at A.R. 4.1466 and not be exactly parallel to μάτηρ μέν).[1]

The repetition is closely linked with another feature of this couplet which has troubled some editors, the 'separation' of ἁ and μάτηρ. To consider | ἁ . . . | μάτηρ as simply article and noun separated from one another is seriously to misunderstand the movement of the sentence. V. 93 ἁ μέν is demonstrative, parallel, e.g., to v. 82 ἁ μὲν ἔφα, picking up the narrative as the speech ends; v. 94 μάτηρ μέν is an addition to this demonstrative: it reinforces ἁ μέν (making the reason for Chariclo's grief as explicit as possible: μάτηρ is almost predicative = 'being, as she was, his mother'), and it also helps sustain the long sentence. Repeated μέν often occurs when an article + μέν is subsequently picked up by a demonstrative (e.g. τῶι μέν . . . τούτωι μέν: see K–G II 268f.): μάτηρ μέν is very similar in function to such a demonstrative.[2]

Such heavy emphasis, ἁ μέν . . . | μάτηρ μέν makes for a very pronounced contrast with v. 95 θεὰ δ' . . .

94–5 In ancient as in modern Greece the nightingale was symbolic not only of melodiousness but also, and especially, of melancholy.[3] The comparison of a mourning relative with the unfortunate wife of Tereus, murderer of her own child, who was metamorphosed into a nightingale,

---

[1] Emendation has not produced any really satisfactory suggestions: Thomas Bentley proposed ὡc for μέν, an anonymous German scholar in the margin of Ernesti's Aldine τᾶν (which Ernesti himself considered).

[2] It is a common epic device to place at the beginning of the sentence an anaphoric article as a demonstrative which is later reinforced by a substantive: with similar articulation again in C. at V 103f. τὸ μέν . . . | ἔργον, IV 61ff. δύω . . . φρουροί | . . . ὁ μέν . . . | . . . | θοῦρος Ἄρης . . . | . . . | ἡ δ' . . . | ἧcτο κόρη, and cf. VI 89f., *E.* 1.9f. Cf. A.W.Bulloch, *CQ* 20 (1970) 263; also F.Bornmann on III intro. p. xxxix and note on v. 68.

[3] For a modern example cf. Seferis' *Helen*.

was a poetic commonplace:[1] in *Od.* 19.518ff. Penelope lamenting Odysseus compares herself to χλωρηὶς ἀηδών . . . ἥ τε θαμὰ τρωπῶcα χέει πολυηχέα φωνήν, | παῖδ' ὀλοφυρομένη Ἴτυλον φίλον . . . ; in Attic drama the nightingale is frequently described or alluded to as a typical mourner,[2] and the topos continues into Hellenistic poetry.[3]

Once again the narrative describes the situation in very grave terms: as, before Chariclo's outburst, the blinding was described almost as if it were Tiresias' death (v. 82 νύξ: see note), so after her speech Chariclo is represented as being like a mother mourning her dead child.

The whole passage is poetically well-worn: the comparison is a stock one, and the expression and movement of the sentence are parallel, e.g., to Soph. *Aj.* 625ff. (Ajax's mother lamenting her son): μάτηρ . . . οὐδ' οἰκτρᾶc γόον ὄρνιθοc ἀηδοῦc | ἥcει δύcμοροc. Only οἶτον and ἄγε refurbish the commonplace (see below).

94 γοερᾶν A poetic adjective (earlier restricted to tragic lyrics but in the Hellenistic period a general poeticism)[4] which provides an appropriate introduction to the nightingale image: Aesch. fr. 749M θρηνεῖ δὲ γόον τὸν ἀηδόνιον, Soph. *Aj.* 629 γόον . . . ἀηδοῦc, Eur. fr. 773N.24f. (= *Phaethon* 68f.) ἀηδών . . . γόοιc. γόοc is particularly used of the lament for the dead: see Fraenkel on Aesch. *Ag.* 57.

οἶτον The normal meaning of this epic/poetic word, 'misfortune', 'fate',[5] is impossible here; the only meaning which gives sense is one of

---

[1] Some of the problems arising out of early versions of the story are discussed by O.Schroeder, 'ΠΡΟΚΝΗ', *Hermes* 61 (1926) 423–36.

[2] Most extensively at Aesch. *Supp.* 60ff. (see Fraenkel on *Ag.* 1526 p. 723), *Ag.* 1142ff., Soph. *Aj.* 625ff.; shorter allusions at Aesch. fr. 749M, Soph. *El.* 107ff., 147ff., 1075ff., *Trach.* 963, Eur. *Hec.* 337f., *Hel.* 1109ff., fr. 773N. 23ff. (= *Phaethon* 67ff.), Aristoph. *Av.* 209ff., *Ran.* 684, Nicom. Alexandrin. fr. 13 (Snell *TGF* I 127 F13). Cf. Hesych. s.v. ἀηδόνειοc· ἐπὶ μὲν ὕπνου τὸ ἐλάχιcτον, ἐπὶ δὲ λύπηc τὸ cφοδρότατον (cf. Nicochares com. fr. 4Dem.).

[3] After C. in [Mosch.] 3.9ff., Parthenius *SH* 646.1–3, and perhaps Nicaenetus fr. 1.9 (Powell, *CA* 1).

[4] In tragedy only at Aesch. *Ag.* 1176, Eur. *Phoen.* 1567, *Hec.* 84, *Hel.* 188. The Hellenistic evidence is slight but widely spread (Giannini, *Dioniso* 37 (1963) 56 is incorrect in suggesting that C. took γοερόc from tragedy): Erinna, *HE* 1796, Call. fr. 323, A.R. 4.19, Dioscorides, *HE* 1707, [Mosch.] 3.15, Nic. *Al.* 301. There are apparently two prose instances: Dion. Thr. *ars gramm.* § 2 (*Gramm. Graec.* I[1] 6) and [Aristot.] *Probl.* 922b 19 (?roughly contemporary with Dion. Thr.?). LSJ's distinction between 'of things' and 'of persons' is not helpful.

[5] See W.Krause, *Glotta* 25 (1936) 143f. (οἶτοc does not necessarily mean 'death'). After Homer in Democr., Soph. (LSJ), Hippon. 77D (128M:

which there is no other certain example extant[1] even though the ancient lexicographers and grammarians give adequate testimony, 'lament': *Et. Mag.* θρῆνος, μόρος, θάνατος, Hesych. μόρος, θρῆνος, κακοπάθεια etc., Theognost. *Can.* (Cramer, *Anecd. Oxon.* II 24.15) τὸ οἶτος ὃ δηλοῖ τὸν ὀδυρμόν, Eustath. 696.21 ἐκ τοῦ οἶ δὲ θρηνητικοῦ ἐπιρρήματος ὁ οἶτος. Possibly the word became at some stage obsolete, and when its Homeric use was debated and variously interpreted the similar sounding οἶκτος provided a possible meaning.

A slight similarity in articulation with *Il.* 9.563f. μήτηρ ἀλκυόνος πολυπενθέος οἶτον ἔχουσα | κλαῖ' (an unclear situation, but a mother appears to be weeping for her daughter carried off by Apollo).[2]

ἀηδονίδων ἀηδονίς is Doric poetic: Eur. *Rhes.* 550 (lyric), Nossis, *HE* 2829, Theocr., *HE* 3484, [Theocr.] 8.38, [Mosch.] 3.46, *P. Oxy.* 2625 fr. 1.8 (undatable choral lyric, = *SLG* 460 fr. 1.8).[3] Only later does it enter general (non-Doric) poetic vocabulary: Parthenius, *SH* 646.2 etc. -ις forms are a feature of Doric poetic vocabulary: cf. ἀμνίς, ἀρβυλίς, κορυδαλλίς, μαλίς, οἰνανθίς, ὀροδαμνίς, χαμευνίς.

95 ἆγε Variously misunderstood. Wilamowitz, *HD* II 21, apparently taking οἶτον with its Homeric sense 'misfortune', seems to interpret 'led the unfortunate life of lamenting nightingales'; Mair's 'led him away' is equally difficult, since it involves taking οἶτον with the delayed κλαίοις'. The verb must be interpreted as 'kept up', governing οἶτον = 'lament'; this application to cries, noises etc. is not common, but can be paralleled in poetry: Pratinas, *PMG* 708.5 κύκνον ἄγοντα . . . μέλος, Soph. *Aj.* 382 γέλωθ' . . . ἄγεις, Eur. *Or.* 181 κτύπον ἠγάγετ'. Hesychius has an entry ἄγω· μέλπω, ἄιδω.[4] The imperfect tense reinforces the sense of continuity in 'sustaining' the lament.

---

not in LSJ); in the Hellenistic period [Mosch.] 3.115 and often in A.R. Cf. μεγάλοιτος in Theocr. 2.72.

[1] Possible instances are: Simon. *PMG* 531 (οἶκτος Jacobs); Soph. *Ant.* 858 (οἶτον in some MSS: see Jebb); Eur. *IT* 1091 (οἰκτρόν Barnes: on οἶτον see D.L.Page in *Greek Poetry and Life* (Oxford 1936) 208); Nicaenetus fr. 1.9 (Powell, *CA* 1: οἶτον based on *Il.* 9.563 but ambiguous in meaning).

[2] The variant οἶκτον preserved in one MS and adopted by Leaf indicates the ease with which the two words could become interchangeable.

[3] Cf. also Theocr. 15.121 ἀηδονιδεύς (cf. Schwyzer, *GG* I 464f.). The fact that ἀηδονίς is Doric poetic seems to make Housman's supplement at fr. 1.16 ἀ̣[ηδονίδες] very unlikely.

[4] Cf. the same application of the verb in other contexts.: Pind. *P.* 9.31 νεῖκος ἄγει, Dem. 9.36 ἐλευθέραν ἦγε τὴν Ἑλλάδα (διάγειν is more common in this usage). The simple verb ἄγειν in the passages quoted above is not 'simple for compound': ἀνάγειν means '*raise* a song etc.', not 'sustain' (cf. Longo on Soph. *Trach.* 210). Cf. also the excellent article by E.K.

βαρὺ κλαίοιcα Reminiscent of the common Homeric formula |–⏑ βαρὺ cτενάχων. Cf. VI 94 κλαῖε μὲν ἁ μάτηρ, βαρὺ δ' ἔcτενον αἱ δύ' ἀδελφαί. Unlike δακρύειν, 'weep tears', κλαίειν denotes primarily a loud cry, often accompanied by tears, expressing strong emotion, grief etc. (Schmidt, *SGS* I 471ff.).

ἐλέηcεν ἐλέειν is normal usage (LSJ): by contrast A.R. uses only the special epic form ἐλεαίρειν (4.738 etc.).

96–106 The second half of the Tiresias narrative consists almost entirely of Athena's long speech, which corresponds to the first half section by section. In this first part of her speech Athena deals directly with Chariclo's grief (vv. 85–95). She does so by putting forward two 'justifications': although the blinding might appear to be personal vindictiveness, responsibility for the punishment is not Athena's but that of ancient divine law, and, secondly, the whole situation was anyway predestined from the moment when Tiresias was born. Athena is rather cool, though not sharp, in tone (vv. 97, 103 δῖα γύναι), and both her diction and her ethics are strongly and conventionally Homeric (see on v. 98 ἀλαόν, vv. 101f., v. 101 ὅκα μή ... ἀθρήcηι, v. 103 παλινάγρετον, vv. 104f.). Technically her two justifications are sufficient to clear her of responsibility, but she fails adequately to match the *emotional* basis of Chariclo's grief; see Intro. Section VI.

96 καί νιν[1] καί μιν ... is extremely common as an opening to lines of this sort in Homer: e.g. καί μιν φωνήcαc ἔπεα πτερόεντα προcηύδα (*Il.* 1.201 etc.: see Schmidt, *PH*).

πρὸc τόδ' ἔλεξεν ἔποc Modelled on the common Homeric formula ... πρὸc μῦθον ἔειπεν | (Schmidt, *PH* 191) which is always preceded by accusative of addressee: e.g. *Il.* 2.156 εἰ μὴ 'Αθηναίην Ἥρη πρὸc μῦθον ἔειπεν. In this formula πρόc is prepositional to the addressee,[2] and here τόδ' ... ἔποc is object of ἔλεξεν and refers to Athena's following speech.

ἔλεξεν Within the formulaic pattern C. exchanges the common ἔειπε

Borthwick, 'Aristophanes *Clouds* 1371' in *CR* 21 (1971) 318–20, who however makes no distinction between simple and compound and interprets ἄγειν as 'strike up' rather than 'keep up'. In the prose examples where Borthwick convincingly suggests retaining the MSS' reading, Theophr. *Char.* 27.2 and Ach. Tat. 5.16.5, the verb makes much better sense as 'keep up', 'intone' than 'start up'; at Aristoph. *Nub.* 1371 ἦγ', if correct the verb is best explained by denoting 'intone', the sense of *starting* up being given by the tense (at Pherecrates fr. 145.23, which B. also cites, simple ἄγων cannot be read because of the metre).

[1] For Meineke's correction of Ψ's non-Doric μιν see on v. 65 νιν.

[2] In effect, that is. Structurally πρόc could equally be a preverb in tmesis: see Ebeling, *LH* II 232 s.v. πρόc.

for the less usual λεγ- form (obsolete in the *koine*)[1] – for a particular effect. In literary Greek the future, aorist, and perfect λεγ- forms ('say') existed alongside the more common ἐρ-, εἰπ- forms not as synonymic doublets but as distinct elements of vocabulary: λεγ- forms stress the action of speaking itself, whereas ἐρ-, εἰπ- forms refer more to the result of the action. λεγ- forms usually mean 'expound', 'recount', 'pronounce' rather than simply 'speak', 'say'.[2] In v. 96 the effect is to give Athena a certain distance and dignity: 'Athena *declared* in reply.'

97 Cf. *Il.* 15.138 (Athena to Ares) τῷ c' αὖ νῦν κέλομαι μεθέμεν χόλον υἷος ἑῆος.

δῖα γύναι Courteous in tone and, especially by comparison later with v. 119 ὦ ἑτάρα, indicative of a certain initial coolness and formality. δῖος is an epic/poetic word (LSJ), vague in meaning and varied in application, but of people expressive, connoting respect and courtesy. (The phrase here is inevitably reminiscent of the common Homeric formula δῖα γυναικῶν.) The absence of ὦ also indicates restraint, as in Chariclo's address earlier (v. 86 πότνια): cf. on v. 81 ὦ Εὐηρείδα.

μετὰ πάντα βαλεῦ πάλιν Usually misinterpreted as 'take back all the words . . .' Athena is not so insensitively cruel: she only denies responsibility for choosing the punishment of blindness ('no, you are wrong'). μεταβάλλεcθαι here has the same meaning as most commonly in all prose authors, 'change one's mind, opinions' (very badly documented in LSJ: see Arndt–Gingrich, *GNT* s.v. and indexes to individual authors). A normal usage verb with poetic tmesis: see on v. 93 περί . . . λαβοῖcα.

πάντα 'internal accusative' = 'as regards everything', since μεταβάλλεcθαι is always intransitive in the sense 'change one's mind'.

βαλεῦ The first example in v of εο contracting to ευ. In v and vi C., like Theocritus, allows both contracted (v 105, 112, 115, 120, vi 53 etc.) and

---

[1] See Mayser, *GGP* I[2] 185, Crönert, *MGH* 267 and cf. Moulton, *GNT* II 247.

[2] Fully discussed by P.Chantraine, *Bull. de la Soc. Ling.* 41 (1940) 39–53 and H.Fournier, *Les Verbes 'dire' en grec ancien* (Paris 1946), esp. pp. 80ff.; also valuable is Schmidt, *SGS* I 83ff. In the Hellenistic poets the λεγ- forms are very rare (never with the simple verb in A.R., Arat., Nic., and only very occasionally in bucolics). Only C. uses them with any frequency and always with the sense 'pronounce': τάδ' ἔλεξε etc. at 7.28, 178.13, 22, 31, 194.97, 384.8, *SH* 257.17, *E.* 12.3, IV 201, usually introducing the pronouncement (cf. Chantraine p. 52 on ἔλεξε in Thucydides: 'ἔλεξε qui annonce le discours qui va se développer présente un sens plus duratif'). Fournier p. 87 on Xenophon remarks 'l'importance de la harangue, la gravité des conjonctures, sont annoncés par ἔλεξεν et non par εἶπεν.' The few examples in the bucolics also introduce declarations: Theocr. 2.94, [Theocr.] 23.48, [Bion] 2.26. Similarly in Isyllus F 72 (Powell, *CA* 134), Rhianus fr. 19 (Powell, *CA* 12), *HE* 3202, epigr. anon. *SH* 971.1.

uncontracted (v 35, 52, 87, 119, 140, vi 48 etc.) forms, and the choice affords useful metrical variety. The mixture of forms has good Homeric precedent (Chantraine, *GH* i 58ff.), but to the Hellenistic writers ευ was almost entirely a Doric feature, and C. and Theocritus have ευ only in their Doric poems, while other non-Doric writers admit it scarcely at all:[1] pre-Hellenistic Greek contracts εο to ου in Attic, and to ευ in Ionic and in some Doric areas (the islands except Crete, Cyrene, and the N.E. Peloponnese), but by the Hellenistic period ευ had become a standard feature of the Doric *koine*. See Monteil, *T* 27f., Thumb, *GD* ii 376 εο > ευ, Boisacq, *DD* 78f., Schwyzer, *GG* i 247f. Cf. on v. 89 ὄψεαι.

πάλιν πάλιν with μεταβαλλ- = 'about', 'round', not 'back to a former state', as is well illustrated by Isocr. *Areop.* 71 ἐγκεκωμίακα τὴν δημοκρατίαν, ὅταν δὲ τύχω, πάλιν μεταβαλὼν ἐπιτιμῶ καὶ κατηγορῶ (Isocrates is suggesting not that he is returning to a previous state of mind, but that he is changing about in relation to opinions just expressed).[2] The placing of the adverb after instead of before the verb is a poeticism: see Mayser, *GGP* ii² 184.

98 εἶπας -ας is a *koine* form, adopted contrary to Homeric usage which has only the -ον, -ες etc. endings for aorist εἶπον. -α- endings, early testified as alternative to εἶπον etc., became well established in the fourth century B.C., and by the third century B.C. had totally displaced the -ο- and -ε- endings in current usage.[3] The Hellenistic poets surprisingly use only *koine* endings in the finite indicative parts of εἶπα;[4] Σ to *Il.* 1.106 records that

---

[1] E.g. A.R. 2.57 is the only instance in the *Argonautica* of contraction in the frequently used imperative middle (Mooney).

[2] Cf. the anonymous Σ to *Il.* 9.56 οὐδὲ πάλιν ἐρέει· τὸ δὲ πάλιν οὐκ ἔστιν ἐκ δευτέρου ὡς ἡμεῖς, ἀλλ' ἀντὶ τοῦ <u>ἔμπαλιν</u> ἐρεῖ, <u>ἐναντίως</u>.

[3] For the gradual establishment of the α conjugation of εἶπον in Attic see in combination: K–B *GG* ii 422f., Schwyzer, *GG* i 745, Meisterhans, *GAI* 183f., Mayser, *GGP* i² 95, 135 (and literature quoted), Moulton, *GNT* ii 208f., and for fourth century B.C. especially Kühner on Xen. *Mem.* 2.2.8. Some dialects have α earlier than Attic, notably Ionic, though Attic in all periods favours -ας, -ατε above -ες, -ετε (the construction by W.G.Rutherford, *New Phrynichus* (London 1881) 219 of an 'Attic' paradigm εἶπον, -ας, -ε, -ομεν, -ατε, -ον is an over-simplification: examples of -ες and -ετε are to be found in almost all Attic authors). A useful list of occurrences in Veitch, *GV* 231–4. See also on v. 65 ἐπεβάσατο.

[4] Often and consistently, including the Homeric A.R. The sole exception is iii 103 ἔειπες which must be suspect, though the Hymn is particularly Homeric in style. Pfeiffer's suggested εἶπον at 75.43 would be plausible only in the form εἶπαν. For the non-finite participle and the optative the Alexandrians freely use the non-*koine* -ο- and -ε- forms as literary alternatives.

Aristarchus there read εἶπας and not εἶπες, and it may be that the Alexandrians considered the -ε- endings to be simply incorrect (cf. M. Van der Valk, *Researches on the Text and Scholia of the Iliad* (Leiden 1963–4) I 174, Chantraine, *GH* I 385f.: the occasional alternative readings in some Homeric MSS of εἶπας and εἴπατε are doubtless a relic of Aristarchus' activity).

ἐγώ The presence of the pronoun and its position as first word give emphasis: 'It was not *I* who made your child blind.'

δ' Here 'explanatory', as commonly in poetry (Denniston, *GP* 169). The simplest kind of connection, δέ is equivalent here to an English colon without a causal conjunction; the connection is slight because the main explanation begins in the next line οὐ γὰρ Ἀθαναίαι . . .

ἀλαόν A rare poetic word (said by one ancient glossography to be of Cypriot origin: Bekker, *Anecd. Graec.* (Berlin 1814–21) 1095) occurring occasionally in the *Odyssey* and the lyrics of Attic tragedy (LSJ).[1] Two of the three Homeric instances are in the phrase | μαντῆος ἀλαοῦ of Tiresias, and ἀλαός appears again in A.R. 2.259 of the prophet Phineus. Athena perhaps hints at the new status that Tiresias will shortly enjoy as a great prophet; again at v. 118.

99 οὐ γὰρ Ἀθαναίαι Emphatic positioning at the beginning of the sentence (and line), taken up by Κρόνιοι δ' similarly placed in v. 100: 'It is not *Athena's* pleasure that . . .' By referring to herself in the third person Athena makes her statement sound more objective.

γλυκερόν may give Athena's disclaimer subtle reinforcement. In the Alexandrian poets γλυκ- is commonly used as an epithet of the eyes,[2] so that here ὄμματα παιδῶν, in itself emotive, perhaps gains additional colouring from the suggestion of the common association of γλυκερόν and ὄμμα.

πέλει For the correption see on v. 89 ὄψεαι.

παιδῶν According to the ancient grammarians Doric accentuation of the genitive plural of third declension monosyllables was perispomenon,[3] and there is some papyrological evidence in support of this.[4] As usual

---

[1] Cf. also the much discussed ἀλαοσκοπίη, for which see *LfgrE* s.v.

[2] Cf. A.R. 2.184 ἐκ δ' ἕλετ' ὀφθαλμῶν γλυκερὸν φάος (of the prophet Phineus), 4.1039 καὶ γλυκεροῖσιν ἔτ' εἰσόψεσθε τοκῆας | ὄμμασιν, Theocr. 6.22 οὐ τὸν ἐμὸν τὸν ἕνα γλυκύν, ὧι ποθορῶιμι, 11.53 καὶ τὸν ἕν' ὀφθαλμόν, τῶ μοι γλυκερώτερον οὐδέν, Herodas 6.23 μὰ τούτους τοὺς γλυκέας.

[3] Ap. Dysc. *de pron.* 33B (*Gramm. Graec.* II[1] 27), Greg. Cor. p. 317 Schaefer; see Ahrens, *DD* 32. The samples quoted by the grammarians are παιδῶν, Τρωῶν, παντῶν.

[4] See Thumb, *GD* I 74ff., Gow, *Theocritus* I lxxv.

there is here no suggestion of the Doric accentuation in any of the MSS.

100 ἁρπάζεν ἁρπάζειν of the MSS is almost certainly a 'normalisation' and should be corrected to the Doric form; see on v. 3 ἕρπεν. To emphasise her innocence Athena uses a striking phrase of some brutality. ἁρπάζειν, here prominently placed, always has connotations of violence and/or suddenness, and, though of wide application, as used here of a faculty is untypical: the only similar usage seems to be Aesch. *Sept.* 259 γλῶccαν ἁρπάζει φόβοc (even more striking and untypical).[1]

Κρόνιοι . . . νόμοι I.e. παλαιοὶ νόμοι. Cronus, head of the *ancien régime*, was symbolic of the old(-fashioned) and connoted great age and antiquity (so, for example, Plato, *Gorg.* 523A ἦν οὖν νόμοc ὅδε περὶ ἀνθρώπων ἐπὶ Κρόνου, καὶ ἀεὶ καὶ νῦν ἔτι ἔcτιν ἐν θεοῖc, *Symp.* 195B Κρόνου καὶ Ἰαπετοῦ ἀρχαιότεροc);[2] furthermore, in the traditional cultural history of Hesiod (*Op.* 109ff.) and Plato (*Polit.* 271C–272D, *Leg.* 713A–714A) ὁ ἐπὶ Κρόνου βίοc was the Golden Age, a period of εὐνομία (*Leg.* 713E).[3]

ὧδε λέγοντι Standard phraseology: cf., e.g., Dem. 22.20 ὡc ὁ νόμοc λέγει, 22.57 οὐ ταῦτα λέγουcιν οἱ νόμοι, 25.27 ταῦτα δ' οἱ νόμοι λέγουcιν; though κελεύειν is more common.

The Doric form of the third plural, -ντι (Buck, *GD* § 138.4), is given by all MSS here and at vv. 115 and 120, except by G which here has -οντο.[4]

101–2 Athena's phraseology is formally legalistic: ὃc ἄν . . . , + qualifying clause + τουτ- (referring to the relative) + infinitive, is a formulation typical of law-code inscriptions. Exactly parallel, e.g., is Gortyn Law Code v 23ff. (Schwyzer, *DGEE* 85, R.F.Willetts, *The Law Code of Gortyn* (Berlin 1967) 43) οἷc κ' ἐπιβάλλει ὄπο κ' ἔι τὰ κρέματα, τούτοc ἀναιλε̄θθαι; cf. v 9ff. ἒ κ' ἀποθάνει ἀνὲρ ἒ γυνά, αἰ μέν κ' ἔι τέκ̣ν̣α ἒ ἐc τέκνον τέκ̣ν̣α̣ ἒ ἐc τούτον τέκνα, τούτοc ἔκε[ν] τὰ κρέματα. In general see W.Larfeld, *Griechische Epigraphik*

---

[1] Aeschylean editors compare Aristoph. *Ran.* 993ff. μόνον ὅπωc μή c' ὁ θυμὸc ἁρπάcαc ἐκτὸc οἴcει τῶν ἐλαῶν.

[2] For documentation of the colloquial usage of κρον- with connotations of stuffiness, foolishness etc. see LSJ s.vv. κρονικόc, κρόνιοc, κρόνιπποc, κρονοδαίμων, κρονοθήκη, κρονόληροc, Κρόνοc. Hesych. glosses Κρόνιον with παλαιόν (cf. s.vv. κρόνιππον and Κρονίωναc). See also Dover on Aristoph. *Nub.* 398. For the semi-proverbial usage see Plato, *Symp.* 195B above and *Paroem. Gr.* II 205 πρεcβύτεροc Κόδρου· ἤτοι Κρόνου, *Suda* s.v. Κρόνου πυγή· τὸ ἀρχαῖον καὶ ἀναίcθητον κρέαc.

[3] Cf. B.Gatz, *Weltalter, goldene Zeit und sinnverwandte Vorstellungen* (Hildesheim 1967) 114–28 ('Das Leben unter Kronos-Saturn'). Athena's statement is no different from that of Theseus (defending the burial of the dead) at Eur. *Supp.* 563 νόμοc παλαιὸc δαιμόνων.

[4] Hyparchetype η read πέλοντι for λέγοντι here, by parablepsis to v. 99 πέλει.

(Munich 1914[3]) 316ff. and *Handbuch der griechischen Epigraphik* (Leipzig 1907) I 451ff.

What Athena here formulates as religious code is part of what had always been traditional belief. An important aspect of a god's power was absolute control over whether or not he was visible to mortals; Odysseus remarks at *Od.* 10.573f. τίς ἂν θεὸν οὐκ ἐθέλοντα | ὀφθαλμοῖςιν ἴδοιτ' ἢ ἔνθ' ἢ ἔνθα κιόντα; Gods could be heard without being seen,[1] appear to some while remaining invisible to others;[2] and it was generally wise to fear their appearance:[3] Ion's immediate reaction at Athena's appearance is typical, Eur. *Ion* 1551f. φεύγωμεν, ὦ τεκοῦςα, μὴ τὰ δαιμόνων | ὁρῶμεν – εἰ μὴ καιρός ἐςθ' ἡμᾶς ὁρᾶν. Cf. Jason's reaction on the appearance of the Libyan nymphs at A.R. 4.1315f. αὐτὰρ ὅγ' εἰς ἑτέρωςε παλιμπετὲς ὄμματ' ἔνεικεν, | δαίμονας αἰδεςθείς. The same taboo was to be found in Israel: *LXX* Exod. 33.20 οὐ δυνήςηι ἰδεῖν μου τὸ πρόςωπον· οὐ γὰρ μὴ ἴδηι ἄνθρωπος τὸ πρόςωπόν μου καὶ ζήςεται.[4]

101 ὅκα μὴ θεὸς αὐτὸς ἕληται Homeric phraseology: *Od.* 16.197f., 23.185f. . . . ὅτε μὴ θεὸς αὐτὸς ἐπελθὼν | ῥηιδίως ἐθέλων . . . ; in particular cf. *Il.* 14.247f. Ζηνὸς δ' οὐκ ἂν ἔγωγε Κρονίονος ἄςςον ἱκοίμην | οὐδὲ κατευνήςαιμ' ὅτε μὴ αὐτός γε κελεύοι.[5]

102 ἀθρήςηι To the Hellenistic poets ἀθρεῖν was apparently an epicism, for like Homer they use only the aorist tense forms;[6] certainly ἀθρεῖν seems to have been avoided in Hellenistic prose, in spite of occasional use by earlier prose authors.[7] The verb is not just an alternative to ἰδεῖν: it usually suggests the engaging of (one's) attention – 'see and recognise',

---

[1] Cf. Soph *Aj.* 14ff., Eur. *Hipp.* 84ff., *IT* 1447.

[2] *Il.* 1.198, *Od.* 16.161, Soph. *Aj.* 91 and 301 (see Jebb on v. 15).

[3] Cf. *Il.* 20.131 χαλεποὶ δὲ θεοὶ φαίνεςθαι ἐναργεῖς. Paus. 10.32.18 remarks τὸ ἔπος οὖν ἀληθεύειν ἔοικε τὸ Ὁμήρου, cὺν οὐδενὶ αἰςίωι τοὺς θεοὺς τῶι γένει τῶν ἀνθρώπων ἐναργῶς ὁρᾶςθαι.

[4] Kleinknecht, *LP* 341 n. 2 compares a statement expressed in terms very similar to C.'s lines in χρηςμοὶ τῶν Ἑλληνικῶν θεῶν (a collection made in the fifth century A.D.: text in Buresch, *Klaros* (1889) 108): θνητοῖς γὰρ χαλεπὸν φύςιν ἄμβροτον ὀφθαλμοῖςιν | εἰςιδέειν ἢν μή τις ἔχηι ςύνθημα θέειον.

[5] Cf. also *Il.* 13.319f. Eur. *Ion* 1244 is one very rare post-Homeric example of ὅτε μή; cf. Monteil, *PR* 280f.

[6] Plato, *Epigr.* 23 ἀθρήςαςα, Call. *E.* 55.4 ἀθρήςας, Timon, *SH* 779.5 ἀθρήςαςθαι, A.R. 4.467 ἀθρήςειε, Theocr. 11.24 ἀθρήςαςα, 15.78 ἄθρηςον, Dosiadas, *Bom.* (Powell, *CA* 175) 9 ἀθρήςας, Nic. *Ther.* 165 ἀθρήςηι, 313 ἀθρήςατο, Antip. Sid., *HE* 616 ἀθρήςας. The present only at Theocr. 16.16, Archimedes, *SH* 201.14, and ἀθρείτω at Herodas 6.33.

[7] Mostly Plato, Aristotle occasionally: otherwise the verb is very rare (once each in Thuc., Isocr. and Xen.). In prose ἀθρεῖν usually means 'consider'.

'catch sight of', 'discern'. Thus at *Il.* 12.391, 14.334 the person seen is, as here, unwilling to be caught sight of.

μιcθῶ . . . μεγάλω μιcθόc figuratively of recompense given for (the moral quality of) an action is rare. Denoting punishment 'the price' is an established but not common poeticism: Aesch. *Ag.* 1261, Soph. *Ant.* 221, Eur. *Hipp.* 1050 (athetised by some), cf. *IA* 1169 (?and 1179?), and once again in C. in a very similar context, III 263 οὐδὲ γὰρ Ἀτρεΐδηc ὀλίγωι ἐπὶ κόμπαcε μιcθῶι.[1] As a reward (for virtue etc.) μιcθόc is almost entirely a feature of the *LXX* and the Christian writers.[2]

Politian and Lascaris, puzzled presumably by the genitive 'of price' with a verb of seeing, read μιcθῶι . . . μεγάλωι: the instrumental dative is not uncommon in Homer with verbs of buying (Chantraine, *GH* II 77), and the dative is anyway often used of the general conditions surrounding an action (e.g. *Il.* 1.418 τῶι cε κακῆι αἴcηι τέκον ἐν μεγάροιcι).

Cf. Prop. 4.9.57 *magno Tiresias aspexit Pallada vates.*

103–4 Cf. Phanocles fr. 2 (Powell, *CA* 108) ἀλλὰ τὸ Μοιράων νῆμ' ἄλλυτον, οὐδέ τωι ἔcτιν | ἐκφυγέειν, ὁπόcοι γῆν ἐπιφερβόμεθα.

103 δῖα γύναι The formal courteous address once more (see on v. 97), introducing Athena's second 'justification'.

τό Demonstrative, not articular. ἔργον is supplementary to τό, added by way of clarification: see above on v. 93f. ἁ μέν . . . | μάτηρ.[3]

τὸ μὲν οὐ παλινάγρετον . . . The rare compound adjective derives from *Il.* 1.526 where it is used, as here, of divine act: (Zeus speaks) οὐ γὰρ ἐμὸν παλινάγρετον οὐδ' ἀπατηλόν | οὐδ' ἀτελεύτητον, ὅτι κεν κεφαλῆι κατανεύcω. The only other pre-Hellenistic example of παλινάγρ. is also epic, Hes. *Scut.* 93,[4] and to the Hellenistic poets παλινάγρ. and its Homeric cognate αὐτάγρετοc provided a source of poeticisms: thus παλινάγρετοc also at A.R. 2.444, Theocr. 29.28, αὐτάγρετοc at A.R. 4.231, 2.326 and in C. a coinage based upon the adjective, 23.20 αὐταγρεcίη.

There is a clear connection by reminiscence between this couplet and A.R. 2.444f. Αἰcονίδη, τὸ μὲν οὐ παλινάγρετον οὐδέ τι μῆχοc | ἔcτ' ὀπίcω, κενεαὶ γὰρ ὑποcμύχονται ὀπωπαί. Similarities in phraseology apart (vocative + τὸ μὲν οὐ παλινάγρετον, a phrase noteworthy both for the rare adjective and for the caesura separating adjective from negative: see below), there is a close affinity between the two contexts which editors have

---

[1] Seemingly the only other examples of μιcθόc = 'punishment' are two isolated and chronologically very separate instances: Hdt. 8.117.1 (?an Ionism?) and D.H. 10.51.2 μετὰ μεγάλων μιcθῶν.

[2] Anticipated by Plato, *Rep.* 614A, cf. 2.363D. '*Il.* 10.304 etc.' (*sic*) in LSJ is wrongly classified.

[3] Cf. also Svensson, *GBA* 63 n. 2.

[4] A similar usage, of Iphicles' ἄτη.

failed to observe. In A.R. the seer Phineus is replying to Jason's suggestion that his sight might be restored; C. makes Athena convey the grim practical truth to Chariclo, that her son's eyes have been permanently put out, through tactful implication, by reminiscence of A.R. (on the chronology of the two passages see below).[1]

οὐ || παλιν- οὐ is normally proclitic, and the separation of the negative from its adjective by the main caesura has no parallel in C.'s hexameters.[2] Theocritus occasionally has article and noun so separated (though only when the article is preceded by a preposition to which it can become enclitic: 2.8, 3.1, 10.29, 21.47), and A.R. has three instances, in addition to 2.444 quoted above, where the caesura comes after a word normally proclitic, though in each case the breaks on either side at the second-foot caesura and the bucolic diaeresis are heavy pauses marked by punctuation (καί at 2.1203 and 3.115; 4.1554 ἐπεὶ οὐ || περιώσιον).[3] It might be argued that since this metrical irregularity can be paralleled in A.R. but not in C., the reminiscence between A.R. 2.444f. and v 103 was of C. recalling A.R. and not vice versa. Cf. A.W.Bulloch, *AJP* 98 (1977) 121f., and see Intro. pp. 41f.

αὖθι 'hereafter'. αὖθι for αὖτις before consonants is a Hellenistic development, if not a Callimachean idiosyncrasy: see Pfeiffer on 197.49.

γένοιτο Not εἴη because the question is of *changing* what has happened, as also in, e.g., *Od.* 1.379, 2.144 αἴ κέ ποθι Ζεὺς δῶισι παλίντιτα ἔργα γενέσθαι.

The optative without κε(ν) to express possibility is an uncommon Homericism (W.W.Goodwin, *Syntax of the Moods and Tenses of the Greek Verb* (London 1912³) §240, Chantraine, *GH* II 217ff., and in general K–G *GG* I 225f.) cultivated by some of the Hellenistic poets: Theocr. 2.34 (where see

---

[1] Some readers might even wish to apply Phineus' next two lines to Tiresias: 446f. ἀντὶ δὲ τοῦ θάνατόν μοι ἄφαρ θεὸς ἐγγυαλίξαι | καί τε θανὼν πάσηισι μετέσσομαι ἀγλαΐηισιν.

[2] Hellenistic writers are less strict over the pentameter diaeresis: see on v. 30 ὧι καί. There are a few examples in C.'s hexameters of caesura separating introductory phrases from their accompanying clause (43.76 μήτ' οὖν ||, IV 163 οὔτ' οὖν ||, VI 53 μή τοι ||, *E.* 44.3 μὴ δή με ||): normally such phrases are proclitic (see A.W.Bulloch, *CQ* 20 (1970) 262 n. 5), but in each case the enclitic makes the separation more acceptable than in οὐ || παλινάγρετον.

[3] For a discussion of prepositions after the caesura going closely with what *precedes* the caesura see Bühler on Moschus' *Europa* pp. 221–8 (Excursus VI). The phenomenon seems to be almost entirely restricted to epic; in many of the examples cited by B. the preposition has the status of a preverb rather than a substantival preposition (in so far as such a distinction can be made).

Gow), 8.20, 89, 91, 16.67, 28.13, 29.38, Arat. 76, 96, 248, Herodas 3.75 (where see Headlam). Not in A.R.[1]

Vv. 103f. are behind Nonn. *D.* 12.144 . . . ἀτρέπτου παλινάγρετα νήματα Μοίρηϲ.

104–5 A direct variation on a Homeric formulaic context: *Il.* 24.209f. τῶι δ' ὥϲ ποθι μοῖρα κραταιὴ | γεινομένωι ἐπένηϲε λίνωι, ὅτε μιν τέκον αὐτή (repeated with slight variations at *Il.* 20.127f. and *Od.* 7.196ff.). The language is distinctively Homeric: ἐπένηϲε[2] appears only in this form and before C. is testified only at *Il.* 20.128 and 24.210;[3] λίνον of the thread of the Fates occurs only in this Homeric formulaic passage before C. Pind. *N.* 7.1 Ἐλείθυια, πάρεδρε Μοιρᾶν Βαθυφρόνων . . .

From the third century B.C. onwards the 'thread of the Moirai' became a poetic cliché in talking of death: cf. Theocr. 1.139f . . . τά γε μὰν λίνα πάντα λελοίπει | ἐκ Μοιρᾶν, Phanocles fr. 2 cited above, and in epitaphs from different parts of the Greek world, e.g. Peek, *GVI* 1606 (Thessaly, third to second century B.C.) λυπρὸν ἐφ' Ἡδίϲτηι Μοῖραι τότε νῆμ' ἀπ' ἀτράκτων | κλῶϲαν . . . , and also Peek, *GVI* 1150, 1549, 1584, 1656, 1680, 1873 (all B.C.).[4]

105 ἀνίκα Here as often particularising the precise moment of an event ('at the time when'): K–G, *GG* II 445, Schwyzer, *GG* II 652, Monteil, *PR* 298.

Ψ had ἡνίκα: Doric ἀνίκα (restored by Lascaris) is testified in VI 21, *E.* 14.1, and often in Theocritus.

τὸ πρᾶτον (τὸ)[5] πρῶτον or πρῶτα added to a temporal conjunction has an intensive effect, 'right at the time when': Ebeling, *LH* II 244.[6] For a

---

[1] For examples in later Hellenistic writers see Schneider, *Callimachea* I 358f., though his list is not entirely reliable.

[2] Bentley's correction of Ψ's ἐπένευϲε is unquestionably correct. Ernesti objected that in spite of the Homeric reminiscence ἐπένηϲε is impossible since spinning is done by Μοῖραι, not by λίνα. However, this variation is typical of C.: λίνα Μοιρῶν is periphrastic for Μοῖραι, and is confirmed by the late (? fourth-century A.D.?) imitation at *AP* 3.15 οὕτωϲ γὰρ Μοιρῶν ⟨τῶιδ'⟩ ἐπέκλωϲε λίνα. Cf. also Diodorus, *GP* 2117 Μοιράων δ' οὐκ ἐμέγηρε λίνα.

[3] Variation (κατά) . . . νήϲαντο at *Od.* 7.198.

[4] Cf. R.Lattimore, *Themes in Greek and Latin Epitaphs* (1962) 159ff.

[5] On the article with neuter pronouns see Schwyzer, *GG* II 23, 70, 617 and K–G, *GG* I 314f.

[6] Temporal conjunction + πρωτ- occurs also in prose, but only occasionally; in poetry it seems to be something of an epic mannerism: cf. A.R. 1.268, 723, 2.420, 3.579, 1230, 4.436, 1080; in C. only here and the strongly Homeric III 23 (temporal participle) and 113: never in Theocritus.

Homeric parallel cf. *Od.* 4.13 ἐπεὶ δὴ τὸ πρῶτον ἐγείνατο παῖδ' ἐρατεινήν (also *Il.* 6.345, *Od.* 19.355). Cf. III 23 γεινομένην τὸ πρῶτον ('right at my birth').

For Brunck's correction of Ψ's πρῶτον see on v. 9 πρατ-.

ἐγείναο On uncontracted -αο see on v. 91 ἐπράξαο.

105–6 νῦν ... ὀφειλόμενον A simple statement invested with a formal poetic dignity (see notes below).

105 νῦν δέ The antithesis, such as it is, is not to the main clause introduced by v. 103 τὸ μέν, but to its subordinate clause ἁνίκα τὸ πρᾶτον ... ('this was fated long ago *in the past*: so *now* ...'); in effect νῦν δέ ... is an extension to τὸ μὲν οὐ παλινάγρετον.[1]

κομίζευ Normal usage = 'receive', 'take' payment due to one (LSJ); the combination with ὀφείλεσθαι is natural: cf., e.g., Lys. 25.11 ὅσοι δὲ τὸν δῆμον πολλὰ κἀγαθὰ εἰργασμένοι εἰσί, κακὸν δὲ μηδὲν πώποτε, ὀφείλεται δ' αὐτοῖς χάριν κομίσασθαι παρ' ὑμῶν ... Here as earlier the metaphorical use of terms of payment is nothing unusual (see on v. 91 ἐπράξαο, v. 102 μισθῶ): for a close parallel cf. *LXX* 2 Macc. 8.33 καὶ τὸν ἄξιον τῆς δυσσεβείας ἐκομίσατο μισθόν.[2]

Ψ has κομίζου, but Lascaris' κομίζευ is certain: contracted εο elsewhere in V produces Doric ευ (see on v. 97 βαλεῦ).

106 ὦ Εὐηρείδα The presence of the interjection ὦ is noteworthy (see on v. 81): at v. 81 it indicated anger, but here, the second time Athena addresses Tiresias directly, the tone is more one of sympathy.

τέλθος Only here and VI 77 τέλθος ἀπαιτησῶν of a 'payment due' of ἑκατὸν βόας. The scholiast to V 106 and Hesychius s.v. gloss with χρέος, and although the word's status must remain uncertain it can reasonably be regarded as a Doric (?poetic?) equivalent of τέλος (= 'dues', 'toll': see LSJ s.v. I 8).[3]

ὀφειλόμενον Continuing the image of the punishment as payment (ὀφείλειν of debts is normal usage: LSJ). The verb also continues the idea that the punishment was something predetermined: ὀφείλεσθαι is general

---

[1] Cf. the idiom of a μέν clause giving the circumstances in which the δέ clause takes place (Denniston, *GP* 370). Comparable is *Il.* 19.65ff. ἀλλὰ τὰ μὲν προτετύχθαι ἐάσομεν ἀχνύμενοί περ | ... | νῦν δ' ἤτοι μὲν ἐγὼ παύω χόλον, where νῦν is antithetical to <u>προτετ.</u>: 'let us leave this to be a thing of the past ... : well *now* I am going to ...'.

[2] Cf. also Xen. *Cyr.* 1.5.10, Plato, *Rep.* 615C, Dem. 18.231, 21.171, and cf. Arndt–Gingrich, *GNT* and Lampe, *PGL* s.v. κομίζω.

[3] For etymological discussion see H.Osthoff, *Indogerman. Forschungen* 4 (1894) 268f., L.Meyer, *Handbuch der griech. Etymologie* (Leipzig 1901) II 851; cf. also Chantraine, *FN* 365, 421, *DE* s.v. τέλος. Etymologists analogise between τέλ-ος/τέλ-θος and ἄχ-ος/ἄχ-θος.

poetic usage of anything fated or inevitable, especially misfortune or death; often so in Hellenistic epitaphs, particularly in a participial phrase in the pentameter as here – e.g. *E.* 16.4 τὸν πάσαις ὕπνον ὀφειλόμενον.[1]

107–18 After giving two justifications Athena turns to consolation of Chariclo: in a passage which corresponds to vv. 70–84, the account of Tiresias' intrusion and punishment, she compares Actaeon's similar intrusion and punishment and remarks that Tiresias' fate could have been a lot worse. This use of a mythological *exemplum* to offer consolation was standard practice in all periods and the earliest and fullest example is Dione's consolation of Aphrodite at *Il.* 5.382–415: on the subject in general see R.Öhler, *Mythologische Exempla in der älteren griechischen Dichtung* (Diss. Basel 1925) esp. 40ff. C. presents the consolation in a typically Hellenistic form: Athena's προνοία becomes fore-knowledge and the *exemplum* is transposed from the past into the future.[2] Doubtless C. had calculated that Actaeon, as a grandson of Cadmus (being son of Autonoe and Aristaeus), was later than Tiresias, who must have been active as a prophet to Cadmus himself (see on v. 125 Κάδμωι).

Actaeon was, like Tiresias, associated with Thebes, and it was in Boeotia on Mt Cithaeron that he disturbed Artemis at her bath (Roscher, *LM* I 214ff., Frazer, *Pausanias* v. 7). This passage is the first indication that Actaeon's punishment was for intruding on Artemis (earlier accounts recorded that he had lusted for Semele, or Artemis herself, or that he boasted of being a better hunter than Artemis) and some editors have suggested that the Actaeon myth was adapted by C. to parallel the Tiresias story (e.g. L.Malten, *Kyrene* (Berlin 1911) 19, 34, Kleinknecht, *LP* 336f.): it is certainly true that mythological *exempla* often innovate in this way (cf.

[1] Many examples in W.Seelbach, *Die Epigramme des Mnasalkes von Sikyon und des Theodoridas von Syrakus* (Wiesbaden 1964) 105 on Theodoridas, *HE* 3551. See also Gow–Page on *HE* 1218 = Call. *E.* 16.4 (Peek, *GVI* 1113a there cited is too late (Apameia: third century A.D.) to be of relevance). The participle again in C. of an event fated by the Moirai at IV 165f. ἀλλά οἱ ἐκ Μοιρέων τις ὀφειλόμενος θεὸς ἄλλος | ἐστί.

[2] See Öhler op. cit. 121, L.Hensel, *Weissagungen in der alexandrinischen Poesie* (Diss. Giessen 1908), L.Deubner, 'Ein Stilprinzip hellenistischer Dichtkunst', *Neue Jahrb.* 47 (1921) 365ff. The example of Actaeon is placed in the future as a rhetorical device and not because Athena is a prophetess: the nearest she comes to μαντεία is at Erythrae where she was worshipped as the goddess of omens, Φημία, and at Delphi where as Προναία she received sacrifice before Apollo (references in Preller–Robert, *GM* I 195 n. 1; cf. Farnell, *CGS* I 306–8). Other examples in C. of narrative in the form of prophecy are *Aetia* frr. 57ff. (Athena's prophecy), *Iambi* fr. 202.54ff. (Apollo's prophecy), *Hecale* fr. 260.47ff. (the crow's prophecy) on which see J.Rea and H.Lloyd-Jones, *HSCP* 72 (1968) 141ff.

M.M.Willcock, *CQ* 14 (1964) 141–54, B.K.Braswell, *CQ* 21 (1971) 16–26). Other editors have argued conversely that the Tiresias story is an extension of the Actaeon myth; see Intro. p. 19. After C. Ovid, *Met.* 3.138ff. deals extensively with Actaeon disturbing Artemis at her bath, and Nonn. *D.* 5.337ff. explicitly recalls C. when his Actaeon says ὄλβιε Τειρεσία, cὺ γὰρ ἔδρακες ἔκτος ὀλέθρου | γυμνὸν ἀναινομένης οἰκτίρμονος εἶδος Ἀθήνης· | οὐ θάνες . . . αἴθε μοι ἄλγος ὄπαςςεν ὁμοίιον, αἴθε καὶ αὐτή | ὄμμαςιν ἡμετέροιςιν ἐπέχραεν ὥς περ Ἀθήνη.[1]

The narration is carefully organised so as to point the moral of the story as forcefully as possible: two self-reinforcing dicola πόςςα . . . πόςςα . . . , τόν . . . τόν . . . end on an antithetical clausula τυφλὸν ἰδέςθαι, and there follows a single long period from v. 110 to v. 116 which describes Actaeon's fate in the climactic final couplet in cruel detail. Athena's language calls on the dignity of Homeric precedent: see on vv. 111–14, v. 111 αἵ τ' ἐν ὄρεςςι, v. 116, v. 117 ὀλβίςταν. Athena's rhetorical elaboration goes almost beyond the limit of acceptability (cf. on v. 107 ἔμπυρα καυςεῖ). Cf. Bacch. 5.94–104 who has the spirit of Meleager express his parents' despair at his death by the same reference to lavish sacrifice, but in the more tasteful conditional: χαλεπὸν θεῶν παρατρέψαι νόον | ἄνδρεςςιν ἐπιχθονίοις. καὶ γὰρ ἂν πλάξιππος Οἰνεὺς | παῦςεν . . . χόλον Ἀρτέμιδος . . . | λιςςόμενος πολέων τ' αἰγῶν θυςίαιςι πατὴρ | καὶ βοῶν φοινικονώτων· ἀλλ' ἀνίκατον θεὰ | ἔςχεν χόλον.

107–8 The elegiac device of articulating the couplet into two complementary cola, with hexameter and pentameter (first half) marked by anaphora, occurs again at, e.g. 388.7f. τόςςα Μάγαṿ βαςιḷῆα . . . | τό]ςςα τὸν ἐν . . . , IV 39f. τόφρα μὲν οὔπω . . . | τόφρα δ' ἔτ' . . . etc.

The corruption of πόςςα in the MSS in vv. 107 and 108 corresponds to the corruption in MSS at the end of v. 78 (see note). The beginnings of vv. 107f. came at the exposed bottom corner of the sheet in Ψ, and scribes coped with Ψ's (possibly progressive) illegibility in different ways.

107 ἁ Καδμηίς Autonoe; C. characteristically leaves her unnamed (see on v. 18 Φρύξ). On the form of the patronymic (-ηίς) see Risch, *WHS* 131. The presence of the article (adding further differentiation to the patronymic) is a common Homericism (Chantraine, *GH* II 163).[2]

ἐς ὕςτερον C. seems to make a point of ensuring, with this explicit phrase, that the reader appreciates that Tiresias can be calculated to

---

[1] Cf. Ovid, *Trist.* 2.105f., [Apollod.] 3.4.4. For a survey of the pictorial material see Paul Jacobsthal, 'Aktaions Tod', in *Marburger Jahrbuch für Kunstwissenschaft* 5 (Marburg 1930), K.Schefold, *Die Göttersage in der klassischen und hellenistischen Kunst* (Munich 1981) 137–46.

[2] *Pace* Svensson, *GBA* 67 on Theocr. 24.1 ἁ Μιδεᾶτις.

antedate Actaeon. The adverbial phrase is not common but is well testified in prose and verse (LSJ: add VI 64, Theocr. 1.145).

ἔμπυρα καυcεῖ To make her point as forcefully as possible Athena details to Chariclo the desperation of Actaeon's parents: they will be so distraught with grief that they will even pray the gods to perform the impossible and restore their son to life. No god could in any circumstances afford such a favour (*Il.* 16.441f. ἄνδρα θνητὸν ἐόντα πάλαι πεπρωμένον αἴcηι, | ἂψ ἐθέλειc θανάτοιο δυcηχέοc ἐξαναλῦcαι;), but Autonoe and Aristaeus will none the less make innumerable fruitless sacrifices to have their son returned even blind. To C.'s discredit, Athena verges on the extreme of rhetorical exaggeration, almost to the point of undermining her own credibility.

108 τὸν μόνον The article is necessary to indicate that μόνον is attributive and not predicative, and in this kind of phrase it is also possessive: 'their only son' (K–G, *GG* I 621: cf. Xen. *Cyr.* 4.6.4 τὸν μόνον μοι καὶ φίλον παῖδα ἀφείλετο τὴν ψυχήν).

109 τὸν ἡβατάν The repeated article, anaphoric to v. 108 τὸν μόνον . . . , helps to suggest the emotional plea by Actaeon's parents (cf. on vv. 89f., repeated ὦ). With the adjective ἡβατάν this (demonstrative) use of the article is Homeric ('the young Actaeon'): see Chantraine, *GH* II 161. The adjective helps to emphasise the closeness of the parallel with Tiresias (vv. 75f. ἄρτι γένεια | περκάζων).

ἡβατάν Ψ's ἁβατάν is probably a hyper-Dorism since the little evidence available indicates that the Doric form of Attic ἡβητήc was ἡβατάc: thus ἡβατάc and ἡβατᾶ at Cyrene (*Berl. Sitzb.* (1927) 160 = *SEG* 9 (1944) 72.34 and 70: fourth century B.C.), and παῖδα hēβατάν at Locri (Schwyzer, *DGEE* 362.7: fifth century B.C.);[1] the Doric forms of Attic ἡβάω and ἥβη are always ἡβάω (or -ίω) and ἥβα.[2] ἁβατάν here is probably the result of 'improvement' by a scribe (rather than a false Dorism by the Cyrenaean C.)[3] Cf. Theocr. 14.45 where most MSS have the hyper-Doric μᾶνεc instead of the correct μῆνεc.

'Ακταίονα All MSS except η and Lascaris had 'Ακταίωνα, the form

[1] Cf. εἰβάτα in Thessaly (Schwyzer, *DGEE* 567.4: third century B.C.).

[2] See LSJ s.vv.; for ἡβάω in Laconia add Collitz, *GDI* 4598a.5, b.5 (? fourth century B.C.?), and for ἥβα add Alcman, *PMG* 1.27 and Simmias fr. 17 (Powell, *CA* 114).

[3] Similarly the MSS of Theocritus have ἅβα at 1.44 and ἄναβοc at 5.87 and 8.3 alongside ἄκρηβοc at 8.93. These α forms too are surely scribal hyper-Dorisms: see A.Fick, *Bezzenbergers Beiträge* 3 (1879) 126 and Buck, *GD* 179f. There is a possibility that early Aeolic had the forms ἅβα and ἅβαμι (see E.-M.Hamm, *Grammatik zu Sappho und Alkaios* (Berlin 1957) §§ 51, 108, 228c).

normally used but here impossible. Ἀκταίόν-, which has been displaced, was occasionally used for metrical convenience (here and Ov. *Met.* 3.243, 244, 720 and also possibly Eur. *Bacch.* 230), but was clearly rare enough to look like a mistake to an unwary scribe; cf. Choeroboscus in Theodos. *Can. Nom.* § 24 (*Gramm. Graec.* IV[1] 273).

110 καὶ τῆνος 'he too'. There is a compression of thought here making for an oblique comparison: although the explicit analogy is between Actaeon and Tiresias, Actaeon here is compared with *Chariclo* as a goddess's companion whose friendship with a divinity is of no avail.

μεγάλας The adjective does not just express vague respect, but emphasises that powerful though Artemis is she too will be able to do nothing to save her companion from being severely punished.

σύνδρομος Actaeon, like Procris (III 209–10), was a ὁμόθηρος of Artemis. The term σύνδρομος is notable here: in the συνδρομ- compounds and the corresponding verb συντρέχειν the prefix almost always means 'so as to meet, encounter', and almost never 'in accompaniment with'. So συνδρομή denotes 'concourse', 'collision', 'coincidence', and the comparatively rare σύνδρομος provides the corresponding adjectival meanings 'coinciding', 'colliding'.[1] C.'s σύνδρομος = 'in accompaniment . . .' is paralleled only at Plato, *Polit.* 266C συνδιαθέων καὶ σύνδρομα πεπορευμένος and possibly Aesch. *Ag.* 1184, where Fraenkel follows Blomfield in regarding the disputed συνδρόμως as 'metaphora a canibus venatricibus sumpta'; the adjective appears not to have this sense again until the late poets and patristic writers.[2] C.'s contemporaries use συνδρομ- in the usual way (Theocr. 13.22, A.R. 2.346, Lyc. 649).

σύνδρομος here is therefore striking (probably rather elevated: certainly not colloquial, *pace* Schmitt, *NDK* 144) in exploiting the technically real but in practice rare alternative meaning of the prefix, especially in a context which gives no supportive preparation:[3] hence the importance in the following sentence of δρόμος and ξυναί to confirm σύνδρομος = 'companion hunter' and not 'encountering'. See further on v. 111 δρόμος.

Note that σύνδρομος is substantival (Ἀρτέμιδος, not Ἀρτέμιδι which adjectival συν- would require): cognates περίδρομος and ὑπόδρομος similarly serve as both adjective and noun; cf. on v. 125 θεοπρόπα.

---

[1] E.g. the famous Pind. *P.* 4.208 σύνδρομοι πέτραι.

[2] E.g. Nonn. *D.* 2.202 (cf. 1.361, 3.431), *AP* 7.585 (Julian), 6.251 (Philip); see Lampe, *PGL* 1313.

[3] The only Classical examples of the verb συντρέχειν denoting 'alongside', 'accompanying' all have preparatory contexts: Plato, *Polit.* 266C ξυνειληχὸς καὶ ξυνδεδραμηκός, Xen. *Cyr.* 2.2.9 . . . δραμόντα . . . ὁ μὲν δὴ ἔτρεχεν, . . . καὶ ὁ ἄλλος δὲ πᾶς λόχος . . . συνέτρεχον, [Xen.] *Cyn.* 6.16 παραθέουσαι, συντρέχουσαι.

111 ἔccεται The Doric form was ἐccεῖται[1] and Wilamowitz suggested reading ἐccεῖτ' in an attempt to preserve the dialect; however, the epic ἔccεται appears in both Pindar and Doric Theocritus (1.103, 4.41, 5.25, and at 7.52 alongside ἐccεῖται at v. 67) and can be retained here as a poetically permissible epicism.

Similar correption of ἔccεται in the same position before a pause in 358.3, IV 98 (cf. also on correption at v. 71 ἵππω ἐπί).

111–14 ἀλλ' οὐκ αὐτόν . . . An evocation of the description in *Il.* 5.51ff. of the death at Menelaus' hands of Scamandrius, a hunter trained by Artemis: δίδαξε γὰρ Ἄρτεμις αὐτὴ | βάλλειν ἄγρια πάντα . . . | ἀλλ' οὔ οἱ τότε γε χραῖcμ' Ἄρτεμις ἰοχέαιρα, | οὐδὲ ἑκηβολίαι, ᾗιcιν τὸ πρίν γε κέκαcτο· | ἀλλά μιν 'Ατρείδηc . . . The similarities of phraseology and expression are confirmed as specific reminiscence by the unique ἑκαβολίαι common to both passages (see note on v. 112).[2] The sentence is similar in articulation to Apollonius' remark on the death of Idmon, 2.816f. Ἴδμονα, μαντοcύνηιcι κεκαcμένον, ἀλλά μιν οὔ τι | μαντοcύναι ἐcάωcαν, ἐπεὶ χρεὼ ἦγε δαμῆναι.

111 ὅ τε . . . αἵ τε . . . The articles are unusual (see on v. 65) and should be interpreted not just as definitive (although αἱ is almost unavoidable with the adverbial ἐν ὄρεccι), but as semi-demonstrative in Homeric fashion: 'but *those* [picking up cύνδρομοc] shared hunts and . . .'. See Chantraine, *GH* II 163f.

δρόμοc 'hunting'; cf. v. 110 cύνδρομοc = 'fellow-hunter'. Like the English 'course' δρόμοc can be used of both the action and the practice of hunting; this usage is rare and not recorded by the lexica but the testimony is sufficient: at Aesch. *Ag.* 1245 Fraenkel follows Headlam in interpreting ἐκ δρόμου πεcών as the image of a bloodhound losing the trail; Aesop, *Fab.* 143 III 8 τὸν τοῦ δρόμου κτύπον ('the sound of the hunt');[3] Philostr. Min. *Imag.* 3.5 ἐν τῶι περὶ τὴν θήραν δρόμωι. These examples are supported by usage of some of the cognates: Eur. *Bacch.* 731f. (Agave addressing the Bacchants) ὦ δρομάδεc ἐμαὶ κύνεc, | θηρώμεθ' ἀνδρῶν τῶνδ' ὕπ', Call. III 16, IV 238 ἐνδρομίδεc = 'Artemis' hunting boots', [Xen.] *Cyn.* 3.7 μεταδρομαί = 'pursuit', 'chase' (cf. Soph. *El.* 1387 μετάδρομοι . . . ἄφυκτοι κύνεc of the Erinyes), Aristoph. *Ran.* 472 περίδρομοι κύνεc = 'prowling hounds'. Cf. also on v. 110 cύνδρομοc.

αἵ τ' ἐν ὄρεccι Same clausula (different context) at *Il.* 16.353; cf. 14.290 and A.R. 2.26, 4.518. Cf. on v. 116 δρυμώc.

---

[1] Bechtel, *GD* II 194, 261, 407, 495 (Argolid) etc.; also occasionally in Homer (Chantraine, *GH* I 290f.).

[2] The echo confirms that Schneider's ἀλλ' οὐδ' for ἀλλ' οὐκ is needless.

[3] Cf. *Fab. Aphth.* 17.6 = *Corpus Fabularum Aesopicarum* (ed. H.Hunger, Leipzig 1959) 332 κυνῶν δρόμοc.

112 ῥυσεῦνται (ἐ)ρύεσθαι is a common epic/poetic word (also in Ionic prose: LSJ s.v. and Veitch, *GV* 497).[1] The verb probably had the same poetic status in the Hellenistic period to judge from its rarity in later prose and frequent use in the poets.

ξυναί The (Ionic) epic/poetic alternative to κοινός is a favourite with C. and A.R.

τᾶμος The standard poetic alternative to τότε, here proleptic to v. 113 ὁππόκα. The Doric form τᾱ- is well attested in Theocritus, and supported both by the parallel Thessalian form (Schwyzer, *GG* I 528) and the common analogous Doric ᾇμος.

ἑκαβολίαι A rare word which before C. occurs only at *Il.* 5.54, a passage to which C. here specifically refers (see above on vv. 111–14): the picking up of ἑκ. is explicit confirmation of the reference. The word is variously used, sometimes to mean simply 'archery', sometimes 'good shooting from a distance' or 'in accuracy':[2] here as at *Il.* 5.54 of the general (repeated) activity. Again at II 99 and Antip. Sid., *HE* 275.

The use of the plural of a first declension feminine abstract to express generality is a Homeric characteristic: Chantraine, *GH* II 31f.[3]

For the Doric ἑκᾱ- see Björck, *AI* 168.

113 ὁππόκα κ' οὐκ Ψ's ὁππόταν οὐκ is improbable for reasons of dialect. A modal particle is necessary even by Homeric practice since the temporal clause refers to a particular situation (Chantraine, *GH* II 257), but elsewhere in V and VI C. uses only the 'Homeric' (Aeolic) κε[4] (close relative of Doric κα), and never Attic/Ionic ἄν; similarly Theocritus never uses ἄν in his fully Doric poems, only κε and κα.[5] Pfeiffer refers to [Theocr.] 23.36 for ὁππόταν in an apparently Doric context, but this poem is of late authorship (see Gow) and the Doric though good is not faultless,[6] so that by itself this reference cannot justify the alien ὁππόταν.

---

[1] Only poetic in Attic: Thuc. 5.63 quoted by LSJ are words of the Spartan Agis.

[2] Cf. Hesych. s.v.: προέσεις τῶν βελῶν, μακροβολίαι, εὐστοχίαι.

[3] Cf. also Gildersleeve, *SCG* I 21ff.

[4] Not, presumably, because he excludes the Doric κᾱ, but because C. like Theocr. uses the Homeric κε as a metrically short alternative (see Gow on Theocr. 2.118–28).

[5] ἄν occurs once at 7.53 χὤταν, and otherwise only in the spurious Doric poems 8, 9, 21. Through the *koine* ἄν eventually displaced κα in Doric inscriptions (see Buck *GD* 106 and for an early Cyrenaic example see *SEG* 9 (1944) 1 (late fourth century B.C.)), but Theocr. and C. consistently avoid ἄν in their Doric poems. On κε/κα and ἄν generally see Schwyzer, *GG* II 305f.

[6] Note, e.g., the blatant hyper-Dorism ἐφαβ- in v. 56.

The simplest solution seems to be to read ὀππόκα κ' οὐκ (= κε οὐκ).[1] Doric conjunctions ending in -κα + modal particle usually conflate to -κκα (thus ὅκκα = ὅκα κα),[2] but conjunction and particle are occasionally kept separate (so ὀπόκα κα in *SEG* 9 (1944) 72.75, 92: fourth century B.C., Cyrene).[3]

The same hybrid with epic/poetic duplication -ππ- and Doric -κα again at Theocr. 5.98 ὀππόκα.

ὀππόκα With τῆμος the corresponding conjunction is usually the cognate ἦμος; not unexpectedly the Hellenistic writers vary the usual pattern: cf. 238.19ff. ὀππ[ότε ...] τῆμος, Arat. 292 τῆμος ... ὁπότ', Nic. *Ther.* 31 τῆμος ὅτ' ... The only Homeric precedent is *Od.* 13.93ff. εὖτ' ... τῆμος (cf. Mosch. 2.6).

οὐκ ἐθέλων περ A crucial phrase: see on v. 52 οὐκ ἐθέλων. Ovid, *Trist.* 2.105 *inscius Actaeon vidit sine veste Dianam.*

χαρίεντα λοετρά For the terminology cf. *Od.* 8.364 (Aphrodite is bathed on Paphos) ἔνθα δέ μιν Χάριτες λοῦσαν ... The adjective indicates the nature of Actaeon's mistake, the intrusion on the forbidden female privacy; Athena's description here corresponds to Chariclo's words at v. 88 'Αθαναίας στήθεα καὶ λαγόνας. Homer always uses plural λοετρά,[4] and uncontracted λ<u>οε</u>- is Homeric as well as Doric (cf. on v. 51 λοετρόν). The noun usually refers to the place or the water, but is occasionally extended as here to the activity (e.g. Hdt. 6.52.7):[5] 'the beauties of the goddess at her bath'.

114 δαίμονος As earlier Chariclo addressed Athena (v. 86 δαίμονες), so Athena here speaks of Artemis, in terms of the force responsible for misfortune (see on vv. 80f. τίς ... δαίμων).

ἀλλ' αὐταί ... κύνες These words spell out Athena's point: Tiresias arrived ἅμᾶι κυσίν (v. 75), and he was lucky not to have been torn apart by them.

For hunting, female hounds were usually considered to be the most important part of the pack, which was generically referred to as feminine:

---

[1] Wilamowitz suggested ὀππόκα κοὐκ: since κᾱ is always elided and never combined in crasis κοὐκ would presumably be crasis of καὶ οὐκ, which however would leave the clause without the necessary modal particle. Meineke's ὀππόκ' ἄρ' also lacks the necessary particle.

[2] See Ahrens, *DD* 382f., Bechtel, *GD* II 359f. and especially E.Hermann, *Griechische Forschungen: I Die Nebensätze in den griech. Dialektinschriften* (Berlin 1912) 304ff. and Schwyzer, *GG* I 265 and literature there cited.

[3] Cf. also ὅκα κα in Schwyzer, *DGEE* 227.227 (Thera *c.* 200 B.C.).

[4] So always A.R.; C. however also uses the non-Homeric singular (68.2, v 51).

[5] Cf. *LXX* Sirach 34.25; often = 'baptism' in *N.T.*

see LSJ s.v. κύων and J.Aymard, *Essai sur les chasses romaines* (Paris 1951) 235ff. (examples of usage in [Xen.] *Cyn. passim*).

The line is echoed by Nonn. *D.* 5.326 οὐκέτι τὸν πρὶν ἄνακτα κύνες μάθον.

τὸν πρὶν ἄνακτα Homeric usage, which has ἄναξ not only of aristocratic position but also more generally = 'master', often of animals (*LfgrE* 788): e.g. *Od.* 10.216 ὡς δ' ὅτ' ἂν ἀμφὶ ἄνακτα κύνες ... | σαίνωσ'.

115–16 Nonn. *D.* 5.545f. similarly (but less effectively) describes Autonoe: ὀστέα δ' ἔνθα καὶ ἔνθα χυτῆι μεμερισμένα γαίηι, | λείψανα πεπτηῶτα, μόγις συνελέξατο μήτηρ.

115 τουτάκι A rare poetic alternative to τότε, apparently rather solemn and particularly suitable for pronouncements (cf. Aristoph. *Pax* 1079a,[1] VI 32, Lyc. 891, Theogn. 844). C. favours the word (260.24, I 44, VI 32), perhaps as a Pindaricism (*P.* 4.28, 255, 9.14, fr. 320).[2]

Omission of final ς (τουτάκις) also in Pind. *P.* 4.28, fr. 320, Isyllus 67, Parthenius, *SH* 609 (a) 10 and at I 44, 260.24: this is perhaps a poeticism (K–B, *GG* I 298), though perhaps originally a Doric dialect form (see G.Meyer, *Griechische Grammatik* (Leipzig 1896³) 398).

δειπνησεῦντι The verb is carefully chosen to maximise the horrific nature of Athena's prediction: δειπνεῖν denotes not eating as such, but the ordered 'civilised' activity of taking a premeditated meal. The contradictory terminology ruthlessly highlights the savage disorder of the hunting hounds (who themselves normally help provide for the table); contrast the ordinary verbs in *Od.* 21.363 τάχ' αὖ σ' ἐφ' ὕεσσι κύνες ταχέες κατέδονται | οἶον ἀπ' ἀνθρώπων, οὓς ἔτρεφες, or Theocr. 5.38 θρέψαι κύνας, ὥς τυ φάγωντι.[3]

115 τὰ δ' υἱέος ὀστέα μάτηρ These words concentrate the pathos: υἱέος and μάτηρ stress the human bond between Autonoe and Actaeon, while the interposed ὀστέα contrasts the useless substance to which Autonoe's son will nevertheless be reduced.

τά ... ὀστέα The article is Homeric, not definitive but 'presentative', placing ὀστέα in opposition to the previous sentence (Chantraine, *GH* II

---

[1] An oracle: Platnauer is surely correct against LSJ.

[2] C.A.Lobeck, *Pathologiae Sermonis Graeci Prolegomena* (Leipzig 1843) 319 on the entry in Hesychius also suggested that τουτάκις may be of Doric origin (cf. the instance in Doric Isyllus 67).

[3] Where Σ remarks παροιμία ἀπὸ τοῦ Ἀκταίωνος τοῦ ὑπὸ τῶν ἰδίων κυνῶν βρωθέντος! Homer and the tragedians use δαίς of birds of prey etc. (see Leaf on *Il.* 1.5 and R.Pfeiffer, *History of Classical Scholarship* (Oxford 1968) 111–13 discussing Zenodotus' controversial reading), but the usage is not comparable with δειπνεῖν since δαίς connotes not orderliness but sumptuousness, and, unlike δειπνεῖν, δαίς of birds etc. is a well-worn metaphor.

161f.: cf., e.g., *Il.* 13.616 λάκε δ' ὀςτέα· τὼ δέ οἱ ὄςςε . . .). As again at VI 93 ὀςτέα is the Homeric (and Attic) form, though Doric sometimes has ὀςτία (bucolics *passim*: cf. Buck, *GD* §9).

116 λεξεῖται Verb and context are thoroughly Homeric. The simple verb λεγ- (active or middle)[1] = 'collect' (prose ςυλλέγειν) is restricted to Homer and later 'epic' writers,[2] and in Homer is used particularly of collecting together the bones of the dead, as at *Il.* 24.793 ὀςτέα λευκὰ λέγοντο καςίγνητοί θ' ἕταροί τε | μυρόμενοι: this was always after cremation, and the verb thus further emphasises by contrast the unnatural manner of Actaeon's death.

δρυμώς δρυμοί (often with ὄρη) are usually a symbol of the wild, 'thicket', 'desert scrub', where untamed animals live (e.g. Eur. *Hipp.* 1127, *Rhes.* 289, Theocr. 1.72, 3.15f., [Theocr.] 25.134f.; the significance is most explicit in *LXX* Ezek. 34.25 καὶ διαθήςομαι τῶι Δαυιδ διαθήκην εἰρήνης καὶ ἀφανιῶ θηρία πονηρὰ ἀπὸ τῆς γῆς, καὶ κατοικήςουςιν ἐν τῆι ἐρήμωι καὶ ὑπνώςουςιν ἐν τοῖς δρυμοῖς).[3] This is where people wander when in distraction: Eur. *Bacch.* 1229 the Bacchants in terrible revel, Theocr. 13.67 οὔρεα καὶ δρυμούς Heracles mad for Hylas, Bion 1.20 Aphrodite lamenting Adonis. V. 118 ἐξ ὀρέων has a similar significance.

As vocabulary δρυμός is uncommon but normal usage: see the spread of references in LSJ and add: Eur. *Bacch.* 1229, *Cyc.* 447, *Rhes.* 289, [Xen.] *Cyn.* 6.5(?), 10.19, Theophr. *H.P.* 4.2.8, Polyb. 3.40.12, 12.4.13, *LXX passim*, [Aristot.] *Mund.* 392b 18, *Mirab.* 837a 24, 839b 10.

Homer uses δρυμός only in the neuter plural form δρυμά, always with short ῠ, but post-Homeric usage lengthens υ in δρυμ- cognates owing to the influence of δρῦς. Some later epic writers occasionally revert to Homeric ῠ (Nic. *Ther.* 222, *Orph. Arg.* 678, Q.S. 2.382 etc.) but mostly Attic ῡ prevails as here (A.R. 3.581, 4.1684, Theocr. 1.72, 117, 3.16 etc., Nic. *Ther.* 489, Rhianus fr. 20P, Bion 1.20, 68). See Wackernagel, *SUH* 184–7, Chantraine, *DE* 300.

Like Pentheus Actaeon will be διαςπαρακτόν, κοὐδὲν ἐν ταὐτῶι πέδωι | . . . ἐν ὕληι κείμενον δυςευρέτωι (Eur. *Bacch.* 1220).

ἐπερχομένα = 'going round' is normal usage (LSJ s.v. III).

117 ὀλβίςταν An irregular superlative form, here for the first time,

---

[1] The middle is more unusual (*Il* 8.507, 24.793), but is the *only* mood used by Hellenistic writers: A.R. 3.899, Nic. *Ther.* 752. Hesychius has a separate entry λέγεςθαι· ςυνάγειν, ἀθροίζειν. The middle also occasionally means 'choose' in Homer (whence A.R. 3.807 which LSJ misclassify).

[2] Once in Pindar in a Homeric context: *P.* 8.53 (Adrastus) θανόντος ὀςτέα λέξαις υἱοῦ.

[3] At Soph. *OT* 1398f. Oedipus describes the place where he killed his father as κεκρυμμένη νάπη | δρυμός τε.

instead of regular ὀλβιώτατος (cf. the Callimachean innovation τέρπνιστος at 369, 536). Though irregular the form is not exceptional: already in Homer -ιστος and -τατος appear sometimes to be alternative suffixes (φέριστος/φέρτατος, ὤκιστος/ὠκύτατος, ῥήιστος/ῥηΐτατος: see Risch, *WHS* 88, Chantraine, *GH* I 259).[1] ὄλβιστος can also be analysed not as a contraction of adjectival ὀλβι-ιστος, but as nominal ὀλβ-ιστος, since -ιστος is occasionally used as an independent intensive suffix on stems which have no adjectival positives: cf. Homeric ἄλγιστος, κάλλιστος, κέρδιστος, ῥίγιστος etc. (Risch, *WHS* 81f.),[2] Attic ὕβριστος, ὕψιστος.[3] ὄλβιστος (like τέρπνιστος) is thus an acceptable innovation by Homeric precedent.[4] The metrical impossibility of ὀλβιώτατος led to ὄλβιστος being taken up by later writers: Alcaeus, *HE* 68, Antip. Sid., *HE* 310, Meleager, *HE* 4418, 4578, Menophilus, *SH* 558.13.

The phraseology is picked up by Nonn. *D.* 6.99, 31.32 ὀλβίστην ἐνέπω σε.

δ' Ψ had no particle here and most editors, including Wilamowitz, have accepted the asyndeton; however E (alone) has δ', and the link between λεξεῖται (116) and ἐρέει is helpful.

ἐρέει The figure of reported speech in dicolon with the verb of saying contained in the first colon is a Callimachean characteristic: 203.55 κα[ὶ] δοῦλον εἶναί φησι καὶ παλίμπρητον, cf. 194.6ff., I 6f. The unequally balanced dicolon is generally a favourite Callimachean figure: Lapp, *TF* 38 (cf. on vv. 19f.).

εὐαίωνα The adjective goes much further than ὀλβίσταν, almost to the point of making Athena's prediction seem extravagant. εὐαίων is a strong word, implying completely undisturbed happiness, usually a gift from or attribute of the gods ('blessed'). So, e.g., Aesch. *Pers.* 711 of Darius (ὑπερσχὼν ὄλβον) . . . βίοτον εὐαίωνα . . . ὡς θεὸς διήγαγες, or at Soph. *Trach.* 81 of the blessed life that Heracles may lead when finally at rest from

---

[1] Attic βέλτιστος, φίλιστος are also doublets to more regular superlative forms.

[2] All of these superlatives have matching comparative forms in -ίων (Risch, *WHS* 82). The formations are mostly made on a nominal or adverbial base: see the list in Schwyzer, *GG* I 539. Cf. H.Seiler, 'Methodologisches zu κέρδιον, κέρδιστος', *Glotta* 51 (1973) 96–8.

[3] On ὕψιστος see Wackernagel, *SUH* 213f.

[4] ὄλβιστος and τέρπνιστος are briefly discussed, but without full reference to the historical context, by Wackernagel, *KZ* 43 (1910) 377f. (= *Kleine Schriften* I 831f.). These coinages were perhaps easier at a time when in the *koine* the -ίων, -ιστος intensive suffixes were becoming obsolete except with very common adjectives (Mayser, *GGP* I² 59, cf. Moulton, *GNT* II 164f.). The Hellenistic writers experimented further and even combined both superlative suffixes together in forms such as τερπνίστατος, κυδίστατος: see Pfeiffer on 93.3 τερπνίστατα.

his labours etc.;[1] Hesychius glosses with ἀγήρως, εὔμοιρος. The word belongs essentially to tragic vocabulary (which also coined δυς- and μακρ-αίων). C. adopts the adjective (IV 292, *E.* 51.3), and after him Leonidas, *HE* 2030, Dioscorides, *HE* 1705, Eratosthenes (?) fr. 35.13P (of Ptolemy Euergetes).

117–18 The pattern of expression seems to be one typically generated by εὐαίων, namely εὐαίων + pentameter detailing the reason for the blessedness, often in a subordinate clause, here in an equivalent participial phrase: Leonidas, *HE* 2030 πῶς οὐκ εὐαίων ὁ Λυκάστιος ὃς καὶ ἔρωτι | ἄρχε καὶ εὖ μολπᾶι καί etc., Eratosth. (?) fr. 35.13 εὐαίων, Πτολεμαῖε, πατὴρ ὅτι παιδὶ συνηβῶν | πάνθ' ὅσα καὶ Μούσαις καὶ βασιλεῦσι φίλα | αὐτὸς ἐδωρήσω.[2]

118 ἐξ ὀρέων A generalising plural (only Helicon is involved), parallel to Autonoe's δρυμώς and also symbolising the wild, where savagery is normal (see on v. 116 δρυμώς) and cf. Archibald Cameron in *Miscellanea . . . Rostagni* (Turin 1963) 296 n. 13). Similarly Theocr. 26.26 describing Bacchants: ἐξ ὄρεος πένθημα καὶ οὐ Πενθῆα φέροισαι.

ἀλαόν The juxtaposition with ἐξ ὀρέων emphatically early in the phrase is effectively equivalent in English to '*only* blind'. See also on v. 98.

παῖδ' Enforcing the parallel with Autonoe (v. 115 υἱέος).

ὑποδεξαμέναν The verb at the end of its period is the final element in establishing the emotive contrast with Autonoe's situation: *she* has to go out and collect her son as bones in the wilds, whereas Chariclo receives Tiresias returning himself (ἐξ ὀρέων) to the human world connoted by ὑποδεξαμέναν (which describes the expression of affection between living people).

---

[1] When the chorus call Ὕπνος εὐαίων at Soph. *Phil.* 829 it is because sleep is about to transform Philoctetes' pain to physical calm: this is also the dramatic point at which Philoctetes believes that his long suffering is about to be relieved – when he wakes, his life will have been changed. The other pre-Hellenistic instances are: Soph. fr. 592.3, Eur. *Bacch.* 426 (not in LSJ), *IA* 550, *Ion* 126, 142, Peek, *GVI* 546 = *SEG* 21 (1965) 856 (fourth century B.C.: not in LSJ). Cf. Wilamowitz on Eur. *Ion* 126.

[2] This recurrent pattern of expression suggests that in *E.* 51 vv. 3f. should be taken closely together: εὐαίων . . . Βερενίκα, | ἇς ἄτερ οὐδ' αὐταὶ ταὶ Χάριτες Χάριτες, the pentameter providing more than simply an additional comment. (The relative clause not only explains *why* Berenice is εὐαίων, it also reinterprets the adjective, implying that in this instance the person described is εὐαίων not because she is a blessed human, but because she is herself divine: ἇς ἄτερ is the phraseology of epicletic hymns listing the god's qualities upon which humans depend. So ἄνευ σέθεν, σοῦ δίχα, σοῦ γὰρ ἄτερ etc. and their opposites διὰ σέ, σὺν δὲ τίν etc.: see E.Norden, *Agnostos Theos* (Berlin 1913) 157 n. 3, 159 n. 1, Nisbet and Hubbard on Hor. *Od.* 1.26.9.)

Meineke's correction ἀποδ. was accepted by both Schneider and Wilamowitz, presumably on the grounds that (a) ὑποδ. usually means 'welcome as a guest', and (b) Chariclo was in fact there with Tiresias, not somewhere else whither he returned after being blinded. But there is no need to change Ψ's reading: (a) ὑποδέχεcθαι basically = 'receive somebody (-thing) from somewhere'. Of people this does usually imply social obligation, hospitality etc. ('take in', 'entertain': see LSJ), and this usage would clearly be inappropriate here for mother and son; but often the verb is used more vaguely = simply 'receive willingly', 'welcome', and in Homer in precisely this context: Thetis of her son Achilles *Il.* 18.59f., 440f. τὸν δ' οὐχ ὑποδέξομαι αὖτις | οἴκαδε νοςτήcαντα (cf. 18.89f.), and similarly *Od.* 19.257f. Penelope of Odysseus.[1] (b) As already suggested on v. 116 δρυμώς and ὀρέων above, Tiresias does indeed return to Chariclo, not geographically but symbolically, from the savage Mt Helicon back alive.[2]

119–36 Athena's gifts. This section balances the description of the friendship with which the narrative began, vv. 57–69: because of her special friendship with Chariclo (v. 119 ὦ ἑτάρα, v. 120 τεῦ χάριν, see on v. 122 μέγα . . . δή τι) Athena gives Tiresias compensation for his blinding.[3] [Apollod.] 3.6.7 (reporting Pherecydes) Χαρικλοῦς δὲ δεομένης ἀποκαταςτῆcαι πάλιν τὰς ὁράςεις, μὴ δυναμένην τοῦτο ποιῆcαι, τὰς ἀκοὰς διακαθάραςαν πᾶcαν ὀρνίθων φωνὴν ποιῆcαι cυνεῖναι, καὶ cκῆπτρον αὐτῶι δωρήcαcθαι κράνειον, ὃ φέρων ὁμοίως τοῖς βλέπουcιν ἐβάδιζεν. Hesiod too received the gifts of a staff and insight into past, present, and future on Helicon: Hes. *Theog.* 30ff. The high tone of Athena's speech is maintained throughout: see on v. 119, 121 ἀοίδιμον ἐcсομένοιcιν, v. 123 οἵ τε πέτονται, v. 124 ἄλιθα, v. 125 θεοπρόπα, v. 129, v. 133 πατρώϊα πάντα.

---

[1] Cf. also *Il.* 9.480f. ὁ δέ με πρόφρων ὑπέδεκτο | καί μ' ἐφίληc' ὡς εἴ τε πατὴρ ὃν παῖδα φιλήcηι, and 6.136 Θέτις δ' ὑπεδέξατο κόλπωι | δειδιότα (Dionysus). Thence [Mosch.] 4.90. In *P. Teb.* 3.28 Asclepiades (?) seems to use ὑποδεξαμένα of the Spartan mother receiving her cowardly son home (cf. *HE* II 151). In itself the verb is in fact very unspecific, as is demonstrated by the wide range of contiguous usages listed in LSJ; Plato uses almost identical words to describe a ditch collecting water: *Crit.* 118D τὰ δ' ἐκ τῶν ὀρῶν καταβαίνοντα ὑποδεχομένη ῥεύματα.

[2] Meineke's own ἀποδ. appears to be impossible since ἀποδέχεcθαι almost invariably implies a choice and a decision made by the receiver: 'accept' (cf. Schmidt, *SGS* III 218). Hdt. 4.33 and Thuc. 5.26 seem to be the only examples of ἀποδ. = 'recover'.

[3] Comparable is Artemis' compensation to Hippolytus in Eur. *Hipp.* 1423ff. cοὶ δ', ὦ ταλαίπωρ', ἀντὶ τῶνδε τῶν κακῶν | τιμὰς μεγίcτας ἐν πόλει Τροζηνίαι | δώcω . . . She, like Athena, is austere in the face of her companion's misfortune: 1396 κατ' ὄccων δ' οὐ θέμις βαλεῖν δάκρυ. See Intro. pp. 49ff.

119 ὦ ἑτάρα Athena's tone changes; her self-defence presented she now relaxes into a more intimate approach (contrast vv. 97, 103 δῖα γύναι, and see on v. 81 ὦ Εὐηρείδα). For the unusual form ἑτάρα see on v. 58.

The placing of the vocative phrase at the beginning of its period, even before a conjunction such as τῶι, is a mark of high style (see K–G, *GG* I 50f., Schwyzer, *GG* II 60 and cf. E.Kieckers, *Indog. Forsch.* 23 (1908–9) 358ff. for a table and list of Homeric instances).

τῶι On form, accentuation etc. see Schwyzer, *GG* II 579 and references there cited.

τῶι μή τι In this position + imperative also at *Od.* 11.486, A.R. 1.1320, 3.1108.

μινύρεο μινυρ- words belong to poetic vocabulary and denote the quietish but high-pitched sound which could be either singing (wailing, warbling mostly of birds, women, or old men) or lamentation (cf. Schmidt, *SGS* III 381ff.); Classical usage is mostly of singing, but the Homeric examples are of lamentation (*Il.* 5.889 and *Od.* 4.719). The word is very suitable of someone whose lament was earlier compared to that of the nightingale (vv. 94f.): Soph. *OC* 671f. μινύρεται . . . ἀηδών, Theocr., *HE* 3484 ἀδονίδες μινυρίσμασιν ἀνταχεῦσι. μινυρ- vocabulary is rare in the Hellenistic poets, who, however, often use the rhyming κινύρεσθαι = 'lament' (especially A.R.).[1]

Line 119 phonetically resembles *Il.* 5.889 μή τί μοι ἀλλοπρόσαλλε παρεζόμενος μινύριζε (though a more than phonetic reminiscence would be counter-effective since Zeus is criticising Ares and says of him ἔχθιστος δέ μοί ἐσσι θεῶν). For other such phonetic allusions to Homer in C. see H.Herter, 'Kallimachos und Homer', *Xenia Bonnensia* (Bonn 1929) 54.

γάρ Here (unnecessarily suspected by Schneider, Meineke and P.Maas) gives an additional reason why Chariclo should not lament (cf. Denniston, *GP* 60f.).

ἄλλα 'Besides' the relative lightness of the punishment Tiresias will receive πολλὰ γέρα (the standard idiom of ἄλλος with an appositive force adding another species or category of things: K–G, *GG* I 275 A.1 b), Gildersleeve, *SCG* II § 599).

120 τεῦ χάριν χάριν with personal pronouns usually converts the pronoun into the possessive (K–G, *GG* I 461 A): τεὰν (σὴν) χάριν would have been more regular, the more so since τεῦ χάριν could be mistaken for τεῦ = τίνος χάριν. Maintenance of τεῦ, however, positioned at the begin-

[1] To LSJ add A.R. 1.883, 3.259, 664, 4.605, 1063, [Mosch.] 3.92, Bion 1.42. μινυρ- and κινυρ- may be historically connected: see H.G.Güntert, *Über Reimwortbildungen im Arischen und Altgriechischen* (Heidelberg 1914) 150f., also the less satisfactory discussion in Leumann, *HW* 241ff.

ning of the line, asserts the pronoun; Athena tries to emphasise her continued affection towards Chariclo. With the following words ἐξ ἐμέθεν too Athena stresses that she does claim responsibility for T.'s special powers of prophecy.

Doric τεῦ is well attested from literary sources: see K–B, *GG* I 583 and add Theocr. 5.19, [Theocr.] 8.83 (VI 99 σεῦ should probably be emended to τεῦ).

ἐμέθεν A common Homeric (Aeolic) form which may also be Doric: Ap. Dysc. *de pron.* 83c (*Gramm. Graec.* II[1] 66) remarks that ἐμέθεν is Syracusan, and quotes Sophron fr. 20 μέθεν (no other evidence available); ἕθεν in Epidaurus may be compared (Bechtel, *GD* II 488). Theocritus always uses the more usual Doric form ἐμεῦ (also ἐμεῖο in [Theocr.]).

μενεῦντι The choice of verb is important since it stresses the certainty of the compensation, the more so because 'predictive' μένειν is mostly used of impending *mis*fortune: see on v. 68 ἔμενε.

Strictly speaking, the future tense is tautological with the futurity of the verb itself: Athena has already decided to give T. various privileges, so there can presumably be no question here of the vague and distant future. However, θησῶ in the next line indicates that the giving of the privileges (or rather their manifestation) is not to be part of the present scene, and the tense fits rhetorically with the series of future tenses in the following ten lines.

γέρα Always of gifts connoting honour or privilege. Delayed to the end of the line and sentence (after early preparation from ἄλλα) to give maximum impact (cf. 384.28 καλά μοι θρ̣ε̣π̣τ̣ὸς ἔτεισε γέρα).

121 ἐπεί Delaying of conjunctions to second, and sometimes third, position is a Callimachean characteristic.[1] Similarly with ἐπεί at 24.1 σκῶλος ἐπεί μιν ἔτυψε and 31c.4, IV 157; delayed conjunction again in V at v. 60 εὖτε.

θησῶ The usual verb for such divine appointments or assignments (cf. Ebeling, *LH* II 331 5): so, e.g., *Od.* 15.252 Πολυφείδεα μάντιν Ἀπόλλων | θῆκε βροτῶν ὄχ' ἄριστον.

ἀοίδιμον ἐσσομένοισιν Athena's claim is made the more cogent by being couched in highly poetic language and appealing to the traditional value of renown in posterity. The phraseology directly recalls *Il.* 6.358 (ὡς καὶ ὀπίσσω) | ἀνθρώποισι πελώμεθ' ἀοίδιμοι ἐσσομένοισι (Helen, of herself and Paris), the only instance of ἀοίδιμος in *Iliad* or *Odyssey*;[2] the sentiment is that expressed at *Od.* 8.580 ἵνα ᾖσι καὶ ἐσσομένοισιν ἀοιδή or 3.204 (οἱ Ἀχαιοί) | οἴσουσι κλέος εὐρὺ καὶ ἐσσομένοισιν ἀοιδήν (cf. 24.200f. στυγερὴ δέ τ' ἀοιδὴ | ἔσσετ' ἐπ' ἀνθρώπους), and in Homeric style Theogn. 251f. καὶ

[1] Cf. Lapp, *TF* 48f.

[2] Once in the Hymns at *H.H.Ap.* 299.

ἐccομένοιcιν ἀοιδή | ἔccηι and Theocr. 12.11 ἐπεccομένοιc δὲ γενοίμεθα πᾶcιν ἀοιδή.

ἀοίδιμον Neutral, = 'renowned', rather than 'famous': apparently a poetic word in Attic, but its appearance in Herodotus and then later prose writers suggests that it was also Ionic whence it became normal (if infrequent) usage in the *koine*.[1]

ἐccομένοιcιν ἐccόμενοι = 'posterity' is entirely epic usage which appears almost entirely in the context of long-lasting renown: see, in addition to the passages quoted above, *Il.* 2.119, 22.305, *Od.* 11.76, 433, 21.255, 24.433, Hes. *Op.* 56, fr. 212 (b) 6, Theocr. 17.137.

122 ἦ Introducing a second stage of thought, syntactically dependent on θηcῶ, but logically an independent addition to v. 121: (1) 'I shall make him a renowned prophet', (2) 'and one who is better than all the others'. Cf., e.g., Aristoph. *Vesp.* 1453f. ἕτερα νῦν ἀντιμαθὼν ἦ μέγα τι μεταπεcεῖται where ἦ similarly 'delayed' syntactically, is properly positioned at the head of the colon which it affirms.[2]

μέγα . . . δή τι Cf. the earlier description of Athena's affection for Chariclo, v. 58 πουλύ τι καὶ περὶ δὴ φίλατο. The phrase is notably Callimachean (see on v. 58) and there may be a direct reference back to v. 58 here, suggesting that Athena will make Tiresias an exceptional prophet, *just as* her friendship for Chariclo was exceptional.[3]

The separation of δή τι from its adverb has no exact parallel in C. (Hertzberg therefore suggested reading τοῦτο), but simple δή is sometimes so delayed by a syntactically related word (Denniston, *GP* 227f.): e.g. Hdt. 9.27.5 οἵτινεc μοῦνοι Ἑλλήνων δή; and transposition, often very much more severe than this, is typical of C. (see Lapp, *TF* 35ff.).

τῶν ἄλλων The article with ἄλλοc or ἕτεροc to mark a distinction or opposition already in Homer: Chantraine, *GH* II 162.

περιccότερον Matching ἀοίδιμον ἐccομένοιcι similarly positioned at the end of its line (and clause). Comparative because all prophets are exceptional, but T. is to be *even more* exceptional. Again in C. in this position in the lacunose 43.9 πε]ριccοτερο.[.[4]

The line is more than usually carefully constructed to make prominent

---

[1] See LSJ and *Thes. Graec.*: add *LXX* 4 Macc. 10.1, 15, Joseph. *A.* 6.165, 19.53.

[2] ἦ, mainly a verse idiom, affirms mostly adjectives and adverbs: Denniston, *GP* 280f.

[3] An internal reminiscence of this kind would add weight to Athena's position: v. 58 was not a claim by Athena which the reader is invited to believe, but a statement by the narrator which he is obliged to believe.

[4] Cf. Aratus, *HE* 765 ἑτέρου δ' ἐcτὶ περιccότεροc.

the last word of the pentameter: ἦ μέγα τῶν ἄλλων is for itself semantically quite unspecific and syntactically opaque, until δή τι and especially the final περιccότερον provide clarification.

123–4 Cic. *de div.* 1.11 *duo sunt enim divinandi genera, quorum alterum artis est, alterum naturae* (see the commentary of A.S.Pease for references to later Greek authors and in particular cf. Soph. *OT* 394ff. μαντείαc . . . ἣν οὔτ' ἀπ' οἰωνῶν cὺ προυφάνηc ἔχων | οὔτ' ἐκ θεῶν του γνωτόν). T. was famous for his powers in both kinds of divination; of the external sort (*Od.* 20.100f. φήμην τίc μοι φάcθω ἐγειρομένων ἀνθρώπων | ἔνδοθεν, ἔκτοcθεν δὲ Διὸc τέραc ἄλλο φανήτω) οἰωνοcκοπία was his special skill: through his sensitive hearing (Aesch. *Sept.* 24ff., Soph. *Ant.* 1000ff. where see Jebb) and/or through the eyes of his daughter Manto (Eur. *Phoen.* 834ff.) or a boy (Soph. *Ant.* 1012ff.). C. alludes here to the skill in general terms without specifying the medium of T.'s observations, though Pherecydes appears to have represented the gift of οἰωνοcκοπία as a cleansing of the hearing to compensate for loss of sight (see on vv. 119–36 above).

T. practised his augury at a particular observatory in Thebes: Soph. *Ant.* 999f. εἰc γὰρ παλαιὸν θᾶκον ὀρνιθοcκόπον | ἵζων, Eur. *Bacch.* 347 θάκουc τοῦδ' ἵν' οἰωνοcκοπεῖ, *Phoen.* 840 θάκοιcιν ἐν ἱεροῖcιν οὗ μαντεύομαι, and the spot was noted by Pausanias in his guide next to temples of Ammon and Tyche (9.16.1).

On οἰωνοcκοπία in general see A.Bouché-Leclercq, *Histoire de la divination* (Paris 1879–82) I 127ff. and Stengel, *GKA* 57ff.

123 γνωcεῖται The standard term for recognising an omen for what it is: so, e.g., *Od.* 15.531f. . . . δεξιὸc ὄρνιc· | ἔγνων γάρ μιν ἐcάντα ἰδὼν οἰωνὸν ἐόντα, Eur. *Her.* 596f. ὄρνιν δ' ἰδών τιν' οὐκ ἐν αἰcίοιc ἕδραιc | ἔγνων πόνον τιν' . . . etc.

ὄρνιχαc The Doric -χ- form restored by Ernesti (Ψ 'normalised' to ὄρνιθαc) is amply documented in literary texts (LSJ), and supported by inscriptional evidence from Cyrene;[1] Theocritus too has ὀρνιχ- in his Doric poems (5.48, 7.47, 60), ὀρνιθ- in the non-Doric poems. The ancient grammarians note the form: Athen. 9.374D οἱ δὲ Δωριεῖc λέγοντεc ὄρνιξ τὴν γενικὴν διὰ τοῦ χ λέγουcιν ὄρνιχοc; similarly Choerobosc. Σ *in Theodos. can.* in *Gramm. Graec.* IV² 292.12f.,[2] and thence Photius, *Lex.* s.v. and Eustath. 1419.16, 1439.38. Doric often has ξ where Attic has c (κλᾴξ/κλεῖc etc.),[3] and this particular Doric form was absorbed into the *koine* as an occasional

[1] *SEG* 9 (1944) 123, 124: two fourth-century B.C. dedications. See also Bechtel, *GD* II 336.

[2] Whence Lentz' 'reconstituted' text of Herodian in *Gramm. Graec.* III¹ 44.

[3] Ahrens, *DD* 91f., Buck, *GD* § 142.

alternative to ὄρνιϲ, whence it was still to be found in Cappadocia in the late nineteenth century.[1]

123–4 ὅϲ . . . οἵ . . . ποίων By the standards of normal Classical usage there is a minor variation here in the train of thought: ὅϲ and οἵ should be adjectival relatives, not interrogatives:[2] 'T. will recognise birds, *those which* are favourable, *those which* are . . .', not 'T. will get to know *what* birds are favourable, *what* birds are . . . '. The first part of the sentence should be describing *re*cognition from prior knowledge, not the acquisition of knowledge; ποίων, however, can only be interrogative (indirect); 'which ones have ill-omened wings'. ὅϲ and οἵ *could* be interrogative,[3] but nowhere else in the Hymns is ὅϲ so used, and the expression of ὄρνιχαϲ as direct object of γνωϲεῖται (not ὀρνίχων) makes ὅϲ and οἵ most natural as adjectival relatives. The change of construction at ποίων involves only minor adjustment, and its occurrence in the final limb of a tricolon in the second line of the couplet (when the sequence of thought seems assured) is a typically Callimachean variation.

123 αἴϲιοϲ A rare but standard technical term = '*faustus*', mostly of omens, and hence often of οἰωνοί as here.[4]

οἵ τε πέτονται Same clausula at *Il.* 13.29, 15.684 (τ)οἱ δὲ πέτονται | (of horses).

124 ἅλιθα 'to no effect', 'with no significance'. The lacunose history of

---

[1] For the *koine* see Mayser, *GGP* I² 31 and especially Crönert, *MGH* 174 n. 5; for the Cappadocian survival see Thumb, *Die griech. Sprache* (Strassburg 1901) 90f. Modern commentators often argue that the Doric nominative ὄρνιξ, of which there is no literary example, was inferred by ancient grammarians from the oblique ὀρνιχ- forms, but the occurrence of ὄρνιξ in the *koine* makes this unlikely, in spite of the apparent instances of ὄρνιϲ in Alcman and Pindar.

[2] Monteil, *PR* 153: 'ὅϲτιϲ sollicite la connaissance d'une identité ignorée; ὅϲ affirme la connaissance d'une identité qui n'est pas nécessairement sollicitée'. Monteil's discussion and conclusions (150–4) are superior to those in K–G, *GG* II 438f.

[3] The clause following a verb of knowing is often indeterminate as between relative and interrogative: see, e.g., *Il.* 2.365, 21.609f., 23.497f., but also cf. Monteil, *PR* 153 n. 2. Third-century B.C. *koine* had lost the distinction between relative and indirect interrogative (Mayser, *GGP* II¹ 76ff., Moulton, *GNT* III 48ff.), but C.'s syntax is usually that of literary Classical Greek.

[4] Gautier's concern (*LX* 90) that αἴϲιοϲ might not be normal usage is unnecessary: the spread of instances illustrates the distribution of the subject matter rather than the status of the term, and the frequency of αἴϲιοϲ in Xenophon (as in later writers: add also Timaeus fr. 149 Jacoby, *FGrHist* 3B 566 (p. 642)) confirms the word's normality.

this adverb is fully discussed by R.Hiersche, *Philologus* 102 (1958) 140–4. An epic word, it occurs only in Homer and the Hellenistic poets (not in the bucolics or epigrammatists). In Homer it is an intensive = 'exceptionally', and so mostly in Hellenistic literature;[1] here, however, and again at A.R. 2.283 and Nic. *Al.* 25, ἤλιθα is used as if it were adverb to the adjective ἠλίθιος in its occasional sense 'purposeless', 'idle', 'vain'.[2] Although this usage may be an established rarity for which earlier testimony happens now to be lost, it is more likely to be an Alexandrian extension of an otherwise dead gloss, interest in which is also shown by Nicander's coinage of the unique adjective ἤλιθος = 'ineffective' (*Al.* 140, and also possibly 25). Mair's otiose 'countless', qualifying πέτονται, illustrates the awkwardness of taking ἅλιθα in its Homeric sense here.

The meaning of ἅλιθα is important. Spanheim adduced Aristoph. *Av.* 170 (ὄρνις) ἀτέκμαρτος where Σ remarks σημεῖον διὰ τῆς πτήσεως οὐκ ἐμφαίνων: more precisely, ἀτέκμαρτος means 'obscure', 'difficult to interpret', as at Hdt. 5.92.3 χρηστήριον ἀτέκμαρτον. This cannot be the meaning of ἅλιθα: T.'s skill will consist in more than being able to recognise obscure omens. Athena's point is that not all birds were equally valuable for augury (see A. Bouché-Leclercq, *Histoire de la divination dans l'antiquité* (Paris 1879–82) I 129f.), and T. will be skilled at distinguishing the ominous from the irrelevant (cf. Aristoph. *Av.* 1330ff. σὺ δὲ τὰ πτερὰ πρῶτον | διάθες τάδε κόσμωι, | τά τε μουσίχ' ὁμοῦ τά τε μαντικὰ καὶ τὰ θαλάττι').

Ψ had ἤλιθα; however, the Doric form of ἠλίθιος = 'purposeless' is ἀλ. (Pind. *P.* 3.11, Theocr. 10.40, 16.9), and ἀλ. is preferable here (the only instance of the adverb in a Doric context).

ποίων A direct interrogative. Strict usage would require ὁποίων, but Homeric usage occasionally (though irregularly) has direct interrogatives in subordinate clauses: e.g. *Il.* 5.85 Τυδείδην δ' οὐκ ἂν γνοίης ποτέροισι μετείη.[3] This interchange was also a feature of the *koine*, in which indirect

---

[1] See LSJ for citations. In Homer always ἤλιθα πολλή(ν), but more freely in the Alexandrians; a frequent user of ἤλιθα is Aratus, who is nowhere mentioned by LSJ or Hiersche.

[2] More often ἠλίθιος = 'silly'; in its rarer sense at Peek, *GVI* 58 (= G.Pfohl, *Greek Poems on Stones* (Leiden 1967) I 40: sixth century B.C. Athens), Pind. *P.* 3.11, Aesch. *Ag.* 366, Theocr. 10.40, 16.9: ἤλιθα = 'to no effect' would thus be a distinct poeticism. Σ to A.R. 2.283 also equates ἤλιθα with ἠλιθίως. Hiersche points out that the various usages of ἤλιθα and ἠλίθιος all fall within the same semantic range ('errant' → 'mad' → 'senseless' → 'fruitless'). Briefer discussions of the adjective in Wilamowitz, *Sappho und Simonides* (Berlin 1913) 176 n. 1 and Fraenkel on Aesch. *Ag.* 366; references to the ancient lexicographers in C.Wendel, *Scholia in Theocritum* (Leipzig 1914) 326.10 on Theocr. 16.9.

[3] Similarly *Od.* 15.423, 17.368 etc.: Chantraine, *GH* II 292.

interrogatives were becoming obsolete (Mayser, *GGP* II[1] 78ff., Moulton, *GNT* III 48f., Meisterhans, *GAI* 237.16). ποίων here, as occasionally in earlier periods and as always in the *koine*, has lost its qualitative value and simply = τίνων.[1]

οὐκ ἀγαθαί The adjective as in phrases such as ἀγαθὸς δαίμων, ἀγαθὴ τύχη = 'favourable', 'propitious'. The periphrasis for κακαί (cf. κακὸς ὄρνις: *Il.* 24.219, Eur. *Hel.* 1051 etc.) balances αἴσιος in the previous line (Hesych. αἴσιος δεξιός, καλός, ἀγαθός: cf. *Et. Mag.* 39.21). Hes. fr. 240.11 σὺν οἰωνοῖς ἀγαθοῖσιν, Call. fr. 608, Plut. *Num.* ὄρνιθες ἀγαθοὶ καὶ δεξιοί.

πτέρυγες An easy metonymy, as suggested by LSJ s.v., of the type *causa pro effectu*, just as at 43.66 μέρμν[ο]υ μọị πτερύγεσςị seems to mean simply 'with the good omen of the *flight* of a hawk' (see Pfeiffer ad loc.); similarly πτερόν at Soph. *OC* 97 = 'omen', and at Eur. *Ion* 377 πτερά is used as πτέρυγες here: in Latin cf. Prop. 3.10.11 *felicibus edita pennis.*[2]

125–6 The superior kind of *divinatio*, that of prophecy by inspiration (see Cicero referred to on vv. 123f.); cf. Plato, *Phaedr.* 244D ὅσωι δὴ οὖν τελεώτερον καὶ ἐντιμότερον μαντικὴ οἰωνιστικῆς . . . τόσωι κάλλιον μαρτυροῦσιν οἱ παλαιοὶ μανίαν σωφροσύνης τὴν ἐκ θεοῦ τῆς παρ' ἀνθρώπων γιγνομένης. T.'s renowned insight into the future as well as the past was the general power of the wise prophet, servant of Apollo (Soph. *OT* 284ff., 300ff.), distinct from the particular gift of οἰωνοσκοπία which he applied on specific occasions.

125 πολλὰ δὲ Βοιωτοῖσι Ov. *Met.* 3.339f. *ille per Aonias fama celeberrimus urbes | inreprehensa dabat populo responsa petenti.* T.'s most famous recorded prophecies concerned the Theban royal family, but he was also regarded as a popular prophet, especially after his death when a χρηστήριον of Tiresias was active at Orchomenus (Plut. *de def. orac.* 44: see in general Roscher, *LM* V 195f.).

---

[1] See LSJ for earlier references, and for the *koine* Mayser, *GGP* II[1] 78, Moulton, *GNT* III 48, and in general Wackernagel, *VUS* II 113f.

[2] See Butler and Barber ad loc. for more examples in Latin. πτέρυγες might arguably be literal and not metonymy since the detail of how the wing itself was held was important for assessing the omen: cf. the instructions on interpretation of bird-flight inscribed at Ephesus in the sixth to the fifth century B.C. (Ditt. *Syll.*[3] 1167 = Schwyzer, *DGEE* 708): . . . πετόμεν]ος, ἢμ μὲν ἀποκρύψε[ι, δε]ξιός, ἢν δὲ ἐπάρει τὴ[ν ε]ὐώνυμον πτέρυγα, κἂν [διά]ρει κἂν ἀποκρύψει, ε[ὐώ]νυμος· ἐγ δὲ τῆς ἀριστ[ερ]ῆς ἐς τὴν δεξιὴν πετό[μ]ενος, ἢμ μὲν ἰθὺς ἀποκρ[ύ]ψει, εὐώνυμος, ἢν δὲ τὴν [δεξ]ιὴν πτέρυγα ἐπάρας[. Also the omen given to Tiberius Gracchus on the day of his murder: Plut. *Tib. Gr.* 17 reports that when the auspice birds were fed they refused to leave their cage, with the exception of one bird, οὐδὲ αὕτη δὲ τῆς τροφῆς ἔθιγεν, ἀλλ' ἐπάρασα τὴν ἀριστερὰν πτέρυγα καὶ παρατείνασα τὸ σκέλος πάλιν εἰς τὸ ἀγγεῖον κατέφυγε.

θεοπρόπα An exceptional poeticism. θεοπρόπος, normally a masculine substantive of people, is here adjectival, and the adjective is passive, not active ('[things] spoken by/from a god'). The usage may ultimately derive from *Il.* 13.70 θεοπρόπος οἰωνιστής, which Sophocles appears to have interpreted as adjective + noun[1] in *Trach.* 822 τοὔπος τὸ θεοπρόπον. θεοπρόπος as adjective presupposes an etymology of the kind θεός + πρέπω producing an ambivalent adjective/noun: the verbal second element allows the compound to be either active (as in Homer) or passive (as in Sophocles),[2] though the passive usage of such verbal compounds which have no explicit passive form (-τος etc.) is a feature restricted to poetry.[3] C.'s neuter plural takes this poetic adjective full circle to serve *as a substantive*, the passive counterpart to θεοπρόπος.

The special category invented by LSJ s.v., 'θεοπρόπον, τό = θεοπροπία' (followed by Chantraine, *DE* 429) is arbitrary and unconvincing.

Κάδμωι No prophecies of T. to Cadmus (grandfather of Actaeon) are known. The founder of Thebes is probably mentioned here simply for neatness: T. was always given a life lasting seven generations, and the arithmetic required that he begin with Cadmus.[4]

126 μεγάλοις Not an otiose adjective: Athena further reassures Chariclo that the family which T. will advise will be one of the great dynasties. For the phraseology cf. on v. 34 μεγάλων.

ὕστερα A rare poeticism. Adverbial neuter of uncompounded adjectives is usually singular, and the plural when used is either quantitative (πολλά etc.) or superlative in form (ὕστατα, πρῶτα etc.: see Wackernagel, *SUH* 87, Schwyzer, *GG* I 621).[5] However, the plural with temporal adverbs is a Hellenistic mannerism, though usually articulated; again unarticulated at Theocr. 8.16 ποθέσπερα.

Λαβδακίδαις Labdacus was Cadmus' grandson, and the patronymic is commonly used to denote not only Labdacus' immediate descendants

---

[1] On two substantives in apposition see Wackernagel, *VUS* II 53–5 and Schwyzer, *GG* II 176.

[2] Cf. Debrunner, *GW* 53: similarly ambivalent are, e.g., θηροτροφος, λιθοβολος etc. (accent according to usage); see also Lobeck, *Paralipomena* 329–88, esp. 366ff. 75.55 μυθολόγωι is the only other example in C. of a verbal compound noun used adjectivally.

[3] Cf. W.Breitenbach, *Untersuchungen zur Sprache der euripideischen Lyrik* (Stuttgart 1934) 84ff. There seem to be no other instances of adjectival θεοπρόπος until Q.S. 12.534, in whom it is undoubtedly a select rarity.

[4] [Apollod.] 3.6.7 says that T. was ἀπὸ γένους Οὐδαίου, one of Cadmus' sown men. Earliest mention of T.'s seven generations is Hes. fr. 276.4f. ὃς μακρόν γέ μ' ἔθηκας ἔχειν αἰῶνα βίοιο | ἑπτά τ' ἐπὶ ζώειν γενεὰς μερόπων ἀνθρώπων: post-Hesiodic references in Roscher, *LM* V 180f.

[5] Hence at 75.66 the adverbial ἠλεά is again a rare and heightened usage.

(Laius and Oedipus), but generally the whole of that family (e.g. Pind. *I.* 3.16; cf. Soph. *OT* 487, 495, Eur. *Phoen.* 800). The final word of the couplet, therefore, predictably completes the syntactical pattern, but also poses a chronological riddle which is explained not immediately, but in the pentameter of the next couplet.

127 μέγα βάκτρον *Od.* 11.91 χρύσεον σκῆπτρον ἔχων: T. kept his staff even in Hades. Pherecydes too listed the staff among Athena's gifts, specifying that it was of cornel-wood: [Apollod.] 3.6.7 καὶ σκῆπτρον αὐτῶι δωρήσασθαι κράνειον (Aegius: κυάνειον MSS). Pherecydes, like C., gave a rationalistic explanation of the symbolic stick (ὃ φέρων ὁμοίως τοῖς βλέπουσιν ἐβάδιζεν),[1] but it could legitimately be inferred that both authors attributed magical powers to the staff (see on ἐς δέον).

βάκτρον A rather rare poetic word, usually denoting a stick to support the old or blind (though LSJ are incorrect in describing it as being limited to tragic lyrics: also in iambics at Eur. *Hec.* 281, *Ion* 743, *Bacch.* 363).[2]

ἐς δέον A standard phrase (LSJ), which could be interpreted as implying that the staff had magical powers. Cf. Theocr. 14.50 τὰ πάντα κεν ἐς δέον ἕρποι.

ἀξεῖ For Lascaris' correction of Ψ's non-Doric ἄξει see on v. 50 ἡξεῖ.

128 The loss of all but πολυχρόνιον in hyparchetypes βδζ corresponds to the loss of the second half of VI 15 in all except F:[3] V 128 was on the recto and VI 15 on the corresponding part of the verso of the same sheet in the gradually deteriorating archetype. See Intro. pp. 68f.

δωσῶ καί The anaphora with v. 127, compounding the anaphora of the previous couplet, makes Athena's promises particularly forceful. For the Doric accentuation of δωσῶ see on v. 50 ἡξεῖ.

βιότω = βίου, a common poeticism (*pace* LSJ: see individual indexes). Ernesti's correction of Ψ's 'normalised' βιότου makes for consistency with the Doric genitive singular elsewhere in V (10, 65, 102); similarly corrupted (and corrected by Ernesti) at v. 140.

τέρμα Common poetic phraseology: e.g. βιότοιο/βίου τελευτή *Il.* 7.104, 16.787, τέρμα βίου Aesch. fr. 708M, Soph. *OT* 1530, Eur. *Alc.* 643.

πολυχρόνιον The adjective is common in Hippocrates and Aristotle (cf. also citations from other authors in LSJ) = 'long-lasting', 'long-lived', and although avoided by other Hellenistic poets is so used by C. again at III

---

[1] On the symbolic nature of the staff see Pfister, *RGR* 314f. and F.J.M. de Waele, *The Magic Staff or Rod in Graeco-Italian Antiquity* (Gent 1927).

[2] Though βάκτρον was apparently a non-Attic word, βακτηρ- being the standard Attic base: Chantraine, *DE* 159, *FN* 331, 332.

[3] γ here has the full line, as F. Pfeiffer, *Proleg.* lxxx maintains that Ψ's source was F or an ancestor, but the explanation is probably more complex: see Intro. pp. 66f.

132 and IV 282.[1] Here, however, with τέρμα, this sense is near impossible, as Meineke saw when he proposed πολυχρονίω (from an untraced Roman MS); however this is equally unsuitable: since the real object of δωcῶ is not the τέρμα itself, but the fact that it is long-delayed, πολυχρονι- must go with τέρμα.[2] Consideration of the antonym ὀλιγοχρόνιος suggests a solution. The latter is used not only of duration, 'for a short time', but also of the specific point following duration, 'after a short time': particularly important testimony is Hipp. *Prog.* 7 cημαίνει . . . κίνδυνον θανάτου ὀλιγοχρονίου (cf. Iam. *Protr.* 20 ὀλιγοχρονίωc ἐπὶ τέλοc ἀγαγεῖν, Galen 18 (2).243). τέρμα πολυχρόνιον makes excellent sense interpreted as 'an end after a long time', and although there seem to be no other examples of this usage for πολυχρ. itself it should probably not be regarded as abnormal.

129 The traditional belief that Tiresias retained his intelligence even in Hades was based directly on the famous Homeric account of Odysseus in the underworld, and writers who mention it always refer to their Homeric source: thus Plato, *Men.* 100A, Cic. *de div.* 1.88, Paus. 9.33.2, and even Aelian, *NA* 2.3. The crucial lines are *Od.* 10.493ff. μάντηοc ἀλαοῦ, τοῦ τε φρένεc ἔμπεδοί εἰcιν· | τῶι καὶ τεθνηῶτι νόον πόρε Περcεφόνεια, | οἴωι πεπνῦcθαι, τοὶ δὲ cκιαὶ ἀίccουcιν. C. too acknowledges his source by the echo μόνοc . . . πεπνυμένοc. [Apollod.] 3.6.7 makes no mention of T.'s retained intelligence in Pherecydes, and making it part of Athena's compensation may be a Callimachean innovation (although Strabo 9.411 notes that at the shrine at Couralios Athena was connected with Hades κατά τινα, ὥc φαcι, μυcτικὴν αἰτίαν). Hermes' son, the herald Aethalides, was similarly privileged with retained memory even after death, but this was achieved by transmigration of his soul into a succession of bodies (including that of Pythagoras): A.R. 1.644–8.

εὖτε θάνηι Metrically a single unit since conjunctions are appositive: C. maintains the usual practice of avoiding a break in the second biceps (Maas, *GM* §95, Wifstrand, *KN* 64f., 74). Cf. the phraseology of Bacch. 1.182f. τ]ε̣λ̣ευταθεῖcα δ' ὀρθῶc | [ἀνδρὶ κ]αὶ εὖτε θάνηι λεί|π̣[ει . . . The

---

[1] The only Homeric instance, *H.Herm.* 125, a problematic line, seems to have the same meaning: LSJ's 'ancient' is improbable. The wording at [Apollod.] 3.6.7 may be echoing C.: ἐγένετο δὲ καὶ πολυχρόνιοc (Tiresias), cf. Pfeiffer's remark on [Apollod.] 1.3.6 at fr. 37.

[2] πολυχρόνιον cannot be interpreted as 'transferred' from βιότω: such a construction would make the sense very strained, and enallage of the adjective is anyway *very* uncommon in C. (see Lapp, *TF* 51, deleting his reference to V 113f.). Schneider compares Q.S. 11.141 Μοῖραι | μακρὸν . . . βίου τέλοc ἐκλώcαντο, but μακρόc, less specific than πολυχρόνιοc, is often used with reference to distance = 'remote', 'far off'.

difficulty which e, Q and ȝ had with their text here perhaps goes back ultimately to another area of increasing damage in Ψ, though equally scribal reluctance to recognise an unusual conjunction may have been the sole cause.

πεπνυμένος ἐν νεκύεςςι Poetic, and especially Homeric, vocabulary (LSJ s.vv.). LSJ s.v. πέπνυμαι incorrectly distinguish the Callimachean and Homeric passages = 'be conscious' from other instances = 'be wise': πεπνῦςθαι denotes intelligence (φρένες), whether of the sort which distinguishes the living from the dead (*Il.* 23.103f. ἦ ῥά τίς ἐςτι καὶ εἰν Ἀίδαο δόμοιςι | ψυχὴ καὶ εἴδωλον, ἀτὰρ φρένες οὐκ ἔνι πάμπαν), or that which makes one man superior to another (Hesych. πεπνυμένος· φρόνιμος, a word which has the same semantic range).

130 φοιταςεῖ φοιτᾶν usually connotes repeated or habitual movement, whether steady or agitated (LSJ, Schmidt, *SGS* I 501; so elsewhere in C. and other Hellenistic authors). Here the verb is used as at *Od.* 11.538f. ψυχὴ δὲ ποδώκεος Αἰακίδαο | φοίτα μακρὰ βιβᾶςα κατ' ἀςφοδελὸν λειμῶνα and Sappho fr. 55 ἀλλ' ἀφάνης κἀν 'Αΐδα δόμωι | φοιτάςηις πεδ' ἀμαύρων νεκύων ἐκπεποταμένα, of the flittering movement often attributed to the dead in Hades (E. Cavallini, *Museum Criticum* 10–12 (1975–7) 49 suggests that C. here looks to the Sappho passage, but the connections between the two are inconsequential). Cf. Cleanthes, *Hymn to Zeus* 12f. κοινὸν λόγον ὃς διὰ πάντων | φοιτᾶι μειγνύμενος μεγάλοις μικροῖς τε φάεςςιν.

μεγάλωι Cf. on v. 126 μεγάλοις: in Hades as in Thebes T. will advise the great.

Ἁγεςίλαι A learned name for Hades, rare enough to be repeatedly commented on in the lexicographical tradition.[1] Before C. only Aesch. is known to have used the name (or epithet), but its rarity appealed to the Hellenistic poets: anon. third-century B.C. *Hymn to Dem.* in *SH* 990.9 Ἀγεςίλας, Hegesippus, *HE* 1916 ἡγεςίλεω . . . Ἄιδος, Nic. fr. 74.72 Ἡγεςιλάου, Peek, *GVI* 1370 (first century A.D.) Ἀγεςίλας. The name has many forms (as has the historical proper name Ἀγηςίλαος: see LSJ) which seem to be used quite arbitrarily.[2] 'The title . . . refers to his character as host of the dead and is to be compared with his titles Πολυδέγμων, Πολυδέκτης, Πολυςημάντωρ, Πανδοκεύς' (Mair).

[1] Athen. 3.99B καὶ Αἰςχύλος τὸν Ἅιδην 'ἀγηςίλαον' (fr. 612M), Lactant. *de fals. relig.* 1.11 *Plutoni, cui nomen Agesilao*, Methodius in *Et. Mag.* 8.32 Ἀγεςίλαος· ἐπώνυμον τοῦ Ἅιδου (quoting Call.: see testimonia to v 130), Hesych. Ἀγεςίλαος· ὁ Πλούτων.

[2] On the various forms see E.Schwyzer, *Rhein. Mus.* 79 (1930) 103–6: the second syllable is always long except in poetry where ĕ must be explained as a metrical convenience. Cf. also F.Specht, *Zeitschrift für vergleichende Sprachforschung* 59 (1932) 54f.

131 ὣc φαμένα κατένευce ὣc φαμεν- + verb | |: Homeric phraseology (e.g. *Il.* 5.290, *Od.* 18.206, 23.85; again at 384.46).

Ψ had been damaged beyond legibility at the beginning of the line by the time the scribes of hyparchetypes ε and ʒ copied their texts (γ perhaps replenishing its text from F or an ancestor: see Pfeiffer, *Proleg.* lxxx and Intro. pp. 66f.): the same damage rendered the end of VI 18 on the other side of the sheet illegible too (Pfeiffer's apparatus criticus is misleading here: see the full description of readings by Smiley in *CQ* 14 (1920) 71f.).

κατένευce The irrevocable divine assent: *Il.* 1.524ff. εἰ δ' ἄγε τοι κεφαλῆι κατανεύcομαι, ὄφρα πεποίθηιc· | τοῦτο γὰρ ἐξ ἐμέθεν γε μετ' ἀθανάτοιcι μέγιcτον | τέκμωρ· οὐ γὰρ ἐμὸν παλινάγρετον οὐδ' ἀπατηλὸν | οὐδ' ἀτελεύτητον, ὅτι κεν κεφαλῆι κατανεύcω. κατανεύειν and ἐπινεύειν are almost identical in meaning: κ. perhaps implies formal assent, whether with the token nod of the head or not, whereas ἐ. has no connotations of formality. Both verbs are normal usage, but κ. slowly became obsolete in the *koine* (LSJ and *Thes. Graec.* s.vv.). The alternation in v. 131 perhaps reflects contemporary philological discussion: at *Il.* 1.524 Σ reports οὕτωc κατανεύcομαι, οὐχὶ ἐπινεύcομαι, 'Αρίcταρχοc ἐν τοῖc πρὸc Φιλήταν προφέρεται (Philetas fr. 54K, cf. *Testim.* A7K).

131–2 A brief *sententia* of the kind often used in Greek narrative poetry to justify or explain a divine action: e.g. Pind. *P.* 3.11f. χόλοc δ' οὐκ ἀλίθιοc γίνεται παίδων Διόc.

131 τό Demonstrative, antecedent to ὧι.

ἐντελέc Again at 203.48 ἐντελέc τε τὸ χρῆμα (context obscure), but otherwise not in the Hellenistic poets. Like English 'complete' ἐντελήc often = 'not deficient in any way', and is so used often of quantities in phrases such as ἐ. μιcθόc etc.; but it also occasionally indicates accomplishment, fulfilment of action and as antonym to ἀτελήc has fairly powerful legal connotations: Polyb. 8.34.1 ἤδη δ' ἐντελεῖc . . . τὰc πρὸc τὴν πολιορκίαν παραcκευάc, Lucian, *Salt.* 17 ἡγούμεθα ἐντελῆ ἡμῶν εἶναι τὴν εὐχήν, Hesych. ἐντελῆ· τετελεcμένα. Cf. Aesch. *PV* 12f. Κράτοc Βία τε, cφῷιν μὲν ἐντολὴ Διὸc | ἔχει τέλοc δὴ κοὐδὲν ἐμποδὼν ἔτι. Meineke's emendation ἐκτελέc is therefore unnecessary.

ὧι κ' ἐπινεύcηι ἐπινεύειν normally takes a direct object, and the dative here has vexed editors; Kaibel proposed ὅττι κε νεύcηι and Wilamowitz ὧι κ' ἔπι νεύcηι. However, the dative can stand as a rare usage which is testified also at *LXX* 2 Macc. 14.20 ἐπένευcαν ταῖc cυνθήκαιc and *P. Giss.* 1.41 ii 9 (second century A.D.) ἐ. τῆι δεήcει.

132–3 Aesch. *Eum.* 827f. καὶ κλῆιδαc οἶδα δώματοc μόνη θεῶν, | ἐν ὧι κεραυνόc ἐcτιν ἐcφραγιcμένοc (cf. Eur. *Tro.* 80), Hor. *Od.* 1.12.19f. *proximos illi tamen occupavit* | *Pallas honores.* The representation of Athena as ἶcον ἔχουcαν πατρὶ μένοc καὶ ἐπίφρονα βουλήν (Hes. *Theog.* 896) is well documented in cult and myth (see Farnell, *CGS* I 412, Preller–Robert, *GM* I 188ff., Nilsson, *GGR* I 438) though the closeness of a divinity to Zeus was always worth emphasising: cf. II 29 δύναται γάρ, ἐπεὶ Διὶ δεξιὸς ἧσται. C. here emphasises the uniqueness of her position (μώναι . . . θυγατέρων) to make Athena's promises and protestations as an innocent and loyal friend as credible as possible. The couplet is formally part of the narrative section, but as a generalising pious statement it also acts as a transition back to the religious ritualistic setting of the poem.

132 τόγε The γε is not redundant: like the extended μώναι . . . θυγατέρων the (proleptic) demonstrative emphasises the exceptional nature of Athena's powers – '*this* is something which to A. alone of (all) his daughters . . .'

θυγατέρων In the oblique cases of θυγατήρ epic regularly lengthens the υ *metri gratia* (Chantraine, *GH* I 99).

133 πατρώϊα πάντα ⏑–– (verb) A Homeric formula (*Od.* 17.80, 20.336, 22.61: cf. Hes. fr. 240.9 ἐπιχθόνιοι μαντήϊα πάντα φέρονται). C. adapts rather than imitates: Homeric πατρώϊα is concrete = 'patrimony', here abstract = 'father's powers'. Theocr. 17.104 also uses the phrase, πατρώϊα πάντα φυλάσσειν, but in the traditional sense.

φέρεσθαι 'Acquire' conveys the vagueness of the Greek. Normal usage has φέρεσθαι (middle) particularly of prizes or respect as a mark of honour (see *Thes. Graec.* s.v.): similarly of privileges bestowed on Artemis by Zeus at III 31 φέρευ, τέκος, ὅσσ' ἐθελημός | αἰτίζεις.

134–6 The strange manner of Athena's birth is constantly remarked on by Greek writers (cf. especially Hes. *Theog.* 886ff., 924ff., fr. 343, *H.H.* 28.4ff., Pind. *O.* 7.36f., A.R. 4.1309ff.) but its use here to guarantee the goddess's trustworthiness is at least in part humorous. V. 135 Διὸς κορυφά. κορυφὰ Διός expresses the logic of the guarantee in its most economical and exposed form: the token of promise is a nod of the head – Athena was actually born from the most trustworthy head of all. The naivety and literalness of the explanation (baldly presented in a chiasmic figure) can be taken only as a literary conceit,[1] though one which is mild enough and academic enough not to undermine Athena's credibility in the poem. In fact the phraseology contains a final reminder that behaviour from Athena which is apparently insensitive to maternal love is not entirely unexpected: v. 134 μάτηρ δ' οὔτις ἔτικτε θεάν is only slightly less explicit than Aesch. *Eum.* 736ff. μήτηρ γὰρ οὔτις ἐστὶν ἥ μ' ἐγείνατο, | τὸ δ' ἄρσεν αἰνῶ πάντα . . . | ἅπαντι θυμῶι, κάρτα δ' εἰμὶ τοῦ πατρός.

With the reintroduction at v. 134 of the Argive celebrants the narrative is clearly about to close, and the story of Athena's birth leads naturally back

[1] The same figure is used with a similar ironical emphasis on the central word at Theocr. 14.24 ἔστι Λύκος, Λύκος ἐστί.

to the Athena of the Argive cult, the warrior goddess: Hes. *Theog.* 924ff. αὐτὸς δ' ἐκ κεφαλῆς γλαυκώπιδα γείνατ' Ἀθήνην | δεινὴν ἐγρεκύδοιμον . . . | . . . ἧι κέλαδοί τε ἅδον πόλεμοί τε μάχαι τε.[1]

135 κορυφά Strictly speaking the crown of the head. The word is often used in describing the birth of Athena (e.g. *H.H.Ap.* 309, Hes. fr. 343. 12, Pind. *O.* 7.36), and later mythographers gave Athena the mother Coryphe.[2]

κορυφὰ Διός The chiasmus binding the two sentences closely together makes a connecting particle unnecessary.

135–6 Orthodox classical theology and phraseology: cf. *Il.* 1.526 (Zeus speaks) οὐ γὰρ ἐμὸν παλινάγρετον οὐδ' ἀπατηλὸν | οὐδ' ἀτελεύτητον, ὅτι κεν κεφαλῆι κατανεύω (see also notes to vv. 103f. and 131); Aesch. *Supp.* 90f. πίπτει δ' ἀcφαλὲc οὐδ' ἐπὶ νώτωι, κορυφᾶι Διὸc εἰ κρανθῆι πρᾶγμα τέλειον, Eur. *Alc.* 978f. καὶ γὰρ Ζεὺc ὅ τι νεύcηι, cὺν coὶ τοῦτο τελευτᾶι.

136 Ψ appears to have deteriorated at this point: the later hyparchetypes could not even make out the first and last words of the line. VI 23, the corresponding line on the other side of the page, was yet more difficult to read and there F (or ancestor) and β read not even the little that γ and ʒ later retrieved (possibly from another source: see Intro. pp.66f.). Bentley, writing before Ernesti had demonstrated that LMNOT should not be classified indiscriminately with the older MSS, accepted the text of LMN with two minor changes: κορυφὰ Διὸc ὧι κ' ἐπινεύcηι | ἔμπεδον, ὡc αὔτωc ὧι κε καὶ ἁ θυγάτηρ (ὡc δ' οὕτωc LM, ὁccαύτωc N: κεν οἷα L, κεν ἅ τε M, κεν οἱ ἁ N).

137–42 Athena's appearance from the temple is announced: the epiphany is at last complete and there remain only brief instructions to the celebrants to receive the deity properly, and the conventional final prayers for the continued protection of Argos by its patron goddess.

137 ἔρχετ' For the elision of -αι see on v. 64 κεῖντ'.

νῦν The placing of an independent monosyllabic word immediately after a masculine caesura is almost unique in C.: only fr. 114.4, 6 offer a parallel (ναί). The rhythmic fragmentation of the line caused by isolating νῦν with a break on each side gives the word exceptional emphasis, appropriately at the climactic moment of the epiphany (cf. Wifstrand, *KN* 56f.).

---

[1] Bergk, *Opuscula* II 187, who argued that 'virginum appellatio hoc loco plane praepostera', failed to see that here, as at v. 27 ὦ κῶραι, the vocative prepares for a transition, recalling to the reader's mind the celebrants, who after a long interval will shortly be brought back into the poem.

[2] First, apparently, in Mnaseas, the euhemerist pupil of Eratosthenes: see Harpocr. s.v. ἱππία Ἀθηνᾶ, Roscher, *LM* II 1394f. and A.S.Pease on Cic. *de nat. deor.* 3.59.

ἀτρεκές An Ionic word occasionally used in the *koine* (LSJ). Usually = 'accurate', 'exact', 'correct', the adjective often qualifies verbs of knowledge or comprehension (so in A.R. and bucolics), and sometimes makes quantities more determinate (*Od.* 16.245 δεκὰς ἀτρεκές, 'just ten', Theogn. 636 ἀτρεκέως ὀλίγοι)[1]. In this sense ἀτρεκές could cohere closely with νῦν = 'right now'; however, there are also a few examples of ἀτρεκής in normal usage used loosely = 'real' ('not illusory or fake'): *Il.* 5.208 ἀτρεκὲς αἷμ' (cf. Nonn. *D.* 4.80), Theogn. 167 τὸ δ' ἀτρεκὲς ὄλβιος οὐδείς, Hipp. *Praec.* 7 διαντλίζονται . . . ἀτρεκέως ἐθέλοντες ὑγιέες εἶναι (cf. Schmidt, *SGS* IV 283ff.). This sense, which would stress that Athena's appearance is not illusory (after the several occasions earlier when the epiphany was urgently believed to be imminent: vv. 3, 33, 43, 55) and would emphasise the identity of the Palladion with the goddess herself, seems much more appropriate than emphasis on the precise moment of her appearance; the sentiment would be the same as in Hermocles' flattering epiphany hymn to Demetrius (Powell, *CA* 173f.) 18ff. cὲ δὲ παρόνθ' ὁρῶμεν, | οὐ ξύλινον οὐδὲ λίθινον, ἀλλ' ἀληθινόν. | εὐχόμεcθα δή coι.[2] Cf. also Pind. *N.* 5.16f. οὔ τοι ἅπαcα κερδίων φαίνοιcα πρόcωπον ἀλάθει' ἀτρεκές.

ἀλλὰ δέχεcθε Announcement of the god's advent is usually coupled with an instruction for celebrants at epiphanies to make welcome, and C. here uses the standard terminology. The god is 'received' (δέχεcθαι; ἀποδοχή, ὑποδοχή): Aristoph. *Av.* 1707ff. ὦ τριcμακάριον πτηνὸν ὀρνίθων γένος, | δέχεcθε τὸν τύραννον ὀλβίοιc δόμοιc. | προcέρχεται γάρ (vv. 1728f. ἀλλ' ὑμεναίοιc καὶ νυμφιδίοιcι δέχεcθ' ᾠδαῖc αὐτόν), Philodamus Scarph. *Paean in Dionysum* (Powell, *CA* 169) 144ff. (the final stanza) ἀλλὰ δέχεcθε Βακχ[ιάcτα]ν Δι[ό]νυc[ον . . ., cf. Isyllus 81f. (Powell, *CA* 135) οἳ δὴ ἐκάρυξαν πάνταc ξενίαιc cε δέκεcθαι | cωτῆρα (Asclepius the new god announced by Isyllus to the Spartans), and Diod. Sic. 4.51 reports that Medea took into Pelias' city a statue of Artemis and παραγγέλλειν πᾶcι δέχεcθαι τὴν θεὸν εὐcεβῶc (see Pfister, *RE* Suppl. IV 312, Kleinknecht, *LP* 304f.).[3]

138 τὦργον ὅcαιc μέλεται 'Whose business the job is' (viz. δέχεcθαι). The phrase specifies the attendants with particular duties, such as the λωτροχόοι just mentioned, without implying that the rest of the crowd will not also provide a welcome.

---

[1] Cf. Pind. *P.* 8.7 καιρῶι cὺν ἀτρεκεῖ.

[2] Note the paraphrase of Σ to *Il.* 5.208 ἀντὶ τοῦ ἀτρεκέωc εἶδον αὐτό, οὐκ ἠπάτημαι, and similarly Eustath. 539.39 ἀληθὲc καὶ μὴ ψεῦδον τὴν ὄψιν. Word-order too suggests that ἀτρεκέc does not qualify only νῦν, since it follows the adverb.

[3] Cf. *H.H.Ap.* 47f. οὐδέ τιc ἔτλη | Φοῖβον δέξαcθαι (v. 64 Delos says δεξαίμην), Eur. *Bacch.* 312, 770, A.R. 2.756.

τῶργον Boissonade's correction of Ψ's τῶργοϲ is surely right: at this stage in the proceedings an appeal to patriotism, which has not featured hitherto, would be quite out of place – the question is one of ritual duty. Contraction of ο + ε in Doric sometimes produces ου, and sometimes ω (Buck, *GD* 42: Argolic has ω). Theocritus contracts always to ω (Monteil, *T* 28f., 32), and in C. again at VI 38 τῶνδιον; cf. on v. 1 λωτροχόοι, v. 4 cῶcθε.

μέλεται μέλειν/μέλεcθαι is a favourite word of C., especially with reference to somebody's sphere of duty or business (cf. 66.2f. Ἥρηc | ἁγνὸν ὑφαινέμεναι τῆιcι μέμηλε πάτοc). Making the object of concern the subject of the verb is a feature of poetic diction (K–G, *GG* I 367), as is also use of middle instead of active (LSJ).

139 The celebrants are told to welcome Athena with acclamation, prayer, and ritual refrain. The anaphora and the ending of each phrase at a major metrical pause reinforce the formality of the instructions (similar patterning at IV 280). Typically this overall regularity is offset by internal variation: -ίαι (sing.) → -αcι/-αῖc (plur.); -αcι (neut.) → -αῖc (fem.).

εὐαγορίαι Acclamation of a formal kind similar to εὐλογία or ἐγκώμιον (Hesych. εὐηγορεῖν· εὐλογεῖν, Σ to Pind. *I.* 1.51 (= 1.71 Drachmann) εὐαγορηθείc: ἐγκωμιαcθείc; cf. *RAC* VI 900ff. s.v. εὐλογία). Much of what has already been said by this stage is in fact εὐηγορία, though the acclamation need be no more than χαῖρε: see *RAC* I 219f. s.v. 'Akklamation'.

εὐηγορ- words are rare (see LSJ and add Pind. *Pae.* 2.67 εὐαγορίαιcι) and are glossed in Hesychius and the *Suda*, but Eubul. 71 (Kock II 189) εὐηγορῶν (Meineke, εὐήγοροc MS, Εὐήγοροc Wilamowitz) might indicate that the term was normal usage.

εὔγμαcι The prayers are the inevitable prelude and accompaniment to the ritual acts. εὖγμα is a rare poetic variation on the normal forms εὐχή/εὖχοc, only at *Od.* 22.249 and five times in Attic drama (mostly lyric): in Hellenistic poetry this is apparently the only instance. Cf. Chantraine, *FN* 183.

ὀλολυγαῖc The ritual cry which comes after the prayers and sacrifice at the climax of a ceremony (cf. Stengel, *GKA* 112: e.g. *Od.* 4.759ff., Aesch. *Sept.* 266ff.). Thus at the moment of an epiphany: *H.H.Ap.* 119 (the birth of Apollo: imitatively Call. IV 258), Eur. fr. 351N ὀλολύʒετ', ὦ γυναῖκεc, ὡc ἔλθηι θεά (Athena), Aristoph. *Eq.* 1327, the stage directions at *Thesm.* 276f., A.R. 3.1218. Cf. Kleinknecht, *LP* 305.

Here as at v. 131 the archetype was partly illegible by the time δ and ʒ copied their texts, though this time the damage did not extend through to the other side of the sheet (v. 109).

140–2 These lines are of a common syntactical pattern, namely the combination of short initial greeting in vocative with an appended prayer for protection (cf. Kleinknecht, *LP* 305 n. 2), and in particular they are an extended version of the formulaic: *H.H.* 13.3 χαῖρε θεὰ καὶ τήνδε cάου πόλιν, VI 134 χαῖρε, θεά, καὶ τάνδε cάω πόλιν, 112.8 χαῖρε, Ζεῦ, μέγα καὶ cύ, cάω δ' [ὅλο]ν οἶκον ἀνάκτων.[1]

140 χαῖρε (. . . | **χαῖρε**) Not just the usual formula for ending a hymn but also the standard greeting at an epiphany (acclamation: see on εὐαγορίαι above): Aristoph. *Eq.* 1333 χαῖρ' ὦ βαcιλεῦ, Hermocles' hymn at the 'epiphany' of Demetrius in Athens (Powell, *CA* 174) 14 παῖ Ποcειδῶνοc θεοῦ, χαῖρε. The greeting from the leader of the celebrants combines with the poet's own standard hymnal clausula.

καδ- The standard Doric form: Björck, *AI* 177 and LSJ.

κήδεcθαι = 'care about' of cities, peoples etc. is standard usage: e.g. Hdt. 9.45.1 μεγάλωc ἐκηδόμην cυναπάcηc τῆc 'Ελλάδοc, Polyb. 3.15.7 'Αννίβαc . . . κηδόμενοc Ζακανθαίων. For divine concern cf. Hdt. 1.209.4 ἐμεῦ θεοὶ κήδονται.

'Ιναχίω The concluding epithet marks the strength of the Argive claim for Athena's protection: her worshippers are about to bathe the goddess in the river Inachus and their εὐcέβεια merits reward.

For Ernesti's necessary correction -ω see on v. 128 βιότω.

141f. *IG* II^2 1006.11 describing the Athenian Plynteria similarly emphasises the return of the goddess: cυνεξήγαγον δὲ καὶ τὴν Παλλάδα Φαληροῖ κἀκεῖθεν πάλιν cυνειcήγαγον μετὰ φωτὸc μετὰ πάcηc εὐκοcμίαc. It would have been ill-omened to mention the goddess's departure without referring to her return also (cf. Theocr. 18.55, 24.7–9). A similarly articulated formulaic ending at *H.H.* 26.11–13 καὶ cὺ μὲν οὕτω χαῖρε, πολυcτάφυλ' ὦ Διόνυcε· | δὸc δ' ἡμᾶc χαίρονταc ἐc ὥραc αὖτιc ἱκέcθαι, | ἐκ δ' αὖθ' ὡράων εἰc τοὺc πολλοὺc ἐνιαυτούc.

141 ἐξελάοιcα The verb in the sense 'drive out' with accusative omitted, as if intransitive, is normal usage (LSJ s.v. I 3 b)), but the ελα-form is poetic (rare: Veitch, *GV* 240f. and LSJ).[2]

ἐc πάλιν αὖτιc ἐλάccαιc Tmesis is especially common in C. when, as here, isolation of the preverb helps to emphasise a repetition or contrast; the intervening words, if not particles, are usually direct objects or adverbs (cf. Lapp, *TF* 47f.). Tmesis of εἰc as preverb is rare in Homer and occurs mostly only with δ' separating preverb and verb: only *Od.* 21.244 shows extensive

[1] F.Spiro, *Hermes* 23 (1888) 199–201 maintained that in these lines C. was looking to, and correcting, Lyc. 1474 cώιζων παλαιὰν Βεβρύκων παγκληρίαν: the slight similarity in wording, however, is due to the formulaic nature of both passages.

[2] Rare in Hellenistic poetry also; most often in the participial form which offers a useful alternative to the metrically awkward ἐλαύνων etc.

tmesis, ἐc δ' ἄρα καὶ τῶ δμῶε ἴτην (cf. *Il.* 8.115 τὼ δ' εἰc ἀμφοτέρω Διομήδεοc ἅρματα βήτην). After Homer tmesis of εἰc is found in the lyric poets but not the dramatists (K–G, *GG* I 530–6). This is the only instance of εἰc in tmesis in C. and it is assisted by the linguistic jingle with ἐξ- earlier in the line (for the same play on opposites see *H.H.* 26.12f. cited above).

πάλιν αὖτιc A common Homeric phrase (Ebeling, *LH* II 125). At *Il.* 5.257 Aristonicus remarked οὐ τὸ αὐτὸ λέγει διὰ τοῦ πάλιν καὶ αὖτιc, ἀλλὰ τὸ μὲν αὖτιc ἀντὶ τοῦ πάλιν, τὸ δὲ πάλιν τοπικόν, ἀντὶ τοῦ εἰc τοὐπίcω.

141–2 ἐλάccαιc | ἵππωc Cf. vv. 61f. ἐλαύνοι | ἵππωc.

142 The Hymn closes on a note of grandeur. Cf. the similar phraseology in the undated Argive hymn to Demeter v. 8 cited by Aelian, *NA* 11.4 (= *SH* 206): καὶ πάντωc θάλλοι κλᾶροc ἐν Ἑρμιόναι (see Intro. p. 37).

Δαναῶν A poetic alternative to Ἀργεῖοι:[1] Paus. 7.1.7 δυνηθέντων δὲ ἔν τε Ἄργει καὶ Λακεδαίμονι τῶν Ἀχαιοῦ παίδων, τοὺc ἀνθρώπουc τοὺc ἐνταῦθα ἐξενίκηcεν Ἀχαίουc κληθῆναι. τοῦτο μέν cφιcιν ὄνομα ἦν ἐν κοινῶι, Δαναοὶ δὲ Ἀργείοιc ἰδίαι.

κλᾶρον 'estate'. The singular of one allotment is normal usage, but of a whole national territory apparently poetic (majestic): Aesch. fr. 744M Κύπρου Πάφου τ' ἔχουcα πάντα κλῆρον, *Pers.* 899 κατὰ κλῆρον Ἰαόνιον. Cf. A.R. 1.162 Τεγέην καὶ κλῆρον Ἀφειδάντειον, Nic. fr. 104 ὦ κλῆρον ἀεὶ πατρώϊον ἴcχων (Attalus), Parmenon in *SH* 604A 4f. οἵ τ' ἄcτυ Λητοῦc καὶ Κυνὸc περὶ κλῆρον | φοιτῶcι . . .

For the Doric form see Björck, *AI* 177 and LSJ.

cάω A rare Homeric imperative of disputed origin and form,[2] favoured by C. (112.8, VI 134) though not used by other Hellenistic writers: Chantraine, *GH* I 307, K–B, *GG* II 545, Schwyzer, *GG* I 728 n. 2.

---

[1] Also poetically of the Greeks generally in the heroic age (like Ἀργεῖοι): see Pape–Benseler, *Wörterbuch der griech. Eigennamen* (Brunswick 1884[3]) s.v. and cf. Strabo 8.369.

[2] Nauck and Schwyzer favour reading cάου wherever MSS have cάω; the reading here is not affected since cάου would become cάω in Doric. At 112.8 the papyrus has cάω, but at *E.* 33.2 *Codex Palatinus* has cάου.

INDEXES

1 GREEK

References are to pages.

(Modern scholars are listed only where their views have been quoted substantially or discussed.) References are to pages.

3 PASSAGES EMENDED AND ELUCIDATED

3 PASSAGES EMENDED AND ELUCIDATED

3 PASSAGES EMENDED AND ELUCIDATED